An Unquiet Mind: A Memoir of Moods and Madness

Touched with Fire: Manic-Depressive Illness and the Artistic Temperament

Manic-Depressive Illness (with F. Goodwin)

NIGHT FALLS FAST

NIGHT FALLS FAST

— *Understanding Suicide* —

Kay Redfield Jamison

ALFRED A. KNOPF   *New York*   1999

THIS IS A BORZOI BOOK
PUBLISHED BY ALFRED A. KNOPF

Copyright © 1999 by Kay Redfield Jamison
All rights reserved under International and Pan-American
Copyright Conventions. Published in the United States
by Alfred A. Knopf, a division of Random House, Inc.,
New York, and simultaneously in Canada by
Random House of Canada Limited, Toronto.
Distributed by Random House, Inc., New York.

www.randomhouse.com

Knopf, Borzoi Books, and the colophon are registered
trademarks of Random House, Inc.

Owing to limitations of space, acknowledgments for
permission to reprint previously published material
may be found following the index.

Library of Congress Cataloging-in-Publication Data
Jamison, Kay R.
Night falls fast : understanding suicide / by Kay Redfield
Jamison. — 1st ed.
p.   cm.
Includes bibliographical references.
ISBN 0-375-40145-8 (hc)
1. Suicide—United States.   2. Children—Suicidal behavior—
United States.   3. Youth—Suicidal behavior—United States.
I. Title.
RC569.J36   1999
616.85'8445'00973—dc21   99-311227
                                        CIP

Manufactured in the United States of America
Published October 10, 1999
Second Printing, November 1999

For my husband,
Richard Jed Wyatt
With deep love
and
For my brother,
Dean T. Jamison
Who kept the night at bay

Night falls fast.
Today is in the past.

Blown from the dark hill hither to my door
Three flakes, then four
Arrive, then many more.

—EDNA ST. VINCENT MILLAY

Contents

ix

Contents

NIGHT FALLS FAST

PROLOGUE

*S*ummer evenings at the Bistro Gardens in Beverly Hills tended *toward the long and languorous. My friend Jack Ryan and I went there often when I lived in Los Angeles, and I invariably ordered the Dungeness crab and a scotch on the rocks. Not so invariably, but from time to time, Jack would use the occasion to suggest we get married. It was an idea with such patent potential for catastrophe that neither of us had much of an inclination to take the recurring proposal with too much gravity. But our friendship we took seriously.*

This particular evening, having hooked and tugged out the last bits of crab, I found myself edgily knocking the ice cubes around in my whisky glass. The conversation was making me restless and uneasy. We were talking about suicide and making a blood oath: if either of us again became deeply suicidal, we agreed, we would meet at Jack's home on Cape Cod. Once there, the nonsuicidal one of us would have a week to persuade the other not to commit suicide; a week to present all the reasons we could come up with for why the other should go back on lithium, assuming that having stopped it was the most likely reason for the danger of suicide (we both had manic-depressive illness and, despite the better and often expressed judgment of others, had a tendency to stop taking our lithium); a week to cajole the other into a hospital; to invoke conscience; to impress upon the other the pain and damage to our families that suicide would inevitably bring.

We would, we said, during this hostage week, walk along the beach and remind the other of all of the times we had felt at the end of hope and, somehow, had come back. Who, if not someone who had actually been there, could better bring the other back from the edge? We both, in our own ways and in our own intimate dealings with it, knew suicide well. We thought we knew how we could keep it from being the cause of death on our death certificates.

We decided that a week was long enough to argue for life. If it didn't work, at least we would have tried. And, because we had years of cumulative experience with lifestyles of snap impetuousness and knew how quick and final a suicidal impulse could be, we further agreed that neither of us would ever buy a gun. Nor, we swore, would we under any circumstances allow anyone else to keep a gun in a house in which we lived.

"Cheers," we said in synchrony, ice and glass clinking. We sealed our foray into the planned and rational world. Still, I had my doubts. I listened to the details, helped clarify a few, drank the rest of my scotch, and stared at the tiny white lights in the gardens around us. Who were we kidding? Never once, during any of my sustained bouts of suicidal depression, had I been inclined or able to pick up a telephone and ask a friend for help. Not once. It wasn't in me. How could I seriously imagine that I would call Jack, make an airline reservation, get to an airport, rent a car, and find my way out to his house on the Cape? It seemed only slightly less absurd that Jack would go along with the plan, although he, at least, was rich and could get others to handle the practicalities. The more I thought about the arrangement, the more skeptical I became.

It is a tribute to the persuasiveness, reverberating energies and enthusiasms, and infinite capacity for self-deception of two manic temperaments that by the time the dessert soufflés arrived we were utterly convinced that our pact would hold. He would call me; I would call him; we would outmaneuver the black knight and force him from the board.

If it has ever been taken up as an option, however, the black knight has a tendency to remain in play. And so it did. Many years later— Jack had long since married and I had moved to Washington—I received a telephone call from California: Jack had put a gun to his head, said a member of his family. Jack had killed himself.

No week in Cape Cod, no chance to dissuade. A man who had been inventive enough to earn a thousand patents for such wildly diverse creations as the Hawk and Sparrow missile systems used by the U.S. Department of Defense, toys played with by millions of children around the world, and devices used in virtually every household in America; a Yale graduate and lover of life; a successful businessman—this remarkably imaginative man had not been inventive enough to find an alternative solution to a violent, self-inflicted death.

Although shaken by Jack's suicide, I was not surprised by it. Nor was I surprised that he had not called me. I, after all, had been dangerously suicidal myself on several occasions since our Bistro Gardens compact and certainly had not called him. Nor had I even thought of calling. Suicide is not beholden to an evening's promises, nor does it always hearken to plans drawn up in lucid moments and banked in good intentions.

I know this for an unfortunate fact. Suicide has been a professional interest of mine for more than twenty years, and a very personal one for considerably longer. I have a hard-earned respect for suicide's ability to undermine, overwhelm, outwit, devastate, and destroy. As a clinician, researcher, and teacher I have known or consulted on patients who hanged, shot, or asphyxiated themselves; jumped to their deaths from stairwells, buildings, or overpasses; died from poisons, fumes, prescription drugs; or slashed their wrists or cut their throats. Close friends, fellow students from graduate school, colleagues, and children of colleagues have done similar or the same. Most were young and suffered from mental illness; all left behind a wake of unimaginable pain and unresolvable guilt.

Like many who have manic-depressive illness, I have also known suicide in a more private, awful way, and I trace the loss of a fundamental innocence to the day that I first considered suicide as the only solution possible to an unendurable level of mental pain. Until that time I had taken for granted, and loved more than I knew, a temperamental lightness of mood and a fabulous expectation of life. I knew death only in the most abstract of senses; I never imagined it would be something to arrange or seek.

I was seventeen when, in the midst of my first depression,

I became knowledgeable about suicide in something other than an existential, adolescent way. For much of each day during several months of my senior year in high school, I thought about when, whether, where, and how to kill myself. I learned to present to others a face at variance with my mind; ferreted out the location of two or three nearby tall buildings with unprotected stairwells; discovered the fastest flows of morning traffic; and learned how to load my father's gun.

The rest of my life at the time—sports, classes, writing, friends, planning for college—fell fast into a black night. Everything seemed a ridiculous charade to endure; a hollow existence to fake one's way through as best one could. But, gradually, layer by layer, the depression lifted, and by the time my senior prom and graduation came around, I had been well for months. Suicide had withdrawn to the back squares of the board and become, once again, unthinkable.

Because the privacy of my nightmare had been of my own designing, no one close to me had any real idea of the psychological company I had been keeping. The gap between private experience and its public expression was absolute; my persuasiveness to others was unimaginably frightening.

Over the years, my manic-depressive illness became much worse, and the reality of dying young from suicide became a dangerous undertow in my dealings with life. Then, when I was twenty-eight years old, after a damaging and psychotic mania, followed by a particularly prolonged and violent siege of depression, I took a massive overdose of lithium. I unambivalently wanted to die and nearly did. Death from suicide had become a possibility, if not a probability, in my life.

Under the circumstances—I was, during this, a young faculty member in a department of academic psychiatry—it was not a very long walk from personal experience to clinical and scientific investigation. I studied everything I could about my disease and read all I could find about the psychological and biological determinants of suicide. As a tiger tamer learns about the minds and moves of his cats, and a pilot about the dynamics of the wind and air, I learned about the illness I had and its possible end point. I learned as best I could, and as much as I could, about the moods of death.

I

Buried Above Ground

— An Introduction
to Suicide —

Encompass'd with a thousand dangers,
Weary, faint, trembling with a thousand terrors. . . .
I . . . in a fleshly tomb, am
Buried above ground.

— William Cowper

English poet William Cowper (1731–1800) on several occasions tried to poison, stab, or hang himself. The self-described "lines written during a period of insanity" were composed after one of his suicide attempts.

CHAPTER 1

Death Lies Near at Hand

— HISTORY AND OVERVIEW —

A tiny blade will sever the sutures of the neck, and when that
joint, which binds together head and neck, is cut, the body's
mighty mass crumples in a heap. No deep retreat conceals the
soul, you need no knife at all to root it out, no deeply driven
wound to find the vital parts; death lies near at hand. . . .
Whether the throat is strangled by a knot, or water stops the
breathing, or the hard ground crushes in the skull of one falling
headlong to its surface, or flame inhaled cuts off the course of
respiration—be it what it may; the end is swift.

—SENECA

NO ONE KNOWS who the first was to slash his throat with
a piece of flint, take a handful of poison berries, or inten-
tionally drop his spear to the ground in battle. Nor do we know
who first jumped impulsively, or after thought, from a great
cliff; walked without food into an ice storm; or stepped into the
sea with no intention of coming back. Death, as Seneca states,
has always lain close at hand; yet it is a mystery why the first to
kill himself did: Was it a sudden impulse, or prolonged disease?
An inner voice, commanding death? Perhaps shame or the
threat of capture by an enemy tribe? Despair? Exhaustion?
Pressure from others to spare common resources of food and
land? No one knows.

It is unlikely that *Homo sapiens* was the first to think of suicide or act on the thought of it; indeed, from an evolutionary perspective this would seem rather arbitrary, given the sophistication of the hominids before us. The Cro-Magnons, we believe, were skilled hunters, makers of blades and spears, plaiters of rope, users of fire, and reflective, ingenious inventors of remarkable art forms and elaborate burial rituals. And, there was *Homo neanderthalensis* before them, and the hunting apes, such as chimpanzees, known to be aggressive, social, and cognitively complex toolmakers. At what point did self-awareness enter into the life of the brain? When did a conscious, deliberate intent to die veer off from the borderlands of extreme recklessness and impetuous, life-threatening taking of risks? Violence and recklessness, profound social withdrawal, and self-mutilation are not, as we shall see, unique to our species. But perhaps suicide is.

We will never know who or why or how the first to kill himself did (or herself; we will never know that either). But it is very likely that once suicide occurred and others were cognizant of it, the act was repeated—in part because the reasons and means would remain integral to the psychological and physical environment, and in part because animals and humans learn, to considerable extent, through imitation. Suicide, dangerously, has a contagious aspect; it has, as well, for the vulnerable, an indisputable appeal as the solution of last resort.

Recorded observations about suicide are, of necessity, far more recent than its first occurrences. Society's attitudes, as captured in its literature, laws, and religious sanctions, provide one window into our collective reactions to self-murder. They give a historical perspective to the evolution of our perceptions about suicide, perceptions that have varied from our seeing it as an accepted and valued event to treating it as a sin or a crime, or conceptualizing it as the consequence of adverse circumstances or pathological mental states.

Certainly, cultures have varied in their notions of self-inflicted death. Several—for example, the Eskimo, Norse, Samoan, and

Crow Indian—accepted, and even encouraged, "altruistic" self-sacrifice among the elderly and sick. Among the Yuit Eskimos of St. Lawrence Island, if an individual requested suicide three times, relatives were obligated to assist in the killing. The person seeking suicide dressed in ritual death garb and then was killed in a "destroying place" set aside specifically for that purpose. To save commonly held resources of food or to allow a nomadic society to move on unhindered by the physically ill or elderly, some societies gave tacit if not explicit approval to suicide.

No early cultural or religious sanctions were attached to the suicides recorded in the Old Testament or to the only one, that of Judas Iscariot, described in the New (attitudes toward suicide hardened during the early years of Christianity). Most of these deaths, like those of the ancient Greeks portrayed by Homer, were seen as matters of honor, actions taken to avoid falling into the hands of a military enemy, to atone for wrongdoing, or to uphold a religious or philosophical principle. Hannibal, for example, took poison rather than be captured or dishonored, as did Demosthenes, Cassius, Brutus, Cato, and scores of others. Socrates, who refused to renounce his teachings and beliefs, drank hemlock. Gladiators thrust wooden sticks or spears down their throats or forced their heads into the spokes of moving carts in order that they might choose their own, rather than another's, time and way of dying.

Beliefs about suicide varied considerably in ancient Greece. The Stoics and Epicureans believed strongly in the individual's right to choose the means and time of his death. Others were less accepting of the idea. In Thebes and Athens, suicide was not against the law, but those who killed themselves were denied funeral rites and the hand that had been used for the act was severed from the arm. Aristotle regarded suicide as an act of cowardice, as well as an act against the state; so, too, did Pythagoras. (Although, according to Heracleitus, Pythagoras starved himself to death.) Roman law actively prohibited suicide and further prohibited the passing on to heirs of the suicide's possessions and estates. The Catholic Church from its earliest days opposed suicide and, during the sixth and seventh centuries, codified its opposition by excommunicating and denying funeral rites to those who died by their own hand. Suicide was never justifiable, wrote St. Augustine in an authoritative argument for the Church, because it violated the sixth commandment of God, "Thou shalt not kill."

Jewish custom forbade funeral orations for anyone who committed suicide; mourners' clothes were not encouraged, and burial was generally limited to an isolated section of the cemetery, so as "not to bury the wicked next to the righteous." The Semachot, the rabbinic text on death and mourning, states that "He who destroys himself consciously ('la-daat'), we do not engage ourselves with his funeral in any way. We do not tear the garments and we do not bare the shoulder in mourning and we do not say eulogies for him." Over time, a greater latitude and compassion was extended to suicides committed while of an unsound mind. "The general rule," states one scholar of Jewish tradition, "is that on the death of the suicide you do everything in honour of the surviving, such as visit and comfort and console them, but you do nothing in honour of the dead apart from burying them." In Islamic law, suicide is a crime as grave as, or even graver than, homicide.

Strong religious and legal sanctions against suicide are scarcely surprising; it would be odd indeed if society had no reaction to such a dramatic, seemingly inexplicable, frightening, frequently violent, and potentially infectious form of death. Dante, writing almost seven hundred years ago in *The Inferno*, assigned a particularly grim fate to those who committed suicide. Condemned to the seventh circle of Hell and transformed into bleeding trees, the damned and eternally restless souls of the suicides were subject to continuous agony and fed upon mercilessly by the Harpies. They who in "mad violence" killed themselves were, unlike all others who resided in Hell, also denied the use of their earthly human forms.

The civil desecration of the corpses of suicides was common, as were attempts to prevent untoward influence upon the living by physically isolating and constraining the body and its potentially dangerous spirit. The bodies of those who killed themselves were, in many countries, buried at night and at a crossroads. The greater traffic over such crossroads was thought to "keep the corpses down," and the intersection of paths, it was believed, would make it more difficult for the spirit to find its way home. In early Massachusetts, cartloads of stones were unloaded at the crossroads where a suicide had been buried. Not uncommonly, a stake was driven through a suicide's heart, a practice that has suggested to at least one scholar its similarity to the fate of a fourteenth-century murderer whose body was discovered years ago in the peat bogs of Sweden. The murderer's captors, in order to stop the dead man from "walking," drove birch stakes through his back, side, and heart; they then sank his body into a fen, at the meeting point of four parishes, in the not altogether unreasonable belief that he would be unlikely to escape.

The Finns believed that because the act of suicide was a sudden one, it was impossible for the living to make peace with the dead, and the soul of the suicide was therefore "particularly restless and spooky." The body of a suicide victim was handled with dispatch and wariness:

The deceased was washed as soon as possible after the death and clad in graveclothes. The male deceased were washed by men while the female ones by women. Epileptics, lunatics and suicides were not washed; on the contrary, they were buried prone on their stomach in the clothes they wore when they died. They were lifted into the coffin with pokers, never with bare hands, since it was feared that diseases and curse would catch hold of the family.

Up to the early 1900's the one who had committed suicide was buried without any funeral services. The grave was located beyond the fence of the churchyard, often even far away in the woods. It was a general opinion that the corpse of the suicide was heavy. Among the common people there were plenty of stories afloat that the coffin of the suicide had been too heavy even for a horse to haul.

In France, the body of a suicide was dragged through the streets, head downward, and then hanged on a gallows. French criminal law in the late seventeenth century also required that the body thereafter be thrown into a sewer or onto the city dump. Clergy did not attend the burial of a suicide, and corpses could not be buried in consecrated ground. In parts of Germany, the corpses of suicides were put in barrels and floated down the rivers so that they would not be able to return to their home territories. Early Norwegian laws dictated that the bodies of suicides were to be buried in the forest with those of other criminals, or "in the tide, where the sea and the green turf meet." Suicide was, strongly and simply put, "an irreparable deed."

Gradually, both religious and legal sanctions against suicide lessened. Although many theologians continued to assert that suicide was among the more unforgivable of sins—Martin Luther, for example, wrote that suicide was the work of the Devil; the Puritan religious leaders deemed it abhorrent, despicable, and an "individual submission to Satan"; John Wesley declared that the bodies of those who killed themselves should be "gibbeted and . . . left to rot"; and philosophers such as Locke, Rousseau, and, more recently, Kirkegaard railed vociferously against any kind of social or religious acceptance of suicide—judicial systems and the public increasingly considered suicide to be an act of an unbalanced mind, rather than the result of weakness or personal sin. Corpses were no longer buried at crossroads; gradually, instead, they were buried on the north sides of churchyards. Rather than suffering damnation in isolation, the bodies of suicides now kept the geographic company of society's other disreputables and non-Christians: excommunicants, unbaptized infants, and executed felons.

Robert Burton's widely read and influential *The Anatomy of Melancholy*, which depicted with compassion the bonds between madness, melancholy, and suicide and argued for mercy for those who were in such despair and agitation as to kill themselves, was published in 1621. Twenty-five years later, *Biathanatos*, a landmark treatise about suicide, was published. Its author, poet John Donne, was also the prominent dean of St. Paul's Cathedral in London. In *Biathanatos*, Donne declared that suicide was, on occasion, justified; certainly, he argued, it ought to be humanly understandable. It was, for him, personal. "Whensoever any affliction assails me," he confessed in the preface to his work, "methinks I have the keys of my prison in mine own hand, and no remedy presents itself so soon to my heart as mine own sword."

Two recent authors of excellent accounts of suicide trace similar patterns in the changing attitudes and laws in England and the United States. Mark Williams, in *Cry of Pain*, reports that in mid-seventeenth-century England fewer than one in ten suicide verdicts was judged to be non compos mentis, or due to insanity. By the 1690s that figure had climbed to 30 percent; in 1710 it was 40. By 1800, essentially all cases of suicide were regarded as being due to insanity.

The Massachusetts Puritans and other early American colonists generally treated those who killed themselves not only as sinners but also as criminals; over time, however, public attitudes and laws changed. In the seven decades from 1730 to 1800, as Howard Kushner has documented in *American Suicide*, the Boston Coroners' Juries made one non compos mentis determination for every two or three felonious ones. By 1801–1828, the ratio had flipped: there were two insanity decisions for every one felony suicide; at century's end, as in

England, non compos mentis was the usual verdict in suicide. (Of historical interest, the earliest suicide of an English settler in Massachusetts was probably that of *Mayflower* passenger Dorothy Bradford, the wife of William Bradford, who became the governor of Plymouth Colony. Dorothy Bradford, it was said, "accidentally fell overboard" from the ship and drowned in Cape Cod Harbor; historian Samuel Eliot Morison and others, however, believe that her death was a deliberate act rather than a mischance. Bradford himself does not mention his wife's death in his own account of the early colony.)

Most European countries formally decriminalized suicide in the eighteenth and nineteenth centuries, although it remained a crime in England and Wales until 1961 and in Ireland until 1993. Certainly, public understanding of suicide has increased over recent years, although not to a degree commensurate with what has been learned from medical and psychological research. The harshness of centuries-old views of suicide still touches the present, both in social policy and in more personal ways. In my copy of the Book of Common Prayer, for instance, in the small print that precedes the burial rites—a service that is at once of such consolation and ancient familiarity: "I am the resurrection and the life. . . . O death, where is thy sting?"—there is a damning reminder of archaic taboos and exclusions: the Order for the Burial of the Dead, the prayer book clearly states, "is not to be used for any that die unbaptized, or excommunicate, or have laid violent hands upon themselves."

HISTORY HAS reflected in its laws and attitudes at least a measure of the complexity of suicide. An act against the self, suicide is also a violent force in the lives of others. It is incomprehensible when it kills the young; it is awful in the old, inexplicable in the physically healthy or the successful, and too glibly explained away in the sick or failed. There are no simple theories for suicide, nor are there invariable algorithms with which to predict it; certainly, no one has ever found a way to heal the hearts or settle the minds of those left behind in its dreadful wake. What we do not know kills.

Yet we know a mastodonic amount about suicide.

We know, for example, a great deal about the underlying conditions that predispose an individual to kill himself—heredity, severe mental illness, an impulsive or violent temperament—and we know, too, that there are some events or circumstances in life that interact in a particularly deadly way with these predisposing vulnerabilities: romantic failures or upheavals; economic and job setbacks; confrontations with the law; terminal or debilitating illnesses; situations that cause great shame, or are perceived as such; the injudicious use of alcohol or drugs. We have much knowledge, as well, about *who* commits suicide: the most vulnerable age groups and the social backgrounds and gender of those most at risk; and we know, too, about the *hows* and *wheres* and *whens* of suicide: the methods used; the places, times, and seasons chosen.

But we are less certain of *why* people kill themselves. Psychological states, complex motives, and subtle biological differences are difficult enough to ascertain in the living; determining their existence, or the role they may play in those who die by suicide, is something else again. Inevitably, the research literature on suicide reflects the complexities, inconsistencies, and shortcomings in our understanding. It also reflects centuries of attempts to explain the incomprehensible act of self-murder. No one who has had close experience of this literature—the fifteen thousand scientific and clinical papers in the last thirty years alone, as well as the hundreds of books and monographs—can come away from it unimpressed by its depth and breadth of knowledge. No single book, or five, could capture the best of the historical literature or the most exciting of the new scientific and psychological studies.

I wrote *Night Falls Fast* with an awareness of these realities and a tremendous respect for the work done by earlier writers and researchers. My hope was to find a way to maintain an individual perspective—through an emphasis on the psychology of suicide and an extensive use of the words and experiences of those who seriously attempted to, or eventually did, kill themselves—but to keep that individual perspective firmly grounded in the sciences of psychopathology, genetics, psychopharmacology, and neurobiology. It is easy to become so focused on individual lives and deaths that one loses sight of the extraordinary scientific and medical advances of recent years—advances that can alleviate great suffering and save lives. Likewise, it is hard not to get so swept up in the excitement of gene hunting, brain imaging, and serotonin pathways that one forgets, as English poet and critic A. Alvarez has put it, that suicide is not only a "desperately sensitive and confused subject," it is also a problem "to be felt in the nerves and the senses."

It should not be necessary, at the end of a century so rich in literature, medicine, psychology, and science, to draw arbitrary lines in the sand between humanism and individual complexities, on the one hand, and clinical or scientific understandings, on the other. That they are bound and beholden to each other should be obvious. Yet it is undeniable that Maginot Lines exist. For many, the aesthetics of complexity—the singular appeal of psychological case histories, especially ones laced with sociological and cultural explanations—are far more compelling than statistical findings obtained from coroners' reports or DNA gels.

But such a focus on psychological complexity, at the expense of understanding psychopathological, genetic, or other biological factors, is as certain to fail as any consideration of biological causations and treatment that does not take into account the range of individual differences in experience, behavior, ability, and temperament. For those whose primary interests are in the arts and humanities, it will almost always be more intriguing to read about psychological conflicts or social determinants of suicide—and certainly, such matters are crucial to the understanding of suicide—but these factors alone may not be terribly helpful in predicting or preventing unnecessary early death in others.

Suicide as an existential issue is a core problem for philosophers, writers, and theologians; it is an issue of importance for most of us, whatever we do or do not believe. (Albert Camus, for one, believed that "Judging whether life is or is not worth living amounts to answering the fundamental question of philosophy.") But this book, although centrally concerned with the psychology of suicide, is also about suicide as a medical and social problem. Specifically, it is about why suicide occurs, why it is one of our most significant health problems, and how it can be prevented.

The book's focus is on suicide in those younger than forty, but this is in no way meant to downplay the terrible problem of suicide in those who are older. Study after study has shown that the elderly are inadequately treated for depression—the major cause of suicide in all age groups—and that suicide rates in the elderly are alarmingly high. Suicide in the older age groups is a topic for a book in its own right, however, and many of the issues raised in the context of geriatric suicide—"rational" suicide and physician-assisted suicide, especially within the context of disabling or life-threatening illness—are much less relevant to those who are younger.

Suicide in the young, which has at least tripled over the past forty-five years, is, without argument, one of our most serious public health problems. Suicide is the third leading cause of death in young people in the United States and the second for college students. The 1995 National College Health Risk Behavior Survey, conducted by the Centers for Disease Control and Prevention, found that one in ten college students had seriously considered suicide during the year prior to the survey; most had gone so far as to draw up a plan.

The figures for high school students surveyed in 1997 are even more worrying. One in five high school students said he or she had seriously considered suicide during the preceding year, and most of them had drawn up a suicide plan. Nearly one student in ten actually attempted suicide during the twelve-month period. One out of three of the suicide attempts was serious enough to require medical attention. These 1997 figures for high school students are substantially the same as those reported for high school students in 1995 and 1993.

Clearly, there is a difference between reporting the presence of suicidal thoughts or plans and actually attempting suicide; so, too, there is a crucial difference between attempting suicide and dying by it. Still, a suicide attempt remains the single best predictor of suicide, and these figures are reason for grave concern. Suicide, by any reckoning, is a major killer of the young.

Perhaps the magnitude of suicide in the young can best be illustrated by comparing the number of deaths from suicide with those from two other highly publicized causes of death in young men in the United States during the past forty years: the Vietnam War and the acquired immunodeficiency syndrome (HIV/AIDS) epidemic. I have graphed the number of deaths, in males under the age of thirty-five, for each of these three causes (see opposite page). Each—suicide, war, HIV/AIDS— has disproportionately killed young men. Obviously, any kind of death in this age group is terrible, whether it is from war, disease, or one's own hand. The Vietnam War took an appalling toll, but after twelve years it was over. A direct comparison of American male war deaths under the age of thirty-five during the official years of the Vietnam War, 1961–1973, with American deaths from suicide in the same age group, during the same time period, shows that there were almost twice as many suicides (101,732) as war deaths (54,708). Most Vietnam War–related deaths occurred during only a portion of those years (1966–1970), however.

A similar comparison of deaths from suicide and HIV/
AIDS, carried out for the ten-year period 1987–1996, shows
that almost 15,000 more young men died from suicide than
from AIDS. (Although some patients with AIDS committed
suicide during this period, they were relatively few.) The
American HIV/AIDS epidemic has fortunately become somewhat less lethal in recent years, due to the availability of combination antiretroviral therapy and public health education
campaigns. (Of interest, the 1995 National College Health
Risk Behavior Survey cited earlier found that one out of two

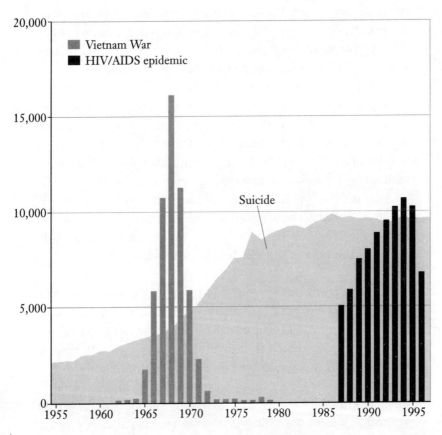

Deaths in males (35 years or younger)

college students received education about HIV/AIDS prevention but fewer than one in five received information about suicide prevention.)

Suicide, however, continues unabated, with little evidence of a decline. Indeed, the sharp increase in suicide in adolescents and young adults since the mid-1950s is obvious in the graph. So, too, is the cumulative death toll. Possible reasons for the increase—more accurate ascertainment of suicide deaths by coroners and medical examiners; an earlier and increased access to particularly lethal means, such as firearms; a younger age of first alcohol and drug use; an earlier age of onset of the severe mental illnesses; and increasing rates of depression—are discussed more extensively later in this book. Thirty thousand Americans kill themselves every year and nearly half a million make a suicide attempt medically serious enough to require emergency room treatment.

Wars come and go; epidemics come and go; but suicide, thus far, has stayed. Why is this, and what can be done about it? These questions are at the heart of this book: understanding why people kill themselves and determining what doctors, psychologists, schools and universities, parents, and society can do to stop it. The public outrage against war deaths and HIV/AIDS has been far more obvious and effective than the advocacy undertaken on behalf of those who have died from suicide, but the horror and the despair are no less real.

Suicide is a particularly awful way to die: the mental suffering leading up to it is usually prolonged, intense, and unpalliated. There is no morphine equivalent to ease the acute pain, and death not uncommonly is violent and grisly. The suffering of the suicidal is private and inexpressible, leaving family members, friends, and colleagues to deal with an almost unfathomable kind of loss, as well as guilt. Suicide carries in its aftermath a level of confusion and devastation that is, for the most part, beyond description.

The same Anglican Prayer Book that excludes from its final rites those who commit suicide speaks elsewhere of a "peace which the world cannot give." It is this peace that lies beyond the suicidal mind. In *The Anatomy of Melancholy*, Robert Burton wrote:

> There is . . . in this [melancholic] humour, the very seeds of fire. . . . In the day-time they are affrighted still by some terrible object, and torn in pieces with suspicion, fear, sorrow, discontents, cares, shame, anguish, etc., as so many wild horses, that they cannot be quiet an hour, a minute of time, but even against their wills they are intent, and still thinking of it, they cannot forget it, it grinds their souls day and night, they are perpetually tormented. . . . In the midst of these squalid, ugly, and such irksome days, they seek at last, finding no comfort, no remedy in this wretched life, to be eased of all by death . . . to be their own butchers, and execute themselves.

It is possible, with what we now know, to provide both comfort and remedy to stop at least some of the butchery. Most suicides, although by no means all, can be prevented. The breach between what we know and do is lethal.

CHAPTER 2

*To Measure
the Heart's Turbulence*

— DEFINITIONS AND MAGNITUDES —

> What a job is this, to measure
> lightning with a footrule, the heart's
> turbulence with a pair of callipers.
>
> —NORMAN MACCAIG

ONE WOULD not expect it to be easy to define or classify suicide, and it is not. Death by one's own hand is far too much a final gathering of unknown motives, complex psychologies, and uncertain circumstance—and it insinuates itself far too corrosively into the rights and fears and despairs of the living—for the definition of suicide to stay locked within the crisp categories chipped out by scientists or for it to adhere to the abstruse elaborations spun out by linguists and philosophers. Yet however permeable its edges, it remains important, as Henry Romilly Fedden observed in 1938, "to discover the elusive boundaries of suicide." The Indian widow dying on her husband's pyre is not, as he put it, "to be linked with the lonely individual strung up in his garret."

The early Greeks used highly active, decisive language to portray the act of suicide. To kill oneself was "to break up life," "to grasp or seize death," "to do violence to oneself," "to leave the light," or to commit "self-slaughter." But the Greeks, in giving words to the act, did not so much define as describe it. Centuries of books and scholarly papers later, the definitions and classification systems for suicide remain diverse, controversial, and subject to ongoing reinvention. Inevitably, a certain intellectual paralysis sets in after reading the hundreds of finely tuned medical, philosophical, and sociological attempts to classify suicide.

All suicide classification and nomenclature systems are, to a greater or lesser extent, flawed; and all, or almost all, have points that are well or uniquely taken. For clarity's sake and consistency, I have adopted the criteria developed by the Centers for Disease Control and Prevention (an agency of the United States Public Health Service in Atlanta) for the certification of a death as suicide, criteria that are used by scientists and public health officials, as well as by medical examiners and coroners. Suicide is defined, succinctly, as a "death from injury, poisoning, or suffocation where there is evidence (either explicit or implicit) that the injury was self-inflicted and that the decedent intended to kill himself/herself." The World Health Organization, whose even simpler definition underlies many of the international studies of suicide, defines suicide as "a suicidal act with a fatal outcome," where a suicidal act is defined as "self-injury with varying degrees of lethal intent."

Society, medical science, and family members require accuracy in determining whether an unnatural death is an accident, murder, or suicide. Families need to know the truth about suicide, as best as that truth can be known, so that they can come to terms with it and so that they can have available to them medical and genetic information that may be important in making treatment decisions about other close blood relatives. Legal and financial issues may be at stake as well, such as property rights, mental competency determinations in disputed estates, life insurance policies, pensions, workers' compensation, medical malpractice suits, and product liability claims.

Accurate suicide statistics are also essential for public health investigators, whose responsibility it is to track trends and correlates of death and disease. (Earlier estimates suggested that suicide rates, based upon information from coroners and medical examiners, were underreported by as much as 25 to 50 percent; more recent studies indicate that the underreporting is now probably less than 10 percent).

It is not always difficult to determine that suicide has occurred. Many instances are unequivocal: a gun is nearby, distinctive powder marks are found, a note has been written, and a psychiatric history or previous suicide attempt is documented. At other times, however, evidence must be pieced together—from autopsy findings, toxicology studies, psychological investigations, and statements from the deceased's family members, or witnesses to the death—to establish that death was, in fact, self-inflicted. Intent must also be established.

Most medical examiners and coroners use scientific and public health guidelines that specify that there must be evidence that the decedent intended to kill himself or herself or wished to die. The evidence may be *explicit*, that is, verbal or nonverbal expression of intent to kill oneself, or it may be *implicit* or *indirect*, such as "preparations for death inappropriate to or unexpected in the context of the decedent's life; an expression of farewell or the desire to die or an acknowledgment of impending death; expression of hopelessness; expression of great emotional or physical pain or distress; effort to procure or learn about means of death or to rehearse fatal behavior; precautions to avoid rescue; evidence that decedent recognized high potential lethality of means of death; previous suicide attempt; previous suicide threat; stressful events or significant losses (actual or threatened); serious depression or mental disorder."

Medical and psychological criteria can go only so far, of course, and many other factors influence the accuracy of suicide statistics. The reporting officials, for example, may be medical examiners who, in addition to being physicians, also have extensive specialist training in forensic medicine, or they may be coroners or elected officials; the latter, in particular, may be more swayed by a family's religious concerns, potential stigmatization or blame by the community, and possible financial repercussions to the survivors. Religious background may also influence the decisions reached by coroners and medical examiners. (In Canadian studies, for example, fewer suicide judgments were rendered by Catholic medical examiners than by non-Catholics, suggesting the possibility that religious views and sanctions continue to play a role in determining whether some unnatural deaths are designated as suicides or accidents.)

Cultural attitudes and practices also have an impact. In one investigation, Danish coroners, using the same case material as their English counterparts, assigned a much higher proportion of equivocal deaths to suicide. Perhaps, as the investigators noted, at least some of the differences were due to the fact that the determination of cause of death in Denmark is carried out in a medical rather than a legal context and that suicide, which was a criminal act in England until 1961, has not been a criminal offense in Denmark since 1866. Too, the Danes believe that they attach less stigma than the English to the primary mental illnesses underlying suicide—depression, manic-depression, and schizophrenia—and therefore to suicide as well.

The method of dying is also important. Coroners and medical examiners, for instance, tend to view hanging as an almost certain indicator of suicide; this is also true when death has resulted from carbon monoxide poisoning from the exhaust pipe of an automobile, plastic bag asphyxiations, and fatal wrist cuttings or throat slashings. Drowning deaths are far more debatable, however, as they may result from suicide, accident, or murder. Indeed, most drownings are accidental, but investigations may be problematic, as sociologist Maxwell Atkinson makes clear in this law enforcement version of "Hearts," where the corpse is played as the queen of spades and shuffled from jurisprudence to jurisprudence:

> For just as it is difficult to imagine ways in which people might end up hanged other than as a result of their own actions, it is very easy to envisage persons slipping, falling or even being pushed into the water from which their body is ultimately retrieved. The consequent difficulty in conducting the investigation and arriving at a definite verdict may be one of the reasons for a practice reported to me by a policeman who worked on one bank of a tidal river, which also marked the border between two police forces. According to him, it was not uncommon for policemen finding a body washed up on their side of the river to push it back into the water so that the tide would wash it up on the other side "so that the other force would have to deal with it." The other force, however, presumably with similar thoughts in mind used to do the same thing, so that a body might float backwards and forwards several times before it was finally taken in and investigated.

Deaths in single-car accidents, or head-on collisions with a large weight disparity between vehicles, also lend themselves to equivocal interpretations about the cause of death, as do some types of pedestrian deaths and deaths resulting from falls from high places. The most important cause of uncertainty in death certification, however, because of the large number of cases involved and the many confounding issues, is self-poisoning or drug overdose. Self-poisoning deaths—unlike cases of strangulation, drowning, gunshot wounds, or falls from heights—may not even look like unnatural deaths; as a result, they may not come to the attention of a coroner or medical examiner. Unless a death is seen as unexpected (for example, in a young person), an overdose death may be mistaken for a natural one.

Intent to die is ambiguous in many drug overdose deaths. Mental states may be clouded by mental illness, especially depression, leading some to take too many pills by accident; others, not fully intending to die, may underestimate the lethal strength of a drug or misgauge its potency in combination with alcohol or other drugs. In these situations, as in other equivocal circumstances surrounding death, a retrospective examination of the life and death of the decedent, a so-called psychological autopsy, can provide critical information about intent and state of mind.

The psychological autopsy is carried out by either an individual or a "Suicide Team" that conducts extensive interviews with family members, friends, physicians, and colleagues of the decedent in order to clarify the intent to die (if any) and the degree to which the death was self-inflicted. This technique was first used, in a more open-ended and less systematic format, by Gregory Zilboorg in an early psychoanalytic study of New York City police officers who had committed suicide. Although developed and most extensively used in the United States, the psychological autopsy is also utilized by researchers in Europe, South America, Australia, and Asia. Eli Robins, a psychiatrist at the Washington University School of Medicine, developed a more standardized interview format in the 1950s and used it to conduct a retrospective, community-based investigation of 134 consecutive cases of suicide in St. Louis. The study, now a classic in psychiatry, remains one of the clearest demonstrations of the almost ubiquitous presence of mental illness in those who commit suicide.

The psychological autopsy as a method of clinical and scientific investigation was most vigorously pursued and developed in the late 1950s and early 1960s by Norman Farberow, Robert Litman, and Edwin Shneidman of the Los Angeles Suicide Prevention Center, who worked in collaboration with

Theodore Curphey, then chief medical examiner for Los Angeles County. Their "death investigation," or psychological autopsy, set as its goal the re-creation of the mental state of the victim during the time leading up to his or her death. Members of the Suicide Team interview friends, family members, and doctors of the victim, covering a comprehensive range of topics: the cause or method of death; the victim's medical and psychiatric history; family background; the personality and lifestyle of the victim, as well as his or her typical patterns of reaction to stress, emotional upheavals, and "periods of disequilibrium"; upsets, pressures, tensions, or anticipation of trouble during the days, weeks, and months preceding death; the role of alcohol or drugs in the lifestyle and death of the victim; the nature of the victim's personal relationships; fantasies, dreams, thoughts, or premonitions relating to death or suicide that the victim may have expressed; changes in personal or work habits and eating or sexual behavior; information about upswings, successes, or plans; an assessment of intention; a rating of the severity of suicidal thinking and behavior; and reactions of those interviewed to the victim's death.

From this information and a detailed analysis of the death itself, the Suicide Team puts together a description of the victim's last days and then presents its findings to the coroner or medical examiner. Often, in seemingly equivocal cases, the recommendation is a persuasive one for a verdict of suicide; in other instances, however, the evidence leads to a decision for accident. The following case, illustrative of the kinds of questions asked and the investigative work involved, is from the files of the Los Angeles Suicide Prevention Center. When first presented to the Suicide Team, the death appeared to be a suicide; after completion of the psychological autopsy, however, the team recommended that it be certified as an accident:

In practically any coroner's office, a death that results from playing Russian roulette would automatically be certified as suicide. Indeed, there is now legal precedent for such certifications. Because of a special interest on the part of the Suicide Team in this type of death, this case was turned over to them by the coroner for investigation, with, as it turned out, extremely surprising results. On the basis of interviews it was ascertained that the victim, a 28-year-old male, was an Army veteran who had a collection of revolvers, which he kept in perfect operating condition. It was determined from his best friend that the victim's favorite activity at parties was to play Russian roulette (following the usual rules of the game by having one chamber of the cylinder loaded) and that he had done this literally dozens of times in the preceding few years. At this point, the Suicide Team wondered about the psychology of a man who would behave in such a fashion: was he psychotic or was he intent on killing himself? Interviews with the widow clarified the situation: the victim had told her that there was no possibility of his hurting himself, as he always glanced at the gun to ascertain that the bullet was in a nonlethal position before he pulled the trigger. If the bullet was one notch to the left of the barrel, he would spin the cylinder again. There had been no suicidal ideation and no evidence of depression, psychosis, or morbid content of thought. What had happened? The Suicide Team knew that the death had occurred in someone else's home. Interviews developed the information that he shot himself with a revolver that was not his own but belonged to his host of the evening. What seemed most important was the fact that, whereas his collection consisted entirely of Smith and Wesson revolvers, he had killed himself with a Colt revolver. The actions of the two guns are different; that is, the cylinder of the Smith and Wesson revolves clockwise. It was believed that the victim, checking and seeing the bullet one space to the right of the barrel, thought that he could not possibly kill himself, whereas in reality pulling the trigger put the bullet in the lethal position and he died immediately.

In the absence of any indication of suicidal affect or any indications of suicidal ideation, and with the additional information about the two types of revolvers, the Suicide Team recommended that this death be considered as accidental. One member of the Suicide Team labeled this case as one of Soviet Roulette, that is, Russian roulette in which one cheats.

The psychological autopsy, in modified and different standardized forms, has been widely used in suicide research, as well as in coroners' and medical examiners' offices. It has proven especially useful in understanding the extent of the link between psychopathology and suicide.

SUICIDE IS the anchor point on a continuum of suicidal thoughts and behaviors. This continuum is one that ranges from risk-taking behaviors at one end, extends through different degrees and types of suicidal thinking, and ends with suicide attempts and suicide. Suicide attempts include not only those acts where there is a clear or likely intent to die but those where there is no intent to die (for instance, acts where the individual wishes to use the appearance of intending to kill himself or herself in order to obtain some other end).

Risk-taking behaviors, while important, almost always involve considerable speculation about underlying intent. They may involve either immediate risk, such as skydiving, or more remote risk, such as smoking or reckless driving. These indirect, or "subintentional," deaths—defined by Shneidman as those "in which the decedent has played a covert, partial, latent, unconscious role in hastening his own death"—have come to include, depending on the clinician or researcher, everything from chronic alcohol or drug abuse or involvement in high-risk sports, to a variety of other activities, such as having unprotected sex with partners at high risk for AIDS, handling poisonous snakes, and provoking rage in those known to be physically violent (so-called victim-precipitated homicide).

Suicidal ideation, which is to say thinking about suicide, is also a problematic concept but one that is more amenable to inquiry and measurement. Thoughts about suicide are relatively common in every age group that has been studied, but the number of people acknowledging such thoughts varies, of course, depending on the nature of the questions asked. The time frame strongly affects the total number of individuals who acknowledge suicidal thoughts or plans: some studies, for example, inquire only about suicidal thoughts during the past week; others ask whether such thoughts occurred during the preceding year; and yet others whether or not the individual has ever, during the course of a lifetime, had suicidal thoughts. Interviewers also ask about the frequency of suicidal thoughts— were the thoughts rare, occasional, frequent, daily, several times a day?—as well as about the severity of intent.

Twenty-five years ago, in an early community-based study of suicidal thinking and behaviors, University of Cambridge psychiatrist Gene Paykel and his colleagues interviewed more than 700 people in New Haven, Connecticut. The results gave a public face to what had been very private thoughts. More than 10 percent of those interviewed said that, at some point in their lives, they had felt that "life was not worth living," and a comparable number said that they had, at one time or another, "wished they were dead." One person in twenty had thought about actually taking his or her own life, and most of those who had thought about suicide had thought about it seriously. One person in a hundred said he or she had attempted suicide.

Approximately twenty years ago, the National Institute of

Mental Health began the largest study ever undertaken of the nature and extent of psychiatric disorders in the U.S. population. It involved extensive interviews of a total of 20,000 people living in the five American catchment areas of Baltimore, Maryland; Piedmont County, North Carolina; Los Angeles, California; New Haven, Connecticut; and St. Louis, Missouri. The study included four questions about suicide, similar to those asked by Paykel and his colleagues, but was more specific in that it required a minimal duration for suicidal thoughts of two weeks. Of the 18,500 individuals who responded to the questions about suicide, 11 percent said they had at some point during their lives felt so low they had thought of committing suicide; 3 percent of the total said they had made one or more suicide attempts. Other investigations conducted in general communities have found that, consistent with these two studies, between 5 and 15 percent of the general adult population acknowledge having had suicidal thoughts at some point in their lives.

College students, asked the same or similar questions, generally report as high or higher rates. The most comprehensive study of university and college students, the 1995 National College Health Risk Behavior Survey (the Centers for Disease Control and Prevention study discussed earlier), questioned 4,600 undergraduate college students across the United States. Ten percent of the students said they had seriously considered attempting suicide during the twelve months preceding the survey, and 7 percent had actually drawn up a suicide plan. Other research, conducted in Europe and Africa as well as in the United States, has shown that mild to severe thoughts of suicide are common, occurring in 20 to 65 percent of college students.

High school students also report disconcertingly high rates of suicidal thinking. The 1997 Youth Risk Behavior Surveillance Survey, cited in the last chapter, canvassed more than 16,000 ninth- through twelfth-grade students (fifteen- to eighteen-year-olds) across the United States. Fully 20 percent, or one in five, said that they had "seriously considered" attempting suicide in the preceding twelve months; 16 percent said they had drawn up a plan. Girls were much more likely to have considered or planned a suicide attempt, and Hispanic students were more likely than either whites or African Americans to acknowledge having thought about suicide. Two other studies of American high school students confirmed that thinking about suicide is far from a rare concern: more than 50 percent of New York high school students reported that they had "thought about killing themselves," and 20 percent of Oregon high school students described a history of suicidal thinking of varying degrees of severity.

Studies in Europe and other parts of North America report similar findings. One in twenty French boys fifteen to eighteen years old, and one in ten French girls of similar age, stated that they had thought about suicide "fairly often, or very often" during the preceding year. In Canada, one in ten high school students reported having thought about suicide at least once during the preceding week. Another Canadian study, carried out in a slightly younger age group (twelve- to sixteen-year-olds), found that thoughts of suicide almost doubled in girls from the time they were twelve or thirteen to the time they were between the ages of fourteen and sixteen (the rates went from 7.5 to 14.5 percent). The boys showed exactly the opposite pattern, dropping from 6.7 to 3.3 percent in the same age groups. These differences between the sexes almost certainly reflect, at least to some extent, the higher rate of depression in girls and women, which is discussed later in greater detail.

These statistics are disturbing, but it is of further concern that there is a wide discrepancy between what children report and what their parents actually notice. In one investigation of suicidal behavior in girls, for example, more than 15 percent of the children reported having had suicidal thoughts or behavior. Very few of their parents were aware that of their children's experiences. This same unawareness of their children's suicidal thoughts and actions has been found for the parents of boys as well. Parents also seriously underestimate the extent of depression in their adolescent children.

It is understandably difficult for parents to believe that young children are in such pain as to wish to die, yet many children are. Cynthia Pfeffer, a child psychiatrist at Cornell University, finds that more than 10 percent of a sample of "normal" schoolchildren, that is, children with no history of psychiatric symptoms or illness, report suicidal impulses. One of the children in her study, a ten-year-old girl, described her thinking explicitly and painfully: "I often think of killing myself. It started when I was almost hit by a car. Now, I want to kill myself. I think of stabbing myself with a knife. When Mom yells at me, I think she does not love me. I worry a lot about my family. Mom is always depressed and sometimes she says she will die soon. My brother becomes very angry, often for no reason. He tried to kill himself last year and had to go to the hospital. Mom was in the hospital once also. I worry a lot about my family. I worry that if something happens to them, no one will take care of me. I feel sad about this."

Another child, a ten-year-old boy, also described his thoughts both specifically and graphically: "I want to hurt myself when I get upset and angry. I bang my head against the wall or punch the wall with my fist. I wish I were dead. I often think about how to kill myself. I think I will go to France to have myself guillotined. It would be quick and painless. Guns are too painful, so is stabbing myself. Once, I put my head into a sink of water and I got scared. My grandmother found me. I told her I was washing my face. Mom was shocked when she heard about this. She began to cry. She worries a lot and always seems sad."

Most instances of suicidal thought, although often frightening and of concern, lead to neither a suicide attempt nor suicide, but some do.

The line between suicidal thoughts and action is not as clear as it might seem. A potentially deadly impulse may be interrupted before it is ever acted upon, or an attempt with mild intent and danger of death may be carried out in full expectation of discovery and survival. Often, people want both to live and to die; ambivalence saturates the suicidal act. Some wish to escape, but only for a while. A few use suicide threats or attempts to make others "pay" for a slight or rejection, yet others to provoke change in the decisions and behaviors of people they know.

Many who attempt suicide later deny or minimize it once the acute crisis or pain is in the past. Novelist Evelyn Waugh, for instance, suffered two professional setbacks, scarcely insurmountable critical reviews of his work, when he was in his early twenties. Desperately unhappy, he decided to end it all. Years later, in recounting his suicide attempt, Waugh questioned how much of what he had done was "real" and how much just "play-acting":

> One night . . . I went down alone to the beach with my thoughts full of death. I took off my clothes and began swimming out to sea. Did I really intend to drown myself? That certainly was in my mind and I left a note with my clothes, the quotation from Euripides about the sea which washes away all human ills. I went to the trouble of verifying it, accents and all, from the school text. . . . At my present age I cannot tell you how much real despair and act of will, how much play-acting, prompted the excursion.
>
> It was a beautiful night of a gibbous moon. I swam slowly out but, long before I reached the point of no return, the Shropshire Lad was disturbed by a smart on the shoulder. I had run into a jelly-fish. A few more strokes, a second more painful sting. The placid waters were full of the creatures.

An omen? A sharp recall to good sense . . . ?

I turned about, swam back through the track of the moon to the sands. . . . As earnest of my intent I had brought no towel. With some difficulty I dressed and tore into small pieces my pretentious classical tag, leaving them to the sea, moved on that bleak shore by tides stronger than any known to Euripides, to perform its lustral office. Then I climbed the sharp hill that led to all the years ahead.

Waugh was not alone in having had his uncertainties about intent and action. There is, in fact, no consistent definition of what is meant by a "suicide attempt"; nor are there universally agreed-upon criteria for distinguishing levels of determination or for classifying the degrees of medical dangerousness from an attempt. Many things need to be taken into account by clinicians and researchers who try to ascertain the seriousness of a person's will to die or who have to assess the extent of the medical complications from a suicidal act.

A Suicide Intent Scale was developed by Aaron T. Beck and his colleagues at the University of Pennsylvania for use with patients who attempt suicide but survive. The kinds of clinical observations and questions asked—whether or not the act took place in isolation, the degree of premeditation, the reasons for the attempt—provide an idea of what clinicians and scientists are interested in when they look at issues of intent and suicide planning.

Suicide Intent Scale

(for Attempters)

I. Objective Circumstances Related to Suicide Attempt

1. Isolation
   0. Somebody present
   1. Somebody nearby, or in visual or vocal contact
   2. **No one nearby or in visual or vocal contact**

2. Timing
   0. Intervention is probable
   1. Intervention is not likely
   2. **Intervention is highly unlikely**

3. Precautions against Discovery/Intervention
   0. No precautions
   1. Passive precautions (as avoiding others but doing nothing to prevent their intervention; alone in room with unlocked door)
   2. **Active precautions (as locked door)**

4. Acting to Get Help During/After Attempt
   0. Notified potential helper regarding attempt
   1. Contacted but did not specifically notify potential helper regarding attempt
   2. **Did not contact or notify potential helper**

5. Final Acts in Anticipation of Death (e.g., will, gifts, insurance)
   0. None
   1. Thought about or made some arrangements
   2. **Made definite plans or completed arrangements**

6. Active Preparation for Attempt
   0. None
   1. Minimal to moderate
   2. **Extensive**

7. Suicide Note
    0. Absence of note
    1. Note written, but torn up; note thought about
    2. **Presence of note**

8. Overt Communication of Intent Before the Attempt
    0. None
    1. Equivocal communication
    2. **Unequivocal communication**

II. Self-Report

9. Alleged Purpose of Attempt
    0. To manipulate environment, get attention, revenge
    1. Components of "0" and "2"
    2. **To escape, surcease, solve problems**

10. Expectations of Fatality
    0. Thought that death was unlikely
    1. Thought that death was possible but not probable
    2. **Thought that death was probable or certain**

11. Conception of Method's Lethality
    0. Did less to self than he thought would be lethal
    1. Wasn't sure if what he did would be lethal
    2. **Equaled or exceeded what he thought would be lethal**

12. Seriousness of Attempt
    0. Did not seriously attempt to end life
    1. Uncertain about seriousness to end life
    2. **Seriously attempted to end life**

13. Attitude Toward Living/Dying
    0. Did not want to die
    1. Components of "0" and "2"
    2. **Wanted to die**

14. Conception of Medical Rescuability
    0. Thought that death would be unlikely if he received medical attention
    1. Was uncertain whether death could be averted by medical attention
    2. **Was certain of death even if he received medical attention**

15. Degree of Premeditation
    0. None; impulsive
    1. Suicide contemplated for three hours or less prior to attempt
    2. **Suicide contemplated for more than three hours prior to attempt**

III. Other Aspects (Not Included in Total Score)

16. Reaction to Attempt
    0. Sorry that he made attempt; feels foolish, ashamed (circle which one)
    1. Accepts both attempt and its failure
    2. **Regrets failure of attempt**

17. Visualization of Death
    0. Life-after-death, reunion with decedents
    1. Never-ending sleep, darkness, end of things
    2. **No conceptions of or thoughts about death**

18. Number of Previous Attempts
    0. None
    1. One or two
    2. **Three or more**

19. Relationship Between Alcohol Intake and Attempt
    0. Some alcohol intake prior to but not related to attempt, reportedly not enough to impair judgment, reality testing

1. Enough alcohol intake to impair judgment, reality testing and diminish responsibility
2. **Intentional intake of alcohol in order to facilitate implementation of attempt**

20. Relationship Between Drug Intake and Attempt (narcotics, hallucinogens, etc., when drug is *not* the method used to suicide)
    0. Some drug intake prior to but not related to attempt, reportedly not enough to impair judgment, reality testing
    1. Enough drug intake to impair judgment, reality testing and diminish responsibility
    2. **Intentional drug intake in order to facilitate implementation of attempt**

Note: The responses most indicative of severe suicide intent are highlighted here in bold print.

Reproduced with permission of Aaron T. Beck, M.D., University Professor of Psychiatry, University of Pennsylvania.

In addition to scales designed to assess the intent to die, there are a number of clinical and research measures that assess the medical seriousness of a suicide attempt. Firearms and hanging are likely to kill and hard to reverse, in contrast to self-poisonings, which are less likely to kill and easier to treat. (Availability and quality of medical care also affect the potential deadliness of a method. In developed countries, where access to emergency treatment is more common than not, death from self-poisoning is less of a risk than in less affluent regions of the world, where deadly agricultural pesticides are more readily available but medical care is not.) The actual medical damage sustained from the attempt can be measured by rating, among other things, the level of consciousness, the extent of permanent injury caused by the suicide attempt, and the extent and nature of the medical procedures required (for example, outpatient care only versus admission to a medical or surgical ward or to an intensive care unit).

Given the disparate views of what constitutes a suicide attempt, it is scarcely surprising that the reported rates for such attempts vary quite widely. In general, however—whether the research is carried out in Europe, North America, Australia, the Mideast, or the Far East—between 1 and 4 percent of all adults state that they have, at some point in their lives, attempted suicide. Adolescents, on the other hand, have higher and more variable rates: between 2 and 10 percent of young people across the world state that they have tried to kill themselves, and a significant number of them report having made more than one attempt. It is unclear why this discrepancy in suicide attempt rates should exist between the older and younger age groups, although several explanations have been suggested.

Myrna Weissman, a psychiatric epidemiologist at Columbia University in New York, has found compelling evidence of a dramatic doubling or even tripling of rates of suicide attempts over recent decades. Some of this may be due to a "cohort effect," that is, a genuine increase in rates of suicidal behavior and depression in individuals born in more recent years; this will be discussed later in more detail. There may also be a tendency to forget or minimize suicide attempts over time. In one study carried out in Australia, for instance, 40 percent of those who acknowledged thinking about suicide at one point in their lives, when asked the same questions four years later denied ever having had such thoughts. Less severe suicide attempts may be particularly susceptible to forgetting, and, of course, some of those who attempt suicide when young will kill themselves before ever reaching adulthood. Too, younger people may simply be more willing to acknowledge suicidal behavior.

THE RELATION between suicide attempts and suicide is murky. There are an estimated ten to twenty-five suicide attempts for every completed suicide. And many, if not most, people who attempt to kill themselves do so more than once.

Gender certainly plays a role in both suicide attempts and suicide. Women in the United States are two to three times more likely to attempt suicide than men. American men, on the other hand, are four times as likely actually to kill themselves. The reasons for this are complicated and will be dealt with at different points throughout this book, but part of the discrepancy may be due to differences in the rates and types of the psychiatric illnesses associated with suicide and attempted suicide. Women and girls, for example, are at least twice as likely as men to suffer from depression, which may account for some of the increase in the rate of suicide attempts. This higher rate of depression in women has been extensively documented in many studies, including the major international investigation led by Myrna Weissman. In each of the ten countries she and her colleagues studied—the United States, Canada, Puerto Rico, France, West Germany, Italy, Lebanon, Taiwan, Korea, and New Zealand—depressive illness was far more common in women than men. Rates for manic-depression, on the other hand, were the same for both sexes.

Although depression is more common in women, their depressive illnesses may be less impulsive and violent than those of men; this in turn may make women less likely to use violent methods and more likely to use relatively safer means such as self-poisoning. There is also evidence that men are more likely than women to feel there is a stigma attached to a "failed" suicide attempt. Women also may remember and report the attempts they do make more accurately.

Men, who may have a more aggressive and volatile component to their depression, are also less likely to seek medical help for psychiatric problems. They further add to their suicide risk by using alcohol and drugs and keeping firearms. (This is not a recent phenomenon, as we shall see later when discussing suicide methods in more detail. The first edition of the *American Journal of Insanity*, published in 1845, reported that more than two-thirds of men who committed suicide used violent and highly lethal means—firearms, throat slashing, or hanging—whereas only one-third of the women used such methods.)

The method used in a suicide attempt clearly has a determining power in whether an individual lives or dies. China, whose citizens accounted for more than 40 percent of the world's suicide deaths in 1990, is the only major country where a comparable number of women and men die by suicide. Although other social factors certainly play a role, the percentage of the population still living on the land and the widespread availability of highly lethal pesticides, coupled with little or no access to emergency medical care, make death from self-poisoning more likely in China than in the Western nations.

There is a crucial overlap between those who attempt suicide and those who commit it: long-term (ten- to forty-year) follow-up studies, for example, show that of those who attempt suicide, 10 to 15 percent will eventually kill themselves. Predicting who will go on to complete suicide is one of the most difficult, frustrating, and essential clinical problems that there is. The borders between thinking, acting, and fatal action are more tenuous, uncertain, and dangerous than any of us would like to believe; this Robert Lowell captured well in his final verses from "Suicide":

> *Do I deserve credit*
> *for not having tried suicide—*
> *or am I afraid*
> *the exotic act*
> *will make me blunder,*

not knowing error
is remedied by practice,
as our first home-photographs,
headless, half-headed, tilting
extinguished by a flashbulb?

Suicide, which kills approximately 30,000 Americans a year, takes a terrible toll across all continents. A recent World Health Organization report estimates that suicide was the cause of 1.8 percent of the world's 54 million deaths in 1998. Suicide figures even more prominently as a cause of death in the young. The ten leading causes of death for males and females between the ages of fifteen and forty-four are shown in the graph on the opposite page. Suicide, it can be seen, is the second major killer of women in this age group and the fourth major killer of men. By any standards, suicide is a critical public health problem.

During the past half century, rates of suicide in the young have been increasing throughout the world. The rapid rise, especially in those below the age of twenty-five, has been a major concern to clinicians, scientists, and public health officials. British researchers, for instance, surveyed the change in youth suicide rates in eighteen countries from the early 1960s to the 1970s. There were significant increases in virtually all of the countries. Researchers at the Karolinska Institute in Stockholm tracked suicide patterns over a thirty-year period, from 1952 to 1981, and found that the risk of a twenty-year-old man committing suicide before the age of twenty-five had increased by 260 percent.

In the United States, between 1980 and 1992, the rate of suicide in children aged ten to fourteen increased by 120 percent. In 1995, more teenagers and young adults died from suicide than died from cancer, heart disease, AIDS, pneumonia, influenza, birth defects, and stroke combined. There are, as Maryland's chief medical examiner has put it, "too many, too young." The strong trend toward higher suicide rates at earlier

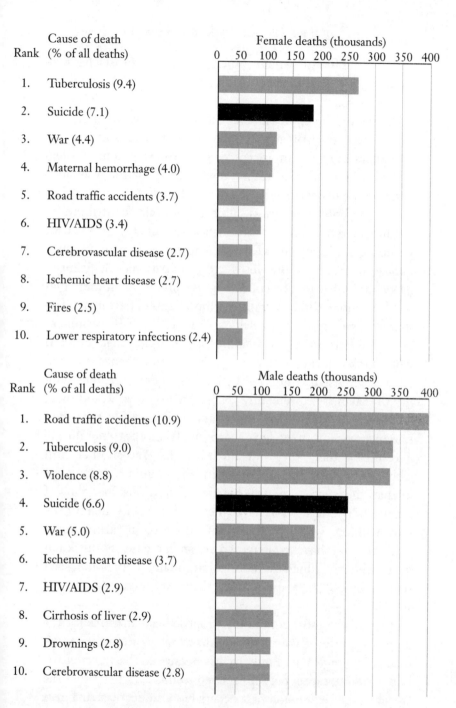

Rank	Cause of death (% of all deaths)	Female deaths (thousands)
1.	Tuberculosis (9.4)	
2.	Suicide (7.1)	
3.	War (4.4)	
4.	Maternal hemorrhage (4.0)	
5.	Road traffic accidents (3.7)	
6.	HIV/AIDS (3.4)	
7.	Cerebrovascular disease (2.7)	
8.	Ischemic heart disease (2.7)	
9.	Fires (2.5)	
10.	Lower respiratory infections (2.4)	

Rank	Cause of death (% of all deaths)	Male deaths (thousands)
1.	Road traffic accidents (10.9)	
2.	Tuberculosis (9.0)	
3.	Violence (8.8)	
4.	Suicide (6.6)	
5.	War (5.0)	
6.	Ischemic heart disease (3.7)	
7.	HIV/AIDS (2.9)	
8.	Cirrhosis of liver (2.9)	
9.	Drownings (2.8)	
10.	Cerebrovascular disease (2.8)	

Leading causes of death in females and males, worldwide, ages 15–44 ages, a trend found by many other groups of scientists, has provoked a great deal of speculation and research about why this should be so.

Some of the increase may be due simply to more accurate reporting of suicide; that is, coroners and medical examiners are now more correctly attributing some violent teen deaths to suicide rather than classifying them as accidents or equivocal deaths. Easier and earlier access to firearms, alcohol, and drugs almost certainly contribute to the higher rates, making those who are vulnerable to suicide yet more so. There is, as well, some suggestion that neurological damage to the fetus from nutritional deficiencies or alcohol, nicotine, or cocaine use in pregnant mothers may result in more children with the mood and behavior patterns that are associated with suicide. (American and Finnish studies published in 1999 found, for example, that mothers who smoke during pregnancy increase the chances of violence, impulsivity, and addictive disorders in their children.) Likewise, premature babies who once would have died are now surviving longer, and it is possible that their nervous systems may have been made more vulnerable as a result of their very low birth weight. Yet another possible reason for the increase in the number of suicides is that the success of psychiatric medications has allowed many individuals who have mental illness to marry and have children who would not have done so in earlier times, and this may have contributed to an increase in the kinds of psychiatric illnesses (depression, manic-depression, and schizophrenia) that carry with them an increased rate of suicide.

One of the most commonly proposed explanations for the increasing rate of youth suicide, however, is the observation that the average age of puberty has decreased sharply over the last several decades; perhaps related to this is the fact that the age at which depression first occurs has also decreased. There is additional evidence that the actual rates of depression may have increased over time.

Because depression and other forms of mental illness are at the heart of many suicides, it is to these disorders of terrible despair, confusion, hopelessness, and reckless impulse that we now turn.

This Life, This Death

A lonely impulse of delight
Drove to this tumult in the clouds;
I balanced all, brought all to mind,
The years to come seemed waste of breath,
A waste of breath the years behind
In balance with this life, this death.

—William Butler Yeats,
"An Irish Airman Foresees His Death"

THERE IS a moment as you watch that your heart stops and you wish you could return the videotape to its owners and forget what you have seen. You know the end of the story; you know that what is done is done; and still there is a terrible sadness in it, more even than you had reckoned on. The tape is difficult to watch, impossible not to, and dreadful in its foretelling.

The home video, no doubt like a hundred others taken that same day, scopes across the Rampart mountain range of the Colorado Rockies, which in turn sets the stage for the man-made jags and triangulars of the buildings of the U.S. Air Force Academy. Lurching, the camera continues to record landscape and people and the day's events, settling at last on the parade ground covered with squadrons of marching cadets in their dress blue jackets, white pants, white gloves, and golden sashes. A thousand, or nearly, graduating seniors; all of them, but one, newly commissioned officers.

The marching ends, and one by one the cadets receive their diplomas, salute, and return to their seats. Each name, a moment; each brisk salute, an exercise in pent enthusiasm.

Slowly, the camera's field becomes more focused, more personal, and a name is called out. It is clear from the crowd's response—a roar of appreciation goes up from his classmates—that the young man is immensely popular; indeed, a fellow cadet has described him as the most respected senior at the Academy, and his squadron has given him its outstanding leadership award.

The young man takes his diploma, raises gloved hand to hat, and salutes sharply, quickly. He smiles gloriously, graciously, contagiously, and you begin to understand the warmth and extent of his classmates' response.

But it is not at this moment that your heart stops, although a certain melancholy seeps in. Rather, it is later, after all the names have been called, all the salutes given and received. For the moment, the martial measures of the Air Force song pound out across the parade field and stadium, and then, suddenly, a thousand freshly minted second lieutenants snap their heads back and watch six F-16s streak overhead in tight formation, the traditional flyover tribute to the Academy's new officers. Before the jet contrails begin to fade, total pandemonium breaks out and hundreds of white hats are flung high into the air, sailing every which way into the sky, creating a higgledy-piggledy of bobbing specks of white. Cheers and embraces obliterate the remaining shreds of order.

The home video focuses once again on the young man whose slowly spreading smile had so captivated, whose appearance had evoked such spontaneous warmth and cheers from his classmates. He, like them, had watched the jets overhead and flung his hat into the air. But this is the moment that causes your heart to stop—his face displays a subtle but chilling confusion. He seems unmoored, not quite sure of what to do next, slightly glassed off from the swirl around him. It is painful to watch because you know the end of the story, and almost unbearable because you know that this is in some way the beginning of that end.

The young man, Drew Sopirak, did not return to the Air Force Academy the night of his graduation, nor did he receive his officer's commission. Although he had dreamed for years of becoming a pilot and had won a highly competitive slot in flight school, he never received his pilot's wings. That evening, instead, he left the celebrations to return to a place in which no one could have imagined him, the psychiatric ward of a nearby military hospital. There he tried to sort out the most recent hand he had been dealt. Unlike all previous hands, which had been flush with love and luck and ability, this one was a nightmare of all things lost. It was unexpected and, ultimately, unplayable.

Success, it would seem, was not a sufficient teacher. Nor, would it seem, were remarkably caring friends and family. Drew Sopirak had all these in full measure. He was, by every account of his friends and instructors, warm, vivacious, and hugely popular with his peers; a natural leader; "drop-dead gorgeous"; and a person for whom no one was a stranger. "There was just something about him," said one of his friends. "I don't think anyone could quite pin it down as to why he was so wonderful—he just was." He had been valedictorian of his Wilmington, Delaware, high school; president of both his junior and senior classes; Homecoming King; captain of his sports teams; and an engaging "Mole" in a community production of *The Wind in the Willows*. It was of little surprise to anyone that Drew was offered appointments to both West Point and the Air Force Academy. He had been expected to succeed, and he had.

Drew chose the Air Force Academy, an easy decision for an eighteen-year-old with a passion for all things that fly and a dream and a determination to become a pilot. Yet within eighteen months of graduating from the Academy, Drew Sopirak somehow found his life so painful and his future so bleak that he went to a gun store, bought a .38-caliber revolver, and pulled the trigger. When it misfired, he pulled the trigger again.

He was twenty-three years old: the way down had been long, and it had been fast.

> Minds of men fashioned a crate of thunder,
>   Sent it high into the blue;
> Hands of men blasted the world asunder;
>   How they lived God only knew!
> Souls of men, dreaming of skies to conquer
>   Gave us wings, ever to soar!
> . . . .
>   Keep the wings level and true.
>
> —"United States Air Force Song"

The Air Force had prepared Drew for many of the things he might expect in life, but it did not, nor could it, prepare him for madness. So when his mind snapped, just a few weeks shy of graduation, he had no equivalent of his earlier survival training to see him through the splintering mania and subsequent, inevitable flameout. His mind pelted first out of bounds and then out of commission; it took along with it his dreams and his life. Manic-depressive illness proved to be an enemy out of range and beyond the usual rules of engagement.

Drew was to mention later that he had experienced occasional problems with racing thoughts and periods of depression prior to his first manic episode. But these he had kept to himself. He was the last person any of his friends would have expected to become psychotic or to have to be confined to a psychiatric hospital. The very unexpectedness and the seeming incongruity, however, were themselves not entirely unexpected, given the nature of the illness that was to kill Drew. Manic-depressive illness usually strikes young, not uncommonly during the college years, and not uncommonly in the apparently invincible—the outgoing, the energetic, the academically successful.

Drew's own academic work, which had been excellent, began to decline significantly during his last months at the Air Force Academy. His roommate noted that at about the same time Drew was making statements "that did not make a lot of sense," and his mother became increasingly concerned that he "sounded paranoid" when she talked to him on the telephone. He was, by his own report, intensely euphoric, sleeping little, and some nights sleeping not at all.

In the midst of his sleeplessness, increasingly manic, Drew became convinced that he had the answers to many or most of the world's problems and that he was a messenger of God. He designed a super spacecraft, based less on his background in aeronautical engineering than on his newly, and delusionally, acquired understanding of UFOs. The spacecraft, as he drew and described it, had spinning lights, a mysteriously increasing energy source, "a new kind of synergy" derived from dry-ice packs and plasma, and a strange force field that created a flow pulse that would somehow "push" the aircraft. The concepts are difficult to follow—indeed incoherent, as manic thinking tends to be—but the notes and drawing clearly had signal importance to Drew as he sketched them out late in April 1994, in his acutely grandiose and delusional state. Painfully, there is also a more personal and prophetic sentence, buried and almost lost in his frenzied notes and sketches: "You will not be happy," Drew had written to himself. "You'll be stressed—about something *important*." There is no clue as to what the source of the stress would be.

Early in June, while in the mountains, he heard the voice of God telling him to "purify" himself; in response to this commandment, he removed all his clothes and ran naked through the woods. Later, frightened, confused, and covered with cuts and bruises, terrified that the world might be ending, he made his way to his chaplain's house. The chaplain's wife put a blanket around him; then, shaken and very psychotic, he was taken to the Air Force Academy Hospital. Still paranoid the next morning and agitated that Russian spies at the Academy, having heard about his superplane, were "out to get him," he was transferred to Fitzsimons Army Medical Hospital.

The military physicians who evaluated Drew were psychiatrically thorough, medically rigorous, and compassionate. His brain was scanned to rule out tumors or vascular disease that might cause a mania-like syndrome; his urine was checked for drugs that might cause paranoid, agitated, or manic states; consultations were obtained from both the departments of neurology and medicine. The doctors concluded that Drew had an extensive family history of manic-depressive (bipolar) illness and that he himself had a classic textbook case of the same disease. They also noted in his medical record that he had many friends, was a very good student, and had been an excellent cadet. "His past history," wrote one of his doctors, "is significant for excelling in any activity that he became involved in."

Drew was started on lithium and within two or three days was decidedly better. By the ninth day of his hospitalization he no longer was delusional, although at one point he became frightened that the hospital might try to do surgery on him to "remove important information from his head." He was able to attend the graduation ceremonies at the academy but within a few days' time had to be air-evacuated for continued treatment at Andrews Air Force Base, near Washington, D.C.

Prior to his transfer, a medical board comprising three military physicians was convened. Their final report, written in the impersonal, if necessary, language of medicine and the military, brought to an end Drew's plans for the future: his commission was denied; he lost his slot in flight school; he would be neither an officer nor a pilot. "This examinee does not meet the medical standards for commissioning due to a mental disorder with psychotic features," wrote the board. The command surgeon agreed, concluding, "I strongly recommend medical disenrollment in this cadet." Drew's active military service was over. His struggle with mental illness was not.

Drew was hospitalized at Andrews for an additional three weeks. The admitting physician, who concurred with the earlier diagnosis of bipolar manic-depressive illness, observed that Drew was still slightly paranoid, anxious, and "trying very hard to make sense of what had happened to him." He noted, as well, Drew's perfectionism (a characteristic mentioned by many who knew him) and the fact that Drew felt guilty about the problems he was causing his family by being ill.

Notes made by the physicians and nurses who treated him throughout his hospitalization make it clear that Drew was struggling to put back together the pieces of his life, struggling to piece together the beginnings of a future. He discussed the possibility of obtaining a Ph.D. in aeronautical engineering, becoming a teacher, or perhaps, he suggested in a less optimistic mood, working at the beach. He didn't know; it was too early to say. He was desperately concerned about paying off the educational debt he felt he had to the Air Force. But his immediate goal was to understand his illness and the medication he was taking to treat it.

Drew's hospitalization at Andrews was difficult, in part because the devastating consequences of his illness were beginning to sink in, in part because it is readily apparent from his medical history that he had a severe form of manic-depressive illness. On his second day at the hospital, one of the nurses found him deeply depressed, rocking in a fetal position. He appeared anxious and stated that he was scared, felt he was being tortured, and was going to die. He was placed on fifteen-minute checks, which ensured that a member of the nursing staff would monitor his safety and whereabouts. His moods cycled rapidly and violently. A few days later, he stated to the other members in his group therapy session that he had the solutions to all of the world's problems, but within a few hours he was tearful and frightened that he could not control his racing thoughts.

Drew's condition gradually improved, and early in July he

was given a two-day weekend pass to visit his parents. When he came back to the hospital, he was angry and agitated at having to return to the ward; he thrashed his arms about and shouted to the staff, "No! I'm not staying! No!"

Thirty minutes later one of the nurses found him lying in bed, where he stated, awfully, "I'm all right. It was just so hard to come back."

Within a few hours, Drew was again agitated. The nurse observed that his face was flushed and that he was pacing back and forth in the hallway. Within fifteen minutes he escaped from the hospital—an escape made easier, no doubt, by his survival training at the Air Force Academy—and was on his way to his parents' home in Delaware. He crawled in through a back window; his parents found him the next morning, sleeping in his own bed.

His mother called the hospital to notify it that Drew had been found and that he was extremely upset by a telephone call he had received. A fellow patient from his days on the psychiatric ward in Fitzsimons Army Medical Center had attempted suicide and been rehospitalized. Under the circumstances, Drew's parents thought it would be better for him to receive his psychiatric treatment closer to home.

Drew arrived home in early July 1994, and his parents arranged for him to get private psychiatric care and counseling. Psychologically shaky for a while, he continued to be preoccupied with guilt because he had been forced to leave the Air Force. He made slow but reasonably steady progress, however, and by midsummer he was feeling better, exercising again, and playing tennis. He had a brief recurrence of his delusions and a short-lived period of sleeplessness, but he was definitely better. In November he began seeing a new psychiatrist, who added an antipsychotic medication to the lithium that Drew already was taking. Both Drew and his doctor noted a dramatic improvement in Drew's mood and thinking, as did his parents.

From late 1994 to August 1995, Drew's mood remained stable and he experienced no psychotic symptoms. He worked at a bank twenty hours a week, was physically active, and talked about going to graduate school. Although he occasionally expressed a desire to stop taking his medications, in the hope that he might someday be able to fly airplanes on a civilian basis, he continued to take his drugs as prescribed.

But Drew's anger about the stigma he felt about having manic-depressive illness was intense, and he felt unable to discuss it with his friends or new acquaintances. "It's the last thing I want to talk about, but it generally comes up when meeting new people or out with friends at bars and parties," he confided to his psychiatrist. He limited his drinking to one or two beers and found that he was questioned about why he didn't drink more. Often asked about why he was no longer in the Air Force, he was too embarrassed to tell the truth and was forced to invent alternative explanations.

Friends were aware that Drew did not want to talk about his problems. One, who went to high school with Drew and described him, as many did, as "Mr. Everything," remarked, "He was still funny and willing to have a good time. I had no idea what he was dealing with inside his head." Another close friend, who is still "looking for explanations I don't even understand," described a change in Drew after his return from the Academy. Drew, he said, had been a loving person, "with a passion for life"; now something had gone wrong; Drew didn't want to talk about it; he "kept a lot of secrets." Still, Drew and his friends were a close-knit, active group. Together they listened to the music of U2, went to rock concerts and the beach, played tennis and volleyball and basketball, yelled exuberantly at ice hockey games, and went to parties in hopes of meeting new women.

Drew remained deeply troubled, however, and utterly convinced that he had disappointed those who mattered most to him. "I never saw bitterness from Drew," says his mother, "only disappointment and regret. He felt he had let everyone down, including the younger cadets, his friends and the Air Force. He was troubled that he could not repay the education he had received. He had a difficult time explaining why he was living at home. He felt he had followed all the rules of the Air Force and still this didn't work out for him. He felt shame at being sick." Like many with manic-depressive illness, Drew had conflicted feelings about his disease. "We told him of all the people who had coped with bipolar disorder and done well," his mother explained, but "he never heard it."

In November 1995 Drew stopped taking his medications and quit his job. For a brief time, it looked as though things might work out. He and two others went to the University of Connecticut to visit a friend, and one of them commented, "Drew was great—meeting people, breaking the hearts of several girls, and generally being Drew." But this same friend also noted, "That was the last time I saw Drew happy."

Drew deteriorated rapidly. "It was during this time that I found out what Drew was really going through," wrote a friend. "We'd talk for hours about his Jesus sightings, UFO theories, or whatever else he was experiencing. Through all his depressive episodes, he still maintained a sense of humor." Another friend commented on Drew's desire for privacy: "He came back from the Air Force broken, I suppose. He was able to hide it pretty well. All I know is that somehow his wings were clipped, and that I shouldn't bring it up—he didn't want to talk about it. It's as if he just didn't want to worry anyone."

Drew's losing battle with manic-depressive illness was profoundly disturbing to the friends who had known, loved, and admired him for so many years. He had been their leader, a person of strong character, an individual of great kindness: he was, said one of them, a person who had "a sweet nature and downright gorgeous looks—a friend we all hope to be, a man who women dream of, and a man who men admire, respect, and almost always befriended." To be privy to such a person's struggle for sanity was almost unbearably difficult and distressing to his friends.

Drew was lucky in these friends, and they in him; their reactions to his sickness are therefore all the more heartbreaking. One who was particularly close to Drew wrote:

I remember trying to talk to him, but conversations were frightening and confusing. He often talked in circles or made no sense or described that his friends were plotting against him. He described to me in horrid detail what ran through his mind and most of it I choose not to repeat. I simply do not know if there is a way to repeat the awful details, and somehow I feel it is my duty still to protect his honor and his name. He would do the same for me.

After he was diagnosed with Bipolar Disorder and I began to try to understand the horror in his mind, I knew he might never be the same. But I did not dream he would commit suicide. It simply did not seem possible. For months after he was hospitalized, his family and Drew told no one but family and me. We wanted to protect him, and perhaps we thought he would get better, and we would never have to speak of it. But Drew did not get better, and the more time dragged on, the more I knew he might never recover.

Drew took his lithium on and off, but I think he never really wanted to believe he needed it. He never wanted to admit it to himself. I think he thought he could recover. But as the months dragged on, I realized that this illness had stolen a part of Drew's soul. It took from him part of his personality and his love of life. I remember when he was hospitalized in D.C. and I went to visit him. His mom left to get dinner, and he laid his head in my lap, curled up in the fetal position. I saw with my eyes the man's face I knew as Drew, but my ears heard another creature. Something else seemed to live in his shell. Someone other than Drew brought words to his lips or created his awkward, disturbing actions. As he rubbed his head, as though to bring his thoughts to some sort of sanity, I looked at him and wondered where my friend had disappeared to. This monster had taken over. He was gaunt and had not shaved in weeks. His skin was sallow and his cheeks sunken; each movement appeared painful. I did not know this person he had become. The more he talked the more my fear for him grew. I went home that evening and cried for two hours straight. Never had I looked horror in the face as I had that evening.

By December, Drew's condition plummeted. He was increasingly depressed, and he kept more and more to himself. The packages he received for Christmas remained wrapped in his room, and he went out with friends only after much inducement and prodding. Temporary solace was to be found in music and in the long baths that he took in a desperate attempt to curb his agitation.

By early January 1996, Drew was almost totally withdrawn from everyone. Finally, he was catatonic in his bed. He was taken by ambulance to a local hospital, where he was admitted on an emergency, involuntary basis. At the time of admission he was mute, his eyes were closed, and he was lying inert on a stretcher. The doctors gave him an antipsychotic drug, which worked rapidly. Indeed, it worked rapidly enough that the next day he escaped from the locked ward and made his way home through one of the worst snowstorms on record. He was taken back to the hospital, where he stayed for another ten days. During this time his physician noted that Drew showed "some improvement," although he was "continuing to struggle with coming to grips with seeing himself as an individual with an illness."

Drew's medical chart paints an unremittingly grim picture. He described himself as "hopeless" to the admitting nurse. His employment history was recorded simply as "unemployed—was working in a bank. Graduated from Air Force Academy." In just over a year and a half, a young man of great promise had gone from a world of academics and athletics, officers and gentlemen, to "unemployed" and "hopeless." Manic-depression had taken no hostages.

Drew was asked during the hospitalization to describe an ideal scenario for his life, once he recovered. He emphasized that he wanted no pity and no medicine. The items he endorsed on a standard psychological test were deeply despairing in nature: "I am so sad or unhappy that I can't stand it," he checked off on the test form; "I feel I have nothing to look forward to." He also endorsed the statement "As I look back on my life, all I can see is a lot of failures" and, most distressingly, "I have thoughts of killing myself, but I would not carry them out."

Drew was discharged to outpatient care five days before he committed suicide. No one knows what he was thinking or feeling during that time, but he did leave behind scattered notes and journal entries. In them, as his mother put it, "you can see him slipping away." The writings are enigmatic, idiosyncratic, flailing; they are at times cohesive, but more often than not the confounding presence of psychosis makes itself felt.

He records unusual dreams, coincidences, and events; there is a sense of a mind trying desperately just to hold on. He mentions falling stars and eagle dreams, dreams of Hell, hurricanes, lightning, jets, death. His instructions to himself compel him to relax, pray, tone down, focus, find peace. He is frightened that his "old beliefs" will come back, and he laments, "I asked God to help me. I didn't deserve his help. Because I cursed God before I asked him for help."

His writings are filled with the sense of a world that is lost, a self that is lost, and a hope that has been entirely abandoned. He is guilt-stricken for the pain he feels he has brought upon others, especially his family, and he enumerates at length the problems he must confront: he must pay off his debts, he has lost his girlfriend, he must take medication, he must see doctors. He is convinced that "everyone will label me as having [an] illness until the day I die," yet he also states, "No one knows the special experiences I have had—so they won't hear what I tell them ever."

The final entry in his journal reflects this pervasive ambivalence toward his disease: "Sick or not?—Medicine reduce[s] symptoms but [I] want [to] be happy."

In his copy of *Moral Issues in Philosophy*, an assigned textbook Drew was reading when he first became ill at the Air Force Academy, different colors of ink accentuate, underline, and emphasize various phrases and ideas. He repeatedly circled and underlined the sentence "There is such a thing as life not worthy to be lived" and underscored yet another sentence, "It is cruel to allow a human being to linger for months in the last stages of agony." Chillingly, the last phrase Drew underlined was "[there is a] moral duty to terminate the life of an insane person who is suffering from a painful and incurable disease."

But the souls of the righteous are in the hand of God, and no torment will ever touch them. In the eyes of the foolish they seemed to have died, and their departure was thought to be an affliction, and their going from us to be their destruction; but they are at peace.

—WISDOM, 3:1–9, read at Drew's memorial service

A few days before Drew's death, two of his closest friends visited him. They did not know that it was to be for the last time. Only recently released from the hospital, Drew was, one of them observed, "unshaven, in black from head to toe, and very sullen. I'm not sure if he had made up his mind by then or not. All I can tell you is that he didn't laugh or smile. As [we] left that night, Drew matter-of-factly said, 'I love you guys.' It was quite strange, and I didn't know how to respond. Sensing this, he just said again, 'I really love you guys,' and shut the door. As far as I know, that's the last thing he said to anyone."

On January 27, Drew Sopirak left his parents' home in Wilmington and drove to a gun store. The state of Delaware required no waiting period to purchase handguns; the clerk sold him a .38-caliber revolver straightaway. A few hours later, Drew shot and killed himself. The police notified Drew's parents that his body had been found inside his jeep at the entrance to the Pennsylvania Turnpike. He was about forty minutes from home.

"We had been on that turnpike so many times," said Drew's mother. "Both our families live in the Pittsburgh area. That road would have taken him to grandparents, aunts, uncles, and cousins and his brother at Penn State. He just never got on it. He must have run out of hope there."

The family was left to do the unimaginable: identify Drew's body at the morgue, notify other family members and friends, plan a funeral and memorial service, mourn him, miss him.

Drew's parents and younger brother received an extraordinary number of condolence letters from Drew's high school friends and teachers, his fellow cadets and instructors at the Air Force Academy, and parents of friends. In reading through them it is striking how many of the letters are in the form of thank-you letters: thank-yous for his life, his presence, his warmth; appreciation of his vitality, friendship, and influence.

"I cannot begin to tell you how sad it makes me to know the world is without one of its great participants," wrote one friend. He continued, "Ovid once wrote, 'Welcome this pain, for some day it will be useful to you.' I don't know how true that is for you concerning your loss, but I know that each time I remember Drew I hurt. What a wonderful gift you gave all of us in Drew. Thank you."

Another said simply, "May your consolation be that he was truly loved in this life." One of Drew's teachers, an instructor in aeronautical engineering at the Air Force Academy, wrote, "I never really understood his illness and he never used it as an excuse. I don't remember the names of most of the hundreds of students I had in my class but a few do stand out. Drew was a stand out guy. Drew made a difference. Drew mattered. I am proud to have known him."

Consolations were of help, but ultimately it was left to Drew's family and friends to attempt to understand why he had done such an incomprehensible, final thing. One friend tried:

> I do not often say this, but after seeing his suffering for so long, I can see how suicide cured Drew's pain. I am not angry for his decision as I am not sure I would have had the strength to continue as long as Drew did. Many did not know his suffering, and he let few close enough to see it. But those of us who loved him and saw his pain do not fault him for leaving this life behind. Still I hate his illness and still I wish I could hear, if just for one last time, his jeep roar up to my house with U2 blaring and see him jump out suntanned and gorgeous and wanting to go for a ride in the valley.
>
> I will never be the same. As I said before, none of us who know him ever will. But I know I have been blessed to have known a soul such as Drew. This is a gift few are given.

Drew's family, whose warmth and understanding of him would have been, in a fairer world, more than sufficient to keep him alive, could not compete with a relentless and ruinous disease. Their funeral notes for Drew end with a perceptive, straightforward statement of fact: "On January 27, 1996 Drew took his life. He had stopped taking his medication. His illness moved faster than his acceptance of it."

The Christmas before Drew graduated from the Academy,

he had placed a small gift for his parents under the Christmas tree; it was the last package to be unwrapped. Inside the box they found a pair of lieutenant's epaulets, which he asked them to pin on his shoulders when he received his officer's commission in six months' time. All the cadets in his squadron received their commissions and epaulets in June. All except Drew.

His parents remedied this by placing the unworn epaulets in his hands the day that they buried him.

> *And He will raise you up on eagle's wings,*
> *Bear you on the breath of dawn,*
> *Make you to shine like the sun,*
> *And hold you in the palm of His hand.*

> *You need not fear the terror of the night.*

The February day of Drew's memorial service at the Air Force Academy was a beautiful, breezy, and sunny one. The flags at the Academy flew at half-mast, and the chapel was filled with young men and women in uniform. They stood, as one, for the opening hymn, "On Eagle's Wings," and listened to their fellow officers and cadets read passages from the Old and New Testaments. The chaplain spoke of Drew's leadership and of how he had been a role model for so many in his class. With obvious emotion, he remarked, "I don't think we know how much pain, how much turmoil, how much anguish Drew experienced as a result of his illness."

Five cadets and officers—sad, young, sober, stricken—went, in turn, to the pulpit to deliver their remembrances. One second lieutenant, a close friend of Drew's, was painfully eloquent: "This chapel," he said, "means a lot to my life. Six years ago I walked in those doors scared as a new basic. A year and a half ago, I walked out of those doors happy as a newly married man. Today, I return to this place sad, as I must say good-bye to a friend."

The young officer paused, his sadness palpable. Then he ended his eulogy with an Air Force pilots' toast that he, Drew, and their fellow cadets had made the night they received their class rings from the Academy. Proposed at the time to the legendary flier and commander of the U.S. air forces in World War I, General Billy Mitchell, the lieutenant now used it to bid farewell to his friend:

> *As we soar among them there,*
> *We're sure to hear his plea,*
> *To take care my friend,*
> *Watch your six,*
> *And do one more roll . . .*
>   *Just for me.*

The congregation rose for the final hymn. "We will run and not grow weary," they sang, "For our God will be our strength, / And we will fly like the eagle, / We will rise again." One by one the young men and women in blue left the jagged triangular chapel.

Their leaving is the last thing you see on the home videotape; there is a terrible sadness in it, even more than you had reckoned on. The only thing that goes through your mind is what you heard a military chaplain say, many years ago:

"I do not know why young men have to die. You would think it would break the heart of God."

II

Just Hope Has Gone

— PSYCHOLOGY AND PSYCHOPATHOLOGY —

Hope now,—not health, nor cheerfulness,
Since they can come and go again,
As often one brief hour witnesses,—

Just hope has gone forever.

— EDWARD THOMAS

Poet Edward Thomas (1878–1917) was twenty-nine years old when he wrote to his wife: "I sat thinking about ways of killing myself. My revolver has only one bullet left. I couldn't hang myself: and though I imagined myself cutting my throat with a razor on Wheatham I had not the energy to go. Then I went out and thought what effects my suicide would have. I don't think I mind them. . . . These thoughts have come to me at least once a week for three or four years now and frequently during the last seven—"

CHAPTER 3

Take Off the Amber,
Put Out the Lamp

—THE PSYCHOLOGY OF SUICIDE—

It is time to take off the amber
Time to change the words,
Time to put out the lamp
Above the door . . .

—MARINA TSVETAEVA

The young boy scrawled a note and pinned it to his shirt. Then he walked to the far side of the family Christmas tree and hanged himself from a ceiling beam. The note was short—"Merry Christmas"—and his parents never forgot or understood it.

E ACH WAY to suicide is its own: intensely private, unknowable, and terrible. Suicide will have seemed to its perpetrator the last and best of bad possibilities, and any attempt by the living to chart this final terrain of a life can be only a sketch, maddeningly incomplete.

We are left with little, as friends or family, as clinicians or scientists: only last bits of conversations; memories of perfectly normal and now suspect behaviors; an occasional note or journal entry; recollections of our own dealings with the dead, fragments we distort through guilt or anger or terrible loss. We are left to make sense of a young boy's Christmas note; a mother of three, whose computer screen reads, "I love you.

I'm sorry. Study Hard"; a successful businessman who jumps in front of a subway train; a brilliant graduate student who kills himself with cyanide from his laboratory; a promising fifteen-year-old African-American boy who provokes his own death by aiming a toy gun at a police officer.

There are sharp limits on our understanding: final signs and messages are subject to a score of readings; and life, once jugulated, cannot be put back in. No matter how much we may wish to reassemble the suicide's psychological world, any light we gain is indirect and insufficient: the privacy of the mind is an impermeable barrier. Everyone has good cause for suicide, or at least it seems that way to those who search for it. And most will have yet better grounds to stay alive, thus complicating everything.

Suicide is not entirely a private act, however; nor is it completely idiosyncratic or unpredictable. We have ways of understanding the psychological underpinnings of suicide, and while they may not provide the final clarity we would like, they give us grounds for a beginning.

Suicide notes—an obvious starting point—often promise more than they deliver. It would seem that nothing could be closer to the truth of suicide than notes and letters left behind by those who kill themselves, but this is not the case; our expectations of how we think people should feel and act facing their own deaths are greater than the reality of what they do and why they do it. Suicide authority Ed Shneidman, for example, in commenting on the disappointing banality of many suicide notes, lets slip his hope, a common one, that the last recorded moments of life will afford a deep or tragic view of dying: "Suicide notes," he writes, "often seem like parodies of the postcards sent home from the Grand Canyon, the catacombs or the pyramids—essentially *pro forma*, not at all reflecting the grandeur of the scene being described or the depth of human emotion that one might expect to be engendered by the situation."

But of course one could argue that most people who decide

to take their own lives have lost their ability to feel things grandly or deeply, to reflect profoundly or originally, to see the world other than monochromatically. Giving words to ultimate, dark, and interior acts is difficult enough for those with keen minds in active gear; for those depressed, confused, hopeless, and mentally constricted, eloquence is unlikely to be much in evidence. When eloquence or pithy insights *do* find their way into suicide notes, they are quoted repeatedly, precisely because of their singular view into the suicidal mind. These notes may be forceful, riveting, or mordantly amusing, but they tend not to be typical.

In fact, few people leave suicide notes. Perhaps one in four does, and it is unclear if these notes represent the emotional states, motivations, and experiences of those who leave behind no written record.

Four thousand years ago, an Egyptian wrote out his despair onto papyrus in the form of a narrative and four short-versed poems. This document, now in the Berlin Museum, is thought by British psychiatrist Chris Thomas to be the first suicide note extant, and he believes it reflects the ruminations of a deeply depressed, probably psychotic mind. In the second of the four poems the ancient writer gives vent to his misery in the images of his time:

> *Lo, my name is abhorred,*
> *Lo, more than the odour of carrion*
> *On summer days when the sky is hot.*

> *Lo, my name is abhorred,*
> *Lo, more than the odour of crocodiles,*
> *More than sitting under the bank of crocodiles.*

> *Lo, my name is abhorred,*
> *Lo, more than a woman*
> *Against whom a lie is told her husband.*

Later, he moves from the pain of his existence to the attractions of death:

> *Death is before me today*
> *As the odour of myrrh,*
> *As when one sitteth under the sail on a windy day.*

> *Death is before me today*
> *As the odour of lotus flowers,*
> *As when one sitteth on the shore of drunkenness.*

> *Death is before me today*
> *As a man longs to see his house*
> *When he has spent years in captivity.*

Suicide notes have been written since, in ink, paint, pencil, crayon, or blood. French artist Jules Pascin, for instance, slit his wrists, wrote a brief note in blood—"*Lucy, pardonnez-moi*"—and then hanged himself. Russian poet Sergei Esenin, who was just thirty when he hanged himself from the heating pipes in the ceiling of his room—a room left in total disarray, with things thrown about and bits of torn-up manuscripts strewn everywhere—wrote an entire poem in his own blood the day before he killed himself:

> *Goodbye, my friend, goodbye.*
> *My dear, you are in my heart.*
> *Predestined separation*
> *Promises a future meeting.*

> *Goodbye, my friend, without handshake and words,*
> *Do not grieve and sadden your brow,—*
> *In this life there's nothing new in dying,*
> *But nor, of course, is living any newer.*

Most notes are not so dramatically drafted. Some note writers, despite being poets, use the words of others. Paul Celan, for example, underlined a sentence from a biography of Hölderlin—"Sometimes this genius goes dark and sinks down into the bitter well of his heart"—and then drowned himself in the Seine. Others leave a more extensive record of their thoughts. Cesare Pavese's diary from the last year of his life is an unbounded history of pain. "The cadence of suffering has begun," he wrote. "Every evening at dusk, my heart constricts until night comes." Then, later, not long before he killed himself, he wrote, "Now even the morning is filled with pain."

The length of suicide notes varies greatly. Ian O'Donnell at the University of Oxford and his colleagues looked at suicide notes written by people who killed themselves on the London Underground railway system and found that the notes ranged in length from one that was only seventeen words long, written on the back of a railway ticket, to an eight-hundred-word "stream-of-consciousness essay written over the course of an hour sitting on a bench in the railway station and ending with a description of the last few steps towards the railway line and the final preparations for the arrival of the train." The average number of words in their series of suicide notes was about the same as the number of words in this paragraph.

Many suicide notes are short and may give only an explicit warning to those who are likely to find the bodies: "BE CAREFUL. CYANIDE GAS IS IN THIS BATHROOM," for example; or "DO NOT ENTER. Call Paramedics." Specific instructions or requests are common, most often detailing how to handle the body, what to tell children or parents about the suicide, how to distribute assets, what to do with a cat or a dog. The reasons given for suicide are often vague and allude to a cumulative pain and weariness—"I could not bear it any longer"; "I am tired of living"; "There is no point in going on"—without going into any further details. Young children are less specific than older adolescents or adults in their reasons for suicide and in what they wish to have done with their bodies and possessions. Both of the younger age groups are less likely than adults to leave notes, but they frequently and explicitly try to relieve their parents, brothers, and sisters of feeling guilty about their suicides. A twenty-year-old girl who jumped from an office building, for instance, wrote, "No one is to blame for my doing this. It's just that I could never become reconciled with life itself. God have mercy on my soul."

The majority of all suicide notes are positive in their remarks about those they are leaving behind. Hostility, when it does occur, however, can be breathtaking. A man whose wife had fallen in love with his brother put a gas tube into his mouth; before he died, he wrote out a note for his wife: "I used to love you, but I die hating you and my brother, too." On the back of her photograph, he wrote, "I present this picture of another woman—the girl I thought I married, may you always remember I loved you once but died hating you." Similarly hostile sentiments were left in another person's suicide note: "I hate you and all of your family and I hope you never have a piece [sic] of mind. I hope I haunt this house as long as you live here and I wish you all the bad luck in the world." Fortunately, these acid notes are unusual.

Suicide notes in general have a concrete, stereotypic quality to them. In a series of studies, genuine suicide notes were compared with simulated ones. The latter were written by individuals (matched for age, gender, and socioeconomic status) who had been asked to write suicide notes as they imagined they would write them if they were planning to commit suicide. The genuine suicide notes were much more specific about giving directives concerning property distribution and insurance policies; more concerned about the pain and suffering they knew would be caused by their acts; more neutral in tone, although also more likely to express psychological pain; and more likely to use the word "love" in their texts. The simulated notes, on the other hand, gave greater detail about the circumstances and thoughts leading up to the (imagined) suicide; more often mentioned the act of suicide itself; and more often used euphemistic phrases for death and suicide.

Even in the midst of great mental suffering, some people before they kill themselves find time to lay out quite explicit instructions to their survivors. Before killing herself with gas from the stove in her kitchen, for example, a fourteen-year-old girl wrote this note:

> *To whom it may concern,*
>
> *If I should die in my childhood, this is my will. I have no money, except $2.95 in the bank, and a little in defense stamps. This is to be given to Robert C———, my nephew. My clothing goes to charity or to anyone that wants them.*
>
> *If I am laid out I would like to be dressed in blue. If I have a funeral all friends and relatives are invited to attend.*
>
> *To my mother I give all I have and everything I possess. To my father and sister all my love and all I possess.*
>
> *No one has killed me. I wish to die. I have committed suicide.*

In 1931, a twenty-five-year-old man who was out of work and despondent about his young wife (whom he had pressured into prostitution so they might live) swallowed poison and died. His suicide note read, in part:

> *Dear Dear Betty*
>
> *Oh how I love you but I am not fit to be your husband or live. I have just gotten the most Deadly Poison there is & When you read this letter I will be gone thank God. I am giving Peggy [their dog] to the Landlady to keep for you and one Dollar to feed her to Thursday & also just Paid the room Thursday. The receipt is enclosed.*
>
> *I am also bringing over to the Detention home $23.00 in Cash, your ring, my ring & my watch for them to give you*

*when you get out. I told the Landlady I would not be here
this week but probably you would be here Monday, if you are
not here I gave her the Attorney's phone number & told her
to ask him to see you & let her know what you want done
with the things.*

*I am also writing him a letter & telling him of the
money & rings that I am bring [sic] over to you & I am also
giving him orders to send you out home or back to my
mother which ever place you want to go.*

A quite different kind of instruction and declaration was left
in the mid-nineteenth century by an Englishman being held in
county jail for indebtedness. Convinced he was the co-Deity, a
son of God, and Elijah, and allowed access to his razor and
knife despite widespread knowledge that he was insane, he was
found dead of self-inflicted wounds to his throat and abdomen.
He left behind letters to the governor of the jail, the coroner,
and his wife. The disturbed state of his mind is apparent, but
despite his delusions he managed to request specific and
rational care in how the news of his suicide would be broken to
his wife. He wrote to the governor:

*I am known to Mr. Herschell, the chaplain, and I have no
doubt he will take the letter addressed to my wife to her
home. I will, however, express my wish, and leave it perfectly
optional with him to comply or not, as he pleases. I should
wish him to ask Dr. Williams to accompany him, by the
eleven o'clock train, to Newham, then take a conveyance and
call on Mrs. Jolly, at Littledean, and request her to
accompany them to my wife at Cinderford. Should she not be
at home, she will be at Drybrook, at my sister's, whither they
must follow, and break the intelligence to her as gently as
they can. I think, when Dr. Herschell reads my dying
affirmation that I am the long-expected Messiah to his
people, he will comply with my request.*

His letter to the coroner addressed the inquest he expected would take place after his death and left even less doubt about his mental state:

> *On the one hand, you will have the solemn assurance that I am the Son of God—the Lamb slain from the foundation of the world, and on the other the oppressive, fearful fact, that I died by my own hand. You will hardly dare bring in a verdict of temporary insanity, because of the deliberation, forethought, and predetermination in which it was accomplished, and because my resurrection from the dead at the end of three days and three nights would manifest such verdict to be an infamous libel and blasphemy.*

Few suicide notes are so overtly peculiar or psychotic; in fact, most reveal little or no evidence of incoherent or delusional thinking. Yet, as we will see, the overwhelming majority of suicides are linked to psychiatric illnesses, so it is not surprising that most of the notes and records left behind reflect the misery, cumulative despair, and hopelessness of these conditions.

Acute mental illness brings pains and dangers, and there is a chronic distress that comes from living with it and dreading its return. The anguish of depression, manic-depression, schizophrenia, and the other major psychiatric disorders cannot be overstated. Suffering, hopelessness, agitation, and shame mix together with a painful awareness of the often irreversible damage done by the illness to friends, family, and careers. It is a lethal mix. One woman wrote in her suicide note about her unsuccessful struggle with mental illness:

> *I wish I could explain it so someone could understand it.*
> *I'm afraid it's something I can't put into words.*
> *There's just this heavy, overwhelming despair—dreading*

everything. Dreading life. Empty inside, to the point of
numbness. It's like there's something already dead inside. My
whole being has been pulling back into that void for months.
   Everyone has been so good to me—has tried so hard. I
truly wish that I could be different, for the sake of my
family. Hurting my family is the worst of it, and that guilt
has been wrestling with the part of me that wanted only to
disappear.
   But there's some core-level spark of life that just isn't
there. Despite what's been said about my having "gotten
better" lately—the voice in my head that's driving me crazy
is louder than ever. It's way beyond being reached by anyone
or anything, it seems. I can't bear it any more. I think
there's something psychologically-twisted—reversed that has
taken over, that I can't fight any more. I wish that I could
disappear without hurting anyone. I'm sorry.

A forty-two-year-old woman who shot herself left a long
note defending her character and pleading with the press not
to sensationalize her death. She was, as are many with mental
illness, concerned about the effects of her illness on others, in
this case on her mother: "I will be of no use to her much longer
with these crazy nerves. No one who has not experienced the
utter discouragement of a nervous collapse is any judge whatever and cannot realize that that alone can make one wish to
die."

Nineteenth-century British painter Benjamin Haydon turned
to Shakespeare for some of his last words. Agitated and sleepless, with a history of violent manic-depression, Haydon
slashed his throat and then put a bullet through his head. His
journal was left open to the final entry:

21st.—Slept horribly. Prayed in sorrow, and got up in
agitation.
22nd.—God forgive me. Amen.

Finis
of
B. R. Haydon

Stretch me no longer on this rough world.—Lear.

"Nerves," agitation, and discouragement with prolonged mental suffering are common themes of suicide notes. Japanese writer Ryuunosuke Akutagawa, paranoid and delusional (believing, among other things, that maggots were in his food), took an overdose of sleeping pills when he was thirty-five. "The world I am living in now," he wrote, "is the icily transparent universe of sickly nerves. . . . Of course, I do not want to die, but it is suffering to live."

James Whale, director of *The Invisible Man*, *Journey's End*, and the classic *Frankenstein* films, also spoke of nerves and suffering in his suicide note. Addressed to ALL I LOVE, he wrote:

> *Do not grieve for me. My nerves are all shot and for the last year I have been in agony day and night—except when I sleep with sleeping pills—and any peace I have by day is when I am drugged by pills.*
>
> *I have had a wonderful life but it is over and my nerves get worse and I am afraid they will have to take me away.* [He had been hospitalized for a nervous breakdown and received shock therapy.] *So please forgive me, all those I love and may God forgive me too, but I cannot bear the agony and it [is] best for everyone this way. . . .*
>
> *No one is to blame—I have wonderful friends and they do all they can for me. . . . I've tried very hard all I know for a year and it gets worse inside, so please take comfort in knowing I will not suffer anymore.*

Morbidly afraid of water, he then drowned himself in his swimming pool. Not too far away, consistent with a lifetime of dark humor, he left out a copy of the book *Don't Go Near the Water.*

The awareness of the damage done by severe mental illness—to the individual himself and to others—and fears that it may return again play a decisive role in many suicides. Those patients with schizophrenia who are more intelligent and better educated, for example, who perform better on measures of abstract reasoning, and who demonstrate greater insight into the nature of their illness, are more likely to kill themselves. Patients who do well socially and academically when young and who then are hit by devastating illnesses such as schizophrenia or manic-depression seem particularly vulnerable to the spectre of their own mental disintegration and the terror of becoming a chronic patient. For them and many others there is a terrible loss of dreams and inescapable damage to friends, family, and self—Randall Jarrell, in describing to his wife the cumulative effects of his manic-depression, said, "It was so queer . . . as if the fairies had stolen me away and left a log in my place"—a sense of being only a shadow or husk of one's former self; an unshakable hopelessness; a feeling of failure and shame; and a terrible anxiety that the illness will return. For others, the fact that the illness *has* come back is in itself unendurable; its recurrence intolerable, one time too many.

Virginia Woolf, who suffered through psychotic manias and depressions, wrote in the first of two suicide notes to her husband, "I feel certain that I am going mad again: I feel we can't go through another of those terrible times. And I shan't recover this time. I begin to hear voices, and can't concentrate. So I am doing what seems the best thing to do." Several days later, she wrote again, and again she blamed her madness for her death:

> *Dearest,*
> *I want to tell you that you have given me complete*
> *happiness. No one could have done more than you have done.*
> *Please believe that.*

*But I know that I shall never get over this: and I am
wasting your life. It is this madness. Nothing anyone says
can persuade me. You can work, and you will be much better
without me. You see I can't write this even, which shows I
am right. All I want to say is that until this disease came on
we were perfectly happy. It was all due to you. No one could
have been so good as you have been, from the very first day
till now. Everyone knows that.*

V.
Will you destroy all my papers?

Woolf then loaded her pockets with heavy stones and
walked into the river.

It is tempting when looking at the life of anyone who has
committed suicide to read into the decision to die a vastly complex web of reasons; and, of course, such complexity is warranted. No one illness or event causes suicide; and certainly no
one knows all, or perhaps even most, of the motivations behind
the killing of the self. But psychopathology is almost always
there, and its deadliness is fierce. Love, success, and friendship
are not always enough to counter the pain and destructiveness
of severe mental illness. American artist Ralph Barton tried to
explain this in his suicide note:

*Everyone who has known me and who hears of this will
have a different hypothesis to offer to explain why I did it.
Practically all of these hypotheses will be dramatic—and
completely wrong. Any sane doctor knows that the reasons for
suicide are invariably psychopathological. Difficulties in life
merely precipitate the event—and the true suicide type
manufactures his own difficulties. I have had few real
difficulties. I have had, on the contrary, an exceptionally
glamorous life—as lives go. And I have had more than my
share of affection and appreciation. The most charming,
intelligent, and important people I have known have liked*

me—and the list of my enemies is very flattering to me. I
have always had excellent health. But, since my early
childhood, I have suffered with a melancholia which, in the
past five years, has begun to show definite symptoms of
manic-depressive insanity. It has prevented my getting
anything like the full value out of my talents, and, for the
past three years, has made work a torture to do at all. It has
made it impossible for me to enjoy the simple pleasures of life
that seem to get other people through. I have run from wife
to wife, from house to house, and from country to country, in
a ridiculous effort to escape from myself. In doing so, I am
very much afraid that I have spread a good deal of
unhappiness among the people who have loved me.

Barton put on his pajamas and a silk dressing gown, got into
bed, opened up his copy of *Gray's Anatomy* to an illustration of
the human heart, and shot himself in the head.

DIFFICULTIES IN life merely precipitate a suicide, wrote
Barton; they do not cause it. There is much evidence to support his belief. But which difficulties are most precipitous? And
why? The reversals of fortune, the deaths or divorces that may
be blamed for a suicide are the same disasters and disappointments that attend us all. Yet few of us kill ourselves in response.
    A. Alvarez describes better than anyone the highly personal
interpretation given to events by those who are suicidal: "A
suicide's excuses are mostly casual. At best they assuage the
guilt of the survivors, soothe the tidy-minded and encourage
the sociologists in their endless search for convincing categories and theories. They are like a trivial border incident
which triggers off a major war. The real motives which impel
a man to take his own life are elsewhere; they belong to
the internal world, devious, contradictory, labyrinthine, and
mostly out of sight."

Each culture has stressed its own motivations for suicide. In classical antiquity, according to scholar Anton van Hooff, shame, grief, and despair were the primary reasons for suicide in young Romans. By the nineteenth century, Bierre de Boismont had classified the causes of nearly five thousand French suicides and concluded that insanity and alcoholism were the most important, followed by incurable disease, "sorrow or disappointment," and "disappointed love." Enrico Morselli, surveying European statistics in the last century, noted that most suicides were attributable to madness; next in order of importance were "weariness of life," "passions," and "vices." Further down the list, but compellingly human in its language, was "despair—unknown and diverse."

The twentieth century has added specificity, although perhaps not eloquence, to the debate about why people kill themselves. In recent years, psychologists and psychiatrists have looked at the relationship between "life events"—an oddly bloodless phrase for catastrophe and heartbreak—and the onset of psychiatric illnesses such as depression, mania, and schizophrenia. Although life events may, of course, be positive (for example, getting married or getting promoted at work), most investigators have focused on adverse events such as medical illness, divorce or separation, death or illness in the family, family discord, and financial or job problems.

There are many reasons to believe that stressful events might bring on or worsen a psychiatric illness. If the underlying psychiatric illness or biological predisposition is severe enough, such events may well play a role in suicide as well. We know that stress has a profound effect not only on the body's immune system and the production of powerful stress hormones but also on the sleep-wake cycle (which, in turn, plays a critical role in the pathophysiology of mania and depression). Tom Wehr and his colleagues at the National Institute of Mental Health, for instance, have demonstrated that psychological stress, certain medications and illnesses,

and significant changes in light and temperature can inter-
fere with circadian rhythms; these disturbances can, in
turn, trigger mania or depression in genetically vulnerable
individuals.

The relationship between the events of life, stress, and psychiatric illness is not a straightforward one, however. People,
when manic or depressed, not only are influenced by the
events in their lives, they also have a strong reciprocal influence on the world and people around them: they often alienate
others with their anger, withdrawal, or violence; act in such
ways as to cause divorce; or get themselves fired from work.
What looks like the cause of a relapse may in fact be brought
about by the illness itself. (There is, for example, no consistent
strong relationship between unemployment and suicide. It is
clear, however, that heavy drinking, mental illness, and personality disorders all contribute to unemployment.) The causal
arrows move both ways, further compounded by the fact that
individuals, when depressed or psychotic, react to stress in very
different ways from those who are not mentally ill. Accordingly, many researchers have narrowed their study of life
events to the so-called independent life events, such as a death
or serious illness in a family. Unlike "events" such as divorce or
financial problems, which are more likely to be affected by
mental illness, these independent events are more genuinely
random.

Most research finds a significant increase in life events prior
to the onset of both manic and schizophrenic episodes,
although the influence of psychosocial stress appears to be less
important in later stages of manic-depressive illness (by which
time the illness has often established a rhythm of its own).
Patients with mood disorders seem, for the most part, to be
more affected by stressful life events then those who suffer
from schizophrenia. Psychologist Sherry Johnson and her colleagues at Brown University found that negative life events
not only increase the rate of relapse in patients with manic-

depression, they also increase the length of time it takes for patients to recover from their episodes of depression or mania. Without significant causes of stress, patients take about four months to recover. If, on the other hand, significant negative life events precede the relapse, it takes, on average, almost eleven months before they are well again. This nearly three-fold increase in recovery time is not only a highly painful time for patients and their families, it is also an extended period of vulnerability for suicide.

Sudden heartbreak or catastrophe is often known to have occurred before a suicide, but the nature and extent of the crisis it causes is unclear. Almost certainly, most of the danger of the event lies in its incendiary effect on the underlying mental condition. But the ultimate impact of psychological stress is different in each individual, depending on his or her own life experiences, ease of access to a means of death, extent of hopelessness, and type and severity of the mental illness. Difficulties and conflicts in personal relationships or imminent threats of arrest or criminal prosecution tend to occur more frequently before the suicides of alcoholics and substance abusers, for instance, than before the suicides of individuals with depression. (Sometimes the reasons for desperation are beyond fathoming. One six-year-old girl who tried to throw herself out of a moving car said simply, when brought into a psychiatric clinic, "I am very hungry. I bite people and try to eat them up. I am a bad girl, and I should die.")

Gender also matters. In a large Finnish study, the partners of those who had killed themselves were asked what they thought was the reason for suicide. Severe mental illness was rated as the most important cause of suicide in the women, whereas medical illness was seen as a more important reason for suicide in the men. For both men and women, intense interpersonal discord was also perceived as an important contributing factor.

Differences in gender exist at a younger age as well. Young

or adolescent boys, for instance, are much more likely than girls to have experienced a crisis event in the twenty-four hours prior to suicide. Particularly common are breakups with girlfriends, disciplinary or legal crises (such as suspension from school or a pending appearance in juvenile court), and humiliating events, such as public failure or rejection. David Shaffer, a child psychiatrist at Columbia University in New York, finds that many male adolescents who kill themselves are not only depressed but aggressive, quick-tempered, and impulsive; they also tend to drink heavily, use drugs, and have difficulties in their relationships with others. Most other clinicians and researchers agree. Depressive illnesses in conjunction with substance abuse are common in these adolescents, providing a combustible fusion when triggered by an adverse or painful event. The fact that most parents are unaware of depression and suicidal thinking in their adolescent children only makes the potential for disaster worse. Recent research shows that adolescents who suffer from depression are much more likely than those with no psychiatric illness to commit suicide when they reach adulthood.

A different but not uncommon profile of an adolescent suicide is that of a high-achieving, anxious, or depressed perfectionist. Setbacks or failures, either real or imagined, can sometimes precipitate suicide. It may be difficult to determine the extent of such a child's psychopathology and mental suffering, due to the tendency to try to appear normal, to please others, not to call attention to oneself. The real reasons for suicide remain fugitive.

One fifteen-year-old boy wrote this poem two years before he killed himself:

> *Once . . . he wrote a poem.*
> *And he called it "Chops,"*
> *Because that was the name of his dog, and*
> *that's what it was all about.*

And the teacher gave him an "A"
And a gold star.
And his mother hung it on the kitchen door,
*   and read it to all his aunts . . .*

Once . . . he wrote another poem.
And he called it "Question Marked Innocence,"
Because that was the name of his grief, and
*   that's what it was all about.*
And the professor gave him an "A"
And a strange and steady look.
And his mother never hung it on the kitchen door
*   because he never let her see it . . .*

Once, at 3 a.m. . . . he tried another poem . . .
And he called it absolutely nothing, because
*   that's what it was all about.*
And he gave himself an "A"
And a slash on each damp wrist,
And hung it on the bathroom door because he
*   couldn't reach the kitchen.*

PSYCHOLOGICAL PAIN or stress alone—however great the loss or disappointment, however profound the shame or rejection—is rarely sufficient cause for suicide. Much of the decision to die is in the construing of events, and most minds, when healthy, do not construe any event as devastating enough to warrant suicide. Stress and pain are relative, highly subjective in their experiencing and evaluation. Indeed, some people thrive on stress and are at sea without it; chaos and emotional upheaval are a comfortable part of their psychological lives. Many individuals at a relatively high risk for suicide—for example, those with depression or manic-depressive illness—function extremely well between episodes of their illness, even when in situations of great pressure, uncertainty, or repeated emotional or financial setbacks.

Depression shatters that capacity. When the mind's flexibility and ability to adapt are undermined by mental illness, alcohol or drug abuse, or other psychiatric disorders, its defenses are put in jeopardy. Much as a compromised immune system is vulnerable to opportunistic infection, so too a diseased brain is made assailable by the eventualities of life. The quickness and flexibility of a well mind, a belief or hope that things will eventually sort themselves out—these are the resources lost to a person when the brain is ill.

We know that the brain's inability to think fluently, reason clearly, or perceive the future with hope creates a defining constellation of depression. We also know that depression is at the heart of most suicides. Neuropsychologists and clinicians have found that people when depressed think more slowly, are more easily distracted, tire more quickly in cognitive tasks, and find their memory wanting. Depressed patients are more likely to recall negative experiences and failure, as well as to recall words with a depressive rather than a positive context. They are also more likely to underestimate their success on performance tasks.

Most of the impaired cognitive functioning in depression is also apparent in highly suicidal patients, including those who have recently tried to kill themselves. Suicidal patients, for example, are less able to generate possible solutions when presented with a series of problems to solve. Their thinking is more constricted and rigid, their perceived options narrow dangerously, and death is seen as the only alternative. Occasionally death is seen not just as the only alternative but as a highly seductive and romantic one. A nineteen-year-old college student illustrates this in drawings she gave to her psychologist, which portray suicide as a tranquil surcease of pain, a lulling alternative to the problems of life.

When suicidal patients undergo psychological testing, the experiences they describe tend to be negative, vague, and diffuse, and they see the future with futility and despair. When asked to think of things they are looking forward to, suicidal patients come up with far fewer than nonsuicidal people do. Often only a sense of responsibility to other family members or concerns about the effects of suicide on their children keep some people alive who otherwise have a strong desire to commit suicide.

In short, when people are suicidal, their thinking is paralyzed, their options appear spare or nonexistent, their mood is despairing, and hopelessness permeates their entire mental domain. The future cannot be separated from the present, and the present is painful beyond solace. "This is my last experiment," wrote a young chemist in his suicide note. "If there is any eternal torment worse than mine I'll have to be shown."

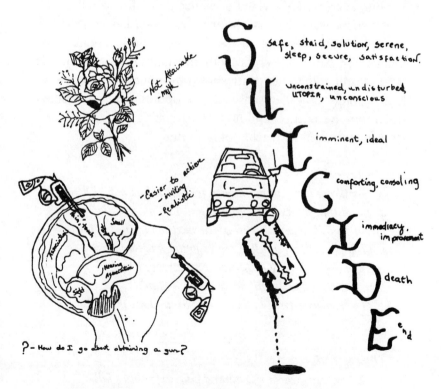

Drawings by a nineteen-year-old college sophomore

This sense of the unmanageable, of hopelessness, of invasive negativity about the future is, in fact, one of the most consistent warning signs of suicide. Aaron Beck and his colleagues at the University of Pennsylvania have shown, in an extensive series of studies, that hopelessness is strongly related to eventual suicide in both depressed inpatients and outpatients. So, too, has Jan Fawcett of Chicago's Rush-Presbyterian Hospital in his long-term prediction studies of suicide. People seem to be able to bear or tolerate depression as long as there is the belief that things will improve. If that belief cracks or disappears, suicide becomes the option of choice.

ON OCTOBER 29, 1995, twenty-year-old Dawn Renee Befano, a talented Maryland freelance journalist who had suffered from severe depression for years, killed herself. She left behind twenty-two journals, which are now in unpublished manuscript form. Excerpts from the journal written in the weeks leading up to her death show how unbearable her world had become, how her sense of her options had constricted them to nonexistence, and how an agonizing, suffusing hopelessness pervaded all reaches of her mind:

October 9th.
I will not last another month feeling as I do now. I do not question that my eyes are brown, and I do not question my fate: I will die a suicide within the next month if relief does not come relatively quick. I am growing more and more tired, more and more desperate. I am dying. I know I am dying, and I know it will be by my own hand. . . .
I am so bone-tired and everyone around me is tired of my illness.

October 10th.
Outside the world is crisp and blue, refreshing fall weather, beautiful weather. I feel like hell, trapped in a black

*free-fall. The contrast between the two makes both seem
more extreme.*

*In a strange way, however, I feel at peace, resigned to my
fate. If I do not feel better by the end of November, I have
decided to choose death over madness. I know, one way or
another, that this will all be over with by the end of next
month. This will all be over and done with. . . .*

*I feel everything and all is pain. I do not want to live, but
I must stick it out until my deadline.*

October 11th.

*I'm terrified. What'll it be, death or madness? In all
honesty, living like this for another two weeks is difficult to
imagine. I can only take so much of this punishment. When
I die, all I leave behind are these journals. . . . I don't think
I'll leave a suicide note, these journals will be more than
adequate.*

October 17th.

*I can't think. All is muddled. I want to sink into sleep, to
escape. I am so tired. To care about anything takes such a
tremendous effort. The fog keeps rolling in.*

*I simply want the world to leave me alone, but the world
slips in through the cracks and crannies. I cannot help that.
The goddamn fog keeps rolling in.*

*Insane. This waiting is truly testing my endurance. I
cannot handle it for much longer. I don't want to have to
handle it. Nobody around me does either. Nobody.*

October 20th.

Behold, I am a dry tree.—Isaiah 56:3

October 23rd.

*I want to die. Today I feel even more vulnerable than
usual. The pain is all-consuming, overwhelming. Last night*

I wanted to drown myself in the lake after everyone in the house had gone to sleep, but I managed to sleep through that impulse. When I awoke, the urgency had vanished. This morning, the urgency is back. I live in hell, day in and day out. Every day, I break down a little bit more. I am eroding, bit by bit, cell by cell, pearl by pearl. I am not getting any better. "Better" is alien to me, I cannot get there. They can try acupuncture, they can try ECT, they can try a frontal lobotomy, none of it will work. I am a hopeless case. I have lost my angel. I have lost my mind. The days are too long, too heavy; my bones are crushing under the weight of these days.

October 24th.
    I am sick, so sick. Impossibly sick. . . .

October 28th.
    So this is what the Tibetan Book of the Dead *calls "bardo," the time between lives. I don't have any taste for life because I am between lives. A more optimistic way of putting things, instead of simply, I don't want to live. . . .*
    I will not go back into a hospital. I will simply take a walk into the water.
    The pain has become excruciating, constant and endless. It exists beyond time, beyond reality, beyond endurance. Tonight I would take an overdose, but I don't want to be sick, I just want to be dead.

The next morning Dawn woke early. She sat at the kitchen table, ate cold cereal, and worked on the crossword puzzle from the newspaper. After a short while, she left the kitchen and was not seen alive again.

The bed in her room was made neatly, according to her mother. There was "a stack of thirteen library books on the floor, and the contents of her backpack, including keys, cash, and her driver's license, stowed in a large envelope. Her great-grandmother's crystal rosary beads were spread out on the bed."

Her body was found months later, floating in a lake.

CHAPTER 4

The Burden of Despair

—PSYCHOPATHOLOGY AND SUICIDE—

One forgets emotions easily. If I were dealing with an imaginary character, I might feel it necessary for verisimilitude to make him hesitate, put the revolver back into the cupboard, return to it again after an interval, reluctantly and fearfully, when the burden of boredom and despair became too great. But in fact there was no hesitation at all.

— GRAHAM GREENE

"MISERABLENESS IS like a small germ I've had inside me as long as I can remember," wrote Graham Greene. "And sometimes it starts wriggling." When the miserableness became intolerable, Greene reached out first for a knife, then for poison, and finally for a gun. Pathological despair came to him early and often throughout his life, cycling—as manic-depression will—with a dangerous, alcoholic, and suicidal ferocity. In his memoir *A Sort of Life*, Greene described his early encounters with suicidal depression and his escalating attempts to numb or die his way out of it. While still at school,

I tried out other forms of escape after I failed to cut my leg. Once at home on the eve of term I went into the dark room by the linen-cupboard, and in that red Mephistophelean glare drank a quantity of hypo under the false impression it was poisonous. On another occasion I drained my blue glass bottle of hay-fever drops, which, as they contained a small quantity of cocaine, were probably good for my despair. A bunch of deadly nightshade, picked and eaten on the Common, had only a slightly narcotic effect, and once, towards the end of one holiday, I swallowed twenty aspirins before swimming in the empty school baths.

Were these "real" suicide attempts, desperate gestures, or simply dramatic responses to the usual glooms of childhood? This is an inevitable question in light of actions taken by a precocious and sensitive schoolboy: How much of what he did was due to his temperament (and, in this case, the quick and finely wired temperament of a child who went on to become a great writer), how much was in response to painful or difficult circumstance, and how much was due to his underlying mental illness, the manic-depression openly acknowledged by Greene and an illness that also ran in his family?

Certainly, thoughts of suicide did not pass as Greene grew older. When he was nineteen, he removed his brother's revolver from the cupboard in their bedroom—"I felt nothing," he said. "I was fixed, like a negative in a chemical bath"—and walked toward the beech woods:

> I slipped a bullet into a chamber and, holding the revolver behind my back, spun the chambers round. . . .
>
> I put the muzzle of the revolver into my right ear and pulled the trigger. There was a minute click, and looking down at the chamber I could see that the charge had moved into the firing position. I was out by one. . . .
>
> This experience I repeated a number of times. . . . The revolver would be whipped behind my back, the chamber twisted, the muzzle quickly and surreptitiously inserted in my ear beneath the black winter trees, the trigger pulled.

Greene did not, in the end, kill himself. But the possibility of suicide was a recurring presence in his life and, as for many with depression, the seeming best and final response to bale and weariness. He continued to wage war against his black depressions, "the hopeless misery of the years," as he put it, using alcohol, the perverse exhilaration and risk of Russian roulette, and dangerous travels abroad into war zones and other areas of high political and social volatility, as antidotes to a bled-out state.

Suicide, at once the most individual of acts, is also a numbingly stereotypic and common end point for many who suffer from severe psychiatric illness. While no one illness or set of circumstances can predict suicide, certain vulnerabilities, illnesses, and events make some individuals far more likely than others to kill themselves.

The most common element in suicide is psychopathology, or mental illness; of the disparate mental illnesses, a relative few are particularly and powerfully bound to self-inflicted death: the mood disorders (depression and manic-depression), schizophrenia, borderline and antisocial personality disorders, alcoholism, and drug abuse. Study after study in Europe, the United States, Australia, and Asia has shown the unequivocal presence of severe psychopathology in those who die by their own hand; indeed, in all of the major investigations to date, 90 to 95 percent of people who committed suicide had a diagnosable psychiatric illness. High rates of psychopathology have also been found in those who make serious suicide attempts.

Work done by Clare Harris and Brian Barraclough in England, shown here in an adapted form, gives a general notion of which kinds of mental illness place an individual at risk. The researchers analyzed the results of 250 clinical studies and compared the number of suicides in people suffering from specific mental illnesses with the number of suicides expected in the general population. To determine suicide risks in schizophrenia, for example, they reviewed thirty-eight studies from thirteen countries; altogether, the suicide rate in more than thirty thousand schizophrenic patients was compared with that of the general population. The patients with schizophrenia, as can be seen in the graph, were more than eight times as likely to die by their own hand.

A history of a serious suicide attempt turned out to be the

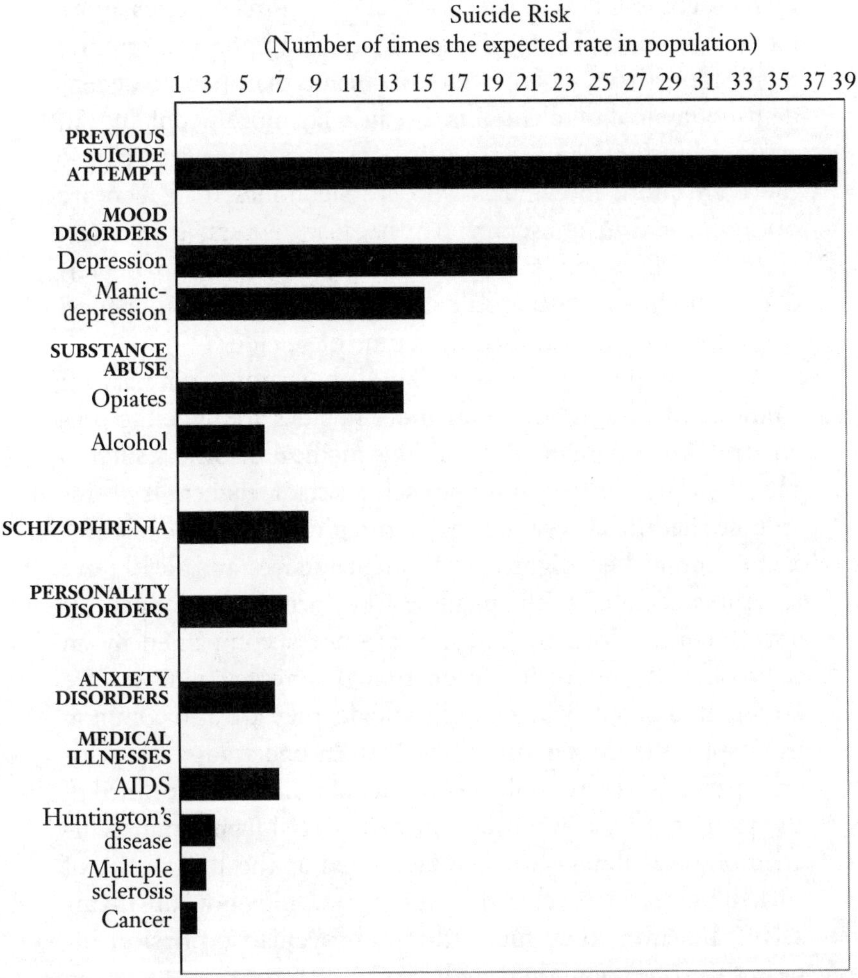

Suicide Risk
(Number of times the expected rate in population)

Suicide risk in selected psychiatric and medical conditions

single most powerful predictor of subsequent suicide, placing an individual at thirty-eight times the expected risk. Mood disorders and substance abuse also carry with them very high rates: those who suffer from depression, or from dependence upon prescription drugs (sedatives, sleeping medications, antianxiety medications), are twenty times more likely to kill themselves than the general population, and individuals with manic-depression (bipolar disorder) are fifteen times more likely. Although people who are dependent upon prescription medications have a higher rate of suicide than people dependent upon alcohol, alcohol is, because far more people use it, responsible for many more suicides. This is in part because there are more individuals who are alcoholics than who are prescription drug abusers; in part because depressive disorders are frequently—and lethally—accompanied by alcohol dependence; and in part because alcohol is often used in conjunction with other methods at the actual time of suicide.

What is perhaps most striking about this summary of studies, however, is how many more suicides are linked to psychiatric illnesses than are to serious medical disorders such as Huntington's disease, multiple sclerosis, or cancer. It seems strange that the latter illnesses, so often tied to pain, disfigurement, diminished dignity and independence, and death, are as little associated with suicide as they are. Most nonpsychiatric medical illnesses, however, are not accompanied by an increased rate of suicide; even though physical illnesses are common in people who commit suicide, they are also common in people who do *not* kill themselves. In one study of psychiatric patients, for example, researchers found that one-third of the patients who committed suicide suffered from nonpsychiatric physical illness; when they looked at the prevalence of such illnesses in psychiatric patients who did not kill themselves, however, they found that nonpsychiatric physical illnesses were as common or more so.

Two things seem to be true: First, although there are exceptions, almost everyone who has a physical illness and subsequently commits suicide also has a psychiatric illness. Second, most of the medical conditions that do show a significant increase in the rate of suicide—temporal lobe epilepsy, Huntington's disease, multiple sclerosis, spinal cord injury, HIV/AIDS, head and neck cancer—originate in or strongly influence the brain and the rest of the nervous system. These medical disorders can cause extreme mood swings and, in some instances, dementia. Other illnesses, such as heart and lung diseases, may be painful, disabling, or life-threatening, but they do not make suicide more likely (some treatments for these illnesses, however, such as coronary bypass surgery and certain medications used to treat high blood pressure, may cause severe, even suicidal depression in vulnerable individuals).

The focus of this book is on suicide in the relatively young and otherwise physically healthy, and therefore the issues surrounding suicides committed in the context of terminal illness are not as relevant as they would be in a discussion of suicide in the elderly. Still, it is important to underscore the fact that even in those with medical illnesses, most suicides or severe attempts are due to coexisting depression. The only condition that actually seems to protect against suicide is pregnancy, a condition of youth or relative youth. During pregnancy and the first year afterward, there is a three- to eightfold decrease in the risk of suicide.

The illnesses most commandingly responsible for suicide are the psychiatric disorders. And nowhere is the danger of suicide more real than in the mood disorders: depression and manic-depression.

Mood disorders, or mood disorders in combination with alcohol and drug abuse, are by far the most common psychiatric conditions associated with suicide. In fact, some type of depression is almost ubiquitous in those who kill themselves. An estimated 30 to 70 percent of people who kill themselves are victims of mood disorders; the rate is even higher when depression coexists with alcohol or drug abuse.

In its severe forms, depression paralyzes all of the otherwise vital forces that make us human, leaving instead a bleak, despairing, desperate, and deadened state. It is a barren, fatiguing, and agitated condition; one without hope or capacity; a world that is, as A. Alvarez has put it, "airless and without exits." Life is bloodless, pulseless, and yet present enough to allow a suffocating horror and pain. All bearings are lost; all things are dark and drained of feeling. The slippage into futility is first gradual, then utter. Thought, which is as pervasively affected by depression as mood, is morbid, confused, and stuporous. It is also vacillating, ruminative, indecisive, and self-castigating. The body is bone-weary; there is no will; nothing is that is not an effort, and nothing at all seems worth it. Sleep is fragmented, elusive, or all-consuming. Like an unstable gas, an irritable exhaustion seeps into every crevice of thought and action.

Sylvia Plath, five years before her suicide, described the seeping, constricting side of her depression: "I have been and am battling depression," she wrote in her journal. "I am now flooded with despair, almost hysteria, as if I were smothering. As if a great muscular owl were sitting on my chest, its talons clenching and constricting my heart." British writer Alan Garner portrayed the cold terror of the beginnings of his manic-depressive breakdown in a different way, but the sense of horror and suffocation is palpable:

> The next thing I remember is that I was standing in the kitchen, the sunlit kitchen, looking over a green valley with brook and trees; and the light was going out. I could see, but as if through a dark filter. And my solar plexus was numb.
>
> Some contraption, a piece of mechanical junk left by one of the children, told me to pick it up. It was cylindrical and spiky, and had a small crank handle. I turned the handle. It was the guts of a cheap musical box, and it

tinkled its few notes over and over again, and I could not stop. With each turn, the light dimmed and the feeling in my solar plexus spread through my body. When it reached my head, I began to cry with terror at the blankness of me, and the blankness of the world.

A scene from Eisenstein's "Alexander Nevsky" swamped my brain: the dreadful passage in which Nevsky dupes the Teutonic Knights onto the frozen lake, and the ice breaks, and their faceless armour takes them under. The cloaks float on the water before being pulled down, and the hands clutch at the ice floes, which flip over and seal in the knights.

All that helplessness, cold and horror comprised me. I was alone in the house, and throughout the afternoon I turned the tinkle tinkle tinkle of the broken toy, which became the sound of the ice. My body was as heavy as the armour and the waterlogged cloaks as I slid beneath the ice.

When the family came home, I was lying on the kitchen settle, in a foetal position, without moving or speaking, until I went to bed at midnight. Sleep was unconsciousness without rest. . . .

I was incapable of emotion except that of being incapable of emotion. I had no worth. I poisoned the planet.

The horror of profound depression, and the hopelessness that usually accompanies it, are hard to imagine for those who have not experienced them. Because the despair is private, it is resistant to clear and compelling description. Novelist William Styron, however, in recounting his struggle with suicidal depression, captures vividly the heavy, inescapable pain that can lead to suicide:

What I had begun to discover is that, mysteriously and in ways that are totally remote form normal experience, the gray drizzle of horror induced by depression takes on the quality of physical pain. But it is not an immediately identifiable pain, like that of a broken limb. It may be more accurate to say that despair, owing to some evil trick played upon the sick brain by the inhabiting psyche, comes to resemble the diabolical discomfort of being imprisoned in a fiercely overheated room. And because no breeze stirs this caldron, because there is no escape from this smothering confinement, it is entirely natural that the victim begins to think ceaselessly of oblivion.

Mania provides a violent contrast to the melancholic states. "The blood," as Austrian composer Hugo Wolf said, "becomes changed into streams of fire"; thoughts cascade and ideas leapfrog from topic to topic. Mood is exultant but often laced with a savage and agitated irritability. One is, said Robert Lowell, "tireless, madly sanguine, menaced, and menacing." Thought is expansive, frictionless, and astonishingly quick; talk is fast and unstoppable; and the senses are acute, engaged, and sharply responsive to the world about them.

The fluidity of thinking in mania is matched by a seductive, often psychotic sense of the cosmic relatedness of ideas and events. (This dazzle and rush of euphoric mania make it hard for many patients to give it up.) Russian poet Velimir Khlebnikov—who was highly eccentric, wildly moody, for a time institutionalized in a mental hospital, and who was described by Mayakovsky as the "Columbus of new poetical continents . . . one of our masters"—believed that he possessed "equations for the stars, equations for voices, equations for thoughts, equations of birth and death." The artist of numbers, he was certain, could draw the universe:

Working with number as his charcoal, he unites all previous human knowledge in his art. A single one of his lines provides an immediate lightninglike connection between a red corpuscle and Earth, a second precipitates into helium, a third shatters upon the unbending heavens and discovers the satellites of Jupiter. Velocity is infused with a new speed, the speed of thought, while the boundaries that separate different areas of knowledge will disappear before the procession of liberated numbers cast like orders into print throughout the whole of Planet Earth.

Here they are then, these ways of looking at the new form of creativity, which we think is perfectly workable.

The surface of Planet Earth is 510,051,300 square kilometers; the surface of a red corpuscle—that citizen and star of man's Milky Way—0.000, 128 square millimeters. These citizens of the sky and the body have concluded a treaty, whose provision is this: the surface of the star Earth divided by the surface of the tiny corpuscular star equals 365 times 10 to the tenth power (365 × 10^{10}). A beautiful concordance of two worlds, one that establishes man's right to first place on Earth. This is the first article of the treaty between the government of blood cells and the government of heavenly bodies. A living walking Milky Way and his tiny star have concluded a 365-point agreement with the Milky Way in the sky and its great Earth Star. The dead Milky Way and the living one have affixed their signatures to it as two equal and legal entities.

With mania, there is a vast, restless energy and little desire or need for sleep. Behavior is erratic, impetuous, and frequently violent; drinking, sex, and the spending of money are excessive. When mania is severe, visual and auditory hallucinations, as well as delusions of grandeur or persecution, may occur. Paranoia, explosive rage, and despair not uncommonly lie beneath the expansive manic exterior.

This weaving together of paranoia and darkness in the

midst of mania is clear in the response of one of my patients to the blank card from the Thematic Apperception Test, a psychological test that requires a patient to make up a story about what he sees on the card. The patient, who was twenty-five years old at the time of testing, was hospitalized for acute mania. The story he reeled off, without pause—again, it should be noted, in response to a blank card—is saturated with paranoid overtones, overt psychosis, and a depression that is mixed with hope:

> It's really clear, except for some spots. There are lots of germs, that's why I'm not holding it close to my face. It would look better with some color. There is an absence of all color except there are bits of color. I identified with the hero, afraid of germs. Color of lithium. Shapes of butterflies. Lots of symmetry, counterparts. Candy-colored bullshit. I feel like I'm being held involuntarily in a fog, don't see much blue. Don't see any flowers. A guy sees a bunch of black guys and weirdies, he follows the man and they find a civilization, walking like robots until they find it. They escape, find a lot of secrets about the trap. They have a run-in with the police, find a guy who looks like God who is arrested for having sex with his wife, who should have been having a test-tube baby. There is a lot of electrocardiac shock in the *fog*, a lot of homosexuals and green and gray people who traveled through fog into an insane asylum. They emerged out into the world and found the sun for the first time in a hundred years.

Earlier in the century, a more exuberant patient described a grandiosity of psychotic proportions, as well as the rapid chase of ideas so characteristic of mania. But underlying the escalating thoughts and feelings were fleeting strands of self-destructiveness:

The condition of my mind for many months is beyond all description. My thoughts ran with lightning-like rapidity from one subject to another. I had an exaggerated feeling of self importance. All the problems of the universe came crowding into my mind, demanding instant discussion and solution—mental telepathy, hypnotism, wireless telegraphy, Christian science, women's rights, and all the problems of medical science, religion and politics. I even devised means of discovering the weight of a human soul, and had an apparatus constructed in my room for the purpose of weighing my own soul the minute it departed from my body. . . .

Thoughts chased one another through my mind with lightning rapidity. I felt like a person driving a wild horse with a weak rein, who dares not use force, but lets him run his course, following the line of least resistance. Mad impulses would rush through my brain, carrying me first in one direction then in another. To destroy myself or to escape often occurred to me, but my mind could not hold on to one subject long enough to formulate any definite plan.

Manic-depression—characterized by episodes of mania (which can be severe or mild) in addition to episodes of depression—is less common than depression but nonetheless quite prevalent. One person in a hundred suffers from the more severe form of the illness, and perhaps another two or three have the milder variations. The average age of its onset, eighteen years, is considerably younger than that for major depression, which is about twenty-six. Unlike depression, which is at least twice as common in women as in men, manic-depressive illness strikes men and women evenly. Bipolar illness is generally a more severe disorder than depression alone, recurs more frequently, and has far more of a genetic component. It is also more likely than depression to be accompanied by drug or alcohol abuse (nearly two-thirds of those with manic-depression have a serious drinking or drug problem, compared with one-fourth of those with depression alone).

Suicide attempts are disproportionately high in both of these mood disorders. At least one person in five with major depression will attempt suicide, and nearly one-half of those with bipolar disorder will try to kill themselves at least once. Individuals with mood disorders tend also to make more serious attempts than those without depressive illnesses, and, despite often using nonviolent methods such as drug or medication overdoses, their attempts usually show more detailed planning and a greater intent to die.

For those with mood disorders, the risk of suicide is highest if the depression is very severe, hospitalization has been required, or suicide has been attempted at some point. Mild or moderate depressions, while often painful and debilitating, do not carry with them the same high risk of suicide. Swedish researchers psychiatrically assessed an entire rural population and then kept track of their mental health for the next fifteen to twenty-five years. Virtually all the men who committed suicide during the follow-up period had been diagnosed during their initial evaluations as having depressive illness. The suicide rate for men with no psychiatric diagnosis at all was 8.3 per 100,000, but for those with depression it escalated to 650. The direct relationship between the severity of depression and suicide was the most compelling finding, however. No one with mild depression committed suicide (although characterized by the Swedish doctors as "mild," such depressions were still sufficiently serious to lead to a radically reduced activity level), but the rate went up to 220 per 100,000 for those who had been diagnosed with moderate depression and skyrocked to 3,900 per 100,000 for those with severe depressive illness (defined by the researchers as depression with impaired reality testing, often of psychotic proportions). The severity of depression—especially when coupled with physical agitation, alcohol or drug use, and profound emotional upheavals, losses, or disappointments in life—is far more predictive of suicide than a diagnosis of depression alone.

Suicide appears to be slightly more common in major depression than in bipolar illness, although many people who are diagnosed with depression turn out to have mild forms of mania as well; these so-called hypomanias generally are not reported by the patients themselves, nor are they always picked up by their doctors or ascertained through psychological autopsies. Individuals who experience these mild periods of mania—usually characterized by high energy, little sleep, and marked irritability—often have coexisting alcohol or drug problems, have chaotic lifestyles, and do not take their medications as prescribed. When irritability and substance abuse are a part of the prolonged depressive phase of the illness, the volatile elements may prove to be a particularly deadly combination.

The violent agitation of some suicidally depressed patients is impossible to comprehend unless it is intimately observed or personally experienced. These high-voltage, perturbed, yet morbid conditions are particularly common in bipolar illness during *mixed states*. Broadly conceptualized as the simultaneous occurrence of both depressive and manic symptoms, mixed states may exist as an independent clinical form (as mania and depression do), or they may occur as transitional conditions, bridging and blending one phase of the illness with another. They are particularly common when depression escalates into mania, mania ratchets down into depression, or depression clears into normal functioning. In the late nineteenth century, psychiatrist Emil Kraepelin captured the violent desperation of many of his manic-depressive patients:

> The patients, therefore, often try to starve themselves, to hang themselves, to cut their arteries; they beg that they may be burned, buried alive, driven out into

the woods and there allowed to die. . . . One of my patients struck his neck so often on the edge of a chisel fixed on the ground that all the soft parts were cut through to the vertebrae.

Behavior and moods during these periods tend to be volatile and erratic. Any combination of symptoms is possible, but the one most virulent for suicide is the mix of depressed mood, morbid thinking, and a "wired," agitated level of energy. Paranoia, extreme irascibility, fitful sleep, heavy drinking, and physical lashing out not uncommonly go along with this particular variant of a mixed state. It is singularly and dangerously uncomfortable. Excess energy produces a kind of unhinging agitation, an "almost terrible energy," as poet Anne Sexton put it:

> I walk from room to room trying to think of something to do—for a while I will do something, make cookies or clean the bathroom—make beds—answer the telephone—but all along I have this almost terrible energy in me and nothing seems to help. . . . I walk up and down the room—back and forth—and I feel like a caged tiger.

Edgar Allan Poe, too, described a "fearful agitation," in a letter written shortly after his suicide attempt:

> I went to bed & wept through a long, long, hideous night of despair—When the day broke, I arose & endeavored to quiet my mind by a rapid walk in the cold, keen air—but all *would* not do—the demon tormented me still. I CANNOT live . . . until I subdue this fearful agitation, which if continued, will either destroy my life or, drive me hopelessly mad.

Mixed states, whether they occur as depressive manias or agitated depressions, make people who experience them more likely to kill themselves. Mania itself rarely kills—and, when it does, it is usually because a patient has acted on a delusional belief that he or she can fly, walk on water, or attack an armed police officer with impunity. The intention of suicide in such situations is highly questionable.

Before the availability of modern medications, many patients died during acute mania due to exhaustion, heart attacks, or widespread infections from unnoticed and unattended wounds in their feet that occurred during prolonged, often barefoot walks. Kraepelin described the frenetic behavior of his manic patients:

> The patient cannot sit or lie still for long, jumps out of bed, runs about, hops, dances, mounts on tables and benches, takes down pictures. He forces his way out, takes off his clothes, teases his fellow patients, dives, splashes, spits, chirps and clicks. . . . [There are] discharges of inner restlessness, shaking of the upper part of the body, waltzing about, waving and flourishing the arms, distorting the limbs, rubbing the head, bouncing up and down, stroking, wiping, twitching, clapping and drumming. . . . [Death may be caused] by simple exhaustion with heart failure (collapse) in long continuing, violent excitement with disturbance of sleep and insufficient nourishment, by injuries with subsequent blood-poisoning.

Psychosis, the presence of hallucinations or delusions, is less clearly associated with risk for suicide in mood disorders than is the actual severity per se of depression or mixed states. Some investigators have found an increase in psychotically depressed patients, but this is by no means a consistent finding. Even though severely depressed patients with auditory hallucinations may hear voices commanding them to kill themselves, they do not appear to be more likely to actually commit suicide. Psychotic patients do, however, tend to use more violent and bizarre methods.

People with depression or manic-depression are particularly likely to kill themselves, or make serious suicide attempts, early in the course of their illness, often after their first attack of severe depression or following their release from a psychiatric hospital. It is not obvious why this should be so, although unfamiliarity with the experience of depression, uncertainty about personal and professional repercussions, and concerns about whether or when it will come back again all certainly play a role. Getting the correct treatment is a gamble and, even with the best of doctors, it often takes a long time to take effect. People often wait until they are most ill before seeking care and may be unable to stay the treatment course long enough to make them feel sufficiently well to continue living.

Disconcertingly, one of the highest-risk periods for suicide is when patients are actually recovering from depression. The transition from hopelessness, lethargy, and despair, on the one hand, to normal mood and existence, on the other, is one freighted with hazard: mixed states are common during this time and bring with them rapid mood swings, perturbations of energy, and disrupted sleep. There may also be sharp disappointments when the jagged pattern of recovery leads to feeling first well and then ill again. A resurgence of will and vitality—ordinarily a sign of returning health—makes possible the acting out of previously frozen suicidal thoughts and desires.

It can be difficult to distinguish between those genuinely getting well from those who may on an impulse, or during a especially hopeless moment, kill themselves. One study, for instance, compared written clinical observations made on patients shortly before they committed suicide with clinical observations made on patients of comparable ages and diagnoses who did not commit suicide. Counterintuitively, those who killed themselves had been assessed by their doctors as calmer and "in better spirits" than those who did not. In fact, nearly one-third of hospitalized psychiatric patients "look normal" to their doctors, family members, or friends in the minutes or hours just before suicide.

This apparent calm before the storm may reflect different things: The suicidal patients may be experiencing a genuine calm in the midst of recovery but then switch precipitously into a severe depression or a mixed state. They may, on the other hand, be calmer because, having decided to kill themselves, they are relieved of the anxiety and pain entailed in having to continue to live. They may also be deliberately deceiving their doctors and families in order to secure the circumstances that will allow them to commit suicide. This latter tendency to deceive in order to die has been recognized for centuries. Among those to make note of this was the great eighteenth-century Philadelphia physician, educator, and patriot Benjamin Rush, surgeon general of the Continental Army and signer of the Declaration of Independence:

> We should be careful to distinguish between a return of reason and a certain cunning, which enables mad people to talk and behave correctly for a short time, and thereby to deceive their attendants, so as to obtain a premature discharge from their place of confinement. To prevent the evils that might arise from a mistake of this kind, they should be narrowly watched during their convalescence, nor should they be discharged, until their recovery had been confirmed by weeks of correct conversation and conduct. Three instances of suicide have occurred in patients soon after they left the Pennsylvania Hospital, and while they were receiving the congratulations of their friends upon their recovery.

Mood disorders, although more linked to suicide than other mental illnesses, are not the only ones to cause early self-inflicted death. Schizophrenia, a terrible psychotic illness, often does as well.

"This is a good-bye letter," wrote poet and composer Ivor Gurney to a friend in June 1918. "I am afraid of slipping down and becoming a mere wreck—and I know you would rather know me dead than mad. . . . May God reward you and forgive me." In a war hospital at the time, diagnosed with a "nervous breakdown from deferred shell-shock," Gurney was acutely suicidal and at the beginning of a long, terrifying descent into paranoid schizophrenia. He threatened suicide on several occasions and at least twice attempted it, once by taking an overdose of sedatives given to him by his doctor, another time by gassing himself. Gurney's agony was scarcely bearable. Imaginary voices told him to kill himself, and he was certain that electrical waves from the radio were bombarding him. The delusions were persistent, as were the voices that threatened and tormented him. His doctor described Gurney's mental condition:

> The electricity manifests itself chiefly in thought. Words are conveyed to him. They are often threatening, [and] they have been obscene and sexual. He has heard many kinds of voices. He sees things when he is awake, faces etc. that he can recognize. He has also had a twisting of the inside. He cannot keep his mind on his work. . . . With regard to suicide he has had such pains in the head that he felt he would be better dead.

There was little change for the better in Gurney's psychiatric condition, and he remained almost continuously in an asylum from 1922 until the time of his death in 1937. He took his pain into his poetry. "There is a dreadful hell within me," he wrote in one of his asylum poems, "And nothing helps. . . . I am praying for death, death, death." In another, he proclaimed, "There is one who all day wishes to die . . . has prayed for mercy of Death."

Schizophrenia is the most severe and frightening of the

psychiatric illnesses. Like manic-depression, it is an illness that first hits when an individual is young (in the late teens or early twenties); is genetic, although not as strikingly so as bipolar disorder; is relatively common (approximately one person in a hundred will get it); and is devastating to relationships, educational plans, and aspirations. Left untreated, it usually gets worse over time. Alienation from friends and family is the rule rather than the exception. Suicide, although less common than in the mood disorders, is still common enough to make it a very lethal disease—lethal and painful, for schizophrenia plays havoc with the senses, reason, emotion, and the wherewithal to act. It is malevolent, and it will kill 10 percent of its victims through suicide.

Hallucinations, the perception of something where nothing exists, and delusions, false beliefs that persist in spite of incontrovertible evidence to the contrary, are only part of the terror of schizophrenia. Often the entire visual and emotional world is transformed into a dark, mapless horror. Auditory hallucinations, especially hearing voices, are common. The voices threaten, condemn, and demand. They may be located anywhere: near or far away; in the heart or head, in the nose or abdomen; in the external world: in birds, telephones, televisions, or the Internet. Usually the voices' content is disturbing; occasionally it is incomprehensible. Sometimes the voice is a solitary one; often there is a conversation or argument between two voices; occasionally there is a cacophonous chorus of sounds and words.

Visual hallucinations are not as common as auditory ones, but they are similarly chameleonic. Emil Kraepelin, an astute observer of psychosis in both mania and schizophrenia, gave examples of some of the many visual distortions and hallucinations experienced by his schizophrenic patients: they saw, he said, death's heads, saints from all eternity, a tumbling clown, black birds of prey hovering overhead, the emperor of China, snakes in their food, Martin Luther, flames, red and white mice in a heart, two tortoises on the shoulder. They saw and heard varied and dreadful things.

Physician and scientist Carol North, now on the medical school faculty at Washington University in St. Louis, described the frightening hallucinations, bizarre delusions, and contorted perceptions in her schizophrenic universe. Here she recalls her experiences in the Quiet Room of the hospital ward:

I lay motionless on the plastic floor mat for hours, till my limbs grew stiff from not moving. The drain in the center of the concrete floor belched up rough voices that laughed at me and called me foul names that reverberated back and forth between the puke-green tile walls several times before dying away. Intermittently, ghoulish faces appeared on the other side of the door's window to observe me as they might observe a reptile behind glass at the zoo. At first I thought those faces belonged to the aides coming back to check on me; then I thought maybe they were really the faces of the voices, finally showing up to meet with me. Later, I wondered if maybe the faces weren't there at all, but just another product of my troubled mind.

I was caught in a limbo or maybe a purgatory, awaiting my place in the Other World. Oh, how I wished something would happen to break up the events and end my discomfort.

Magically, the three-inch-thick door swung open.

"Carol." Dr. Falmouth's voice. "I'd like to talk to you."

"Talk ... walk, balk, chalk, gawk, squawk," the voices echoed, rhyming Dr. Falmouth. That coded message meant we were now traveling toward the sun with supervelocity. We had emerged from special relativity into special-special-relativity. My body was electric, buzzing: a sixty-cycle hum, serving as conductive material in a communications network that allowed forty billion messages to zoom back and forth between parallel universes and Other Worlds. Without me to transfer their messages and hold them together, all of these systems would fall into chaos. Dr. Falmouth would never be able to hold strong against the awesome powers before us.

Dr. Falmouth raised my arm into the air. My finger bolted themselves into a new mold, ready for firing off ray beams into multidimensional space.

Grossly disorganized behavior and language also characterize schizophrenia; speech may become incoherent and meaningless. The gradual disintegration of a mind is almost incomprehensible. To observe its unwinding from within is surely intolerable. To be frightened of the world; to be walled off from it and harangued by voices; to see life as distorted faces and shapes and colors; to lose constancy and trust in one's brain: for most the pain is beyond conveying. Robert Bayley, a patient with schizophrenia, put into words some of the awfulness of his day-to-day struggles:

> The reality for myself is almost constant pain and torment. The voices and visions, which are so commonly experienced, intrude and so disturb my everyday life. The voices are predominantly destructive, either rambling in alien tongues or screaming orders to carry out violent acts. They also persecute me by way of unwavering commentary and ridicule to deceive, derange, and force me into a world of crippling paranoia. Their commands are abrasive and all-encompassing and have resulted in periods of suicidal behavior and self-mutilation. I have run in front of speeding cars and severed arteries while feeling this compulsion to destroy my own life. As their tenacity gains momentum, there is

often no element of choice, which leaves me feeling both tortured and drained. I also hear distorted sounds that modulate and contort from the very core of my brain. There are times when these sounds can erupt from nowhere as the voices continue to propel me into a crazed inner world.

The visions are extremely vivid, provoking fear and consternation. For example, during periods of acute bombardment, paving stones transform into demonic faces, shattering in front of my petrified eyes. When I am in contact with people, they can become grotesquely deformed, their skin peeling away to reveal decomposing inner muscles and organs.

Contortions of reality are not the only sources of pain. A malignant apathy is pervasive; emotions that are intense or pleasurable for others are often flat or blunted for those with schizophrenia; intellect, memory, and the ability to concentrate and think logically are eroded. (Not surprisingly, brain-imaging studies reveal pronounced differences in structure and functioning between individuals who have schizophrenia and those who do not.) These symptoms, although they overlap with those of depression, tend to be more permanent, less likely to remit over time. For many, mood is also affected: at least one in four schizophrenic patients suffers from serious depression, which in turn makes them far more likely to kill themselves.

Schizophrenic patients who commit suicide, like those with mood disorders, are very likely to be depressed, intensely irritable, and restless. They are also more likely to have attempted suicide at some point (30 to 40 percent of schizophrenic patients attempt suicide at least once; as with depressed patients, a history of a serious suicide attempt is the single best predictor of subsequent suicide). They also tend to be in the early stages of their illness or recently released from a psychiatric hospital. Although hallucinations and delusions are clearly a source of distress to psychotic patients, the actual role they play in precipitating suicide is unclear.

Several other psychiatric conditions, most significantly the anxiety disorders and the borderline and antisocial personality disorders, also carry with them a higher-than-expected risk of suicide. (Although the eating disorders anorexia nervosa and bulimia nervosa result in many medical complications and even death, the actual suicide rate is unclear. A review of more than thirty studies found that approximately 1 percent of those with eating disorders die by suicide.)

Anxiety disorders, on the other hand, especially when accompanied by panic attacks or severe depression, definitely increase the chances of suicide. The defining symptoms of these disorders—excessive anxiety and worry, disturbed sleep, muscle tension, irritability, fatigue, and restlessness—tend to be long-standing features of an affected individual's life. Symptoms of depression are common. Panic attacks are also associated with an increased rate of suicide and suicide attempts, although there has been a spirited debate about the extent of the increase. These attacks are discrete periods of intense fear or discomfort, accompanied by an abrupt onset of a number of unpleasant physical and mental symptoms such as palpitations or a pounding heart, sweating, shaking, a sense of being smothered or shortness of breath, chest pain, and an acute fear of dying or losing one's mind. These symptoms often lead to emergency room visits because the people experiencing them are frightened they are having a heart attack. If panic attacks occur too often, they may lead to a sense of despair and hopelessness, as well as to self-imposed social isolation in an attempt to avoid situations that might trigger subsequent attacks. Severe anxiety, like severe agitation, is a potent predictor of suicide.

Surprisingly, and uniquely among the major mental illnesses, obsessive-compulsive disorder seems not to put those who suffer from it at an increased risk for suicide. Although the persistent and intrusive thoughts and impulses and the highly repetitive behaviors—such as hand washing until the hands are raw, counting, repeatedly checking the door to ensure that it is locked—that are the hallmarks of this illness are not only deeply distressing to those who have them but also time-consuming (often taking up hours of every day) and highly disruptive to virtually all aspects of life, most studies find that suicide is rare in obsessive-compulsive disorder unless it is extremely severe or complicated by depression.

A final broad category of psychiatric conditions, the so-called personality disorders, include two that result in a disproportionate number of suicides. Borderline personality disorder is broadly defined as a pervasive life pattern of stormy relationships and impulsive, self-destructive behaviors; symptoms can include unstable job history, chronic feelings of emptiness and fears of abandonment, intense periods of anger, rapid mood swings, wrist slashing, skin carving or burning, head banging, self-cutting, and suicidal behavior. Antisocial personality disorder, which often starts as a conduct disorder in childhood, is characterized by a pervasive pattern of disregard for the rights of others, a lack of empathy, excessive aggression, pathological lying, little or no capacity for remorse, and physical cruelty.

Although these disorders are dissimilar in many significant respects (for example, antisocial personality disorder is three times as common in males; the reverse is true for borderline personality disorder), there are several features they share: both are familial disorders, that is, first-degree relatives (parents, siblings, and children) are far more likely to have borderline or antisocial personality disorders than would be expected by chance; both are relatively prevalent; and both have a tendency to diminish in severity over time. Other features shared by antisocial and borderline personality disorders probably also contribute to their increased risk of suicide: markedly impulsive behavior; uncontrollable fits of rage; frequent physical fights or unprovoked assaults; reckless behaviors, such as high-risk sexual promiscuity or substance abuse; highly unstable moods, and extreme irritability. The virulent instability of mood and behavior, coupled with the diagnostic hallmarks of manipulativeness and a disregard for the feelings and rights of other people, essentially guarantees combative relationships, an impoverished and solitary personal life, and occupational chaos, unemployment, or imprisonment.

Reckless and violent behaviors, which we will look at more closely in the next several chapters, have been associated time and again with suicide and serious suicide attempts in those with psychiatric illnesses. When the unstable elements that define borderline and antisocial personality disorders mix with depression, alcoholism, or substance abuse, the combination can be explosive, dangerous, and not uncommonly lethal. Nearly three-quarters of those with borderline personality disorder attempt suicide at least once, and 5 to 10 percent do kill themselves. With these patients, suicidal behavior is more bound to their conflicts in relationships with other people than it is with patients who have major depression, schizophrenia, or manic-depression. Borderline patients are exquisitely sensitive to actual or perceived rejection, and their depressed moods, although short in duration, are far more responsive to setbacks in relationships. (Suicide itself often takes place in the physical presence of another person. In one study, more than 40 percent of suicides committed by borderline patients were witnessed by other people; in individuals with other diagnoses, only about 15 percent of suicides were witnessed.)

A clinician who has worked a great deal with borderline personality disorder, Howard Wishnie, described a thirty-two-year-old mother of three children who had been hospitalized for depression and brief psychotic episodes:

> During the first hours of hospitalization she appeared as a neatly dressed attractive young woman who was immediately comfortable with staff and patients. There

was no objective evidence of depression. Over the weekend she overdosed with alcohol and sedatives. On Monday when she reappeared at the hospital, medications were immediately discontinued. The patient made many attempts to have her medications restored to her and refused to recognize that her inappropriate use of medication could be sufficient grounds for the discontinuance. By Monday afternoon she had become openly seductive with the resident therapist and demanded sexual relations. Her appearance and behavior had become more disorganized and bizarre. Attempts to discuss the rapid fluctuation in the patient's appearance and mental status were explained as evidence of her "illness," for which she had no understanding. When the therapist pointed out that the patient's ability to manage her own life and deal with her intense feelings seemed better prior to hospitalization, the patient became enraged and stated that she would go to another hospital where the doctors understood her better and would be less distant. She stormed out of his office and left the building

After several minutes the therapist left his office. He returned ten minutes later and found the patient standing in a pool of blood. She had smashed the windows in his office and cut herself with the glass. Several months later she explained: "You were supposed to be in your office for me, even if I said I was leaving. I knew you would be there. When you weren't, I suddenly saw my father's face appear on the glass coming at me. A great tear appeared in his face. The world was being turn apart. I began to smash out the images."

The brief psychotic episode was followed by a second one on the same day when a meeting was held with the patient's husband. In spite of the patient's demonstrated capacity for regression, the conditions for treatment and hospitalization in terms of the patient's responsibility for her own behavior were restarted. The patient began telling her husband of the doctor's callous indifference to her. When this failed to alter the stated conditions for continuing treatment in the hospital, the patient fell to the floor, began chewing on the chair leg and making bizarre moans and cries. He pulled her off and angrily stated that her behavior clearly demonstrated her need for intense treatment and her inability to be responsible for herself. The therapist maintained his position, and the patient assumed a trancelike appearance. She and her husband left the office to seek hospitalization elsewhere.

One hour later the therapist received a phone call from the patient. Her voice was clear and direct, as upon admission. She said, "Doctor, I agree." Her agreement was to continue treatment as initially stated. She was immediately discharged and seen as an outpatient for the next one and one-half years. Several brief psychotic episodes occurred during subsequent therapy sessions. Each related to real or suspected object loss. The identification of the loss in each case was followed by the lifting of the psychosis within the treatment hour. Had this patient been seen during one of her regressed states without the benefits of previous history she could easily have been diagnosed as schizophrenic.

The major clue of her actual diagnosis was the open and dramatic discussion of symptoms coupled with the mobilization of numerous people in the environment on her behalf.

All the psychiatric conditions we have been discussing—the mood disorders, schizophrenia, and the anxiety and personality disorders—are not only painful and terrible illnesses to have, they also have profound, usually alienating and destabilizing, effects on the ability of the affected person to have meaningful relationships, to engage in satisfying and economically viable work, and to believe in the point of living. All these disorders are also made infinitely worse by using alcohol or drugs.

Schizophrenia and the mood, anxiety, and personality disorders are at the heart of many suicides, but by no means all. Alcohol and drug abuse, either in their own right or, more commonly, in combination with depression and other mental illnesses, take a terrible toll as well. Substance abuse, like manic-depression and schizophrenia, usually begins early in life, often in adolescence or the early twenties, and, once it has set in, has a stubbornly progressive course. Despite massive and often irreversible personal, financial, social, legal, and professional problems, people with a drinking or drug abuse problem typically continue compulsively to use the substances that are destroying them.

It is not always easy to sort out dependence on drugs or alcohol from the depressive illnesses that can precede, accompany, or follow the onset of substance abuse. Both kinds of problems involve disturbances in mood, thinking, behavior, sleep, and appetite. Alcoholism can cause most of the symptoms of depression, and very serious depression can follow prolonged periods of drinking. The reasons for this are both obvious and subtle. Psychiatric illnesses such as depression, mania, and schizophrenia are painful and frightening. Drugs and alcohol can, in the short term, bring relief from the despair and blot out, for a while, a sense of hopelessness and ragged nerves. Drinking increases not only during depression but most pathologically so when people are manic or experiencing agitated mixed states. These perturbing conditions invite the use of alcohol or other drugs, such as sedatives and hypnotics, to tamp down the restlessness, afford the possibility of sleep, and cloak, however briefly, the unpleasant sensations that are such a large part of these psychological and physical conditions.

Self-medication to lessen disturbing thoughts and grisly moods tends to be quite specific in practice. Cocaine, for example, is used by many who are depressed not only as an antidepressant—albeit an exceedingly costly and ultimately damaging one—but also, in those with manic proclivities, to induce mild manias or prolong existing ones. Opium has served a lulling, numbing function for centuries, and alcohol, although pharmacologically a depressant and a killer of all but fractured sleep, is used by millions to erase the moment, give the slip to depression, and induce senselessness.

The relationship between alcohol, drugs, and mental illness is a looping-back-upon-itself, reverberating one. Drugs, at first use, work well and often enough to have been employed for thousands of years throughout the world as a core means for grappling with anxiety, distress, depression, and psychosis. Fermented grains, rolled coca leaves, and the juice of poppies have been the commonest choices to chase the blues, resurrect the deadened senses, obliterate pell-mell thoughts, or stifle intrusive voices. But the use of such drugs has always been risky. To the extent that they work, they do so by altering the fine tuning of the brain and muffling its consciousness. As such, they are blunt agents that, with prolonged use, alter or damage the brain's delicate chemistry. In doing so, they work huge damage in the relationships, jobs, health, and pride of those who are dependent on or addicted to them.

Alcohol and drugs, used to contend with the pain of mental illness, more often worsen it. Independently or together they can precipitate acute episodes of psychosis, worsen the overall course of the underlying illness, and not only undermine the individual's willingness to seek out and receive good clinical care but also sabotage the effectiveness of prescribed treatments. Substance abuse loads the cylinder with more bullets. By acting to disinhibit behavior, drugs and alcohol increase risk taking, violence, and impulsivity. For those who are suicidal or potentially so, this may be lethal. So too may the savage mood swings that often accompany substance abuse or withdrawal from drugs. With judgement warped, personal relationships made chaotic or destroyed, and an escalating desire for the substances that, over time, work decreasingly well, it is perhaps not surprising that when drug and alcohol abuse combine with psychopathology they form an intensely volatile environment for suicide.

Research tends to support the idea that in those who have both, mental illness usually precedes the addictive disorders. Edgar Allan Poe, no stranger to turbulent moods chased back by wine and cider, observed, "I am constitutionally sensitive—nervous in a very unusual degree. I became insane, with long periods of horrible sanity. During these fits of absolute unconsciousness I drank, God knows how much or how long. As a matter of course, my enemies referred the insanity to the drink rather than the drink to the insanity." His description is a telling one.

Unfortunately, mental illness and alcoholism or drug abuse often go together. Two of every three people with manic-depression, and one of every four with depression, have substantial alcohol or drug abuse problems; the rates for those with schizophrenia are nearly as high. More dangerously, those who are both mentally ill and have such a problem are at far greater risk of attempting or committing suicide. The combination of alcohol and depression is implicated in the majority of all suicides. Drugs and mood disorders tend to bring out the worst in one another: alone they are dreadful, together they kill.

Poet John Berryman, in and out of hospitals for both his alcoholism and his manic-depression, saw his drinking and mental illness pull down the pilings of his life and erode the foundations of his marriage, friendships, and writing. Two years before he jumped to his death from a bridge—ending his own life, as his father and aunt had done before him—he wrote of the futility of his mental state. Returning to his home after yet another wild bender and ill-considered sexual entanglement, Berryman found himself confronted by his wife, an official from the university at which he taught, and police officers who were about to take him, in restraints, to a psychiatric hospital:

> He knew he was standing in his entry-hall. Wife facing him, cold eyes, her arm outstretched with a short glass—a little smaller than he liked—in her hand. Two cops to his left. His main Dean and wife somewhere right. . . . The girl had gone. He was looking into his wife's eyes and he was hearing her say: "This is the last drink you will ever take." Even as somewhere up in his feathery mind he said "Screw that," somewhere he also had an unnerving and apocalyptic feeling that this might be true.

CHAPTER 5

What Matters It,
If Rope or Garter

— METHODS AND PLACES —

Since we can die but once, what matters it,
If rope or garter, poison, pistol, sword,
Slow-wasting sickness, or the sudden burst
Of valve arterial in the noble parts,
Curtail the miseries of human life?
Though varied is the cause, the effect's the same:
All to one common dissolution tends.

— THOMAS CHATTERTON

THE PARTICULARS of suicide hook our imagination in a dark way. Intrigued by even the banal ways of self-inflicted death and riveted by the bizarre, we try to reason backward from the choice of method and place to the anguish and weariness leading up to them. We assign meaning to the logistics of the act—a hanging in the woods, a slashed throat in the bathroom—in the hope of entering an inaccessible state of mind. Yet only a few methods—gunshot, jumping, poisons, gas, hanging, drowning—account for nearly all suicides.

Seneca, in the first century, spoke of the ways: "In whatever direction you may turn your eyes," he wrote, "there lies the means to end your woes. See you that precipice? Down that is the way to liberty. See you that sea, that river, that well? There sits liberty—at the bottom. See you that tree, stunted, blighted, and barren? Yet from its branches hangs liberty. See you that throat of yours, your gullet, your heart? . . . Do you ask what is the highway to liberty? Any vein in your body!"

Yet, as Yale surgeon and author Sherwin Nuland points out, when it actually came time to kill himself Seneca found it more difficult than he had imagined or had advised others: "He plunged a dagger into the arteries of his arm," writes Nuland, and "when the blood did not come fast enough to suit him, he cut the veins of his legs and knees. That not sufficing, poison was swallowed, also in vain." Death came finally with steam suffocation in a bath.

The sheer horror of the act of suicide tends to elicit anxiety and fear in those who have little personal familiarity with the bleak hopelessness underlying it. For those with familiarity, however, a grim wit can sum up the options. Dorothy Parker's "Résumé" is one of the more mordant and famous contributions to the subject:

> *Razors pain you;*
> *Rivers are damp;*
> *Acids stain you;*
> *And drugs cause cramp.*
> *Guns aren't lawful;*
> *Nooses give;*
> *Gas smells awful;*
> *You might as well live.*

Parker lived what she wrote. Her first suicide attempt was with a razor to her veins, the second with an overdose of veronal, the third with barbiturates. Her depressions, not helped by her prodigious drinking, were frequent and awful, but she was able to use her deadly wit to deflect the pain, at least with her friends. Biographer Marion Meade captures Parker's arch black humor poignantly:

> When Dorothy was sufficiently recovered to receive visitors, she prepared her performance. Even though she looked wan and still felt weak from crying, she greeted her Round Table friends with a cheerful grin and her customary barrage of four-letter words. Pale-blue ribbons were gaily tied around her bandaged wrists, and she waved her arms for emphasis as if she were proudly sporting a pair of diamond bracelets from Cartier's. Had she been candid about her despair, they might have been forced to acknowledge the depth of her suffering and probably would have responded in a manner more suitable to the occasion. Playing it for laughs, she gave them an easy out.

Edna St. Vincent Millay was born within a year of Parker, though lifestyles away; she too spent time in mental hospitals and wrote her share of gallows verse on suicide. Her "I Know a Hundred Ways to Die" was, rather strangely, published in a collection of poems for young people.

> *I know a hundred ways to die.*
> *I've often thought I'd try one:*
> *Lie down beneath a motor truck*
> *Some day when standing by one.*
>
> *Or throw myself from off a bridge—*
> *Except such things must be*
> *So hard upon the scavengers*
> *And men that clean the sea.*
>
> *I know some poison I could drink.*
> *I've often thought I'd taste it.*

What Matters It, If Rope or Garter

But mother bought it for the sink,
And drinking it would waste it.

Millay and Parker dashed off in rhyme the familiar ways of suicide, but emergency room doctors, police officers, undertakers, psychiatrists, and medical examiners keep a morbid trove of far more dreadful means of dying. In his 1840 book *The Anatomy of Suicide*, physician Forbes Winslow described a man who stabbed himself to death with his spectacles, another who threw himself to the bears in the Jardin du Roi in Paris, and yet another who suspended himself from the clapper of a village church bell. One Frenchman, who had been betrayed by his mistress, called his servant and informed him that he was going to kill himself. He asked him to make a candle of his fat, once he had died, and "carry it lighted to his mistress." In his final letter to her he wrote, "As he had long burnt for her, she might now see that his flames were real; for the candle by which she would read the note was composed of part of his miserable body." He then committed suicide.

Later in the century, the superintendent of the New York State Lunatic Asylum described patients who had committed suicide by drinking boiling water, pushing broom handles down their throats, thrusting darning needles into their abdomens, or gulping down leather and iron.

To kill themselves, the suicidal have jumped into volcanoes; starved themselves to death; thrust rumps of turkeys down their throats; swallowed dynamite, hot coals, underwear, or bed clothing; strangled themselves with their own hair; used electric drills to bore holes into their brains; walked off into the snow with no provisions and little clothing; placed their necks in vices; arranged for their own decapitation; and injected into themselves every substance known to man, including air, peanut butter, poison, mercury, and mayonnaise. They have flown bombers into mountains, applied black widow spiders to their skin, drowned in vats of beer or vinegar, and suffocated themselves in their refrigerators or hope chests. One of Karl Menninger's patients tried repeatedly to kill himself by drinking raw hydrochloric acid; he survived those attempts and died only after swallowing lighted firecrackers.

Henry Romilly Fedden, writing about suicide earlier in this century, described a Polish woman who swallowed "four spoons, three knives, nineteen coins, twenty nails, seven window-bolts, a brass cross, one hundred and one pins, a stone, three pieces of glass and two beads from her rosary." Another woman, a Parisian, applied a hundred leeches to her body.

More recently, there have been several reports of suicidal men deliberately trying to infect themselves with the AIDS virus, and a disconcerting number of people who provoke police officers into killing them, a practice known to the police as "suicide by cop." This baffling endgame, as it has been described by the *New York Times*, is now responsible for nearly 10 percent of fatal police shootings in the United States.

Like the police, undertakers and medical examiners are often first or early witness to nightmarish death scenes. These scenes are terrible to consider when drugs or drowning are involved but mentally unshakable if a particularly bizarre or violent method has been used. In his book *The Undertaking*, poet and undertaker Thomas Lynch makes this explicit in a harrowing account of one suicide he tended:

> The cuckolded householder had sat up drinking after his wife had gone to bed announcing her intention to put spongy rollers in her hair. This had become an intimate code which meant to him she did not want to have sex with him but wanted to look good for the boss tomorrow. He'd finished the bottle of Dunphy's Irish and raided her stash of Valium, then gone to the drawer where the Black & Decker electric carving knife was kept between Easters and Thanksgivings and Christ-

mases. He'd plugged it into the wall socket on his side of the bed, locked his jaw against any utterance and, lying down beside her, applied the humming knife to his throat, severing his two ascending carotid arteries and jugular veins and making it half through his esophagus before he released his hold on the knife's trigger. It had not been his coming to bed, nor the buzz of the knife, nor any sound he'd made, if, indeed, he'd made any that woke her. Rather, it was the warmth of his blood, that gushed from his severed blood vessels halfway up the master bedroom wall and soaked her and her spongy rollers and saturated the bed linen and mattress and box springs and puddled in the carpet beneath the bed that woke her wondering was it just a dream.

These singular methods of suicide are far from being just a sideshow of freakish death; they give testament instead to the desperation and determination of the suicidal mind. Their very bizarreness somehow makes the act more real. They evoke horror, certainly, but they also give us a glimpse into otherwise unimaginable misery and madness.

The logistics of suicide in antiquity were not dissimilar to those used in the centuries since. Weapons—knives, swords (the "Roman death"), razors, scalpels, and daggers—were the most common means, then hanging, jumping, and poisoning by hemlock, opium, or other drugs. Less often, but not rarely, the Romans starved to death by refusing to eat, set themselves on fire, or provoked murder in others who were in a position to kill them (not unlike the modern "suicide by cop"). Anton van Hooff, who more than anyone has described the suicide practices of classical antiquity, notes that in Rome, as now in most countries, far more men than women killed themselves. Only in the ancient myths did more women commit suicide.

Hanging, though a frequent method of suicide for young people and women, was regarded by the Romans as "unclean" and shameful; weapons were thought to be the honorable way to die. Euripides, as quoted by van Hooff, makes this clear:

> *To die were best. How then with honour die?*
> *Unseemly is the noose 'twixt earth and heaven:*
> *Even of thralls 'tis held a death of shame,*
> *Noble the dagger is and honourable,*
> *And one short instant rids the flesh of life.*

Over the succeeding centuries, weapons continued to be a prominent method of suicide. Firearms, as they became more available, gradually overtook knives and swords as the weapons of preference. Hanging, however, remained popular, and poisons and drowning were used by an increasingly large number of people. By the late nineteenth century in Europe, hanging and poisons were by far the most common ways to kill oneself in France, England, and Prussia; drowning was next in preference. Cultural differences, however, were significant. Firearms, for example, were quite commonly used in suicides in Italy, France, and Prussia but far less often in England, where a wide assortment of drugs and poisons—prussic acid, caustic acid, mercury, opium, laudanum, potassium cyanide, arsenic, vermin killers, chloroform, strychnine, and belladonna—was put to use. After firearms, poisoning was the most common means of suicide in the United States during the same time period.

The rivers and sea, and even the waters in city parks (such as the Serpentine in London's Hyde Park, where many, including Percy Bysshe Shelley's first wife, drowned themselves) were frequent sites of suicide; they also became a darkly romanticized part of literature and folklore.

Langston Hughes, in this century, described the river's lure in his succinct poem "Suicide's Note":

What Matters It, If Rope or Garter

The calm,
Cool face of the river
Asked me for a kiss.

National preferences for modes of suicide tend to vary. "Thus," wrote sociologist Emile Durkheim in 1897, "each people has its favorite sort of death and the order of its preferences changes very rarely." Nineteenth-century Russians took to hanging, the English and Irish to poison, the Italians to firearms, the Americans to firearms, poisons, and illuminating gas. Proclivities for certain methods tended to go with immigrants wherever they went, or at least until they assimilated into their new countries. "Even away from their own country," wrote Morselli, "the English and Irish preserve their predilection for poison and the pistol, whilst the German always retains his pre-eminence in hanging." Over time, however, German immigrants to the United States tended more toward poisoning and guns, taking on the preferred means of suicide in North America; likewise, the English, Scottish, and Irish immigrants to Australia gradually assumed the suicide preferences of their adopted country.

Within the same country, suicide methods often vary by geographical region. In Belgium, for example, poisons are used more in the southern districts, while guns are used in the wooded regions, which have a stronger cultural history of hunting. Brussels, with its taller buildings, is more frequently the site of deaths by jumping. Poisoning and hanging are the most popular means of suicide in much of India, except for Punjab, where 55 percent of suicides are by lying down on railway tracks or jumping in front of trains.

Not surprisingly, methods of suicide change over time. During the years 1960 to 1980, for example, a study of suicide methods in sixteen countries found that deaths from domestic gas had decreased, while deaths from motor vehicle exhaust, hanging, and firearms had increased. There were no changes in the use of poisons, cutting, or drowning. The decrease in suicides from domestic gas was due to a change in government policy that lowered carbon monoxide levels in gas, thereby undercutting its deadliness. This raises critical questions about the impact of decreasing the availability of a particular suicide method—such as gas, prescription drugs, or firearms—on the overall suicide rate. Is there a genuine reduction in suicides, or do suicidal individuals simply substitute another method? This issue will be discussed later in the context of suicide prevention policies.

In the United States, firearms are now responsible for more than 60 percent of all suicides; no other method comes close. Strangulation (hanging, strangulation, and suffocation) and overdoses (drugs, medications, and poisons) together account for another 25 percent or so. Inhalation of gases and vapors, falls, cutting, and drowning make up the remainder of self-inflicted deaths.

What, for the suicidal, determines the method of death? Is it pragmatic? Symbolic? Or imitative? Is the method chosen for its availability, its painlessness, or is it meant, as well, as a final reflection of style or desperation? In his suicide note, Japanese writer Ryuunosuke Akutagawa laid out some of his reasoning for why he chose to die as he did:

> The first thing I considered is how to die without suffering. For this purpose, probably hanging is the best, but when I picture a person hanged to death, I feel an aesthetic abhorrence. . . . Drowning is not good either, because . . . drowning will involve more suffering than hanging does. Suicide by running into a rushing train also is aesthetically abhorrent to me. Suicide by gun or knife does not seem to work well for me because my hands shake. Jumping from a high building produces an ugly sight. Considering thus, I have decided to die with

pills. To do so implies longer suffering than hanging but it has advantages. My body would appear better and there would be less risk of failure than with other methods. Its only disadvantage is the difficulty of obtaining pills. Since I have determined to use pills, I have tried to acquire them at every opportunity. At the same time, I have attempted to increase my knowledge of drugs.

Then I considered the place of my suicide. My family members must depend on what I leave for them. My possessions are a piece of land of 100 *tsubo* [about 100 feet square], my home, the royalties from my books, and savings of 2,000 yen. If I commit suicide in my house its value will drop. I want to commit suicide in such a way that my body will be seen as little as possible by others—other than my family members.

Although symbolic meanings and vivid interpretations have been given to different methods of suicide—Karl Menninger took drowning to represent a desire to return to the womb, and Freud conjectured that the various means of suicide represented sexual wish fulfillments (to poison oneself was to desire to become pregnant, to drown was to wish to bear a child, and to throw oneself from a height was to be delivered of a child; Freud did not specify whether these interpretations were equally applicable to both sexes)—the inventiveness of the interpretations would appear to outweigh the available evidence. Personality traits, as measured by standard psychological tests and administered to individuals in the months or years preceding their suicides, do not correlate with the type of suicide method chosen. Nor have any differences in intelligence level been found between those who choose to die by gunshot, poison, jumping, hanging, or drowning.

Many factors undoubtedly play an important role in the choice of methods. The availability of the method is obviously critical. In countries in which firearms are readily available, such as the United States, or in professions that have easy access to guns, such as the police and the military, firearms are used disproportionately. Where toxic plants and fruits grow abundantly—for example, poisonous alary seeds from the yellow oleander in Sri Lanka, or the fatal sachasandia fruit in Argentina—or where deadly germicides, pesticides, and other agrochemicals are used freely, as they are in China, Singapore, Western Samoa, Sri Lanka, Guyana, India, and many other countries, suicide deaths reflect their ease of access.

Where rail and metro systems flourish and other methods are less at hand; where seas and rivers, cliffs, or tall buildings are easy to find and take advantage of, these ways will be used by those wishing to die. If you are a doctor or a chemist and can lay hands upon a lethal drug, you will choose it more often than those who do not have access to or information about it. And if you are a patient on a psychiatric ward, the right of access to the more obviously lethal means removed, necessity will provoke the use of shoelaces, coat hangers, bedsheets, or a rushed jump from an unprotected stairwell. If you are a psychiatric patient outside the hospital and you have been prescribed potentially lethal medications (such as antidepressants, lithium, or barbiturates), you may opt to poison yourself with the drugs you have been given to treat your illness.

The availability of a method is far from the only significant consideration in its choice. The perception of an act's deadliness is clearly crucial to decision making. Some methods of suicide, such as jumping, hanging, or gunshot, leave little or no chance for detection or rescue by others. Nor do they allow the opportunity to change one's mind. Other methods, however, such as drug overdoses or cutting, offer a more extended period of time between the suicidal act and death. Discovery of the attempt, or seeking help oneself, are more than viable possibilities; this is especially true now that highly sophisticated emergency medical services are available at large urban trauma centers and at many local hospitals.

One person's estimation of a method's effectiveness is not another's, however. Forensic pathologists, for example, when asked to rate twenty-eight methods of suicide in terms of their deadliness, ranked gunshot wounds, cyanide, explosives, being hit by a train, or jumping from a height as the most effective. The ratings made by the pathologists were highly consistent with one another. Laypeople, on the other hand, were wildly variable in their understanding of different methods. They overestimated (when compared with the pathologists) the effects of prescription drug overdoses and wrist cutting and underestimated the deadliness of gunshot. Women tended to overestimate the lethal consequences of most methods, especially medication overdoses, which suggests that many more women who survive overdoses may have intended death than is commonly thought. There is further evidence that people err in their estimates of the deadliness of suicide methods. American adolescents, who have easy access to over-the-counter medications and who use them in up to one-half of their drug overdoses, tend to greatly underestimate their potential for toxicity.

In general, women use less violent and final means, although increasingly in recent years they have turned to firearms. One study conducted in the 1970s found that both women and men regard drugs and poisons as the "most acceptable" form of suicide, but men perceive firearms as more "masculine," efficient, and easy to use. Women's preference for drugs and poisons centers on their perceived painlessness, accessibility, and ease of use. Fear of disfigurement has been suggested as another possible reason to explain women's preference for nonviolent forms of suicide, although the evidence for this is slight.

Age also plays a role in the choice of suicide method. Now, as in antiquity, hanging tends to be used more often by younger people. So, too, does jumping from heights or leaping in front of oncoming trains. Firearms are used by both the young and the old, but increasingly by the young. The type and degree of psychopathology are also factors in the method chosen. Severely mentally ill patients are more likely than others to immolate themselves, leap in front of trains, or choose particularly bizarre and self-mutilative ways to die.

Some individuals avoid a particular suicide method because of concern about risking the lives or psychological well-being of others: they will not use carbon monoxide poisoning, for example, because gas may seep into places where other people live; cyanide, because traces of it on the lips may endanger would-be rescuers who use mouth-to-mouth resuscitation techniques; jumping, for fear of landing on other people; and gunshot or jumping, because of the traumatic visual effects on survivors. However, most who kill themselves, for reasons of pain or impulse or crippled thought, are not able to act on any such altruistic concerns they may have. As a result, that which may appear as anger or malevolence to those left behind—a disfigured body left in a familiar or intimate place—may reflect only a desperate or precipitate act. Revenge and anger play a role in the circumstances of some suicides, but probably not most. It is next to impossible, as Morselli wrote more than a hundred years ago, to discover the reasons, "sometimes noble and weighty, sometimes shameful and thoughtless, why the suicide goes to cut his throat on his own bed, or to suffocate himself in the darkest recess of the house."

Symbolism and suggestion also play their part in the circumstances of self-inflicted death. Louis Dublin, former chief statistician for the Metropolitan Life Insurance Company and, as such, keenly interested in the prediction and prevention of suicide, wrote of the individual's "psychological constellation and personal symbolism." These conditions of thought, memory, and desire, persuaded by impulse and irrationality, are influenced as well by personal aesthetics and private meanings. They are directed, too, by the accounts of the suicides of others, accounts that are often enhanced or romanticized by newspaper and television reporting or portrayals in books or films. Some methods and places become "suicide magnets," drawing to them not only the impulsive and the acutely disturbed but the more chronically suicidal as well.

Leaping into a river or the sea seems always to have had both an aesthetic and practical draw. Eons ago, the Greeks—including, it is said, Sappho and Phobos—leapt to their deaths from the high cliffs of Leucas; others jumped from bridges and riverbanks into the Tiber or Euphrates. More recently, the Thames held a pragmatic allure, and by 1840 nearly 15 percent of suicides in London were individuals who had thrown themselves off Waterloo Bridge. Wading into the sea was an "easeful death" made strangely alluring by the Romantics. Drowning became such a popular way to commit suicide in nineteenth-century Paris that in order to avoid public health problems, the city paid fishermen a bounty for every body they retrieved.

At Beachy Head, the cliffs on the eastern end of the South Downs of the English coast, suicides have been reported since the sixth century. Recent years have witnessed sharp peaks in the number of self-inflicted deaths here, suggestively related to intensive media coverage. More than 120 people threw themselves off the Sussex cliffs between 1965 and 1979. British researchers believe that the publicity given to the suicides at Beachy Head increased the likelihood that others would occur there. They cite, as an example of the effects of publicity, a fifty-six-year-old man who, while in a hospital recovering from a suicide attempt by overdose, read a newspaper report about the spate of suicides at Beachy Head. He remarked, "Fancy putting something like that in the paper for people like me to see." Two weeks later he made his way to Beachy Head and jumped to his death. (Jumping from public monuments has also had a contagious allure—the Eiffel Tower in Paris, St. Peter's Basilica in Rome, the Duomo of Milan, the Campanile of Giotto in Florence, the Empire State Building in New York City—an allure that resulted in the construction of protective barriers on many such buildings.)

Publicity given to particular ways and places of suicide can certainly have a bearing on the methods chosen by vulnerable individuals. Alary seeds, from the yellow oleander plant, were unknown as a means of suicide in Sri Lanka before 1983. Newspaper coverage and a south Indian film broadcasting their use, coupled with easy public access to the plants, increased by orders of magnitude the number of poisonings in subsequent years. Similarly, press coverage of the terrible deadliness of the herbicide paraquat, noting that it took only a single mouthful to kill, greatly increased its use as a means of suicide in Fiji. An Indian film gave parallel prominence to a waterfall at Hogenakal in south India, as did television and newspaper publicity to suicides from high-rise apartment buildings at Takashimadaira, near Tokyo, and fatal jumps from multistory car parks in Australia.

In the year following the 1991 publication of *Final Exit*, Derek Humphry's best-selling book, which presented in detail a variety of ways to commit suicide (including, prominently, suffocation by plastic bag), suicidal asphyxiations involving plastic bags increased by 31 percent. Peter Marzuk and his colleagues at Cornell University Medical College in New York noted that although the total number of suicides did not increase, the publicity surrounding this particularly lethal method may have had a deadly impact on impulsive and ambivalent individuals. They suggest, with good cause, that clinicians include in their assessments of suicide risk questions not only about actions of potential concern, such as writing suicide notes or drawing up wills, but whether patients have obtained and read literature about euthanasia or assisted suicide.

An epidemic of suicides by burning occurred in England and Wales in 1978 to 1979 after a twenty-four-year-old Australian heiress, deported from England the week before after having threatened to kill herself in Parliament Square, set fire to herself in front of the Palais des Nations in Geneva. Three days later, a director of Fortnum and Mason committed suicide in a similar manner on the banks of the Thames at Windsor. By month's end, there had been ten immolations, and within a year eighty-two people had killed themselves by burning. This was in stark contrast to an annual average of twenty-three such suicides in the years 1963 to 1978 (in no year had there been more than thirty-five). The tremendous media coverage of the self-immolations led the researchers who wrote up these findings to conclude that there was a need for some form of voluntary restraint on the part of the press. "In a free society," they wrote, "there is a conflict between the need for a free press and the use of the press of reports of horrifying deaths as spectacles for entertainment purposes." They also stressed the need to deromanticize death by burning. Far from being quick and painless, they pointed out, only one-third of those who set fire to themselves died immediately. Another one-third lived longer than twenty-four hours, and all the victims experienced great pain and suffering.

AT THE FOOT of Mount Fuji, Japan's highest mountain and a sacred site, there is a dense forest called Jukai, the "sea of trees." The forest, which grew over a lava plateau, is unpopulated and essentially without roads. The first recorded suicide in Jukai was in the fourteenth century; since that time, the thick "black forest" has enticed hundreds to their deaths. Yoshitomo Takahaski, of Yamanashi Medical College, contends that there is an almost mythic belief that once in the forest there is no coming out: the magnetic composition of the igneous lava plateau renders a compass virtually useless, and because visibility is nil, it is next to impossible to navigate by sun or stars.

In the early 1960s, a popular Japanese writer wrote a best-selling novel that described the heroine's attempt to kill herself by entering the forest. Streams of people followed her example. Television, films, newspapers, and magazines added to the attraction by calling further attention to Jukai as a suicide site. Regular police patrols had to be put in place in order to rescue potential suicides, and wide-scale searches for bodies are now conducted in the spring and fall. At least thirty still die in the forest each year, most by hanging or overdoses; a few kill themselves with carbon monoxide poisoning or die from exposure.

Of all the suicide sites romanticized in literature, however, of all of those given ink and airtime by the media, two stand out for their hold on both the popular and suicidal imaginations: Mount Mihara, on the Japanese island of Oshima, and the Golden Gate Bridge in San Francisco.

Mount Mihara, an active volcano in Japan, was almost entirely unknown until January 1933, when two classmates from an upper-crust Tokyo school climbed to the top of its crater. Meiko Ukei, at twenty-four the older of the two, announced to her friend that she intended to throw herself into the volcano. She would, she explained, be cremated instantly and sent heavenward in smoke and beauty. After extracting a vow of secrecy from her friend, she jumped.

Masako Tomita was only twenty-one, and understandably unable to keep the promise she had made. She confided in another friend, who then insisted that Masako take her to Mount Mihara so that she, too, could "follow Meiko to paradise through Mihara's gateway." Masako was unable to persuade her friend otherwise, and in early February the two young women climbed to the top of the volcano. The friend jumped alone, Masako returned alone, and soon the story was a major force in the cultural life of Japan. People swarmed to Mihara, first by steamer and then by a larger boat that was required to handle the curious. On an April Sunday not long after the deaths of the two young women, six people leaped into the volcano; twenty-five others had to be physically restrained from doing so. Tourists lined up to watch the suicides, which were now occurring several times a week. By year's end, at least 140 people had committed suicide.

The following year, 1934, more than 160 plunged to their deaths and another 1,200 had to be restrained by the police from following suit. In January 1935, three young men jumped to their deaths within ten minutes of one another. The police maintained a twenty-four-hour watch at the crater, and a high barbed-wire fence was erected; yet in 1936, at least 600 people killed themselves in Mihara. The crater and its surrounding area and local commerce took on a ghoulish, surreal quality, as Edward Ellis and George Allen recount in *Traitor Within*:

> The suicide epidemic brought to Oshima a boom comparable to the Florida land craze of 1925–26. From a barren, desolate place, it blossomed into a combination national shrine, Coney Island, Atlantic City, and Niagara Falls. The island's population increased greatly. Fourteen hotels and 20 restaurants opened within two years. Horses were imported to carry tourists to Mihara's summit. Five taxicab companies opened for business. By 1935 the island's photographers had increased from two to 47. A post office was opened at the crater's edge. A strictly amusement-park touch was added with the construction of a 1,200-foot chute-the-chute down Mihara's slope to provide the visitors a final thrill. . . .
>
> The Tokyo Bay Steamship Company replaced the *Kiku Maru* with two new large ships, declared a 6 percent dividend on stock which had paid no dividends for the previous three and a half years, and reported that its net profit was now running to $280,000 a year. Part of this income was provided by a spectacular addition which the steamship company made to Mihara's attractions. The company had imported three camels to carry tourists across the mile-wide strip of volcanic desert which surrounds Mihara's crater. The first of

these animals most Japanese had ever seen, they were an instant, money-making success.

In an effort to escape the onus of profiting on suicide, the steamship company refused to sell one-way tickets to Oshima. The government backed the company with a law making it a criminal offense to attempt to purchase a one-way passage. Plain-clothes men were assigned to mingle with the passengers on the ships, with instructions to arrest anyone who appeared to them to be bent on suicide.

Access to the mountain was eventually closed, but not before at least a thousand people had thrown themselves into the crater.

A year or so later, on the other side of the Pacific Ocean, the Golden Gate Bridge was opened. A graceful structure in San Francisco Bay in a staggeringly beautiful part of the world, it soon took on the siren call of Mount Mihara. Three months after the bridge opened in May 1937, the first of more than a thousand, and some estimate nearly twice that number, committed suicide by jumping over the side. Leaping to death from the Golden Gate Bridge soon entered into American folklore, much as Mihara had seeped into Japanese cultural awareness. Psychologists Richard Seiden and Mary Spence, of the University of California at Berkeley, observe that a language and mythology soon grew up around the bridge: if the stress gets too great, they quote city residents as saying, "one can always go off the bridge." In San Francisco, Gray Line Tour bus drivers cited Golden Gate Bridge suicides as a part of their tours, and jokes on the subject ended up in greeting cards. The *San Francisco Chronicle* reported a lottery whose players bet on the date of the next suicide from the bridge.

The jump from the Golden Gate Bridge is 250 feet and almost invariably fatal. Trauma from water impact is extreme, ripping apart the great blood vessels, demolishing the central nervous system, and transecting the spinal cord. A few have died from drowning and one from a shark attack, but mostly death is caused by the crushing impact of body on water. In the word of one of the doctors who investigated the causes of death in the suicide victims, the trauma rips the internal organs "asunder."

In fact, only 1 percent of those who jump from the Golden Gate Bridge survive. David Rosen, a psychiatrist at the University of California, San Francisco Medical School, interviewed six of those survivors, and all said that for them it was only the Golden Gate Bridge that they considered as a suicide site; as one put it, "It was the Golden Gate Bridge or nothing." Another remarked, "There is a kind of form to it, a certain grace and beauty. The Golden Gate Bridge is readily available and it is connected with suicide." One man, suffering from depression, also emphasized the bridge's accessibility. In the suicide note he left before jumping off the bridge, he asked, "Why do you make it so easy?"

All the survivors favored the construction of a suicide barrier, an idea resisted by bridge officials until very recently. Most of the survivors also stressed the importance of somehow deromanticizing suicide from the bridge. One survivor, understandably, if naively, said, "Newspaper editors should voluntarily stop all press coverage of the Golden Gate Bridge suicides—extensive press coverage put the idea into my mind." This is debatable, but it is an important and complicated debate to which we will return.

Far more people actually kill themselves in psychiatric hospitals than they do in highly publicized or exotic places. Five to 10 percent of all suicides, in fact, take place in mental hospitals. It may seem strange that such high rates should exist in places specifically designed to protect patients from harming or killing themselves. But in many ways, it is no more strange than the fact that there are high death rates in intensive care units or on oncology wards. Psychiatric hospitals exist to take care of the most severely ill and those most at risk for suicide.

A common reason for admission to a mental hospital is having attempted suicide, and attempted suicide is, as we have seen, the single best predictor of subsequent suicide. A substantial risk of suicide is also one of the few reasons people can be held in hospitals involuntarily.

Although many precautions can be taken by medical staff to protect patients, there is no way, short of intolerable violations of privacy and freedom, to protect everyone. The line between civil liberties and preservation of life is a controversial one. Acutely suicidal patients are kept under close observation, often on a locked ward. Windows on such wards are usually unbreakable and unopenable, electrical cords are kept as short as possible, and "breakaway" hooks and shower rods, designed to break off at low weights, are used. Patients are searched for sharp objects and drugs, and matches, lighters, nail polish remover, mirrors, bottles, scissors, belts, and shoelaces are removed from their possession.

Physical observation of suicidal patients is intense, with levels varying according to the assessment of the suicide risk. In one-to-one observation, the patient is continuously watched and accompanied by a staff member even when the patient is showering or using the toilet. The physical proximity is kept close, sometimes no further than arm's length, in order to allow a quick response in case of a sudden or impulsive move. Occasionally, a single nurse may observe two or three suicidal patients at the same time; if the suicide risk appears to lessen, a patient will then be put on five-, fifteen-, or thirty-minute "checks." These checks consist of staff members monitoring the whereabouts and well-being of the patient on a frequent but not continuous basis.

Were suicidal patients able or willing to articulate the severity of their suicidal thoughts and plans, little risk would exist. But this is not the case. Patients determined to die may present a clinical picture greatly at variance with how they actually feel or what they intend to do. They may move quickly and with desperate ingenuity. As nineteenth-century psychiatrist Emil Kraepelin wrote in his classic text, *Manic-Depressive Insanity:*

> Only too often the patients know how to conceal their suicidal intentions behind an apparently cheerful behaviour, and then carefully prepare for the execution of their intention at a suitable moment. The possibilities at their command are numerous. They may, while deceiving the vigilance of the people round them, drown themselves in the bath, hang themselves on the latch of the door, or on any projecting corner in the watercloset, indeed even strangle themselves in bed under the cover with a handkerchief or strips of linen. They may swallow needles, nails, bits of broken glass, even spoons, drink up any medicine, save up sleeping-powder and take it all at one time, throw themselves downstairs, smash their skull with a heavy object and so on. A female patient by sticking in pieces of paper managed to prevent the upper part of a window, where there was no grating, being properly shut, and then threw herself down from the second storey in an unwatched moment. Another who was shortly to have been discharged, was alone for a few minutes in the scullery; she took a little bottle of spirit and a match from the cupboard, which had been left open through negligence, and having poured the spirit over herself set herself on fire.

In the 1930s, Gerald Jameison and James Wall, at Bloomingdale Hospital in New York State, described the varieties of suicide methods used by patients in their hospital: twisted cords round the neck; two neckties attached to plumbing fixtures in the toilet; three handkerchiefs attached to the hinge of a closet door; a curtain tied around the throat and then attached to a window sash; cut throats from razors or window glass; and a cut femoral and radial artery with a piece of glass from a tumbler. (Sylvia Plath, who had been hospitalized after a nearly lethal suicide attempt, described in her autobiographical novel, *The Bell Jar*, the guile attendant to suicidal thought: "A maid in a green uniform was setting the tables for supper," she wrote. "There were white linen tablecloths and glasses and paper napkins. I stored the fact that they were real glasses in the corner of my mind the way a squirrel stores a nut. At the city hospital we had drunk out of paper cups and had no knives to cut our meat.")

Hanging and jumping are by far the most common methods of suicide used by psychiatric inpatients, and being under staff supervision is no guarantee against self-inflicted injuries and death. Psychiatrists Jan Fawcett and Katie Busch, in a Chicago-based study of patients who had committed suicide while in the hospital, found that more than 40 percent had been on fifteen-minute checks at the time they killed themselves. Fully 70 percent of those who killed themselves had denied, prior to the act, any suicidal thinking or plans.

The reality of treating seriously ill and potentially suicidal patients is that difficult clinical decisions have to be made each step of the way. When should a patient first be taken off constant nursing observation and placed on fifteen- or thirty-minute checks? At what point can a patient first be allowed off the ward unaccompanied or given a pass to go home for the weekend? Prediction is imperfect, and patients who are desirous of dying dissemble.

Research indicates that more than half the patients who kill themselves in psychiatric hospitals had been described by nursing or medical staff, just before their suicides, as "clinically improved" or "improving." Indeed, nearly 50 percent of those who commit suicide while on a ward, or immediately after discharge from the hospital, had been assessed as nonsuicidal at the time of admission. The days early in hospitalization and those leading up to discharge are particularly high-risk periods for suicide. The time prior to leaving the hospital is often laden with concerns about rejection by family and friends, loneliness, a still turbulent clinical course (often characterized by volatile mood cycling and an exceedingly uncomfortable restlessness, agitation, and irritability), concerns about job problems or unemployment, and fears about being able to manage outside the hospital. Often caught in the dilemma of being too well to be in the hospital but not well enough to deal with the realities and stresses of life outside, as well as having to contend with the personal and economic consequences of having a serious mental illness, patients sometimes feel utterly hopeless and overwhelmed, and kill themselves. Hospitals can provide sanctuary and medical care; they can save the lives of many who are suicidal. But they cannot save everyone.

THE LION ENCLOSURE

The world goes by my cage and never sees me.

—RANDALL JARRELL,
"The Woman at the Washington Zoo"

THE CAUSE of death, said the medical examiner, was suicide: the dead woman had died from sharp- and blunt-force injury associated with massive blood and soft-tissue loss. No doubt this was true. More to the point, however, the thirty-six-year-old woman with long dark hair had been mangled, shredded, and partially eaten by one or both of the lions in their outdoor enclosure at the National Zoo in Washington. Mauling was the reality. Mauling, with all of its attendant visual horrors, was what people conjured. Not blunt-force injury. Not soft-tissue loss. A woman was violently dead, in a manner handpicked and appalling.

Her body, still wet from swimming across a twenty-six-foot moat—only one of several barriers separating the public from the four-hundred-pound cats—was discovered by a zoo worker on a cold March morning in 1995. Face up, mutilated beyond recognition, the body was dressed lightly for the winter day. It lay on a grassy terrace near the place where the lions went for their usual feeding; the arms and hands had been chewed off. Bite marks covered the corpse. Certainly, as the medical examiner put it—certainly and terribly—"this was not an instantaneous death."

No one doubted the immediate cause of death. The lions, a young male and older female, would have responded predictably to an intruder in their territory. Out of curiosity or a sense of threat, instinct would dictate a deadly or near-deadly outcome. No one questioned that the powerful and dangerous carnivores had killed the young woman. The questions that, for a day or two, kept the nation's capital spellbound were, instead: Who was she? *And why?*

Intense public interest in the macabre circumstances of the woman's death provoked an inevitable round of speculation: Was it suicide? Murder? Had she fallen into the lion enclosure by accident? The bizarreness of the circumstances, the savagery of her death caught everyone's imagination in the darkest, most primitive of ways.

The *Washington Post*, in one of five stories it ran on the subject, captured the city's shock at the act: "Suddenly," wrote journalist Phil McCombs, "this city of smooth diplomacy with its false beaming smiles and barely sheathed fangs, this town where Arafat and Rabin could shake hands and lobbyists blandly testify under oath that their deadly products won't harm you, this place of careful spins and cloaked motives and paper death, was mesmerized by the sudden fierce savagery of real slaughter. . . . It was, in a way, a death too simple for Washington to swallow. By yesterday afternoon [two days after her death had been reported], at least one caller to talk radio was speculating that the sad event at the zoo must be related to the Whitewater investigation."

The police, on the other hand, suggested on the basis of their own casing that the woman's decision to seek out the lion enclosure was somehow tied to her religious ideas. Christians in ancient Rome, after all, as wages for their belief, had been thrown to the lions, and Daniel, in the Old Testament, had come back triumphant and whole from his test of faith in the lion's den. Based on what later came to be known about the dead woman's history, it was as reasonable a guess as most. Her mind, as further inquiry would show, was not entirely her own. She shared it with voices and visions and other sundry by-products of madness.

Then the king commanded, and they brought Daniel, and cast him into the den of lions. Now the king spake and said unto Daniel, Thy God whom thou servest continually, he will deliver thee.

And a stone was brought, and laid upon the mouth of the den; and the king sealed it with his own signet, and with the signet of his lords.

—DANIEL, 6:16–17

The clues the woman left behind were fragmentary. Near her body, investigators found a Sony Walkman that contained a cassette of Christian singer Amy Grant's "House of Love." A barrette from her hair lay on the ground not far from where the lions had killed her. Tucked into her shoes was a money order, and a business letter was stuffed into a pocket. No suicide note was found and no fingerprints remained.

An Arkansas Transit Authority bus pass identified the dead woman as Margaret Davis King, a transient from Little Rock. Three days before her death she had checked into a cheap hotel room in northwest Washington, where police later discovered a single suitcase and scattered religious writings. Little emerged about the last days of her life other than a quixotic late-afternoon visit she had made to the U.S. District Court the day before she died. There, according to the clerk who assisted her, King said she wanted to file a lawsuit to get her daughter back.

It was soon clear to the clerk that King was mentally disturbed; she claimed to be the sister of Jesus Christ and declared that she and Jesus had grown up together in the same household with President Clinton. It was the president's intervention she now sought in her child custody case. King was, the clerk reported, "clean, attractive, and well-spoken"; and although she seemed upset, she was upset in a "controlled way." In fact, the clerk said, she appeared "very calm." She quoted the Scriptures as she petitioned and clasped a packet of papers to her chest.

She left the District Court building about 5 p.m., and no one knows what she did or where she went until she entered the zoo and made her way to the lion and tiger exhibit. She may have hesitated, but at some point she was certain enough of her decision to climb over a three-and-a-half-foot barrier, walk across a buffer zone of dirt, scramble down a nine-foot wall, and swim the moat to the grassy home grounds of the lions. Who was she? *And why?*

Margaret Davis King, the medical examiner and journalists would discover, was twice married and the mother of three young children. She was also an honorably discharged veteran of the U.S. Navy, homeless, and a paranoid schizophrenic. Over the years she had been confined to psychiatric hospitals in California, Georgia, and Arkansas. She claimed to be not only the sister of Jesus Christ but, on occasion, Jesus himself. As evidence of the latter, she would point out what she thought to be nail holes in her hand from the Crucifixion. She said she received messages directly from God and placed telephone calls to people in cities across the country, commanding them to leave their homes and jobs and follow her. God, she assured them, would provide their transportation.

She had been arrested for making threats and for aggravated assault. At one point, according to the sheriff's office in Arkansas, she swung a broomstick at a deputy and told another officer to shoot her. She was hospitalized, released, rehospitalized, and released yet again. She was prescribed medication that she took for a while and then stopped. She had no governance over her thoughts, there was no tolerable flow to her mood or energy. Gradually, the pattern of her life became indistinguishable from that of tens of thousands of others with schizophrenia; she became part of the urban netherlands, the homeless mentally ill.

The lions had the mastery of them,
And brake all their bones in pieces.

—DANIEL, 6:24

We have filled these netherlands past any pretense of civilization; we have swollen their ranks with the psychotic and the incapacitated, taken the hopeless and made them more so, and then we have disregarded what they need to survive. We have released the severely mentally ill onto our streets, and they have come to make up a third to a half of our country's homeless. They disturb the well who share their streets and perplex city managers. They make us uncomfortable, but not so uncomfortable that we protect or house, insure or tend or heal them.

They die on the streets, in parking lots, in shelters, or in vacant buildings, in the park or on the sidewalks. They die younger than the rest of us, and they die of causes tied to neglect: tuberculosis, HIV/AIDS, hepatitis B, alcoholism and drug abuse, and injuries. Nearly 10 percent kill themselves.

The decision to release psychiatric patients onto the streets was not a malevolent one; it was just thoughtless and ill considered. The 1963 Community Mental Health Centers Act, signed into law by President Kennedy, was meant to counter the warehousing of the severely mentally ill in large institutions. It was hoped that the newly available antipsychotic and antidepressant medications would allow patients to return to their communities, and it was assumed, too optimistically, that those communities would be able to—and want to—take care of these patients. Society sent itself on a fool's errand.

Richard Wyatt, chief of neuropsychiatry at the National Institute of Mental Health, along with other physicians and scientists, has been a vehement critic of the national execution of this consequential social policy, which hadn't the scientific basis to back it up. In a 1986 editorial in the journal *Science*, Wyatt wrote:

America's homeless crisis began in 1963 when deinstitutionalization became law. . . . Hundreds of thousands of disabled patients with schizophrenia, affective [mood] disorders, alcoholism, and severe personality disorders were released from large institutions to the streets. Once deinstitutionalized, those individuals created their own communities of isolation, alienation, hopelessness, and despair. By law, the former residents of structured institutions became the homeless. This situation occurred because a social welfare movement, based on virtually no scientifically gathered data, became public policy. Remarkably, only one controlled pilot study performed in England was available at the time the law was passed. The country undertook a noble, but unfeasible, and ultimately unjustifiable project because the essential research had not been done.

No one who treats schizophrenia or the homeless mentally ill would claim to have the solution to such knotted and bewildering problems. Certainly, no one could say why Margaret Davis King, homeless and schizophrenic, delusional, and unlikely to recover custody of her children, would choose to end her life as or when she did. Public interest in her death soon paled; quips about lions and suicide made their way to Washington dinner parties. The capital city moved on.

King was unknown, little tolled, and less understood. Why did she die? Was she despairing and beyond hope or exultantly psychotic and beyond fear? Why did she choose such an awful way? We do not know these things; we do not know her. She left only the slightest trail of human intimation. But for the public recollection of zoo lions in a national park, there would have been an even slighter trace, a fleeting chalk-out of just one of the million suicides in the world that year.

III

Pangs of Nature,
Taints of Blood

—THE BIOLOGY OF SUICIDE—

O, yet we trust that somehow good
Will be the final goal of ill,
To pangs of nature, sins of will,
Defects of doubt, and taints of blood.

—ALFRED, LORD TENNYSON

Generation after generation of the Tennyson family was afflicted with debilitating melancholia, uncontrollable fits of rage, and manic-depression. Alfred, Lord Tennyson (1809-1892), referred to the "black blood" of the Tennysons, and the themes of suicide, suicidal despair, and inherited madness are at the heart of some of his most powerful poetry.

CHAPTER 6

A Plunge into Deep Waters

— GENETIC AND EVOLUTIONARY PERSPECTIVES —

It was, he said, a constitutional and a family evil, and one for which he despaired to find a remedy.

—EDGAR ALLAN POE

But it is always a question whether I wish to avoid these glooms. . . . These 9 weeks give one a plunge into deep waters. . . . One goes down into the well & nothing protects one from the assault of truth.

—VIRGINIA WOOLF

PRECISELY ONE year before General Robert E. Lee surrendered the Confederate Army of Northern Virginia to General Ulysses S. Grant at Appomattox Court House, Professor John Ordronaux delivered a major lecture to the students of Columbia College in New York. Human conduct, he told them, is not always the reflection of human reason. Original instincts, "however much they may be modified by intellectual culture, or repressed by circumstances forbidding their expression, are rarely, if ever, entirely eradicated." Nature, he said, quoting Francis Bacon, "is often hidden, sometimes overcome, seldom extinguished."

Ordronaux, although deeply affected, as were all his colleagues and fellow citizens, by the Civil War, was not addressing it in his lecture. He was, rather, speaking about the irrational and violent roots of an internal war, forces that seemed to pass from one generation to the next. He was addressing at length and with some vehemence the arguments for the inheritance of suicide. Like many other mid-nineteenth-century doctors who treated mental illness, he was impressed by the predisposing temperaments underlying both insanity and suicide:

> Observations show that the question of temperament enters quite extensively into the problem of suicide. While the sanguine and plethoric are predisposed to diseases of accelerated circulation, like mania, and may, and often do commit acts of sudden frenzy, either against others, or themselves, the nervous, bilious, and lymphatic temperaments are those in whom the predisposition to suicide most usually assumes the chronic and inveterate form. In them the morbid tendency seems easily awakened and of difficult eradication; and when slumbering as a predisposition, hereditarily transmitted, requires but a slight exciting cause to develop itself into the full-blown malady. So potent in fact is the influence of hereditary transmission in the production of suicide, that not less than *one-sixth* of all recorded cases have been directly traced to this source.

It is unclear where the "one-sixth" estimate came from as there were no reliable figures then and only slightly better ones now. But certainly it had long been believed—indeed, for more than two thousand years—that madness and suicide run in families. And twenty-five years earlier, in 1840, British physician Forbes Winslow had stated unequivocally, "With reference to suicide, there is no fact that has been more clearly established than that of its hereditary character. Of all diseases to which the various organs are subject, there is none more generally transmitted from one generation to another than affections of the brain. It is not necessary that the disposition to suicide should manifest itself in every generation; it often passes over one, and appears in the next, like insanity unattended with this propensity."

Benjamin Rush, professor of medicine at the University of Pennsylvania, was likewise impressed with the hereditary aspects of suicide and included in his widely published and influential 1812 textbook, *Medical Inquiries and Observations upon the Diseases of the Mind*, a letter he had received from a colleague recounting a case of suicide in identical twin brothers:

Captains C. L. and J. L. were twin brothers, and so great was the similarity in their countenances and appearance, that it was extremely difficult for strangers to know them apart. Even their friends were often deceived by them. Their habits and manners were likewise similar. Many ludicrous stories are told of people mistaking one for the other.

They both entered the American revolutionary army at the same time. Both held similar commissions, and both served with honour during the war. They were cheerful, sociable, and in every respect gentlemen. They were happy in their families, having amiable wives and children, and they were both independent in their property. Some time after the close of the war, captain J. removed to the state of Vermont, while captain C. remained in Greenfield [Massachusetts], in the vicinity of Deerfield, and 200 miles from his brother. Within the course of three years, they have both been subject to turns of partial derangement, but by no means rising into mania, nor sinking into melancholy. They appeared to be hurried and confused in their manners, but were constantly able to attend to their business. About two years ago, captain J. on his return from the general assembly of Vermont, of which he was a member, was found in his chamber, early in the morning, with his throat cut, by his own hand, from ear to ear, shortly after which he expired. He had been melancholy a few days previous to this fatal catastrophe, and had complained of indisposition the evening previous to the event.

About ten days ago, captain C. of Greenfield, discovered signs of melancholy, and expressed a fear that he should destroy himself. Early in the morning of June fifth he got up, and proposed to his wife to take a ride with him. He shaved himself as usual, wiped his razor, and stepped into an adjoining room, as his wife supposed, to put it up. Shortly after she heard a noise like water or blood running upon the floor. She hurried into the room, but was too late to save him. He had cut his throat with his razor, and soon afterwards expired.

The mother of these two gentlemen, an aged lady, is now in a state of derangement, and their two sisters, the only survivors of their family, have been subject, for several years, to the same complaint.

The assumed familial nature of suicide continued as a thread throughout much of the nineteenth- and twentieth-century suicide literature. In June 1906, Charles Pilgrim, the president of the New York Commission on Lunacy, read a paper to the American Medico-Psychological Association in Boston. In it he declared, "There is nothing more firmly established than the fact of the transmission of the suicidal tendency. This tendency is not only very apt to reappear in the offspring but it is not unusual for it to appear at the same age that it appeared in the parent, and often the same means are sought to accomplish the end." He went another disturbing step: "Therefore, it seems reasonable to expect the accom-

plishment of considerable good by the efforts of our own pro-
fession to prevent marriage where any hereditary taint exists."

Several pedigrees of families with heavy burdens of suicide
appeared in the medical literature at about the same time as
Pilgrim's remarks. Two British physicians published four generations of a pedigree of a seafaring family that was saturated
with suicide and insanity: of sixty-five family members, six
committed suicide, four threatened it, eight were "markedly
peculiar in mental condition," and six were "idiotic or insane."
The language of the doctors leaves no doubt about their views:
"The evil results in the case of Family C² are specially
apparent, a deeply affected father having mated with an habi-
tual drunkard. . . . The rapid method of suicide has accounted
for two of the cousins, the asylum will protect Family C² from
further disasters, the antisocial tendencies of Family C³ will
diminish the chances of procreation, and Family C⁵ has begun
badly, and will no doubt leave its mark in asylum records."

In 1901, the *Medical Record* noted an even more alarming
concentration of suicides in one family:

> A man named Edgar Jay Briggs, who hanged himself on
> his farm, near Danbury, Connecticut, a few days ago,
> was almost the last surviving member of a family which
> has practically been wiped out of existence by suicide.
> The history of self-destruction in this family extends
> over a period of more than fifty years, and in that time,
> so it is stated, at least twenty-one of the descendants and
> collaterals of the original Briggs suicide have taken their
> own lives. Among these were the great-grandfather,
> grandfather, father, brother, and two sisters of the one
> just dead.

More recently, in Iraq, five suicides—four by self-
immolation and one by gunshot—were reported in the two sisters, brother, and two nephews of a woman who had herself

attempted suicide by pouring kerosene over her body and lighting a match.

Many other "suicide families" have been cited in the medical literature, but, while compelling, they by no means establish a genetic basis for suicide. The odd or striking case history is more likely to be noticed and written up for scientific publication, and other factors—such as family exposure to suicide or learning from another family member's behavior that suicide is a tenable, even desirable, way of handling the problems of life or illness—may be important as well. Ferreting out a biological predisposition to suicide from psychological influences is difficult. And even assuming that it can be shown that suicide is hereditable, or partially so, new questions immediately arise: What exactly is being genetically transmitted from one generation to the next? Are there specific genes that make an individual more likely to commit suicide? Or is an increased tendency to commit suicide due only to the passing on of the genetic predispositions to the psychiatric conditions most intimately linked to suicide—depression, manic-depression, schizophrenia, and alcoholism—all of which, especially the mood disorders, we know to have a strong genetic basis? Are there specific genes associated with certain aspects of temperament—impulsivity, aggression, and violence—that we know also to be predictive of suicide? A particularly lethal combination of genetic liabilities may well result from an underlying volatile temperament mixed with, or triggered by, mania, psychosis, or alcoholism.

Medicine and science have evolved several strategies to help unskein the effects of heredity from influences of the environment: family studies, which examine familial patterns of suicide and suicide attempts; twin studies, which look at rates of suicide in identical and nonidentical twins; adoption studies, which are designed to tease apart "nature-nurture" issues by comparing suicide in adopted individuals with suicide in their biological and adopted relatives; and molecular genetic studies, which look at alterations in specific genes in individuals who do and do not commit suicide. Each of these strategies gives us a different kind of information.

There have been more than thirty family studies of suicide, and almost all of the ones completed in recent years find a greatly elevated rate of suicide and suicidal behaviors in the family members of those who commit suicide and those who make a serious attempt. In studies of children and adults, as well as in studies of patients with psychiatric illness, those who commit suicide are at least two or three times as likely to have a family history of suicide as those who do not. Individuals who commit or attempt suicide in a violent manner—by gunshot, hanging, or jumping—are particularly likely to have a strong family history of suicide, often of violent suicide.

One of the most important and interesting of the family studies of suicide was carried out by Janice Egeland and James Sussex in their work with the Old Order Amish, a conservative Protestant religious sect that settled in southeastern Pennsylvania in the early eighteenth century. The community is agrarian, socially cohesive, and protected against many of the risk factors that ordinarily permeate urban culture. Alcohol is prohibited; serious crime is essentially nonexistent; and loneliness and isolation are relatively unusual due to the emphasis on extended families living together in the same homes. Social support is exceptionally strong, and unemployment is not a significant problem. Suicide—known by the Amish as "the abominable sin" or "that awful deed"—is socially unacceptable and strongly censured by the community; until recent times, Amish who killed themselves were buried outside the boundaries of the community cemetery.

The Amish have kept extensive genealogical and medical records of their ancestors that extend back through thirty generations; because of this, Egeland and Sussex were able to identify all of the suicides that occurred during the hundred-year period between 1880 and 1980. Twenty-five of the twenty-six confirmed suicides (92 percent) were diagnosed with depression or manic-depression (of necessity, some of the symptoms of mania were culturally bound and included, in addition to the more traditional diagnostic criteria, "racing one's horse and carriage too hard . . . buying or using machinery or other worldly items . . . excessive use of the public telephone"), and most were situated in families that had, for many generations, been suffused with mood disorders. Twenty of the twenty-six suicides were by hanging, four by gunshot, and two by drowning. Most of those who killed themselves were married with children, and most were in the prime years of their life.

The most dramatic and scientifically interesting finding in the Amish study of suicide was the extent to which the suicides clustered in only a few families. Just four families accounted for 73 percent of all suicides; these, in turn, made up only 16 percent of the total Amish population. The suicides clustered in families with mood disorders, but most families with heavy loadings for mood disorders did not show a heavy concentration of suicides. This tendency for suicides to cluster in some families heavily loaded with depression and manic-depression but for there to be many with mood disorders and no suicides was later replicated in an Austrian study.

The evidence from family studies is suggestive of a genetic influence on suicide but it is not conclusive. A clustering of suicides in a family may be due to other, nongenetic factors as well: a child whose parent kills himself may suffer extremely from the loss and, if inclined to depression, respond in a desperate and similar way; exposure to violence or suicide may have a particularly deadly impact upon some family members; or suicide may be imitated or learned as the seemingly best solution to severe pain, privation, or stress. One way to tease out environmental and psychological effects from genetic ones is to look at the rates of suicide in identical and nonidentical twins.

Identical twins come from the same egg and therefore share the same genetic material. Nonidentical twins, on the other hand, come from two eggs and share only half their genes (in this sense, they are no different from their other siblings). If genetic influences are present, one would expect a far higher concordance rate for suicide—that is, if one twin commits suicide, the other does as well—in identical twins than in nonidentical ones. This turns out to be true.

Alec Roy, a psychiatrist at the Veterans Administration Hospital in New Jersey, has written more about the genetics of suicide than anyone else. He recently reviewed all of the twin studies published in the psychiatric literature and found nearly four hundred pairs in which at least one twin had completed suicide. Of the 129 identical twin pairs, 17 committed suicide, and of the 270 nonidentical pairs, only 2 did. This, from a statistical point of view, was a highly significant difference. In a different study, of attempted suicide, Roy found that nearly 40 percent of identical twins whose co-twin had committed suicide themselves attempted suicide; no surviving nonidentical twin did so. Recent research from Australia found likewise: if one identical twin made a serious suicide attempt, nearly 25 percent of the co-twins did as well; none of the nonidentical twins did. The authors noted that although it could be argued that identical twins share a closer psychological and social world than nonidentical ones—they are, for example, more likely to dress alike and be treated in a similar manner—the social and psychological closeness between nonidentical twins was also very strong.

The concordance rate for suicide in identical twins, approximately 15 percent, suggests several things. First, although the rate is much higher than it is for nonidentical twins, it is not formidably high. Even in individuals who are genetically most similar, the odds are overwhelming that if one identical twin kills himself the other will not. Second, the concordance rate for suicide in identical twins is far less than the concordance rate observed for manic-depression (70 to 100 percent, depending on whether suicide and recurrent depression are included as concordant diagnoses), or schizophrenia (40 to 50 percent). The genetic influence may simply be stronger in the severe mental illnesses than it is in suicide. It is also possible that the devastating impact of suicide on the surviving twin actually *lessens* the chances that he or she will commit suicide, either because of a heightened awareness of the psychological pain caused to others or because the twin is now more apt to seek out and receive medical care.

The findings from the twin studies provide strong evidence for a genetic effect, but family dynamics and other psychological issues inevitably confound their interpretation. One way of further isolating environmental from genetic influences is by conducting an adoption study. Individuals who are adopted share their genes, but not their environment, with their biological parents; conversely, they share their environment, but no genes, with their adoptive parents. Adoption therefore creates a unique natural experiment. If there is a significant genetic influence on suicide, one would expect a much higher rate of suicide in the biological parents of adoptees who commit suicide than in the adoptive parents. This is exactly what was found in two studies done in Denmark, a country that for years has maintained excellent and comprehensive medical records.

The first study, based on all Copenhagen adoptions between 1924 and 1947, revealed that fifty-seven of the adoptees eventually committed suicide. These fifty-seven adoptees were matched with a control group of other adoptees for such factors as age, sex, social class, and the amount of time spent in institutions or with their biological parents. An extensive examination of the causes of death in biological relatives established that twelve of the biological relatives of the adoptees who committed suicide had also committed suicide; only two of the biological relatives of the adoptees who had not committed suicide had killed themselves (this was a highly significant statistical difference). None of the adopting relatives of either the suicide or control group committed suicide. Although the authors of the study found that only six of the twelve biological relatives who committed suicide had had any contact with psychiatric services and therefore concluded that the genetic predisposition for suicide may, at least to some extent, be independent of major psychiatric disorders, this may or may not be true. In the United States, for example, more than half of those who meet the diagnostic criteria for mood disorders never seek or receive psychiatric treatment.

In a second study of Danish adoptees, seventy-one adoptees were identified as having suffered from a mood disorder. They were then matched with seventy-one adoptees who had no history of psychiatric illness. Fifteen of the nineteen suicides that occurred in the relatives of the two groups of adoptees occurred in the biological relatives of the adoptees suffering from depression or manic-depression. The rate of suicide in biological relatives was especially high in adoptees who had a strongly impulsive quality to their depressive episodes.

Together, the family, twin, and adoption studies make a strong case for a strong genetic influence on suicide and suicidal behaviors. Genes are, of course, only a part of the tangle of suicide, but their collision with psychological and environmental elements can prove, as we shall see later, to be the difference between life and death.

If suicide has a genetic underpinning and the illnesses most associated with it—depression, manic-depression, schizophrenia, and alcoholism—have even stronger ones, it is natural to ask why—with all their pain, maladaptiveness, and early death—they should survive in the gene pool at such high rates. Is there any evolutionary reason for suicide, or is it simply random splicings of and realignments in DNA? Is it the result of a deadly interaction between a stressful world and vulnerable wiring, or is there some common element that drives both life and death? Is suicide always conscious and therefore a uniquely human behavior, or do we share with other animals the capacity for self-destructiveness and the deliberate ending of life? How, in short, does suicide fit into and serve the rest of the natural world?

The construing of suicidal acts as consciously determined and therefore uniquely human is both obvious and problematic, as psychiatrists Ivor Jones and Brian Barraclough point out:

> Suicide poses a special problem in relating animal studies to man: man can visualize his death and arrange it, no animal has ever been shown to do that. In this sense suicide is uniquely human. However, this formulation implies that the processes leading to suicide are rational, which may be untrue: depression in most suicides probably impairs the capacity for rational thought while at the same time inducing suicide impulses. We suggest that suicide may be a uniquely human attribute only because our definition of it makes it so; in other words, if suicide were to be defined as a destructive act inflicted on the self leading to death, then animal analogies do exist. However, even by this changed definition, man's suicide and animal self-destruction are different in the following ways: Man may defer the event, the animal does not. Man may use an instrument, the animal does not. Man may manipulate his environment to do the act for him, the animal does not. It seems, therefore, that if animal behaviour is relevant to suicide it provides only one component—a disposition to self-injury—which becomes incorporated into a syndrome with other uniquely human components.

No one disputes that some animals under conditions of acute stress—isolation, overcrowding, confinement, alterations in habitat—inflict great damage, even death, upon themselves. They may gnaw through their limbs or tails, gouge out their eyes, otherwise mutilate their bodies, or ceaselessly bang their heads against the walls of their enclosure. Severe self-inflicted injuries and death from stress have been reported in many zoo animals, including deer, lions, hyenas, and jackals; in a variety of captive primate species; in mice, rats, octopi, opossums, platypuses, and numerous other animals; and in domestic pets when separated from their owners. Macaque monkeys will slap and bang their heads and use their teeth and claws to gash their limbs and body. On occasion, domestic pigs and some wild animals, when captured or transferred to new environments, make violent attempts to escape; if unable to get away, a few fall into a stupor. Many ranch mink chew through their tails when kept in captivity.

The most severe forms of self-injury in animals seem to occur when a confined animal or an animal reared in isolation encounters acute stress; this in turn typically precipitates an agitated, aggressive, or frustrated state. "In all known instances," Ivor Jones says, "the severe class of self-injury and some headbanging is associated with acute agitation." The agitation and frustration appear to arise from limitations in the type and extent of physical activity, alterations in or elimination of usual feeding and grooming behaviors, or a lack of social or sexual contact with other animals. Acute agitated states can also be induced surgically or pharmacologically by creating lesions in the brain or by administering drugs and alcohol.

To some extent, self-injurious behavior in animals substitutes for the aggression normally directed at other animals or energy that would otherwise be expended in coping with the natural world. Self-injuries also seem reduce the level of acute agitation experienced by the animal, in a way not dissimilar to the defusing of tension that allows self-mutilative or cutting behavior in humans who suffer from particular forms of psychopathology (such as borderline personality disorder). Severe social isolation and confinement in humans, such as that experienced by prisoners, can lead to analogous destructive behavior. Prisoners, for example, have amputated their toes, fingers, and genitals; occasional disembowelings have also been reported.

Overcrowding in the wild also often results in behaviors that end in injury or death for an individual animal. Rats, when too populous for the environment in which they find themselves, exhibit grossly abnormal behavior: aggression increases precipitously, as do premature deaths; fertility declines in adaptation to dwindling resources; and maternal behavior, including nest building, suffers. Cannibalism occasionally erupts, as it does in frogs and alligators and other species when they become too densely populated. Snowshoe hares, even when removed from overcrowded spaces and placed in safe environments with plenty of food and water, often die from stress and refusing to eat. Prolonged psychopathology is rarely observed among animals other than humans, because, as primatologist Henry Harlow and his colleagues point out, such animals do not survive very long in the natural world.

Lemmings, the poster animals for suicide, do not in fact commit suicide. They do, however, abandon highly populated areas, and in the course of their migrations to new, less densely populated sites, many die. Their deaths are an inevitable price of their travels to new lands. This dispersal of animals, which both extends their territorial range and ultimately increases their genetic diversity, is advantageous to the species but not necessarily to the individual: the lemmings' "suicidal march to the sea" is in no meaningful sense suicidal.

Animals engage in risky behaviors other than emigration to new territories. Years ago, Harvard biologist E. O. Wilson set out the case for "altruistic" behaviors, demonstrating that some animals sacrifice their own shelter or food to close kin. The enhanced survival of kin in turn makes more likely the survival of the family genes. In social insects, for example, protection of the group by soldier wasps or ants may bring death to the individual but, through that death and others, allow the group to survive. Animals that travel in herds, such as bison or elk, often protect their young by surrounding them with older and stronger members of the group. The mountain gorilla, which travels in a small social group, uses subordinate males to protect the infants and females. These animals, which stand guard at the edges or position themselves between predators and the group's most vulnerable, are necessarily at risk of injury or death.

Within most species, including humans, there is a range in the ability and willingness to take such risks. Temperaments and capacities vary. Some animals move faster and are more curious, more impulsive, more restless. Highly energetic, grasping, and aggressive, they are drawn to new regions, different foods, and disparate mates. Others wait, stand back, move collectively, and act less impetuously. The diversity of styles and temperaments serves the needs of the group, allowing it, as necessary, to push forward, or pull back, or to expand or conserve its collective energies.

Like other animals, human beings are diverse in their capacities and temperaments. Adaptive behaviors lurch with dispatch into maladaptive ones, a perhaps inevitable price that must be paid for a biological system that maintains the capacity to ratchet its responses—flight, aggression, cooperation—rapidly to survive in a changing or dangerous environment. The balance between adaptive and pathological is often a tottery one, and it makes evolutionary sense that it should be so. George Schaller observed in his studies of the Serengeti lion and its prey that "a galloping animal is precariously balanced": speed is necessary to save life but carries with it the risk of losing it.

Aggression, likewise, is subject to jeopardous overshoot. "We are strongly predisposed to slide into deep, irrational hostility under certain definable conditions," writes E. O. Wilson in *On Human Nature*. "With dangerous ease hostility feeds on itself and ignites runaway reactions that can swiftly progress to alienation and violence. Aggression does not resemble a fluid that continuously builds pressure against the walls of its containers, nor is it like a set of active ingredients poured into an empty vessel. It is more accurately compared to a pre-existing mix of chemicals ready to be transformed by specific catalysts that are added, heated, and stirred at some later time." Human beings, he continues, "are strongly predisposed to respond with unreasoning hatred to external threats and to escalate their hostility sufficiently to overwhelm the source of the threat by a respectably wide margin of safety."

We have, then, within ourselves the capacity for extremes that will serve us well on occasion and badly on others. These extremes encompass not only rage and aggression but sadness and ecstasy, inertia and frenzied energy states, dullness and exploration. But why should the proclivity for suicide survive? Why do the genes and the volatile brain chemistry that underlie the suicidal potential remain in our genetic makeup? Is suicide a part of the price we pay for diversity? Are the reckless and impulsive behaviors associated with many acts of suicide also associated with capacities integral to the survival of the species? Or do these pathologies exist independent of any adaptive value? The fact that a condition is widespread does not necessarily mean that it is adaptive.

The recently emerging field of evolutionary psychiatry has been looking at an important and closely related question: Why do the severe psychiatric illnesses—schizophrenia, manic-depression, and depression—persist in humans? The persistence of the genes for schizophrenia—a terrible, debilitating, and painful disease—is perplexing. It would seem that over tens of thousands of years, protection against or elimination of such a maladaptive genetic mutation should have occurred. Yet schizophrenia not only survives, it survives at a relatively high rate, in 1 percent of the population. Why? Some have argued that perhaps the same cognitive and social behaviors that, in their extreme forms, mark or destroy the lives of those with schizophrenia—bizarre and unpredictable thinking, strange or altered patterns of attention, paranoia, resistance to physical pain, acute sensory awareness, intense apprehension, isolation from others, resistance to certain inflammatory disorders or the infectious agents that precede them—may in their milder forms (watchfulness, novel thought, a heightened attentiveness to possible danger) have benefits not only to individuals but, if in an attenuated form, to their kin. Timothy Crow, a psychiatrist at the University of Oxford, creatively and controversially argues that language and psychosis have a common evolutionary origin and that schizophrenia may be the price that *Homo sapiens* pays for having language.

It is easier to understand, and more vigorously argued by many, that mood disorders may give an advantage to both individuals and their societies. Depression, characterized as it is by a conservation of energy during times of scant resources, a reduction of activity at times of nonnegotiable threat, or a slowing or cessation of sexual behavior when environmental conditions are poor, is a not surprising biological reaction during times of change or stress. Its existence in mild forms may act as an alerting mechanism to other animals to act similarly and may, as some have argued, help to maintain a stable social hierarchy as well. (Less dominant animals, for example, may submit to more dominant ones in order to increase their own chances for survival and reproduction.) The discontents and darkness of the depressive mind may also create—through the arts and philosophy—a useful perspective in the collective social awareness.

It is the temperamental, cognitive, and behavioral elements of manic-depressive illness that provide the strongest evidence for a possible link between the infrequent adaptive advantages of a severe illness, on the one hand, and suicide, on the other. American poet Anne Sexton, who committed suicide after a long struggle with manic-depression and alcoholism, wrote in one of her poems that high-flying Icarus

> *. . . glances up and is caught, wondrously tunneling*
> *into that hot eye. Who cares that he fell back to the sea?*

The "wondrous tunneling" into the sun and subsequent falling back into the sea conjure an image of the dangerous relationship between exploration and recklessness. Mania, we know, is an aggressive and volatile state, but it is generative as well, an influential condition of contagious enthusiasms and energies. The elements that in part define mania—fearlessness, a fast and broad scattering of thoughts, an expansiveness of moods and ideas, utter certainty, the taking of inadvisable risks—often carry with them the power both to destroy and to create. When the high-voltage manic brain slows, as it must, and its mood seeps down into depression, the crackling together of manic impetuousness with a black mood can be lethal. Suicide is the not-uncommon end point of a short-lived, violent, and yet, on occasion, fertile time.

The boldness and violence of the manic temperament may come at a cost, but there is strong evidence that manic-depression and its milder forms can provide advantages to the individual, his or her kin, and society at large. (An interviewer once asked me if a manic was not perhaps the first to throw a spear into the heart of a mastodon. The mastodon may have been brought down, but so too may have been the manic.) Several studies have shown that both manic-depressive patients and their relatives are uncommonly creative and academically successful. At least twenty studies have found that highly creative individuals are much more likely than the general population to suffer from depression and manic-depressive illness. Clearly, mood disorders are not required for great accomplishment, and most people who suffer from mood disorders are not particularly accomplished. But the evidence is compelling that the creative are *disproportionately* affected by these conditions.

Suicide is also more common in highly creative or successful writers, artists, scientists, and businessmen than it is in the general population. Most are related to underlying depression, manic-depression, or alcoholism in combination with these mood disorders. Percy Bysshe Shelley, who attempted suicide when young, said, "But mark how beautiful an order has sprung from the dust and blood of this fierce chaos," and this perhaps is true. Extremes in emotions and thinking, when tightly yoked with a disciplined mind and high imagination, certainly can advance the arts, sciences, and commerce. Suffering that may benefit a work of art or move the direction of a spiritual life— "Is the shipwrack then a harvest," asked Gerard Manley Hopkins, "does tempest / carry the grain for thee?"—may not be of such benefit to the life of the artist. Immoderate thought, and behavior on the remotest ridges of experience, may end in death, yet some artists and explorers feel no choice but to go there. The pull between a life at the extremes and one in more moderate zones is fierce for many. "It isn't possible to get values and color," wrote Vincent van Gogh. "You can't be at the pole and the equator at the same time. You must choose your own line, as I hope to do, and it will probably be color."

The toll of suicide on artists, writers, scientists, mathematicians, and others strongly influential on their societies is powerful. The rates of suicide in these groups have been examined in a series of studies conducted by researchers in the United States, Britain, Europe, and Asia. Eminent scientists, composers, and top businessmen were, in these investigations, five times more likely to kill themselves than the general population; writers, especially poets, showed considerably higher rates. Many of the artists, writers, and scientists who committed suicide are listed in the endnotes; the list is a long and disturbing one and gives credence to these lines from Dylan Thomas:

> *The hand that whirls the water in the pool*
> *Stirs the quicksand; that ropes the blowing wind*
> *Hauls my shroud sail.*

CHAPTER 7

Death-Blood

—NEUROBIOLOGY AND NEUROPATHOLOGY—

I have a violence in me that is hot as death-blood. I can kill myself or—I know it now—even kill another. I could kill a woman, or wound a man. I think I could. I gritted to control my hands, but had a flash of bloody stars in my head as I stared that sassy girl down, and a blood-longing to [rush] at her and tear her to bloody beating bits.

— SYLVIA PLATH

EVERYWHERE IN the snarl of tissue that is the brain, chemicals whip down fibers, tear across cell divides, and continue pell-mell on their Gordian rounds. One hundred billion individual nerve cells—each reaching out in turn to as many as 200,000 others—diverge, reverberate and converge into a webwork of staggering complexity. This three-pound thicket of gray, with its thousands of distinct cell types and estimated one hundred trillion synapses, somehow pulls out order from chaos, lays down the shivery tracks of memory, gives rise to desire or terror, arranges for sleep, propels movement, imagines a symphony, or shapes a plan to annihilate itself.

From its beginning in the DNA architecture twisted within a single cell, the brain owes its development not only to the tens of thousands of genes it inherits, but also to the constantly shifting environment within which it finds itself. While still in the womb, the brain's evolution is beholden to a mother's actions and experiences: if she drinks too much or smokes, eats poorly, or uses drugs, if she is infected by a damaging virus or bacterium, or if she is greatly stressed, the fetal brain registers the effects.

If susceptible genes are exposed to one of these additional stresses, or "second hits," from the prenatal environment, a lasting cost—certain forms of mental retardation or epilepsy, perhaps even autism or schizophrenia—may arise. Once a child is born, its exposure or lack of exposure to stimulation from its environment—through sounds, light, shapes, move-ment, nutrition, touch, and smell—determines which brain cells are pruned and which networks of nerve cells are put into place. The molding of the circuitry of the brain, the formation of its pathways and connections, will remain throughout an individual's life a product of both inheritance and experiences derived from interactions with the world.

The essence of the brain, its nerve cells (or neurons), communicate with one another electrochemically by sending information out across fibers called axons. These axons branch off into a number of small fibers that end in terminals; between terminals are the slight gaps known as synapses, across which messages are sent. Electrical stimulation of a nerve cell causes the release of neurotransmitters—such as norepinephrine, glu-tamate, acetylcholine, dopamine, and serotonin—from storage areas in vesicles located at the end of the neuron. The release of these neurotransmitters into the space between the nerve cells allows the transfer of information from cell to cell.

Neurotransmitters are the lifeblood of the brain, governing the interactions from cell to cell, brain region to brain region, and brain to body. No one knows how many transmitters there are, nor does anyone fully understand the actions of the more than one hundred identified to date. We are only just learning about the profusion of transmitters that exist, and we have only the merest notion of their tangled relationships with one another. For scientists to focus on one or two substances at the expense of the others known or yet to be discovered, or to minimize the complexity of the chemical interactions within the brain or at the synapses, would be a damning mistake, a late-twentieth-century equivalent of earlier, primitive views that deranged minds were caused by satanic spells or an excess of phosphorous and vapors.

Many neurotransmitters and hormones are critical to the regulation of mood and to the activation of the many behaviors involved in suicide. It is impossible to discuss or even mention all of them here. The primary focus here is on only one of the dozens of transmitters known to be involved in the complex activities of the brain, serotonin, but it is a central one and illustrative of the role of the brain's chemistry in suicide and suicidal behaviors.

Serotonin, a chemical found in plants as well as in ancient invertebrate nervous systems, is widespread in the bodies and brains of mammals, including humans. It acts in diverse ways: it controls the diameter of blood vessels, affects pain perception, influences the gut, plays a role in the body's inflammatory responses, and causes platelets to clump. More significant from a psychiatric and psychological perspective, however, serotonin is deeply implicated in the roots of depression, sleep regulation, aggression, and suicide.

Several lines of evidence link abnormalities in serotonin functioning to suicidal behavior. First, we have known for a long time that the neurotransmitters serotonin, norepinephrine, and dopamine are intricately involved with the origins of mood disorders, and we have also known that drugs that have an impact on these transmitters can precipitate or ameliorate depression or mania. Reserpine, a drug derived from the plant *Rauwolfia serpentina*, furnished an early illustration of this phenomenon. Used centuries ago in India as a remedy for insomnia and insanity and more recently in this century as a treatment for psychosis and high blood pressure, the drug had a disturbing effect on some patients who took it. A significant number became profoundly depressed; as it was subsequently shown, the depression was due to a dramatic depletion in the brain of serotonin, dopamine, and norepinephrine.

In the mid-1950s a quite opposite clinical observation was made. Some patients who were being treated for tuberculosis with a drug called iproniazid became strangely cheerful and animated; despite their grim circumstances and prognoses, they were almost defiantly optimistic. A few were strikingly euphoric. It was not long before iproniazid, pinpointed by the clinicians and scientists who were studying it as the cause of the mood elevation, was in widespread use as an antidepressant. In short order the mechanism of its action was discovered: it worked because it inhibited the action of monoamine oxidase, an enzyme that inactivates norepinephrine, serotonin, and dopamine after they have been released at nerve synapses. This inhibition of monoamine oxidase in effect increased the availability of the neurotransmitter substances. It was becoming clear to researchers that the availability and distribution of neurotransmitters were critical to the expression and regulation of mood. This was underscored by Nobel laureate Julius Axelrod's discovery that another antidepressant, imipramine (a tricyclic antidepressant, also known as Tofranil), worked by inhibiting the reuptake of neurotransmitters from the synaptic cleft back into the synapse that had first released them, thus increasing their availability.

More recently, the "third-generation antidepressants," drugs that act much more specifically on individual neurotransmitters, have not only radically altered clinical practice by their widespread popularity and use but have also provided further evidence for the role of neurotransmitters in the origins or perpetuation of depression. Classified as selective serotonin reuptake inhibitors, they act primarily by blocking the removal of the serotonin at the synapses. This in turn increases the availability of serotonin in the brain.

In addition to the link between neurotransmitters and

depression, there is another line of evidence implicating serotonin in suicidal behavior; this is its entanglement with impulsive behavior, aggression, and violence. We know from studies
of rodents and nonhuman primates that if the availability of
serotonin is curtailed or its transmission impeded, animals
become more aggressive and impulsive. Rats with low serotonin levels attack and kill other rodents, and "knockout"
mice—mice that are lacking a gene necessary for normal serotonin functioning—attack faster, acquire addictions more
quickly, and press levers more rapidly and erratically. Rats and
other animals selectively bred for docility, on the other hand,
have higher levels of serotonin.

Monkeys with low levels of serotonin's breakdown product,
5-hydroxyindoleacetic acid (5-HIAA)—a metabolite that is
presumed to reflect serotonin functioning in the central nervous system—are far more likely than those with higher levels
to assault other monkeys, increase their alcohol intake, and
engage in highly risky behaviors such as leaping long distances
at perilous heights. If serotonin levels in monkeys or other animals are artificially elevated by drugs or by adding tryptophan
(a precursor of serotonin) to their diets, their aggressive and
impulsive behaviors sharply decrease.

Psychologist J. Dee Higley and his colleagues at the
National Institute on Alcohol Abuse and Alcoholism followed
the lives of forty-nine free-ranging rhesus monkeys on a South
Carolina sea island. When the monkeys were two years old,
the scientists measured their 5-HIAA levels by drawing sam-
ples of cerebrospinal fluid (CSF). The animals were ranked
from lowest to highest in their levels of aggression, and a
record was made of all existing scars and wounds. Four years
later, the scientists recaptured and reassessed the animals.
Eleven of the monkeys were dead or presumed missing; the
correlation between the primates' survival and their 5-HIAA
levels was stunning. Nearly half of the monkeys with low CSF
5-HIAA concentrations, as determined at the initial assess-

ment when the monkeys were two years old, had died as a result of violence. None of the monkeys with high concentrations had died or was missing. Low levels of serotonin were predictive not only of premature death but of excessive aggression and risk taking as well.

Studies of serotonin levels and violence are of direct relevance to humans, who share with other group-living primates most of the genes that are involved in violent, aggressive, and impulsive behavior. And as Higley and other primatologists point out, nonhuman primates and humans share many critical infant-rearing patterns, relatively stable personality traits, and similar serotonin pathways and chemistries. Serotonin functioning in the central nervous system, as measured by CSF 5-HIAA, appears to be an enduring trait in individual animals and humans, and it correlates well with impulsive and aggressive behavior. Interestingly, however, Higley and his collaborators conclude from their primate studies that low CSF 5-HIAA concentrations are not correlated with rates of aggression in a simple way. They are correlated only with aggression that is impulsive and unrestrained. High rates of impulsive behavior, the scientists believed, were associated with "severe, unrestrained aggression, but not with competitive, restrained aggression used to maintain social status or aggression that seldom escalated out of control."

Primates with low CSF 5-HIAA levels are not only more likely to be inappropriately aggressive, they are not well accepted by their peers and they are less likely to breed. Often forced to live apart from their natural social groups, many end up living in isolation. The impact of serotonin functioning on aggression and social behavior is powerful and potentially life-threatening. An animal's biology, behavior, and physical and social environments link together and influence one another in complex and subtle ways we are just beginning to understand.

There are many lines of evidence to suggest that serotonin functioning in the brain is determined by both genetic and environmental factors. Genes certainly are important. Rhesus monkeys separated from their biological parents and raised by an unrelated "wet nurse" monkey have CSF 5-HIAA levels similar to those of their biological parents. Impulsivity and aggressiveness are strongly heritable in both humans and other animals. And specific genes (such as the tryptophan hydroxylase, or TPH, gene) have been isolated that appear to be involved in CSF 5-HIAA concentrations, as well as being associated with impulsivity and suicide attempts.

But rearing patterns and the social environment exert a strong influence as well. Adult male vervet monkeys, for example, appear to show a day-to-day consistency in their blood serotonin concentrations as long as they are living in stable group environments. When there is a shift in a group's dominance pattern, however, the transition from a lower to a higher position is accompanied by an increase in serotonin. When dominant male vervet monkeys are isolated in cages and have no visual or tactile contact with other members of their group, their serotonin concentrations drop by 50 percent. If they are returned to their original social group, their serotonin concentrations rise to their original levels.

Studies of rhesus monkeys have shown the importance of maternal influences on serotonergic functioning and social behavior. If infant monkeys are separated at birth from their mothers and reared with other infants of their own age—thus allowed to grow up without any adult influence on their behavior—several things happen. First, they are unable to control their impulses as well as monkeys that are raised by their mothers: their aggression escalates out of control much more quickly; they are more likely to consume alcohol in excess; and they are more likely to be aggressive toward infant monkeys. They also have more difficult relationships with their peers and are more likely to be wounded and to have to be removed from their social group.

The mother clearly plays an important modulating role

in the infant's developing serotonergic system. Critically, when the CSF 5-HIAA levels of peer-raised monkeys are examined, they are significantly lower than in monkeys raised by their mothers. If the peer-raised monkeys are given serotonin reuptake inhibitors (antidepressant drugs that increase the availability of serotonin in the brain), their levels of aggressiveness and alcohol intake are reduced. While it is unlikely that any single explanation, such as elevated or decreased serotonergic functioning, can begin to explain the highly complex chemical events and interacting neurotransmitter systems in the brain, primate experiments provide an exceptionally interesting and valuable way of looking at aggressive and self-destructive behaviors.

The evidence is strong that serotonin inhibits violent, aggressive, and impulsive behavior, but what do we know about the connection between these behaviors and suicide? Several lines of observation converge to support a compelling association. First, we know that suicidal acts are often impulsive; that is, they are undertaken without much forethought or regard for consequence. More than half of suicide attempts occur within the context of a premeditation period of less than five minutes, and many researchers and clinicians, as well as patients who survive medically serious suicide attempts, lay stress on the role of impulse in the decision to commit suicide. (Although many suicidal patients have well-formulated plans for suicide, the ultimate timing and final decision to act are often determined by impulse.) Professional handwriting analysts, when asked to distinguish between suicide notes written by those who have actually committed suicide and notes using the same wording but written by nonsuicidal individuals, are easily and consistently able to differentiate the two groups; the writing of those who kill themselves is judged by the graphologists to be highly "impulsive," "aggressive," and "agitated."

Suicidal patients, in addition to being more impulsive, are also more likely to commit violent or aggressive acts than nonsuicidal patients. In one English study, those who actually killed themselves were three times more likely to have had a history of violent behavior than individuals matched with them for age, gender, and social class. The argument for a relationship between violence and suicide is further bolstered by many international investigations that demonstrate that homicide is frequently followed by suicide. In England and Wales, for example, murder is followed by suicide 33 percent of the time. Most other countries show high murder-suicide rates as well: Denmark (42 percent), Australia (22 percent), and Iceland (9 percent). (However, in countries with very high homicide rates and easy access to firearms, such as the United States, the murder-suicide rate is much lower—for example, 1 to 2 percent in North Carolina and Los Angeles and 4 percent in Philadelphia.)

In addition to the evidence for a relationship between violence and suicide, there is evidence of heightened irritability and violence in several of the major psychiatric conditions most associated with suicide. Although the majority of people who suffer from depression, manic-depressive illness, schizophrenia, or personality disorders are not more violent than the rest of the population, there are some phases of illness that are not infrequently accompanied by physical violence. This is particularly true for the acutely paranoid and agitated phase of schizophrenia and for the mixed states associated with manic-depressive illness and for mania itself. Nearly 50 percent of all manic episodes are characterized by at least one act of physical violence; this proclivity to violence is further compounded by the drinking that frequently accompanies mania. Extreme irritability is also a hallmark of mood disorders, present in 80 percent of episodes of mania and depression and virtually always during mixed states.

Given the connection between neurotransmitter functioning and depression and the impressive series of studies demonstrating a link between serotonin functioning and impulsive, aggressive behaviors, it is not surprising that clinical researchers next turned to comparing serotonin functioning in suicidal and nonsuicidal psychiatric patients. The result of their studies were unexpectedly consistent. In fact, one of the most replicated findings in psychiatric research is the association between suicide risk and low levels of CSF 5-HIAA, the serotonin metabolite. Although some scientists have questioned the methods and findings, more than twenty studies document that across diagnostic groups (mood disorders, alcoholism, personality disorders, and schizophrenia), low concentrations of CSF 5-HIAA are associated with a significant increase in suicide risk. The lifetime severity of aggressive behaviors and the severity of suicide attempts both are correlated with CSF 5-HIAA levels.

Marie Åsberg and her colleagues at the Karolinska Institute in Sweden, as well as scientists from other countries, have shown, for instance, that if CSF 5-HIAA is measured in patients with mood disorders after they have attempted suicide, those with very low concentrations of the serotonin metabolite are far more likely to be dead from suicide within a year than are those with higher levels. It is possible that a low CSF 5-HIAA level is correlated with a tendency to act impulsively and violently while in acute emotional turmoil or during a severe episode of psychiatric illness.

Low CSF 5-HIAA levels are found in many psychiatric and behavioral syndromes other than heightened suicidality, but most of them, like suicide, are associated with problems of impulse control: for example, children who are impetuously aggressive or who are cruel to animals; alcoholics who are particularly aggressive, even when sober; depressed patients with histories of marked argumentativeness, frequent clashes with colleagues or employers, or sporadic contacts with the police; individuals with bulimia or Gilles de la Tourette's disease; and impulsive arsonists or others who engage in a pattern of impulsive criminal behaviors. People who are highly obsessive and inhibited, on the other hand, such as those suffering from anorexia nervosa or obsessive-compulsive disorder, tend to have relatively elevated levels of CSF 5-HIAA. (Interestingly, obsessive-compulsive disorder, unless it is accompanied by severe depression, is one of the few major psychiatric illnesses that do not seem to place their sufferers at an increased risk for suicide.) Smoking cigarettes, which is far more common in those who commit suicide than those who do not—and also more common in patients with schizophrenia, alcoholism, depression, and antisocial personality disorder—appears to be associated with low CSF 5-HIAA levels. It is unclear whether smoking causes the reduction or a low level of serotonin functioning increases the likelihood that an individual will take up or persist in smoking.

The association between serotonin and suicide is further supported by postmortem studies of the brains of individuals who have killed themselves. The evidence is strong that there are serotonin abnormalities in the prefrontal cortex of the brain, an area strongly implicated in the inhibition of behavior. Reduced serotonergic functioning in this part of the brain may cause disinhibition, which may in turn result in acting precipitously on suicidal thoughts and feelings.

The number of noradenergic neurons in the brains of completed suicides also appears to be markedly depleted, suggesting a pathology in the circuitry of norepinephrine, a transmitter implicated in sleep regulation, depression, attention, and the sleep-wake cycle. These changes in the noradenergic system may be due to abnormalities in the development of the brain or to the effects of acute or chronic stress. An acute or chronic stress, such as depression, alcoholism, or a shattering emotional setback, may trigger the serotonergic vulnerability, precipitating a lethal cascading of biological events within the brain.

The hypothalamus, pituitary, and adrenal glands are primary actors in generating the chemicals regulating the body's response to stress. Under normal circumstances, the release of stress hormones such as cortisol and adrenaline (epinephrine) will increase heart rate, suppress hunger, and pulse more blood to the muscles; in short, it will mobilize an animal's adaptive response to stress. But if for some reason—early trauma, genetic factors, mental illness—this stress response cannot be shut off, the result may be prolonged and dangerous. Rats, if subjected to stressful experiences at the time of birth or prematurely separated from their mothers, may show irreversible social and cognitive damage. If, on the other hand, rat pups are exposed to more intensive grooming and licking from their mothers, their later ability to learn, explore, and interact with other rats is enhanced.

In humans, a hyperactive stress response, which is set into play by both biological factors and experience, may adversely affect mood, immune activity, and serotonin functioning. Pathological levels of anxiety and agitation, both implicated in suicide, are not uncommon. Autopsy studies of suicide victims reveal evidence of hyperactivity in the hypothalamo-pituitary-adrenocortical axis, lending further support to the role of stress in suicide.

Scientists have repeatedly found significant brain pathology when conducting imaging studies (pictures taken of the brain, such as positron-emission tomography, or PET, scans) of the anatomy and functioning of the brains of patients with depression, schizophrenia, or manic-depression—showing, for example, in bipolar patients that there is an enlargement of the amygdala, which is involved in generating emotions and regulating mood; an increase in white-matter lesions, known as hyperintensities, which are associated with the water content of brain tissue; and severe depletions in the number of glial cells, which are involved in the development of the brain and also provide growth factors and nutrients to the nerve cells— and it is possible that repeated psychosis or depression may exacerbate the already fragile chemistry of a vulnerable brain.

There is some evidence that structural changes in the brains of patients with chronic schizophrenia may correspond with suicide attempts and that white-matter lesions in patients with Alzheimer's disease may be associated with the presence of suicidal thinking. Eileen Ahearn and her colleagues at Duke University are currently studying the relationship between suicide attempts and hyperintensities in the periventricular region of the brain, an area concerned with, among other things, stress response and biological rhythms. These studies are preliminary only and complicated by possible changes to the brain brought about by psychiatric medications, but they are indicative of the direction of an important field of suicide research.

Scientists have also been looking at the possible effects of serum lipids, such as cholesterol and polyunsaturated essential fatty acids, on depression and suicide. Concerned by reports that individuals who had low cholesterol levels (either naturally or because they had made dietary changes, exercised more, or taken cholesterol-lowering medications) were more likely to die prematurely from suicide, investigators sought to understand the link. Not every study showed an association between suicide and low cholesterol levels, but enough did to warrant taking it seriously.

Several explanations were set forth. Some researchers suggested that low cholesterol levels were simply an artifact of the real cause of suicide, namely, depression; many people, when depressed, lose weight, and their cholesterol levels drop accordingly. What looks causative may therefore, in fact, be incidental. However, a few studies, which controlled for weight loss and diet, still found a link.

Other scientists, including Jay Kaplan at the Bowman Gray School of Medicine in North Carolina, believe that cholesterol intake affects serotonin functioning and behavior in critical ways. In a series of intriguing studies on macaque monkeys, he and his colleagues studied social behavior and plasma lipids. For two years, monkeys were fed diets either high or low in saturated fat and cholesterol. Their behavior was rated for fleeing, attacking, grooming, and social isolation. The monkeys fed a low-fat diet exhibited more extreme physical violence than those that were not. Other studies conducted by the same scientists confirmed that cholesterol-lowering diets potentiate aggressive or antisocial behavior. Low cholesterol was also linked to low serotonergic functioning in other investigations.

Kaplan and his colleagues propose that the links among cholesterol, aggression, and serotonin functioning may have served an important evolutionary role: When foods high in animal fat were abundant, the resultant relatively high serotonergic activity in the brain may have created "behavioral complacency." In times of food scarcity, on the other hand, especially when the scarcity involved foods rich in animal fat, a low plasma cholesterol level may have precipitated impulsive, risk-taking behavior such as aggressive hunting and foraging.

The links among cholesterol, serotonergic functioning, and suicide are an important theoretical concept, as well as one that has potentially critical clinical implications. But the evidence so far is mixed, and much more research is necessary before any conclusions can be reached.

Among the scientists disputing the centrality of cholesterol in depression and suicide is Joseph Hibbeln, a researcher in the Laboratory of Membrane Biophysics and Biochemistry at the National Institutes of Health. He strongly believes that the important lipid players are actually the omega-3 essential fatty acids, not cholesterol, and speculates that one reason for the increasing rates of depression and suicide during recent decades may be due to an increase in society's consumption of saturated fatty acids, coupled with a decrease in the intake of omega-3 essential fatty acids, found in fish. Low plasma concentrations of these fatty acids, which are selectively concentrated in neural tissue, are associated with low concentrations of CSF 5-HIAA. Societies that consume a large amount of fish (for example, Japan and Taiwan) appear to have lower rates of depression, though not necessarily suicide, than those that do not (for example, Germany and New Zealand).

Paleolithic and modern hunter-gatherer populations, Hibbeln and others argue, consumed a diet much lower in saturated fats (and higher in polyunsaturated ones) than the modern diet. As agriculture became more specialized and focused on raising fewer plant species, the animals that were used as the basis of our food supply had a commensurately lower proportion of the necessary fatty acids. Hibbeln and others estimate that during the earlier periods of human evolution the ratio of saturated to polyunsaturated fats was perhaps one to one; in current diets that ratio is as high as twenty-five to one. Over the past fifty years, the widespread use of infant formula, which, unlike breast milk, contains virtually no polyunsaturated fats, may have resulted in subtle neurological deficits that have had an effect not only on mood and behavior but possibly on rates of suicide as well. The results from the studies of omega-3 essential fatty acids are preliminary, and await replication before their significance can be established.

Studies of cholesterol and essential fatty acids raise core questions about the development of the nervous system, the possible effects of diet on depression, aggression, and suicide, and potentially critical issues of clinical assessment and treatment. (There may be a link between impaired fatty acid metabolism and schizophrenia as well, as suggested by researcher David Horrobin in Scotland.) The findings so far are by no means definitive, but by all means fascinating.

CERTAINLY, MUCH is decided by our biology. Genes, in the main, determine our temperaments, and our temperaments in turn influence our choices about which environments we seek out or avoid. Our temperaments also mold how we respond to our environments and how we are shaped by them. For those who are low-key and stable, a disappointment or rejection, the loss of a job or the end of a marriage, or an extended bout of depression will be painful and distressing but not life-threatening. For those with a short wick, a savage temper, and impulse-laden wiring, life's setbacks and illnesses are more dangerous. For them, it is as though the nervous system had been soaked in kerosene: a fight with a lover, a gambling loss or a run-in with the law, or an irritable flash from a mental illness can ignite a suicidal response.

Most who encounter the ordinary, if awful, stresses and losses handed out by life handle them well or reasonably well. In fact, very few people commit suicide under even the most terrible and prolonged situations of physical or mental suffering. Yet there are others who are impelled by the seemingly slightest of reasons to reach for a gun or throw a rope across a beam. For these more biologically vulnerable, the threshold for suicide is very low; their flash point may be triggered by the inconsiderable. For yet others, the threshold may be low but not dangerously so; in the presence of depression, schizophrenia, alcoholism, or crippling anxiety, however, the threshold may drop precipitously.

A genetic predisposition to suicide by no means implies that suicide is inevitable. It simply makes it more likely that given enough cumulative stress or a devastating, acute one, suicide may be an option more readily summoned. In this respect, it is no different from the "two-hit" model that characterizes many other medical conditions. A genetic vulnerability for heart disease, cancer, or asthma, for example, or for diabetes or sickle-cell disease, does not ensure that the illness will occur. It does mean that it may be more readily triggered by behavior or the environment, for example, through smoking, a sedentary lifestyle, diet, aging, or stress. Depending on the strength of the genetic vulnerability, the predisposing genes may or may not ever be triggered. If an illness is overwhelmingly determined by genetic factors—for example, Huntington's disease—possession of the responsible gene essentially guarantees that the disease will eventually develop. If, on the other hand, the genetics are more complex or the underlying predisposition is less strong (or protected against by yet other genes), the environment and an individual's behavior has more sway in whether or not he or she becomes ill.

For some, suicide is a sudden act. For others, it is a long-considered decision based on cumulative despair or dire circumstance. And for many, it is both: a brash moment of action taken during a span of settled and suicidal hopelessness. Sudden death often waits in the wings for those whose family histories or brain chemistries predispose them to impulsive suicide; they are like dry and brittle pyres, unshielded against the inevitable sparks thrown off by living. If by temperament they are impetuous and volatile, their cast to risk taking will make them generators and throwers of sparks as well: they become instigators of brawls; participants in and perpetuators of tumultuous affairs; gamers and gamblers; high-wire acts; and dealers in discord. They are like the Australian aborigines who, as Stephen Pyne describes them in his book *World Fire*, "on this, the hottest and driest of the vegetated continents . . . habitually walked around with flaming firebrands that dribbled embers everywhere." They are the ones vulnerable to impulsive suicide: those who are volatile and fractious by nature, those who are subject to the Catherine wheel instability of mania or who live the tossed-and-turning lives associated with personality disorders or alcoholism.

Others kill themselves only after great deliberation and after having lived a long time with pain, mental illness, or chronic stress. Joseph Conrad, who shot himself in the chest when he was a young man but luckily survived, wrote, "Suicide, I suspect, is very often the outcome of mere mental weariness—not an act of savage energy but the final symptom of complete collapse." For many the cumulative despair simply becomes unendurable; there is a steady erosion in the brake linings of the mental system that apply force against self-murder. Although it is tempting to imagine suicide as obituary writers often do—as an "understandable" response to a problem of life, such as economic reversal, romantic failure, or shame—it is clear that these or similar setbacks hit everyone at some point in their lives. Unless someone lives an unthinkably boring life, has no hopes that can be shattered, no love that can be lost, or transits from birth to death in a bubble above the frays of earth, he or she experiences the same griefs or strains that, for a few, become the "cause" of death. For every grief or strain that appears to trigger a suicide, thousands of other people have experienced situations as bad or worse and do *not* kill themselves. The normal mind, although strongly affected by a loss or damaging event, is well cloaked against the possibility of suicide.

John Mann and his colleagues at the New York State Psychiatric Institute have proposed a "Stress-Diathesis" model to explain the relationship between the underlying biological predisposition to suicide and the precipitants that trigger it. Several factors influence the predisposition to commit suicide, and together they act to establish a threshold for suicidal behavior. These include genetic vulnerabilities such as family history and compromised serotonergic functioning in the brain; temperamental variables, such as aggressiveness and impulsivity; chronic alcohol and drug abuse; chronic medical conditions; and certain social factors, such as the early death of a parent, social isolation, or a childhood history of physical or sexual abuse. To some extent, the threshold of suicidal behavior can be raised (that is, suicide can, to a limited extent, be protected against) by religious beliefs, the presence of children in the household, financial security, strong social supports, or a good marriage. In the presence of a strong predisposition to suicide, however, these protective factors may be of limited value.

The precipitants of suicide, known rather oddly as "triggers," include stressors such as psychiatric illness, acute intoxication from drugs or alcohol, personal or financial crisis, or contagion from another suicide. The interactions between the threshold factors and the triggers are, of course, complicated. A man who is born with a genetic predisposition to manic-depressive illness, has impaired serotonergic functioning, and comes from a family with a history of suicide is at high risk to kill himself. But his risk may increase even further if he drinks when he is depressed or manic, because this will increase the likelihood that he will have problems with his relationships and his work. It will also make it more likely that his illness will get worse, that his treatment will be less effective, and that his serotonin functioning will be compromised even further.

Alone, a single risk factor—either predisposing or precipitating—may only slightly increase the odds that an individual will kill himself. But some, such as a genetic or other biological predisposition, especially when coupled with a severe psychiatric disorder, are particularly ominous. When the threshold is set low from birth and the triggers kick in, the likelihood of suicide may become unstoppably high. A slight affront or loss may quickly create a flash point from a lethal mix of elements. It is as with fire: dry grass and high winds may remain, in themselves, only dangerous possibilities, elements of combustion. But if lightning falls across the grass, the chance of fire increases blindingly fast: it leaps from slim to given.

ACUTE PSYCHIATRIC illness is the single most common and dangerous trigger of suicide. Most people who suffer from depression, manic-depressive illness, alcoholism, or schizophrenia do not kill themselves, but a vastly disproportionate number of them do. For some, the threshold of suicide is lowered because of the characteristics of the illness itself—for example, the extreme irritability and impulsivity associated with mixed states or the mental and physical agitation of severe depression as it begins to clear or as it worsens—but for others, those who even when well have endangeringly low CSF 5-HIAA levels and who are aggressive and reckless by temperament, mental illness may trigger the underlying chronic propensity to commit suicide. Many things in the environment or a person's behavior may in turn precipitate or worsen psychiatric illness. We saw earlier, for example, how psychological stress can play a pivotal role in vulnerable individuals.

Sleep loss is probably the strongest element in triggering a manic episode, and mania in turn puts the individual at a very much increased risk for depression, mixed states, and subsequent suicide. A sharp reduction in sleep—from stress, grief, childbirth, jet lag, work that involves sudden alterations in sleep patterns (such as military training, shift work, war, or medical internships), acute seasonal changes in light, alcohol or drug abuse—sets in motion powerful biological changes in the brain. Medications such as antidepressants and steroids can also induce profound mood changes or provoke agitated and restless states in vulnerable individuals; so, too, can many medical conditions, such as thyroid disorders, Cushing's disease, myocardial infarctions, postoperative states, hemodialysis, AIDS, head trauma, stroke, and infections. A diet that results in low levels of cholesterol or is deficient in omega-3 essential fatty acids may also have an impact on the suicide threshold, although the extent of its importance is unclear. Even though, as Emil Kraepelin described nearly a hundred years ago, "the attacks of manic-depressive insanity may be to an astonishing degree independent of external influences," there is no question that there is a complex causal relationship among the major mental illnesses, behavior, and the physical environment. These in turn exert a strong influence on the underlying biological and temperamental vulnerabilities to suicide.

There are other major influences on suicide as well. Age is

particularly significant. Suicide, we know, is rare before the age of twelve. One percent of all suicides occur in the first fifteen years of life, but 25 percent occur in the second. What causes this abrupt upturn in rates?

Several researchers have suggested that very young children do not commit suicide because they have highly unrealistic notions of death—more than half of six- to eleven-year-olds, for example, believe that death is reversible—but it is not obvious why such a belief would protect a child against killing himself (indeed, it could be argued that thinking of death in such terms would make suicide more likely). Of more relevance, perhaps, is the fact that the planning and carrying out of suicide are cognitively quite complex, and young children usually lack the necessary ability. Most important, major psychopathology (mood disorders, alcohol and drug abuse, and the psychotic illnesses) is uncommon in very young children. The severe mental illnesses are far more likely to occur first after puberty than before.

Puberty, which generally begins between the ages of twelve and fourteen, coincides with the first significant rise in the rate of suicide. It brings with it a whirlpool of hormones and a steady increase in the prevalence of major psychiatric disorders. The average age of onset for manic-depression is eighteen; for drug and alcohol abuse and schizophrenia, twenty-one; and for major depression, twenty-six. The rise in the prevalence of severe mental illnesses parallels the rise in suicide, making increasing age a significant risk factor.

Gender, as well as age, plays a determining role in suicide. Some of the differences in suicide between men and women were discussed earlier: women, although they are more prone to depressive illness than men and are more likely to attempt suicide, do not actually kill themselves nearly as often. To some extent, this is because men are less likely to recognize depression in themselves and to seek treatment for it, but it is also because they are more inclined to drink heavily when mentally ill and to reach for firearms or other highly lethal means in order to kill themselves. Impulsivity and violence, which predispose to suicide, appear to be more innately characteristic of males, although the differences between the sexes in terms of serotonergic functioning have not been well studied.

There is some evidence that blood levels of serotonin rise during pregnancy, which may partially account for the lower rate of suicide during this period. (Unlike cerebrospinal fluid measures of serotonin, which measure serotonergic functioning in the brain, blood levels of serotonin are strongly influenced by dietary and other factors). The risk for suicide in women in the year following childbirth is generally very low, except in those who have a history of severe psychiatric illness. (For these women the risk of postpartum suicide is much higher.) The evidence is somewhat conflicting for changes in the rates of suicide during different phases of the menstrual cycle, but most studies find an increase in suicides, suicide attempts, and calls to suicide prevention centers during the week immediately preceding menses or during menstruation itself. A London autopsy study of twenty-three women who had killed themselves found, from endometrial examination, that all but one of the women was in the luteal phase of her cycle (that is, in the fourteen days preceding menstrual bleeding). Autopsies of Hindu women who had committed suicide by burning themselves with kerosene revealed that nineteen of the twenty-two were menstruating at the time of death. There is some evidence that suicide attempts during the first week of the menstrual cycle may be associated with low levels of estrogen.

Although there is a strong male predominance in completed suicides across the world, there are a few countries where this is not true, for example in Malta, Egypt, Papua New Guinea, western Ethiopia, and China. In 1990, more than 180,000 Chinese women committed suicide (during the same time period, 159,000 Chinese men killed themselves), which was more than one half of the world's female suicides. Most of the five hundred Chinese women who kill themselves every day are young, in their early twenties, and live in rural parts of the country.

The explanations for such a high rate of suicide in young Chinese women are many and controversial. Among the most logical, although by no means entirely explanatory, is the easy access that rural Chinese women have to deadly pesticides. An impulsive act that would be far less life-threatening if the substance ingested were instead a medication, or if emergency medical care were more readily available, under these circumstances becomes lethal. An impulsive suicide attempt is quickly transformed into suicide.

Some have suggested that the rapid shift to a market economy may be partially to blame for the high suicide rate, although this is not a situation unique to China, nor is it clear why such a shift should affect women more adversely than men. Others speculate that China, which does not have strong sanctions against suicide, may make it psychologically easier for young women to make the decision to commit suicide. Social scientists have stressed that Chinese society places a low value on women, but while this perception of women's low status may be true, China is not very different in these attitudes from many other countries that have far lower suicide rates. Family disputes, arranged marriages, and other domestic problems are also important factors, but these or similar stresses and conflicts exist in all societies. They may play a precipitating role, but it is unlikely that they are the primary cause of suicide.

There is a spirited debate now under way about the extent to which mental illness is central to suicide in China. Michael Phillips, a Canadian psychiatrist based in Beijing, believes that only 50 percent of suicides in China are linked to psychiatric illness, unlike in other countries, which report at least 90 percent. Most of the others, he believes, are impulsive in nature.

Andrew Cheng, a Taiwanese doctor, whose studies conclude that more than 95 percent of suicides in Taiwan are closely tied to mental illness—and whose findings are more consistent with those reported elsewhere throughout the world—strongly disagrees with Phillips. It will be some time before these differences of opinion are sorted out, but in the meantime everyone is in agreement that something needs to be done. Recently, Chinese doctors have begun to focus on identifying and treating depression; access to pesticides is being curtailed; suicide prevention programs have been started; and young girls are being taught better ways to handle the stresses they encounter.

WE ARE, with the rest of life, periodic creatures, beholden for our rhythms to the rotations of the earth around the sun and the moon around the earth. The chemistry of our brains and bodies oscillates in adaptation to the earth's fluctuations in heat and light, and probably its electromagnetic fields as well. Like other mammals, our patterns of eating, sleeping, and other physical activities sway with the seasons, varying in accordance with changes in day length and temperature. A master biological clock, genetically determined, controls the cycling of our brain's constituent chemicals and shapes our responses to our physical environment.

Suicide is far from immune to the effects of the earth's daily rhythms and yearly seasons. Most suicides occur between 7 a.m. and 4 p.m., which one nineteenth-century scientist (who had observed a similar pattern in a large number of European countries) explained by saying, "Shocks and reverses are most frequently met with in the busiest hours, and to those already sick of the toils and worries of life, entrance upon a new day, no brighter than its predecessors, is often more than they can bear." Hospital suicides tend to be committed very early in the day, most often between 5 a.m. and 7 a.m. Some of this may be an artifact of activity on the wards and the availability of nursing staff, but more likely it reflects the well-established diurnal variation that exists in moods, particularly in those who suffer from major depression or manic-depression. Mood, especially in individuals with manic-depression, tends to be much worse in the morning and then improve as the day wears on. Cognitive impairment, including attention, memory, and concentration, reaction time, and physical strength also show profound diurnal fluxes in those with mood disorders. These mood and cognitive changes, and their relationship to diurnal patterns in suicidal behavior, will be discussed more fully in the context of diurnal rhythms in the brain's chemistry. There is no evidence for a link between suicide and the lunar cycle although the moon may have had a more powerful influence on moods and behavior in the time before modern lighting came into existence. Nor is there a link between suicide and birthdays or national holidays such as Thanksgiving and Christmas. (One study in Britain did find an increase in suicide *attempts* on Saint Valentine's Day.) There is, however, a fairly consistent increase in suicides on Mondays. This has been attributed by some to a "broken-promise" effect, a sense of despair or betrayal when the beginning of the new week, which ought to be a psychological beginning, proves not to be any different from the days preceding it. For others, if severely depressed or disturbed, the tasks of the new week, laid out on a desk or in an appointment book, may prove to be crushing.

The seasonal variation in suicide is one of the most robust and consistent findings in the research literature. In the late 1800s, Enrico Morselli studied suicide in eighteen European countries and showed that in seventeen of them the maximum suicide rate occurred in the spring or summer months. (Conversely, in virtually every country, the minimum occurred in the winter.) Several years ago, I reviewed more than sixty studies of seasonal patterns in suicide and found a similar pattern. The peak months for suicide were, with rare exceptions, in the late spring and summer. Likewise, the lowest rates were always found in the winter months. This late-spring-to-summer peak has also been found in a series of Belgian, Finnish, American, and Chinese studies completed since the time of the review. Seasonal variation in suicide appears to correlate not with the dark and dismal months but with the brightness and extended duration of spring and summer light instead. Consistent with this, studies carried out in the Southern Hemisphere—in Australia, Chile, Uruguay, and South Africa—show that suicide peaks in the months making up their springs and summers. In the Northern Hemisphere, men have one peak in suicide—in April, May, and the summer months—whereas women appear to share that peak but to have a second smaller one in October and November as well.

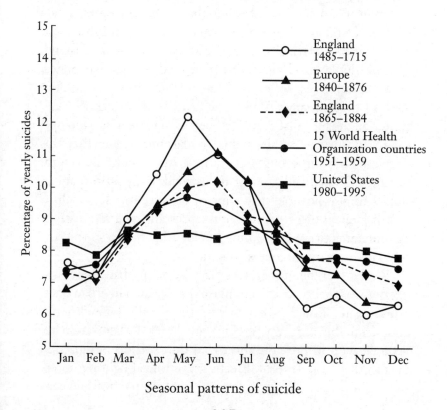

Seasonal patterns of suicide

The peaking of suicide in the spring and summer can be demonstrated in data collected as long ago as the fifteenth century and as recently as the last few years. The graph on page 207 shows monthly patterns of suicide in several populations: England, 1485–1715; Europe (France, Italy, Belgium), 1840–1876; England, 1865–1884; fifteen World Health Organization countries, 1951–1959; and the United States, 1980–1995. Across all time periods and all countries the spring-to-summer peak and the winter trough were found.

It is clear, as well, from looking at the graph, that the seasonal effect was more pronounced in earlier centuries—for example, in England (1485–1715) and Europe (1840–1876)—than it has been in later ones, such as the fifteen World Health Organization countries (1951–1959) and the United States (1980–1995). This lessening in amplitude over time was also apparent in a major Danish study that examined seasonal patterns in Denmark between 1835 and 1955 and in subsequent investigations carried out in Australia and New Zealand, Canada, Finland, Hungary, Sweden, and the United States. The explanations for this "deseasonalization," as Jürgen Aschoff of Germany's Max Planck Institute has described it, center on the idea that there has been a decrease in our biological responsiveness to the natural environment and that this decrease has been brought about by artificial lighting, central heating and air-conditioning, industrialization, and urbanization. It is also possible that some of the recent deseasonalization has taken place because antidepressant medications may be more effective in preventing suicides that have a strong seasonal component than those that do not.

Emile Durkheim observed last century that there was greater seasonality in suicides in rural areas than in urban ones, a finding replicated earlier this century in the United States and within the past few years in South Africa. Urbanization has brought with it more distance from the rhythms of light and heat in the natural world. Electricity, artificial lighting, interrupted sleep patterns (including less total sleep time), and central heating all have decreased the impact of the natural seasons on the brain and body. Yet the seasonal impact remains strong.

Why should suicide ebb and flow with the seasons? And why should suicide occur more often in the months of sunlight, instead of during the bleak, drizzly months of winter? We know, of course, that the daily rest-activity cycles are deeply affected by changes in daylight and temperature. Hibernation of animals is the most obvious example of this relatedness. Profound behavioral, endocrine, and other physiological changes are common in response to seasonal changes in light. In humans, variations in mood, energy, sleep, and behavior are also strongly affected by the seasons, but they are far more pronounced in patients with mood disorders. In fact, many neurobiological systems of relevance to mood disorders, and presumably to suicide as well, show pronounced seasonal patterns; these include levels of neurotransmitters, sleep and temperature regulators, melatonin, testosterone, estrogen, thyroid, and other hormones. During the winter, for example, which has the lowest rate of suicide, plasma L-tryptophan (a precursor of serotonin) is at its peak, as are melatonin and thyroid hormones and possibly cholesterol as well. All are thought to be deeply involved in the regulation of mood, activation, or the sleep-wake cycle. The effect of seasonal changes on serotonin and other transmitters remains unclear.

Of particular relevance in discussing seasonal patterns in suicide, however, is the strong seasonal variability in the occurrence of the major psychiatric disorders, depression, mania, and schizophrenia. More than two thousand years ago, Hippocrates observed that melancholia was more likely to occur in the spring and autumn, and other ancients noted a strong tendency for attacks of mania to occur during the summer months. These observations have been replicated by the more systematic work of recent scientists. Hospital admissions for mania, it has been shown by many investigators, are far more common in the late spring and summer. Schizophrenia, likewise, appears to be likely to occur or recur during the summer months.

Depressive episodes show a more diverse seasonal pattern. There are generally two broad peaks for hospital admissions for depression: during the spring and during the autumn. Hospitalizations for depression are more likely to reflect the severity of the depression—including suicidality—than the beginning of the episode per se. In fact, many depressive episodes begin in winter but reach their maximum severity or dangerousness in the early spring. Hospital admission dates for mania, on the other hand, are more immediately tied to the actual onset of manic episodes than they are for depressive ones because of the more quickly emergent nature of mania.

Several things are likely to contribute to the seasonality of both the severe mental illnesses and suicide. The biological changes brought about by alterations in temperature and the length of daylight are likely to underlie both phenomena. Seasonal fluctuations in the brain's chemicals, importantly serotonin, may have a forceful effect not only on an underlying predisposition to suicide but also on psychopathological states such as mania, violence, depression, and psychosis. This is also true of their effect on suicide. Violent suicides show a far stronger seasonal pattern than do nonviolent ones; they, like homicide and other violent behaviors, are much more likely to occur in the late spring and summer months. A seasonal effect on factors likely to change levels of omega-3 essential fatty acids—such as fluctuating availabilities of foods and vegetables and an increased intake of fat-rich foods during winter solstice holidays—has been suggested by scientist Joseph Hibbeln.

Manic and schizophrenic episodes during the summer months precipitate highly volatile, agitated, and paranoid states that may in turn lead to impulsive and violent acts such as suicide. Too, because most individuals who become manic also go through a depression before or after their mania, they are at increased risk of suicide during those times as well. Mixed states, that is, coexisting depression and mania, are also likely to increase during this time and are among the most deadly of psychopathological conditions. These may occur independently, as part of the transition between depression and mania, or in the transition between mania and normal psychological functioning. There is an overlap in depression and mania peaks in the spring and fall that in turn correlates with the peaks in suicide.

Depression carries with it a greatly increased risk of suicide not only during its acute phase but also during its slow and often tempestuous period of recovery. Suicide is not at all uncommon at the end of the worst part of the depression, when mood seems to be improving and energy has returned. Nor is it rare during the early stages of the descent into despair. Depression is often subtly mixed with perturbing manic symptoms, and many patients initially diagnosed as depressed turn out, on closer clinical evaluation, to experience mixed states as well.

Severe depression, manic-depression, and schizophrenia may additionally act as a "second hit" for those genetically vulnerable to suicide; that is, the pain and agitation of psychosis, the biological events it sets into play, or the anguish and frustration at again becoming ill may interact lethally with a susceptible constitution. Spring and summer are deceptive notions and contain a capacity for self-murder that winter less often has. Or, as Edward Thomas believed, winter lingers far past its season:

> *But these things also are Spring's—*
> *On banks by the roadside the grass*
> *Long-dead that is greyer now*
> *Than all the Winter it was;*

> *The shell of a little snail bleached*
> *In the grass; chip of flint, and mite*
> *Of chalk; and the small birds' dung*
> *In splashes of purest white:*

All the white things a man mistakes
For earliest violets
Who seeks through Winter's ruins
Something to pay Winter's debts,

While the North blows, and starling flocks
By chattering on and on
Keep their spirits up in the mist,
And Spring's here, Winter's not gone.

THE COLOURING TO EVENTS:
THE DEATH OF MERIWETHER LEWIS

We were now about to penetrate a country at least two thousand miles in width, on which the foot of civilized man had never trodden; the good or evil it had in store for us was for experiment yet to determine. . . . However, as the state of mind in which we are, generally gives the colouring to events. . . . I could but esteem this moment of my departure as among the most happy of my life.

—Meriwether Lewis, April 7, 1805

THE YOUNG red-haired Virginian had thought hard and well about the provisions his men should take with them, but the planning cannot have been easy. A few dozen men were about to set out on an eight-thousand-mile journey across the unmapped American wilderness. There was little they could draw upon to predict the quick variability of the land or to grasp its vastness. The expedition would be far afield from usual calculation and experience, but because of this it would in the end be unmatched for what it discovered about the country, its inhabitants, and its resources.

The trip would be dangerous, it would be arduous, and it would take more than two years to complete, but the expedition's leader was anything but bowed or intimidated. He had the confidence of the president who had chosen him, as well as a firm, well-placed belief in his own ability to command men and to carry out the scientific work at the heart of the expedition's mission. He had prepared for the trip with care and intelligence, and he was exhilarated to have the chance to explore and chart the unknown lands.

His country had just, overnight, doubled in size. On July 4, 1803, the U.S. Congress had purchased the Louisiana Territory from Napoleon. For three cents an acre, the government had acquired the vast, murkily bordered lands stretching from the Mississippi River to the Rocky Mountains. It was clear to some that it was only a matter of time until America pushed past the western mountain ranges and took the nation's expanding borders to the Pacific Ocean. In the meantime, the country needed knowing.

Captain Meriwether Lewis, the young Virginian who had drawn up the plans for the westward expedition, was a U.S. Army officer who had lived in the wilderness frontier and was well acquainted with Indian cultures. He was six feet tall, restless, intrepid, and profoundly and wide-rangingly curious; he knew life not only from the frontier but, more recently, from the inside of the president's house as well. Thomas Jefferson, two weeks before taking office in February 1801, had written to Lewis asking that he help with the "private concerns of the household" and, more intriguingly, "to contribute to the mass of information which it is interesting for the administration to acquire." Lewis's "knoledge of the Western country, of the army and of all of it's interests & relations has rendered it desirable" that he join Jefferson as the president's private secretary.

Meriwether Lewis accepted the position with speed and delight, and for two years the fellow Virginians, separated in age by nearly thirty years, shared meals, confidences, and several hours of most days together. Both men were singularly inquisitive by nature, and both were passionate for the exploration of the country's vast lands—the young officer for the exploration itself, the president for what could be learned from it. In 1802, Jefferson decided that Lewis should command an expedition to the Pacific Ocean; he then set out for the young officer a remarkable course of tutelage in subjects ranging from geography and natural history to medicine, botany, and astronomy.

Jefferson had high expectations for the westward journey, and he had a thousand questions and requests: "The object of your mission," the president wrote Lewis in June 1803, "is to explore the Missouri river, & such principal stream of it, as, by it's course & communication with the waters of the Pacific Ocean, may offer the most direct and practicable water communication across this continent, for the purposes of commerce." Lewis was to "take observations of latitude & longitude . . . with great pains and accuracy," and he was to make several copies of all notes and observations—one to be written "on the paper of the birch, as less liable to injury from damp than common paper"—in order to guard against damage or loss. Lewis was to determine the names of the Indian nations, "& their numbers; the extent & limits of their possessions . . . their language, traditions, monuments; their ordinary occupations in agriculture, fishing, hunting, war, arts . . . the diseases prevalent among them, & the remedies they use . . . peculiarities in their laws, customs and dispositions."

Lewis and his men were also to record the "soil and face of the country, it's growth & vegetable productions . . . the animals of the country generally . . . the mineral productions of every kind . . . Volcanic appearances." Climate was to be carefully noted "by the proportion of rainy, cloudy & clear days, by lightening, hail, snow, ice, by the access & recess of frost, by the winds prevailing at different seasons, the dates at which particular plants put forth or lose their flowers, or leaf, times of appearance of particular birds, reptiles or insects."

Jefferson's instructions to Lewis could not have been written by anyone else. As Donald Jackson, the editor of the correspondence and documents of the Lewis and Clark expedition, has put it: "They embrace years of study and wonder, the collected wisdom of his government colleagues and Philadelphia friends; they barely conceal his excitement at realizing that at last he would have facts, not vague guesses, about the Stony Mountains, the river courses, the wild Indian tribes, the flora and fauna of untrodden places."

The president had no doubt that if anyone could be trusted to carry out his requests, it would be Meriwether Lewis. "Capt. Lewis is brave, prudent, habituated to the woods, & familiar with Indian manners & character," Jefferson wrote to Benjamin Rush, the eminent Philadelphia physician from whom Lewis was to learn medicine in order to look after his men on the expedition. "He is not regularly educated, but he possesses a great mass of accurate observation on all the subjects of nature which present themselves here, & will therefore readily select those only in his new route which shall be new." After Lewis died, Jefferson elaborated further upon his friend's temperament and character: "No season or circumstance could obstruct his purpose," Jefferson wrote. He possessed a passion for "dazzling pursuits"; had "enterprise, boldness, and discretion," "courage undaunted," and a "firmness and perseverance of purpose which no thing but impossibilities could divert from its direction." His fidelity to truth was "scrupulous."

In the final paragraph of the president's extraordinary and detailed instructions to Lewis, Jefferson requested that he designate a second in command who could take over Lewis's responsibilities should he die on the expedition. Lewis decided to appoint a co-leader instead and chose for the position William Clark, an officer he greatly admired and liked and under whom he had previously served.

By the late summer of 1803 the expedition was under way. The leaders and their men set out with fishing hooks and tents; mosquito netting, whiskey, and salt pork; Pennsylvania rifles and axes; sextants and telescopes; lamps and kettles and saws. They left with provisions for most imaginable contingencies, and they took, as well, items of exchange for the Indians they would encounter: boxes of fabrics and bright things—500 brooches, 72 rings, 12 dozen looking glasses, 3 pounds of beads—tomahawks and knives; striped silk ribbons and calico shirts; and 130 rolls of tobacco. There were, for the inevitable fevers and injuries along the way, tourniquets, lancets, and medicinal teas. Laudanum, an ease for almost any ailment, was boxed up as well, as were cloves and nutmegs to disguise the acrid taste of improvised brews and tonics. Peruvian bark, containing quinine, was included to fight malaria.

With what they had and knew, the men could cross rivers and plains, build boats, and survive in the mountains. They could barter for goods, and they could defend themselves. But two of the men, Lewis and Clark, could also measure, describe, and write down what they had observed and where their journey had taken them. They had provisions for history—100 quills, 1 pound of sealing wax, 6 papers of ink powder, and 6 brass inkstands—and with their quills and ink they filled red morocco-bound journals and an elk-skin field book with precise and captivating scientific records of their twenty-eight-month journey across the American continent.

The Corps of Discovery—Lewis and Clark and their small contingent of soldiers, hunters, woodsmen, blacksmith, cook, and carpenters—went into the country's unmapped territories and mapped them; explored its rivers and mountains; dug canoes out of cottonwood trees; did commerce with the Indians; and at times stayed among them. They caught fish and shot game. They walked forever, took the measure of the lands and rivers they crossed, and then, after extracting from the stars what they needed for their bearings, the leaders of the expedition would start to write. They filled their journals with detailed descriptions of the plants and trees they had discovered, new animals encountered, the flowings of waters and the structure of the mountains, and the medicines or the discipline they had doled out to their men.

The journals of Lewis and Clark are vivid and immediate; they pull the reader into the unexplored continent and wildlife of wilderness America. Here, for example, is Lewis writing about weather, the taste of a beaver tail, and the gait of porcupines. It is May 1805, and the expedition is making its way upstream on the Missouri River:

Thursday May 2nd, 1805.

The wind continued violent all night nor did it abate much of it's violence this morning, when at daylight it was attended with snow which continued to fall untill about 10 A.M. being about one inch deep, it formed a singular contrast with the vegitation which was considerably advanced. some flowers had put forth in the plains, and the leaves of the cottonwood were as large as a dollar. sent out some hunters who killed 2 deer 3 Elk and several buffaloe; on our way this evening we also shot three beaver along the shore; these anamals in consequence of not being hunted are extreemly gentle, where they are hunted they never leave their lodges in the day, the flesh of the beaver is esteemed a delecacy among us; I think the tale a most delicious morsal, when boiled it resembles in flavor the fresh tongues and sounds of the codfish, and is usually sufficiently large to afford a plentifull meal for two men.

Friday, May 3rd, 1805

We saw vast quantities of Buffaloe, Elk, deer principally of the long tale kind, Antelope or goats, beaver, geese, ducks, brant and some swan. near the entrance of the river mentioned in the 10th. course of this day, we saw an unusual number of Porcupines from which we determined to call the river after that anamal, and accordingly denominated it Porcupine river. . . .

I walked out a little distance and met with 2 porcupines which were feeding on the young willow which grow in great abundance on all the sandbars; this anamal is exceedingly clumsy and not very watchfull I approached so near one of them before it percieved me that I touched it with my espontoon.—found the nest of a wild goose among some driftwood in the river from which we took three eggs. this is the only nest we have met with on driftwood, the usual position is the top of a broken tree, sometimes in the forks of a large tree but almost invariably, from 15 to 20 feet or upwards high.—

Neither Lewis nor Clark was a professional naturalist or geographer, but they were fastidious in their measurements and descriptions of the places they had been and the wildlife they had seen. Along the way, they sent back to Jefferson and scientists in Philadelphia the moon rocks of their time: nearly two hundred different specimens of trees and plants—grasses from the plains, currants, wildflowers, sagebrush, flax, Mariposa lilies, spruce, and maples—most of which had been, until that time, unknown to leading botanists. They shipped crates full of roots, seeds, and bulbs, as well as the skins and skeletons of weasels, coyotes, squirrels, badgers, birds, antelopes, mountain rams, and scores of other animals. "Few explorers have undertaken a larger task or achieved greater success in carrying it out," observed one writer. "Their survey notes were meticulously recorded, and their maps of the areas explored were the best available for fifty years."

In September 1806 the Corps of Discovery completed its journey. Jefferson's initial hope of finding a Northwest Passage that linked the Atlantic with the Pacific was not realized, but the exploration was otherwise a success beyond the imaginations of imaginative men. When Lewis and Clark and the rest of their expedition arrived in St. Louis, they stepped from their boat into a swirl of acclaim, society balls, and national celebration. "Never," declared Thomas Jefferson, "did a similar event excite more joy in the United States." Meriwether Lewis, however, only thirty-two years old, began the descent into the last three, deeply unsettled years of his life.

It is nearly two hundred years since Meriwether Lewis died of gunshot wounds in a cabin seventy miles from Nashville. The circumstances of his death remain charged with controversy and rancor, although suicide seems by far to be the most likely explanation for his death. But suicide is at odds with a country's notion of what a hero should be. Thomas Jefferson, who for two years had lived intimately with Lewis and who had treated him like a son; William Clark, who had shared leadership, adversity, and triumphs with him for at least as long; and those who were with Lewis during the last hours and days of his life had no doubt that his wounds were self-inflicted. Yet the possibility that Lewis might have killed himself proved unthinkable to many who had never even met him. Derangement, as several who observed his mental state toward the end of his life described it, seemed, for some, inconsistent with courage, honor, and accomplishment of the first rank. Conspiracy theories and speculation about murder cropped up to "protect" the blackened reputation of the explorer. But what was the evidence of suicide? Who could imagine that Lewis's reputation needed defending? And why should suicide be seen as a dishonorable rather than just dreadfully tragic act?

Contemporary accounts of the weeks leading up to Lewis's death make a compelling case for a deeply distraught and troubled man who was drinking heavily, spending and investing money irrationally, and acting in a way that caused others to be concerned for his safety and well-being. His position as governor of the Louisiana Territories, taken up after his return from the West, was marred by conflict and questionable judgment, and he was hopelessly behind in preparing the journals of the expedition. Jefferson was clearly exasperated: "I am very often applied to know when our work will appear," he wrote to Lewis. "I have so long promised copies to my literary correspondents in France that I am almost bankrupt in their eyes. I shall be very happy to receive from yourself information of your expectations on this subject." The inordinate delay in forwarding the highly awaited information about the journey was not the first time there had been gaps in Lewis's writing. Most of them, interestingly, showed a similar seasonal pattern, occurring during August and/or September; some extended through late fall or early winter, as well (Lewis died in early October 1809). In that same time of the year, in August 1805, Lewis also wrote the only introspective and rather melancholic entry into his journal:

> *This day I completed my thirty first year, and conceived that I had in all human probability now existed about half the period which I am to remain in this Sublunary world. I reflected that I had as yet done but little, very little indeed, to further the hapiness of the human race, or to advance the information of the succeeding generation. I viewed with regret the many hours I have spent in indolence, and now soarly feel the want of that information which those hours would have given me had they been judiciously expended. but since they are past and cannot be recalled, I dash from me the gloomy thought, and resolved in future, to redouble my exertions and at least indeavour to promote those two primary objects of human existence, by giving them the aid of that portion of talents which nature and fortune have bestoed on me; or in future, to live for* mankind, *as I have heretofore lived* for myself.

In early September 1809, the month before he died, Lewis set off for Washington and Philadelphia to straighten out his financial affairs and to work on the publication of his expedition journals. William Clark, who had tried to help Lewis sort out his expense accounts, was clearly concerned about the state of Lewis's mind: "Several of his Bills [to the government] have been protested, and his Crediters all flocking in near the time of his Setting out distressed him much, which he expressed to me in Such terms as to Cause a Cempothy which is not yet off—I do not believe there was ever a honester man in Louisiana nor one who had pureor motives than Govr. Lewis. if his mind had been at ease I Should have parted Cherefuly."

A week after leaving St. Louis, Lewis drew up a will, and

a few days later he arrived at Fort Pickering (Memphis). The commanding officer of the fort, Captain Gilbert Russell, heard from the crew on Lewis's boat that Lewis had twice attempted to kill himself. Russell himself observed that Lewis had been drinking heavily and was, at the time he arrived at the fort, "mentally deranged." The commander, afraid that Lewis would take his own life, unloaded Lewis's boat so that he could not escape and kept him under constant surveillance for several days:

> In this condition he continued without any material change for about five days, during which time the most proper and efficatious means that could be devised to restore him was administered, and on the sixth or seventh day all symptoms of derangement disappeared and he was completely in his senses and thus continued for ten or twelve days. . . . In three or four days he was again affected with the same mental disease. He had no person with him who could manage or controul him in his propensities and he daily grew worse untill he arrived at the house of a Mr. Grinder . . . where in the apprehension of being destroyed by enemies which had no existence but in his wild imagination, he destroyed himself in the most cool desperate and Barbarian-like manner, having been left in the house intirely to himself.

The U.S. agent to the Chickasaw Nation, James Neelly, who was with Lewis for the last three weeks of his life, wrote to President Jefferson shortly after Lewis's death: "It is with extreme pain I have to inform you of the death of His Excellency Meriwether Lewis, Governor of Upper Louisiana who died on the morning of the 11th instant and I am Sorry to Say by Suicide." He reported, as Russell had, that Lewis had been mentally "deranged" off and on for some period of time.

The details of Lewis's suicide were later recorded in detail by his friend, the eminent ornithologist Alexander Wilson. He wrote his account after interviewing the woman at whose inn Lewis had died:

Governor Lewis, she said, came hither about sunset, alone, and inquired if he could stay for the night; and alighting, brought his saddle into the house. He was dressed in a loose gown, white, striped with blue. On being asked if he came alone, he replied that there were two servants behind, who would soon be up. He called for some spirits, and drank a very little. When the servants arrived . . . he inquired for his powder. . . . [He] walked backwards and forwards before the door, talking to himself.

Sometimes, she said, he would seem as if he were walking up to her; and would suddenly wheel round, and walk back as fast as he could. Supper being ready he sat down, but had eaten only a few mouthfuls when he started up, speaking to himself in a violent manner. . . . He smoked for some time, but quitted his seat and traversed the yard as before. He again sat down to his pipe, seemed again composed, and casting his eyes wistfully towards the west, observed what a sweet evening it was. Mrs. Grinder was preparing a bed for him, but he said he would sleep on the floor, and desired the servant to bring the bear skins and buffalo robe, which were immediately spread out for him; and, it now being dusk, the woman went off to the kitchen and the two men to the barn which stands about two hundred yards off.

The kitchen is only a few paces from the room where Lewis was, and the woman being considerably alarmed by the behavior of her guest could not sleep, but listened to him walking backwards and forwards, she thinks, for several hours, and talking aloud, as she said, "like a lawyer." She then heard the report of a pistol, and something fall heavily to the floor, and the words "O Lord!" Immediately afterwards she heard another pistol, and in a few minutes she heard him at her door calling out, "O madam! give me some water and heal my wounds!"

The logs being open, and unplastered, she saw him stagger back and fall against a stump that stands between the kitchen and the room. He crawled for some distance, and raised himself by the side of a tree, where he sat about a minute. He once more got to the room; afterwards he came to the kitchen door, but did not speak; she then heard him scraping in the bucket with a gourd for water; but it appears that this cooling element was denied the dying man.

As soon as the day broke, and not before, the terror of the woman having permitted him to remain for two hours in this most deplorable situation, she sent two of her children to the barn, her husband not being home, to bring the servants; and on going in they found him lying on the bed. He uncovered his side, and showed them where the bullet had entered; a piece of his forehead was blown off, and had exposed the brains, without having bled much.

He begged they would take his rifle and blow out his brains, and he would give them all the money in his trunk. He often said, "I am no coward; but I am so strong, so hard to die." He begged the servant not to be afraid of him, for that he would not hurt him. He expired in about two hours, or just as the sun rose above the trees.

Captain Russell's account of Lewis's last hours was even more dreadful. After twice shooting himself with his pistol, Russell reports, Lewis "got his razors from a port folio which happened to contain them and siting up in his bed was found about day light, by one of the servants, busily engaged in cuting himself from head to foot."

William Clark was stricken at the news of his friend's death, but he was not entirely surprised by the accounts that Lewis had killed himself: "I fear O! I fear the weight of his mind has overcome him," he wrote to his brother two weeks after Lewis died. And Thomas Jefferson, in a short memoir about Meriwether Lewis, wrote:

> Governor Lewis had, from early life, been subject to hypochondriac [depressive] affections. It was a constitutional disposition in all the nearer branches of the family of his name, and was more immediately inherited by him from his father. They had not, however, been so strong as to give uneasiness to his family. While he lived with me in Washington I observed at times sensible depressions of mind: but knowing their constitutional source, I estimated their course by what I had seen in the family. During his western expedition, the constant exertion which that required of all the faculties of body and mind, suspended these distressing affections; but after his establishment at St. Louis in sedentary occupations, they returned upon him with redoubled vigour, and began seriously to alarm his friends. He was in a paroxysm of one of these, when his affairs rendered it necessary for him to go to Washington. . . .
>
> About three o'clock in the night he did the deed which plunged his friends into affliction, and deprived his country of one of her most valued citizens. . . . It lost too to the nation the benefit of receiving from his own hand the narrative . . . of his sufferings and successes, in endeavoring to extend for them the boundaries of science, and to present to their knowledge that vast and fertile country, which their sons are destined to fill with arts, with science, with freedom and happiness.

Jefferson's account of his friend's death would seem to many, myself included, a thoughtful and compassionate portrayal of the death of a courageous man. But others have felt differently. Some simply cannot reconcile the outward realities of Lewis's life with his desire to leave it. Olin Dunbar Wheeler, historian and editor, was one of these. "It seems impossible," he wrote, "that a young man of 35, the Governor of the vast Territory of Louisiana, then on his way from his capital to that of the nation, where he knew he would be received with all the distinction and consideration due his office and reputation, should take his own life." Biographer Flora Seymour, writing in 1937, thought suicide totally out of character: "Many believed that Governor Lewis, ill, dejected, despairing of justice, had died by his own hand. . . . But those who had been with the brave young captain on the long journey West felt that this could not be the solution. The Meriwether Lewis they knew did not lose his courage nor his head in times of trial."

A more recent biographer, Richard Dillon, takes Seymour's argument further, determined to clear Lewis's name of the "crime" of suicide:

> Is it likely that the cause of Lewis's death was self-murder? Not at all. If there is such a person as the anti-suicide type, it was Meriwether Lewis. By temperament, he was a fighter, not a quitter. . . . Sensitive he was; neurotic he was not. Lewis was one of the most positive personalities in American history.
>
> Not enough has been made of the factors weighing against his taking his own life. His courage; his enthusiasm; his youth (thirty-five); his plans—to return to St. Louis, after seeing his mother and setting things straight in Washington; to engage in the fur trade with his brother, Reuben, and his best friend, Will Clark. . . .
>
> In a democracy such as ours—to which Meriwether Lewis was so strongly dedicated—it is held in the courts of justice that a man is presumed innocent of a crime

until proved guilty. Meriwether Lewis has not been proven guilty of self-destruction at Grinder's Stand in the early hours of October 11, 1809. Therefore let him be found NOT GUILTY of the charge—the crime of suicide.

Yet others have stated that Lewis's death was somehow "beclouded" or "tainted by dishonor"; some, believing that Lewis was murdered, have impugned Jefferson's integrity for concluding that Lewis's death was self-inflicted: "It seems to me that Jefferson's ready acceptance of Lewis's death by suicide was a disgraceful way to treat a man," wrote physician and historian E. G. Chuinard a few years ago. David Leon Chandler, a Pulitzer Prize–winning journalist, put Jefferson in the center of a convoluted conspiracy (the title of his book is *The Jefferson Conspiracies: A President's Role in the Assassination of Meriwether Lewis*) and states, among other things, that "Thomas Jefferson's complicity is a substantial one and includes his endorsement of the suicide theory. . . . He accepted the stigma of suicide because he feared a greater scandal." Less darkly, William Clark's son, Meriwether Lewis Clark, said simply that he wished no stigma "upon the fair name I have the honor to bear."

Underlying the suicide-murder controversy run several streams of thought: it is a disgrace to die by suicide; that Lewis was too young or too successful to kill himself (neither of which, of course, protects against suicide); or that committing suicide is intrinsically a cowardly act and therefore a great and courageous man could not have done such a thing. Others have argued that Jefferson would not have appointed Lewis to command the westward expedition had he actually known of any mental instability in Lewis or his family line. This argument has been further buttressed by repeated assertions that, in any event, Jefferson could have had no way of knowing of any mental illness in Lewis's family, despite the fact that Jefferson and Lewis had lived together for two years and presumably had had many intimate discussions which neither of them committed to paper. There is, in fact, no way of knowing what confidences about family and self they shared. It is difficult, short of weaving an elaborate conspiracy net, to imagine why Jefferson would write what he did about Lewis and his father's family unless he believed it to be true. (Interestingly, there may have been instability on both sides of the family. Lewis's half brother, Dr. John Marks, his mother's son by her second marriage, at one point had to be confined because of "mental problems"; there was also a great deal of intermarriage, nearly a dozen marriages, between the Meriwether and Lewis families.)

Jefferson's conjecture that Lewis's melancholic tendencies were put on ice as long as he was actively and physically engaged but emerged later during slower, more sedentary times is perceptive, telling, and completely consistent with what is known about restless, energetic, and impetuous temperaments that have an obverse inclination to despair. Stephen Ambrose, in his excellent biography of Meriwether Lewis, *Undaunted Courage*, discusses at some length Meriwether Lewis's occasional quickness of temper: "He had, however, four times lost his temper and twice threatened to kill. His behavior was erratic and threatening to the future of the expedition. . . . He had a short temper and too often acted on it. . . . [He] could not keep his 'boisterous' passion in check."

Lewis, then, had a family and personal history of depression, a quick temper and a restless disposition, and a tendency to drink heavily and, toward the end of his life, to be financially reckless and rather unaccountable in his professional obligations. He twice attempted suicide and was placed on a close suicide watch by a fellow officer. His closest friends, William Clark and Thomas Jefferson, believed the eyewitness accounts of his last days and hours, all of which had concluded that he had killed himself.

Why, then, the convoluted theories of conspiracy, of malaria, or of syphilis, all of which have been offered as "explanations" for his death? There is little credible evidence for the "Jefferson conspiracy"; improbable speculation only for the theory of murder (much of it based on the magnification of inevitable inconsistencies in the accounts of witnesses); and next to no evidence at all for syphilis, although it is possible he had it. He may well have suffered from malaria, which was endemic along the frontier; this has been suggested by some as the explanation for his "derangement." Cerebral malaria, which occasionally results in impulsive and self-destructive acts, is very uncommon. (Of the malaria cases reported in the nineteenth century, as well as the tens of thousands detailed in World Wars I and II and the Vietnam War, fewer than 2 percent were cerebral malaria; of those that were, suicide was a rare outcome.) A medical cause for irrational behavior may be more palatable to some historians, but it is not more plausible.

Douglass Adair and Dawson Phelps of the Oregon Historical Society raise, I think, the critical question: "Apparently," they write, "most of Lewis's contemporaries who knew him well . . . were either not surprised to learn that he had killed himself, or had extremely persuasive evidence that his death was suicide. Does the murder theory reflect the unwillingness of American scholars (the frontier specialists in particular) to admit that a man as great as Lewis had shown himself to be . . . could become so spiritually desolated or mentally ill that he could kill himself?"

I think the answer is yes, that scholars and laypeople alike find it hard to hold in their minds the thought that a great man could have been deranged or that a courageous man could have killed himself. But such men do. And the same bold, restless temperament that Jefferson saw in the young Meriwether Lewis can lie uneasily just this side of a restless, deadly despair. It is to the great credit of Jefferson that he was able to understand this complexity of human nature and to Lewis's credit that he chose as his co-leader and explorer William Clark, a man of a complementary, more even disposition.

In recent years, there has been a rumbling to disinter the

remains of Meriwether Lewis. It is argued that doing so would settle the truth of his death once and for all, and perhaps it would. One reader of the *Washington Post*, for example wrote, that if it could be proved that Meriwether Lewis had been murdered, "then a blot is removed from the name of the explorer." I wrote a letter to the *Post* in response. I thought it was extraordinary that suicide should be seen as a "blot"; that there was a compelling case that Lewis had suffered from manic-depression and had killed himself; and that however Lewis had died, he had lived a life of remarkable courage, accomplishment, and vision. Suicide is not a blot on anyone's name; it is a tragedy. I believe, as do many others, that he should be allowed to keep such undisinterred peace as he might have. He has earned his rest. And, in the end, for all of us, it is his life that remains. Lewis was, as Ambrose writes, an explorer first, last, and always:

> He was a man of high energy and was at times impetuous, but this was tempered by his great self-discipline. He could drive himself to the point of exhaustion, then take an hour to write about the events of the day, and another to make his celestial observations.
>
> His talents and skills ran wider than they did deep. He knew how to do many things, from designing and building a boat to all the necessary wilderness skills. He knew a little about many of the various parts of the natural sciences. He could describe an animal, classify a plant, name the stars, manage the sextant and other instruments, dream of empire. But at none of these things was he an expert, or uniquely gifted.
>
> Where he was unique, truly gifted, and truly great was as an explorer, where all his talents were necessary. The most important was his ability as a leader of men. He was born to leadership, and reared for it, studied it in his army career, then exercised it on the expedition.

. . .

MERIWETHER LEWIS was a great man and the circumstances of his death unbearably sad. Shakespeare, in writing of the suicide of Mark Antony, said it best: "The breaking of so great a thing should make / A greater crack: the round world / Should have shook lions into civil streets, / And citizens to their dens."

IV

Building Against Death

— PREVENTION OF SUICIDE —

But suicides have a special language
Like carpenters they want to know which tools.
They never ask why build.

—ANNE SEXTON

Anne Sexton (1928–1974) received the 1967
Pulitzer Prize for *Live or Die*, a collection of
poems that included the one excerpted here. She
attempted suicide on several occasions, and eventually died in 1974 from carbon monoxide poisoning. Her sister and aunt also committed suicide.

CHAPTER 8

Modest Magical Qualities

—TREATMENT AND PREVENTION—

For melancholy, take a ram's head that never meddled with a ewe . . . boil it well, skin and wool together . . . take out the brains, and put these spices to it, cinnamon, ginger, nutmeg, cloves. . . .

It may be eaten with bread in an egg or broth.

—ROBERT BURTON

Lithium . . . is the lightest of the solid elements and it is perhaps not surprising that it should in consequence possess certain modest magical qualities.

—G. P. HARTIGAN

MARIGOLD IS "much approved against melancholy," wrote Robert Burton in 1621; so too are dandelion, ash, willow, tamarisk, roses, violets, sweet apples, wine, tobacco, syrup of poppy, featherfew, and sassafras. A ring made of the hoof of an ass's right forefoot is "not altogether to be rejected," and "St. John's wort, gathered on a Friday in the hour of Jupiter . . . mightily helps."

The treatment of melancholy and the prevention of suicide have moved on since tamarisk and featherfew, but still it is from the natural world—a light metal, the third element in the periodic table—that we have extracted lithium, our most demonstrably effective treatment against suicide. We have, as well, found other medications that stabilize mood, fight psychosis, or tamp down anxiety, agitation, and impulsivity. We have antidepressant medications that aggressively treat the depressions often responsible for suicide. We have built hospitals to provide a sanctuary against madness and self-inflicted death, and developed psychotherapies to ameliorate pain and to help the suicidal navigate through the darkest times of their lives. We know a great deal about how to prevent suicide, but not enough. And what we do know, we do not use as well or widely as we could.

The causes of suicide lie, for the most part, in an individual's predisposing temperament and genetic vulnerabilities; in severe psychiatric illness; and in acute psychological stress. Addressing only one of these causes at the expense of others is unlikely to be enough to keep suicide at bay. Misdiagnosing or ineptly treating a potentially lethal psychiatric illness, or underplaying the gravity of a suicide risk, can and often does have tragic consequences. Together, doctors, patients, and their family members can minimize the chances of suicide, but it is a difficult, subtle, and frustrating venture. Its value is obvious, but the ways of achieving it are not. Anyone who suggests that coming back from suicidal despair is a straightforward journey has never taken it.

Most who commit suicide explicitly, and often repeatedly, communicate their intentions to kill themselves to others— to their doctors, family, or friends—before doing so. Many never do: they act on impulse or cloak their plans; they give no chance to themselves or others. But for those who do make clear their desire to die, it is fortunate; it allows at least the possibility of treatment and prevention. Eli Robins and his colleagues at the Washington University School of Medicine in St. Louis concluded in their landmark study of 134 suicides:

If we had found that suicide was an impulsive, unpremeditated act without rather well defined clinical limits, then the problems of its prevention would present insurmountable difficulties using presently available clinical criteria. The high rate of communication of suicidal ideas indicates that in the majority of instances it is a premeditated act of which the person gives ample warning.

In a clinical setting, assessment of suicide risk must precede any attempt to treat psychiatric illness or prevent suicide. Asking a patient directly about suicidal thoughts or plans is an obvious and essential part of history taking. In addition to an individual's stated plans about suicide, there are other major risk factors that need to be evaluated: the presence or absence of severe anxiety, agitation, or perturbance; the pervasiveness, type, and severity of psychopathology; the extent of hopelessness; the presence or absence of a severe sleep disturbance or of mixed states; current alcohol or drug abuse; ease of access to a lethal means, especially firearms; lack of access to good medical and psychological treatment; recent severe causes of stress, such as a divorce, job loss, or death in the family; a family history of suicidal or violent behavior; social isolation, or a lack of friends and family; close proximity to a first episode of depression, mania, or schizophrenia; and recent release from a psychiatric hospital.

It is difficult but essential to obtain from a potentially suicidal patient an accurate and comprehensive history of violence and impulsivity, because, in conjunction with psychiatric illness, they can create a flash point for suicide. Many patients, especially women, are reluctant to acknowledge such behaviors; others, for whom violent feelings and relationships are an integral part of their lives, may not realize that their violent behaviors are sufficiently unusual to report them to a doctor or therapist. Patients need to be asked whether or not they have a quick or violent temper; how frequently they find themselves in the middle of tempestuous relationships or participants in repeated scenes of vitriolic verbal abuse; and whether or not they experience frequent and pronounced irritability or engage in impulsive behaviors, such as bolting from social situations or attempting to jump out of moving cars.

Treatment decisions follow from the clinical evaluation of suicide risk and psychiatric diagnosis. A clinician's first responsibility is to evaluate the risk of imminent suicide and, if necessary, to arrange for hospitalization. Such an assessment is occasionally straightforward, but often it is not. Acutely suicidal patients who are at high risk often need to be hospitalized, both as a protective measure and in order to diagnose and treat severe mental illness, and to evaluate the patient's psychological assets and social resources.

Psychiatric hospitalization is generally both frightening and reassuring to suicidal patients. It continues to carry a heavy stigma and to create personal, economic, and professional difficulties for many individuals. And as we have seen, it does not prevent all suicides. Hospitals do, however, save many lives, and they relieve not only patients, but also their family members and friends, of the terrible burden of feeling responsible for their own or another's life. Hospitalization is too often seen by both patients and their doctors as a symbolic defeat or as the treatment of last resort, rather than as an occasional necessity for a serious problem. These beliefs, which tend not to accompany decisions to hospitalize people who have other medical conditions, are pervasive and dangerous, and they stand in the way of good clinical care.

William Styron, who described his hospitalization for suicidal depression as a "way station, a purgatory," strongly regretted his doctor's reluctance to admit him to a psychiatric ward:

Many psychiatrists, who simply do not seem to be able to comprehend the nature and depth of the anguish their patients are undergoing, maintain their stubborn allegiance to pharmaceuticals in the belief that eventually the pills will kick in, the patient will respond, and the somber surroundings of the hospital will be avoided. . . . I'm convinced I should have been in the hospital weeks before. For, in fact, the hospital was my salvation, and it is something of a paradox that in this austere place with its locked and wired doors and desolate green hallways—ambulances screeching night and day ten floors below—I found the repose, the assuagement of the tempest in my brain, that I was unable to find in my quiet farmhouse.

Whether or not acutely suicidal individuals are hospitalized, they need intensive care: a greater time and emotional commitment from their clinicians; specialized and aggressive use of medications; intensified psychotherapeutic or other clinical contacts; and an increased involvement between their doctors and their family members and friends. Later, we will deal in some detail with psychotherapy and with family education and involvement. Here we delve into what is known about the effectiveness of different kinds of medication in preventing suicide.

Suicide usually requires multiple "hits"—a biological predisposition, a major psychiatric illness, and an acute life stress—but only some of these "hits" are amenable to change. There is, for example, relatively little a doctor can do to control many of the major stresses in a patient's life: they occur too randomly, and thus are difficult to predict and even more difficult to govern. But there *are* things that can be done to influence or treat the underlying biological vulnerabilities to suicide, as well as the mental illnesses closely linked to suicidal behavior.

Lithium is the most effective, most extensively studied, and best-documented antisuicide medication now available. It has been used since 1949 to stabilize the dangerous mood swings and erratic behavior associated with manic-depressive illness and, by Europeans particularly, to prevent recurrent depressions. Its effectiveness in preventing suicide is probably due to its impact on two of the most potent risk factors for suicide: its putative capacity to enhance serotonin turnover in the brain (as well as its effects on other neurotransmitters)—and thereby to decrease aggression, agitation, and impulsivity—and its power to decrease or eliminate mania and depression in most people who have manic-depressive illness.

Recently, two researchers from Harvard Medical School, Leonardo Tondo and Ross Baldessarini, and I reviewed twenty-eight published treatment studies that together included more than seventeen thousand patients with major depression or manic-depressive illness. Patients who had not been treated with lithium were nearly nine times more likely to commit or attempt suicide than those who had been treated with it. (In a separate investigation, Tondo and his colleagues found that suicidal acts rose sixteenfold in the first year after discontinuing lithium treatment.) A 1999 study from Sweden concluded that lithium treatment resulted in a 77 percent reduction in the risk of suicide. The authors, while cautioning that patients who remain on lithium for several years make up a self-selected population, noted that patients were nearly five times more likely to kill themselves when they were not taking lithium than when they were.

If lithium works so well to prevent recurrences of mania and depression, and if it has such a potent effect in decreasing suicidal behaviors, why isn't everyone who suffers from a major mood disorder taking lithium? Indeed, why isn't everyone who is suicidal taking lithium? The answers reflect the problems, as well as the promise, of psychiatric medications. First, not everyone responds well to lithium. Some who take it respond only partially or, more unusually, not at all. Others cannot take it for medical reasons, or they find the side effects intolerable. Many others, as we shall see later, are simply noncompliant;

that is, they do not take the medication as prescribed. For whatever reasons, lithium is seen by many patients as a stigmatizing treatment, or else it is seen as toxic, an attitude not helped by the attitudes and practices of many in the medical community. The difficulty was captured in a letter written to the editors of *The Lancet*: "Psychiatrists and other practitioners regard the use of lithium as arcane, difficult, and potentially dangerous for all but the specialist to administer," wrote the concerned practitioners, who also noted that there was "poor quality and reliability of lithium information from official sources" and that the plasma lithium concentrations recommended by many doctors were often far too high, reflecting clinical practice that was fifteen to twenty years out of date. These attitudes are subtly pervasive in clinical practice, especially in the United States, and are the result of many factors: lithium requires monitoring of blood levels to prevent toxicity, and side effects—such as blunting of emotions, slowed thinking, and problems in coordination—affect a number of patients.

Some of the marginalization of lithium is due to other important advances in medical research. Many new medications used for treating mood disorders—the anticonvulsant drugs (which were first used to treat epilepsy, but now are used to treat manic-depression, as well) and the newer antidepressants, for example, the selective serotonin reuptake inhibitors, such as citalopram, fluvoxamine, paroxetine, fluoxetine, and sertraline (Celexa, Luvox, Paxil, Prozac, and Zoloft, respectively)—are more easily administered than lithium by general practitioners, internists, and psychiatrists. This ease of prescription is largely to the good, although it makes it more likely that highly effective and relatively inexpensive drugs such as lithium—which, in fact, is generally *not* that difficult to prescribe or monitor properly—will be bypassed for other, better-marketed drugs. It also increases the likelihood that the more popular and easier-to-prescribe antidepressants may be given to patients who would benefit more from a mood-stabilizing drug such as lithium and who may actually get worse on antidepressants (that is, their episodes may increase in frequency and intensity, and they may experience severely agitated or mixed states). Often antidepressants and mood-stabilizing drugs need to be used together in order to obtain the best therapeutic results.

In recent years, advances in psychiatric research have made the highly profitable marketplace for mood-altering drugs far more competitive. Patients unresponsive to lithium or unwilling to take it now have good alternatives available to them. The most commercially successful of these, valproate (Depakote), an anticonvulsant, has now overtaken lithium as the most widely prescribed, and often the first prescribed, medication for bipolar disorder, or manic-depressive illness. This is a striking reversal in prescription patterns. There has also been a marked increase in the total number of prescriptions written for depression and bipolar disorder over the course of the past five years (a trend even more dramatic for the prescription of antidepressants), which reflects an increase in media and public awareness of the availability of effective medical treatment for mood disorders; impressive educational work on the part of patient advocacy groups; and highly effective physician and public marketing campaigns financed by the major pharmaceutical companies.

The ability of the anticonvulsant medications (valproate, carbamazepine, gabapentin, lamotrigine, and topiramate) to prevent suicide is unproven, however. Hypothetically, because they stabilize moods and have an impact on agitated and aggressive states, they should have an impact on suicide rates as well. In the one direct comparison of lithium and an anticonvulsant (carbamazepine, or Tegretol), however, this did not prove to be true. German doctors studied 378 hospitalized patients who suffered acute major depression (one-half suffered from bipolar manic-depression) and, at the time they were discharged from the hospital, randomly assigned them to lithium, carbamazepine, or amitriptyline (an antidepressant) treatment. Over the subsequent two and one-half years, five patients killed themselves and four made very serious suicide attempts. All the patients who killed themselves, or tried to, were in the carbamazepine or antidepressant treatment group. Despite the fact that there had been more prior, pretreatment suicide attempts in the group that received lithium, none of the suicides or suicide attempts that occurred during the treatment period were made by patients taking lithium. The authors of the study concluded that their research demonstrated that lithium had "antisuicidal effects which may have been specific, which markedly exceeded its prophylactic efficacy, and which were superior to the effects of carbamazepine and antidepressants on suicidal behavior."

The same researchers also believe that lithium appears to protect against suicide even in those patients who do not show a good mood-stabilizing response to the drug. In a recent study, patients who had attempted suicide at least once were classified as excellent, questionable, or poor responders to lithium when it was given to prevent severe depressive episodes. There was in each group, despite the variability in recurrence rates, a significant decrease in the number of suicide attempts. Bruno Müller-Oerlinghausen of the Free University of Berlin summarized his group's findings: "Discontinuing lithium or switching to other medications in apparently nonresponding patients may be considered a rational step toward optimizing medication, but it may result in the death of the patient."

It may well be that future research will show an antisuicidal effect of the anticonvulsant medications. Certainly they provide a real and important alternative to lithium for many patients. But in light of the many studies demonstrating lithium's ability to prevent suicide in high-risk patients and the utter dearth of studies documenting this for the anticonvulsants, caution is in

order. The clinical problem is complex, however. Not everyone who has depression or manic-depression is suicidal. If a
patient refuses to take lithium or does not respond to it, anticonvulsants provide an important and often more agreeable
treatment alternative. Lithium is effective in preventing suicide only if patients are willing to take it and if they respond to
it. Not everyone will take it. Not everyone will respond to it.

Ultimately, the best course of treatment for many patients
may be a combination of lithium, used as a hedge against suicide, with another mood stabilizer or with an antipsychotic,
antidepressant, or antianxiety medication. Because the cost of
lithium is far less than that of valproate, the economic factor is
a further issue, although the additional expense for the newer
antidepressant, anticonvulsant, and antipsychotic medications

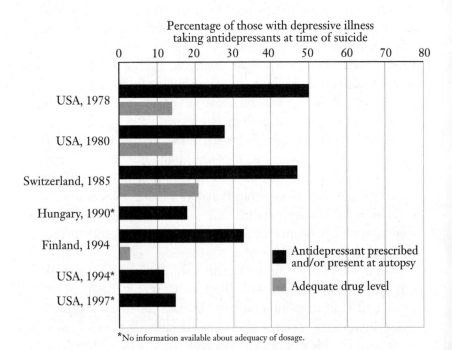

*No information available about adequacy of dosage.

Antidepressant use at time of suicide

is often cost-effective and clinically warranted due to increased compliance and greater safety and efficacy.

Antidepressant medications are not as obviously effective in lowering suicide rates as lithium is, although there are many practical problems in showing a clear-cut impact of antidepressant medications on suicide rates. (One reason for this is simple: suicidal patients are almost always excluded from clinical drug trials.) But there is persuasive evidence that the newer antidepressants, the selective serotonin reuptake inhibitors (or SSRIs), not only alleviate and prevent depression but also decrease angry, aggressive, and impulsive behaviors. These effects on such dangerous risk factors for suicide are immensely important. Some epidemiological and clinical studies have shown a decrease in the number of suicides and serious suicide attempts in patients taking antidepressants, but the extent of the decrease remains equivocal.

What is unequivocal, however, is that in every investigation of individuals who have committed suicide, researchers have demonstrated that depression has been underdiagnosed and antidepressants have been underprescribed. Even when antidepressants have been prescribed, they have been given at inadequate dosages or for too short a period of time for them to take effect. This gross undertreatment of depression is shown in the graph on the opposite page, a summary of seven American and European toxicology and autopsy investigations that calculated the percentage of depressed individuals actually taking antidepressants at the time they committed suicide. The majority of patients had not been taking antidepressants at all, and far fewer still had been taking a therapeutic amount. The undertreatment of depression is consistent with research showing that doctors in general woefully underprescribe antidepressants and lithium for patients who could benefit from them.

Several additional interpretations are possible. In the earlier studies, more individuals with depressive illnesses were taking antidepressants at the time they committed suicide than those in recent years. This may reflect the fact that the earlier antidepressants worked less well, or it may reflect the fact that, because the tricyclic antidepressants were far more toxic than the modern SSRIs, very suicidal patients had access to a more deadly means of suicide.

There have been other difficulties in demonstrating a clear effect of antidepressant medications on patterns of suicidal behavior. There is, we know, a high rate of suicide in patients with bipolar II disorder, a variant of manic-depressive illness characterized by extended periods of depression and shorter, mild episodes of mania. These patients are frequently misdiagnosed as suffering from depression only; this is in part because the mild manias are not experienced by the patients as pathological and in part because doctors are inadequately trained to make the differential diagnosis. Many clinicians are unaware that mood volatility and irritability are often signs of bipolar illness, and they do not inquire specifically enough about other sleep, mood, and behavioral symptoms that are important in making the diagnosis. Doctors also make the diagnostic error because depression is far more likely than mild mania to motivate a person to seek clinical care. This underdiagnosis of bipolar manic-depressive illness is widespread—perhaps one-third of patients are inaccurately diagnosed as depressed, rather than bipolar—and it can result in treatment that makes the illness worse over time. Antidepressants, if prescribed alone, rather than with mood stabilizers such as lithium or the anticonvulsants, can precipitate mania and, occasionally, highly agitated and potentially suicidal mixed states.

Accurate diagnosis and the appropriate treatment of psychiatrically ill children and adolescents are material problems. A 1999 survey of pediatricians and family doctors found that only 8 percent of those prescribing antidepressants for children felt they had received adequate training in treating childhood depression. Many children with early-onset manic-depression, or bipolar disorder, are mistakenly diagnosed as suffering from attention deficit disorder with hyperactivity, either because doctors do not recognize the symptoms of manic-depression in children or because they are unduly sensitive to subtle pressures from parents and teachers who feel there is less stigma attached to attention deficit disorder than there is to a major psychiatric illness. Although there are overlapping symptoms—hyperactivity, distractibility, and irritability, for instance—and the differential diagnosis can be difficult, there are many distinguishing features: bipolar children are more likely to have a family history of bipolar illness or depression, to have mood lability, euphoria, grandiosity, hypersexuality, less need for sleep, and racing thoughts, and to be suicidal. Their pre-illness social and academic histories tend to be good and their illness is often a sharp departure from their normal level of functioning. The correct diagnosis is important because the primary treatment for attention deficit disorder is stimulant medication, which may aggravate the condition of a child with bipolar disorder (a disorder that generally requires a mood stabilizer such as lithium or an anticonvulsant). The long-term effect of the combined use of antidepressants and stimulants in a child or adolescent with bipolar illness is unclear but problematic.

The role of antidepressants in actually precipitating suicidal behavior is controversial and unresolved. From a broad clinical and public health perspective, the evidence is strong that antidepressants do not increase the number of suicide attempts or actual suicide. On the contrary. But there is almost certainly a vulnerable subgroup of individuals who become agitated, restless, and virulently sleepless as a result of taking antidepressants. Although this is an uncommon reaction, it is potentially dangerous, and all patients need to be advised in advance of taking antidepressants that these side effects can occur, and if they do, they should be reported to their doctors. (The manufacturers of antidepressants generally include a warning to this effect in their product information in the *Physicians' Desk Reference:* "The possibility of a suicide attempt is inherent in depression and may persist until significant remission occurs. Close supervision of high risk patients should accompany initial drug therapy. Prescriptions . . . should be written for the smallest quantity of capsules consistent with good patient management, in order to reduce the risk of overdose." The manufacturers also include in the list of adverse effects anxiety, nervousness, insomnia, agitation, akathisia, and central nervous system stimulation.)

The newer SSRIs, although no more effective against depression than the older tricyclic antidepressants, tend to be better tolerated by patients because their side effects (occasional insomnia, agitation, nausea, or sexual problems) are less difficult to live with than those caused by the tricyclics (dry mouth, blood pressure changes, constipation, or dizziness). The SSRIs have also been used to good effect in suicidal patients who are dependent on alcohol. Their major clinical advantage, however, is that they are much less toxic and therefore less likely to cause death in deliberate overdose. Lethal drug overdoses in British women, for example, have declined by a third over the past two decades, despite an increase in the rate of nonfatal overdoses during this period. Most of this decline is attributable to the wider use of the newer, less toxic antidepressants.

There are other treatments for depression. Some existing drugs have effects on both norepinephrine and serotonin reuptake, while others exert their primary influence on serotonergic neurotransmission. Many new antidepressant medications are under development. (The Pharmaceutical Research Manufacturers of America reported that at the end of 1998 there were eighty-five psychiatric drugs in the research pipe-line: twenty-three for Alzheimer's disease, nineteen for substance abuse, eighteen for depression, fifteen for schizophrenia, and ten for other disorders.) Some of these drugs, like the existing SSRIs, are designed to affect the serotonergic pathways in the brain; others have been developed to focus not only on serotonin but a variety of other neurotransmitters; yet others target different neurochemical systems, including norepinephrine. One drug in the pipeline, for instance, decreases the level of "Substance P," a chemical that is highly concentrated in the amygdala and the hypothalamus, areas of the brain that are intricately tied up with the regulation of mood and emotion.

Additional drugs that may ultimately have an effect on suicidal behaviors are under development. Some focus on the neurotransmitter glutamate and will, it is hoped, decrease alcohol and drug cravings in individuals who are dependent on those substances. Yet other drugs, known as CRH receptor antagonists, have been developed to reduce the stress response, which, if it is severe, and if it occurs in vulnerable persons, can trigger suicide.

Omega-3 fatty acids, implicated by some (but by no means all) researchers in both depression and suicide, have been tested in recent clinical studies at Harvard. On discharge from a psychiatric hospital, patients with bipolar illness were, in addition to their regular dosages of valproate or lithium, given either omega-3 fatty acids or a placebo. After four months, 64 percent of those taking fatty acids were in remission but only 19 percent of those on placebo remained well. The results were sufficiently significant that the researchers were obliged to "break the blind" of the experimental condition, in order that those who were on the placebo could be treated with the omega-3 fatty acids. To date, although the research is very preliminary, there have been no serious adverse effects from the fatty acids given to the patients in the study. A seventeen-year epidemiological study of fish consumption in 265,000 Japanese adults—which found a 19 percent reduction in suicides in those who consumed large amounts of fish rich in omega-3 fatty acids—adds further suggestive evidence to the fatty-acid hypothesis of depression. Still, the theory remains unproven until the research findings are replicated.

St. John's wort, a mild to moderate antidepressant taken from the yellow-flowered plant *Hypericum*, is currently under study in a large clinical investigation coordinated by Duke University Medical Center. It is widely used as an antidepressant in Europe and more recently in the United States, but its usefulness in preventing suicide is unknown. Because it is not considered a drug, its purity and potency are unregulated by the Food and Drug Administration. Without doubt, it is helpful to some individuals who are depressed, but because it is usually taken without clinical supervision, there are several potential difficulties. Many people assume that St. John's wort and other herbal treatments are safe simply because they are "natural" substances (as indeed, one should add, are lithium and arsenic), but there have been reports, although rare, of rapid mood swings, mania, and suicidal thinking induced by the herb. (These adverse reactions have also been rarely observed in another unregulated treatment for depression, light therapy.) More problematically, buying over-the-counter treatments for potentially lethal medical conditions, such as severe depression, may give the illusion of treatment and thereby prevent people from seeking out more effective drugs if the depression or suicidal thoughts do not abate.

The antipsychotic medications used to treat schizophrenia and, occasionally, manic-depressive illness share some of the same problems and promise in preventing suicide that the antidepressants do. Used ineptly or without adequate clinical supervision, they can cause akathisia, an extremely uncomfortable state of agitation, muscle discomfort, and a difficulty in sitting still (often described by patients as feeling as if they are "jumping out of their skin"). But used carefully, in moderate doses, the antipsychotic medications—especially the more recently developed ones that have fewer side effects, such as clozapine, risperidone, and olanzapine (Clozaril, Risperdal, and Zyprexa, respectively)—may reduce the rate of suicide in psychotically ill patients.

Electroconvulsive therapy (ECT), sometimes known as "shock therapy," has been used for decades to treat severely suicidal patients. Although there is little evidence of a long-term effect on suicide, profound and often rapidly induced short-term improvements in suicidal mood are common in deeply depressed patients. Keeping patients alive through an acute suicidal crisis is the most important clinical priority; ECT not only can save lives, but it buys time to work out the best long-term treatment.

Although ECT is the most effective and rapid treatment for severe depression, it remains controversial and, particularly in the United States, underutilized. This is due in part to the highly negative media coverage of ECT (some of which was clearly justified several decades ago, when abuses of shock treatments were rampant) and in larger part to the availability and ease of use of alternative treatments for depression. For many doctors, ECT remains the treatment of last resort, even with highly suicidal patients. This has led Jonathan Himmelhoch, a psychiatrist at the University of Pittsburgh, to write, "The narcissistic ponderings of psychiatrists whose political agenda supersedes their clinical experience must not be allowed to keep patients who are suffering the most severe form of pain from relief." This is some truth in this remark, although the controversy over ECT is unlikely to disappear. A new, noninvasive treatment technology, transcranial magnetic stimulation, which involves placing a small, powerful electromagnetic coil on the scalp and sending repetitive pulses of high-intensity current to the brain, is now being tested in depressed patients. Transcranial magnetic stimulation has antidepressant capabilities, but clinical efficacy and safety studies are still in the very early stages. Unlike ECT, it does not require anesthesia and does not involve inducing a seizure;

so far at least, memory impairment has not been reported as a significant adverse effect. It may or may not have an effect on suicidal thinking and behavior.

Medications and other medical treatments are effective—often remarkably so—in preventing or diminishing the pain and suffering of the major psychiatric illnesses most closely linked to suicide. Less clearly, except in the case of lithium and probably the antidepressants and the newer antipsychotics, they lessen the chances that a suicidal individual will kill him- or herself. Medications, hospitalization, and ECT save many but by no means all lives. Psychotherapy or a strong therapeutic relationship with a doctor can make all the difference in whether some patients ultimately live or die. The very success of psychopharmacology in treating serious mental illness has had the unfortunate effect of minimizing the importance of psychotherapy in healing patients and keeping them alive. Most managed health care companies, for example, cover the costs for medication visits, although often only very brief ones, but do not provide any meaningful coverage for psychotherapy. Despite the extensive and elegant series of studies conducted by Myrna Weissman and Gerald Klerman at Yale University, which showed that the combination of psychotherapy and antidepressants was more effective in treating depression than either treatment alone, and despite convincing recent work from many groups in the United States and Britain demonstrating better outcomes in bipolar and schizophrenic patients who receive a combination of medications and psychotherapy rather than drugs only, there remains a pervasive belief in many psychiatric and research quarters that medication by itself is sufficient to deal with serious mental illness.

Some of the reluctance to aggressively encourage psychotherapy in patients who suffer from depression, manic-depression, severe personality disorders, or schizophrenia is understandable. Psychotherapy is expensive, difficult, and time-consuming to do and to study, and there are deep conflicts within the psychotherapeutic community about which kinds of therapy work best for which kinds of patients and illnesses; what the nature of clinical training should be; and for how long psychotherapy should last. Territorial and economic disputes between psychiatrists and clinical psychologists are legendary and often riven with mistrust and resentment. It has been too easy to draw an arbitrary distinction between psychological and biological factors in mental illness, and nowhere has this divisiveness been more destructive than in the conceptualization of the causes and treatments for suicidal behavior.

The complexity of the suicidal mind and brain demands for its care a complexity of clinical thought and treatment. Psychotherapy alone, if used without addressing or treating the underlying psychopathology or biological vulnerabilities, is generally unlikely to prevent profoundly suicidal individuals from killing themselves. The ability to diagnose psychopathology accurately and to refer patients to colleagues for medication when necessary is a nonnegotiable fundamental of good clinical practice. Not to do this is malpractice.

The polarization of opinions about the correct treatment of suicidal patients was highlighted by a 1994 court ruling against Thomas Szasz, an influential psychiatrist and vehement critic of the concept of mental illness, as well as an adamant opponent of the use of "coercive" efforts to keep an individual from committing suicide. Szasz's philosophical opposition to "coercive" prevention of suicide is based, in part, on his strongly held belief that there is no connection between suicide and mental illness, a belief supported neither by the clinical and scientific literature nor, indeed, by any data presented by Szasz himself. His views, which had a strong professional and popular following in the 1960s and 1970s and are still widely cited, can best be conveyed by his own words:

Why do we now give psychiatrists special privileges to intervene vis-à-vis suicidal persons? Because, as I have noted, in the psychiatric view, the person who threatens or commits suicide is irrational or mentally ill, allowing the psychiatrist to play doctor and thereby, like other doctors, to save lives. However, there is neither philosophical or empirical support for viewing suicide as different, in principle, from other acts such as getting married or divorced, working on the Sabbath, eating shrimp, or smoking tobacco. These and countless other things people do are the result of personal decisions. . . . Psychiatrist and patient are both lost in the existential-legal labyrinth generated by treating suicide as if it constituted a psychiatric problem, indeed a psychiatric emergency. If we refuse, however, to play a part in the drama of coercive suicide prevention, then we shall be sorely tempted to conclude that the psychiatrist and his suicidal patient richly deserve one another and the torment each is so ready and eager to inflict on the other.

For those who disagree with Szasz, and I obviously am one (and am grateful that my psychiatrist was another), and believe that committing suicide is not altogether the same thing as eating shrimp or working on the Sabbath, it was of no little interest to read that in 1994 Szasz agreed to pay $650,000 to the widow of one of his patients, a physician who had suffered from manic-depressive illness and killed himself. The legal complaint filed against Szasz charged that he instructed and advised his patient to stop taking lithium in June 1990; in December of the same year, the doctor, after beating himself in the head with a hammer and inflicting lacerations to his neck, hanged himself with battery cables. The complaint further charged that Szasz had failed to render "psychiatric medical care and treatment in conformity with the customary and accepted sound standards of medical care," "failed to properly diagnose and treat," "failed to provide proper therapy to treat manic depression," and "failed to keep adequate and proper medical records." Although Szasz's attorney maintained that the patient had stopped taking lithium of his own accord and Szasz himself did not concede he had committed malpractice, the court ruled that the widow was to receive $650,000 in settlement. Szasz, despite his distaste for the psychiatric establishment, was a member of the American Psychiatric Association, and it was the organization's malpractice insurance carrier that ended up paying the settlement.

Philosophical views and assumptions about the causation of suicide, while strongly held and necessarily and importantly debated, are not sufficient to disregard the massive and credible medical, psychological, and scientific research literature about suicide. Ignoring the biological and psychopathological causes and treatments of suicidal behavior is clinically and ethically indefensible. But so too is disregarding the psychological and social roots of suicide and ignoring potentially useful psychological and social treatments. The mental pain of the suicidal condition is engulfing and unbearable. The therapist, as Ned Cassem at Harvard points out, must have the "capacity to hear out carefully and to tolerate the feelings of despair, depression, anguish, rage, loneliness, emptiness, and meaninglessness articulated by the suicidal person. The patient needs to know that the therapist takes him seriously and understands." Directness on the part of the clinician is important, as is clear communication about treatment, about expectations about the time course and problems of recovery, and about ways to contact the therapist in case of emergency.

Morag Coate, a British writer who suffered from severe, recurrent psychosis, described the doctor's role in saving her life:

> Because the doctors cared, and because one of them still believed in me when I believed in nothing, I have survived to tell the tale. It is not only the doctors who perform hazardous operations or give life-saving drugs in obvious emergencies who hold the scales at times

between life and death. To sit quietly in a consulting room and talk to someone would not appear to the general public as a heroic or dramatic thing to do. In medicine there are many different ways of saving lives. This is one of them.

Most of the studies of psychotherapy, or of psychotherapy combined with medication, have focused on the treatment of psychiatric illness; few have dealt specifically with measuring changes in suicidal thinking or behavior. Marsha Linehan, a psychologist at the University of Washington, recently reviewed twenty controlled clinical trials utilizing different forms of psychotherapy with patients at high risk of suicide. In most studies, the patients were selected on the basis of having made at least one suicide attempt. The psychotherapeutic interventions that seemed to be most effective, particularly in patients with borderline personality disorder, sharply focus on changing specific suicidal behaviors and thoughts. These therapies, especially those that are based on identifying and modifying maladaptive behaviors and thinking, appear to work reasonably well in decreasing deliberate self-harm. Keith Hawton at the University of Oxford, in a comprehensive review that included studies of both psychotherapy and medication effects, also found promising results in altering suicidal behaviors. Specific emphasis in several investigations was placed on teaching patients to more effectively handle situations of interpersonal conflict, which, for many of them, had preceded their suicide attempts. It remains unclear whether these therapies prevent actual suicide or suicide attempts only.

Psychotherapy can be extremely helpful not only in sustaining patients through times of terrible psychological suffering and encouraging them to learn better ways of handling suicidal impulses but also in helping them to deal with the critical and gnarly problem of treatment noncompliance. An unwillingness to take medications as prescribed or to keep psychotherapy or medical appointments is a pervasive and potentially life-threatening problem.

Many patients never fill even their initial prescriptions, either because they do not want to take medication or because they cannot afford it; many more stop taking their medication after a few days, weeks, or months of treatment because they experience unpleasant or disabling side effects, feel well and see no point in continuing in treatment, find their dosage schedules too confusing, or simply do not believe they have a psychiatric illness. Perhaps 20 percent of all medical patients on long-term maintenance medications take "holidays" (that is, they stop their medications for a period of time); this can be catastrophic, especially with drugs such as lithium that clear from the body very rapidly.

Compliance is less than ideal in most patients who have any kind of chronic illness. (By way of comparison, in medical conditions such as epilepsy, chronic lung diseases, hypertension, and glaucoma, overall compliance rates range between 50 and 75 percent.) For patients taking antidepressants, the compliance rate is between 65 and 80 percent; for antipsychotic medications, about 55 percent; and for lithium, about 60 percent. (The one study that directly compared one-year compliance rates with lithium and valproate, the anticonvulsant, found compliance rates of 59 percent and 48 percent, respectively.) Compliance rates are even lower in patients who have attempted suicide and who have been given follow-up appointments by emergency room staff or by nurses, doctors, or social workers on the inpatient wards of psychiatric hospitals.

Psychotherapy increases medication compliance in many patients with psychiatric illnesses, and some, but not all, of the programs designed to facilitate follow-up treatment—programs that actively involve and educate patients and their families, as well as emergency room doctors and nurses, about the gravity of suicide attempts and the need for ongoing treatment; programs that facilitate follow-up care through home visits or keeping in touch through letters or telephone calls—have increased the likelihood that adolescents and adults at risk of future suicidal behavior will enter—and stay—in treatment.

Individuals who are at risk of killing themselves because they have in the past attempted suicide or been severely suicidal, who have psychiatric illnesses that are closely linked to suicide, or who have a strong family history of suicide can do several things to make suicide less likely. Being well informed about mental illness, actively involved in their own clinical care, and very assertive about the quality of medical and psychological treatment they receive is a good start. Patients and their family members can benefit by actively seeking out books, lectures, and support groups that provide information about suicide prevention, depressive and psychotic illnesses, and alcoholism and drug abuse. They should question their clinicians about their diagnosis, treatment, and prognosis and, if concerned about a lack of collaborative effort or progress in their clinical condition, seek a second opinion.

Those who are on medications should request, when possible, written information about the drugs, their potential side effects, and which of the side effects need to be reported to the doctor immediately. Certain medication side effects, or flare-ups of symptoms in the underlying psychiatric illness, are of particular concern if someone is suicidal, and these symptoms and side effects—agitation, severe anxiety, marked sleeplessness, restlessness, delusions, feelings of violence, or impulsivity—should be openly and quickly communicated to the clinician. Several recent clinical studies have shown that teaching patients to recognize early symptoms of their illnesses and drawing up written plans that specify emergency steps to follow in case of relapse are helpful in avoiding the kinds of escalation of illness that can lead to hospitalization, loss of jobs and close relationships, or suicide.

If someone is acutely or potentially suicidal, guns, razor blades, alcohol, knives, old bottles of medications, and poisons should be removed from the home. Medications that can be used to commit suicide should be prescribed in limited quantities or closely monitored, and alcohol use, which can worsen sleep, impair judgment, provoke mixed or agitated states, and undermine the effectiveness of psychiatric medications, should be discouraged.

The recovery from severe depression or psychosis is a deceptively difficult and dangerous time. This has become especially true in recent years because the length of psychiatric hospitalizations has gone from years or months to only days. Patients leave the relative safety of a hospital, often still very ill, and return to their disruptive lives and chaotic moods.

More than forty years ago, Sylvia Plath wrote in her journal, "And, when our lives crack, and the loveliest mirror cracks, is it not right to rest, to step aside and heal?," but few now have the time or financial resources to heal as they should. Medications take a painfully long time to take hold, and the recovery period is jagged, discouraging, and never easy. A setback after finally feeling better again can be devastating, if not lethal. The frustration and rockiness of this period can be predicted, and the clinician's doing so can take away some of the sting.

Almost inevitably, family members and friends are drawn into the painful world of possible suicide. They, too, can be most helped, and helpful, by being educated about the clinical situation; learning about the illness and its treatments; inquiring about reasonable expectations for recovery and the likely time course involved; and seeking out information and help from patient support and advocacy groups. If a family member or friend is acutely suicidal, it may be necessary to take away their credit cards, car keys, and checkbooks and to be supportive but firm in getting them to an emergency room or walk-in clinic. If the person is violent, it may be necessary to call the police. These are difficult things to do but often essential.

The National Depressive and Manic-Depressive Association,

a national patient-run advocacy and support group based in Chicago, makes the following specific recommendations to family members and friends who believe someone they know is in danger of committing suicide:

- Take your friend or family member seriously.
- Stay calm, but don't underreact.
- Involve other people. Don't try to handle the crisis alone or jeopardize your own health or safety. Call 911 if necessary.
- Contact the person's psychiatrist, therapist, crisis intervention team, or others who are trained to help.
- Express concern. Give concrete examples of what leads you to believe your friend [or family member] is close to suicide.
- Listen attentively. Maintain eye contact. Use body language such as moving close to the person or holding his or her hand, if it is appropriate.
- Ask direct questions. Find out if your friend [or family member] has a specific plan for suicide. Determine, if you can, what method of suicide he or she is thinking about.
- Acknowledge the person's feelings. Be empathetic, not judgmental. Do not relieve the person of responsibility for his or her actions.
- Reassure. Stress that suicide is a permanent solution to temporary problems. Provide hope. Remind your friend or family member that there is help and things will get better.
- Don't promise confidentiality. You may need to speak to your loved one's doctor in order to protect the person. Don't make promises that would endanger your loved one's life.
- If possible, don't leave the person alone until you are sure they are in the hands of competent professionals.

There are several excellent advocacy and research organizations, many of which have patient and family support groups and all of which are actively involved in issues having to do with suicide prevention and mental illness. (Further information about these groups is given in the Appendix.)

Often it is helpful, when a potentially suicidal person is improved or well, to have a contingency planning meeting that involves the doctor or therapist, family members, and friends. Not only is the individual who is at risk less likely to be guarded or confused, he or she is better able to express clear and highly specific wishes for treatment: who is to be contacted and how, what others can do that is helpful, what others may do that is not helpful. Patients who decide, when rational, that if they again become suicidal they wish to be hospitalized or receive antipsychotic medications or undergo electroconvulsive therapy, but who also know that they are unlikely, when ill, to consent to this, may in some areas of the country draw up "Odysseus" arrangements. Based on the mythic character's request to be strapped to the mast of his ship so that he might avoid the inevitable call of the Sirens, Odysseus agreements (or advanced instruction directives) allow patients to agree to certain treatments in advance.

Parents, if there is a history of mental illness or suicide in the family, can help their children who may be at risk. By knowing their family's psychiatric histories, being educated about the symptoms and available treatments for mental illness, and discussing these issues openly and in a matter-of-fact way with their children, parents make it more likely that the children will seek help if they become depressed or start using alcohol or drugs. College-age children are at particular risk for mental illness and suicide because first episodes of depressive illnesses or schizophrenia are most likely to occur at this time; they are away from home for the first time and subject to new stresses; they may use alcohol or drugs more heavily; or they may radically alter their sleep pattern, which can, in turn, precipitate a psychotic episode.

I am often amazed at how many parents who will check into the social and athletic facilities of a college, visit the libraries and residence halls, and request the success rates of the college in getting its graduates into law school, medical school, or doctoral programs do not inquire into the quality and accessibility of its student health facilities. Counseling and psychiatric services vary enormously in quality from campus to campus, and it can be helpful to make inquiries about how well the student health center deals with students who have mental illness. It is also a good idea to obtain from the psychiatry department of the nearest teaching hospital or medical school a list of clinicians who are specialized and competent in the treatment of psychiatric disorders. Mental health advocacy groups such as the National Alliance for the Mentally Ill and the National Depressive and Manic-Depressive Association also can be helpful in providing information about local clinicians and support groups. The list will hopefully never be used, but getting it in advance makes sense. The same parents who have ensured that their children are educated about AIDS, sexually transmitted diseases, and drug abuse often do not discuss the symptoms of depression, an illness that is common, potentially lethal, and highly treatable. Yet only accidents are more likely than suicide to cause death in this vulnerable age group.

Fortunately, students are beginning to take it upon themselves to educate their fellow students about mental illness. (University and college administrations are now somewhat more aware of the prevalence of mental illness in their undergraduates and graduate students and increasingly shaken into action by the too-frequent suicides of young people. But they are not nearly aware or active enough.) I have had the pleasure and privilege of meeting with hundreds of students across the country, many of whom have struggled for years against severe depression, manic-depressive illness, or alcoholism. A disturbing number have nearly died from their suicide attempts. Rarely do their parents or professors have any idea of the extent of their suffering or what it takes for them simply to show up for class, take their examinations, or write their papers.

I recently met with a group of students at Harvard University who had established a mental illness awareness program for students on campus. They sponsor lectures, work with a professor from the psychiatry department who acts as their adviser, maintain a Web site, and run a support group for students who suffer from mental illness. The founder of the group, Allison Kent, is a gutsy, lively, and warm young woman who has turned her own pain from manic-depression into a great source of hope and support for others. She has described her own experience as a student:

> I have a mental disorder. When I got sick my freshman year, I remember flipping through *The Unofficial Guide to Life at Harvard* and other publications, frantically looking for a peer group addressing mental illnesses. I had thought Harvard had a group for just about everything. I mean there couldn't be a Free Thought Society, a Texas Club, and an Anime Society and not one addressing an issue as basic as mental health. But I was wrong. The only thing I found was that the stigma that mental illnesses have in society was just as prevalent and pervasive here at Harvard. . . .
>
> Take a look around at your fellow students some day. Realize that I am not unusual. We are often hidden, the mentally ill, but we are hidden both in homeless shelters and at Harvard. Help reduce our burden by educating yourself and your friends about the pervasiveness of mental illness and learn about how it can be successfully treated. As we acknowledge our own vulnerability and accept vulnerabilities in others, we make the world easier to live in for all of us, not just the mentally ill. No one should need to cry herself to sleep alone.

CHAPTER 9

As a Society

— THE PUBLIC HEALTH —

As a society, we do not like to talk about suicide.

—DAVID SATCHER, M.D., PH.D.,
Surgeon General of the United States

MORE THAN three thousand people turned out for the funeral of John Wilson in May 1993, and thousands more lined the streets of Washington to watch as his coffin passed. Wilson's death stunned the nation's capital, where he had served with impatient intelligence as chairman of the D.C. Council. Those of us who live in Washington and who were hopeful that he would some day be elected mayor were horrified to hear that the blunt, charismatic Wilson, only forty-nine years old, had hanged himself. Rumors of mercurial outbursts and erratic behavior had circulated for months, but his suicide was a shock. It forced an uncharacteristically reflective pause in the city's rushing ways and, within hours, provoked a rash of questions: How could so admired and well loved a man—elegant, vivacious, and scathingly witty—do such an irremediable thing? Did he know, or was he just past caring, that his suicide would be devastating to those whose hopes and lives he represented? Would his suicide have an imitative, cascading effect, especially on other African-American men in the city? Had he been in treatment? Was he taking medication? If so, what kind? Most of all, could society—or the medical system—have prevented Wilson's suicide?

John Wilson was no stranger to depression. The illness ran in his family, and he had, on at least four earlier occasions, tried to kill himself—he had slashed his wrists, played Russian roulette, taken an overdose of his antidepressant medications, and attempted to hang himself. During the course of his last illness, his psychiatrist, family, and close friends had pleaded with him to check into a hospital, but he had refused. Perhaps he thought there was nothing that could help him; but he also hoped to be mayor some day and believed, at a visceral level, that hospitalization would be political suicide. Probably he was right, but possibly not. In any event, he killed himself before the city could show its subtler colors.

Accounts of Wilson's last few weeks reveal a man captured by private despair and slowly unraveling in public. Peter Perl, in the *Washington Post*, describes his final days:

What was constant, his friends say, was an unrelieved grayness seeping into him, taking over. "What finally closed in on John . . . was bigger than just the question of running for mayor" or pursuing other career options. "He was more depressed, and depressed more consecutively. . . . He became darker and less shakable from the grip of depression."

Only once did Wilson talk in public about the pain of his depression. On May 7 [less than two weeks before he killed himself] he scrapped a prepared text on children and violence, and instead began revealing his own illness to a group of psychiatrists and other professionals at a meeting of the D.C. Mental Health Association. "We can talk about me being a politician, but we can also talk about me as a person who deals with depression, a very painful, very difficult disease . . . [that] leads to a great feeling of being lost, of a hole in your body," he said. He told them the disease was particularly deadly in the black community, where people played "Russian roulette" with their lives, and said, "I believe that more people are dying of depression than are dying of AIDS, heart trouble, high blood pressure, anything else, simply because I believe depression brings on all of those diseases." The audience was stunned, but according to association director Anita Sheldon, none of the people who came up to Wilson afterward talked to him about his illness.

Wilson became increasingly strange and morose in public appearances, but most people attributed his behavior to his customary moodiness. In his final taping of a TV show he hosted on D.C. cable, Wilson was alternately laughing, stuttering and rambling . . . he concluded the monthly show by saying, "We'll be back next week, I guess."

At a May 12 hearing on Capitol Hill on the D.C. budget, he discarded his prepared speech—"the people who wrote this would die if I didn't read it, so they are going to die"—and proceeded to ramble extemporaneously before the House District of Columbia appropriations committee: "Mr. Chairman, I am at the end of a political career, I am arriving at the end of a political career and I have served this government, I think, well for 18 years. . . . So, Mr. Chairman, I come to you today as a tired, weary old man, who is losing his hair, who is becoming extremely, extremely frightened to death of the District of Columbia's financial situation. . . . I am frightened. I don't know what to do anymore."

The day before he killed himself, Wilson presided over a crowded city hearing; he was intermittently lucid and volatile. At one point, in front of television cameras and a room full of people, he exploded with rage and stalked out of the hearing room. Later he returned to the meetings but was rambling and incoherent. Despite this, at least one close friend remarked that he had looked upbeat and jovial, "like he didn't have a care in the world." The next day, when he did not show up for work, his chauffeur and his wife drove to Wilson's house, where they found him hanging dead in the basement.

A superb politician and a prominent civil rights leader, the ambitious and wildly successful son of a porter for the Baltimore & Ohio Railroad was dead by his own hand. He was dead from depression, dead from his concerns about how the public would respond if they knew of his mental illness or if they knew that he had been hospitalized for it. Dead, too, because the illness he had made it difficult for others to know how to reach out to him: no one knew how to deal with a public figure who was unstrung and unpredictable. Dead because psychiatric commitment laws protect civil liberties but not necessarily lives. And dead because we as a society fail to deal in a tolerant or informed way with serious mental illnesses, addictions, or suicide.

What could society have done to have made it acceptable to sign into a hospital, and what could it have done to make it unnecessary and unimaginable to throw a rope over a pipe?

DOCTORS, WHO ought to be in the best position to help the public, are not distinguished by their own ability to help one another or themselves. They are, to start with, twice as likely to kill themselves as other people are. Psychiatrists and anesthesiologists are especially vulnerable, and women physicians even more so; in fact, women doctors are three to five times more likely than the general public to kill themselves. (Women psychologists and chemists, but not teachers, have similarly elevated suicide rates. Men in these professions do not. It may be that there is a selection factor—high energy and volatility, with an associated mood disorder—for women who go into, and succeed in, highly competitive and male-dominated fields. Women also probably experience greater levels of stress due to the demands of bringing up children, the prejudice of colleagues and patients, and loyalties torn between personal and career lives. Those in medicine and science also have a familiarity with, and access to, highly lethal methods of suicide.)

Doctors, more often than not, are left alone to struggle with their suffering. Many find it hard to ask for help or, indeed, to acknowledge needing it: they are trained to be independent, to be accountable for decisions that cost or save lives, and to assume an undue portion of the miseries of others. They function within a closed system that too often discourages seeking treatment and has, as well, the power to deny or rescind medical licenses and hospital privileges and to affect the flow of patient referrals. Highly addictive and lethal drugs are readily available, stress and depression are common, and sleep deprivation—a source of fatigue and bad judgment, as well as a potential precipitant of mental illness—is pervasive. Self-medication with alcohol, drugs, or mood-altering medications can be, and often is, disastrous.

Doctors must recognize and take care of their own problems and those of their colleagues, in addition to those of the patients they treat. They must attend to deeply ingrained attitudes and prejudices about mental illness and suicide as well. The compassion and scientific knowledge they bring to the care of other medical illnesses are not always a part of treating the mentally ill. Doctors confronted with suicide or suicidal behavior often find it incomprehensible or threatening. Yale surgeon Sherwin Nuland, for example, observes that for the family members or friends of someone who has killed himself, "things seem inexplicable. . . . But for the uninvolved medical personnel who first view the corpse, there is another factor to consider, which hinders compassion. Something about acute self-destruction is so puzzling to the vibrant mind of a man or a woman whose life is devoted to fighting disease that it tends to diminish or even obliterate empathy. Medical bystanders, whether bewildered and frustrated by such an act, or angered by its futility, seem not to be much grieved at the corpse of a suicide. It has been my experience to see exceptions, but they are few. There may be emotional shock, even pity, but rarely the distress that comes with an unchosen death."

Yet nearly a third of those who kill themselves visit a physician in the week before they die, and more than a half do so in the month prior to committing suicide. Most do not say they are suicidal, and most are not asked. Even for mental health professionals, as we have seen, recognizing and appropriately treating a suicidal patient are not always easy things to do. Some doctors remain skeptical that general medical practitioners can or should be put in the position of screening for or treating suicidal patients; others persevere in the erroneous believe that if they ask their patients about suicide, they will somehow encourage the act. Accumulating evidence suggests, however, that educating doctors about recognizing and treating depressive illness may have an impact on the suicide rate.

In the early 1980s, the Swedish Committee for the Prevention and Treatment of Depression introduced an educational program for all general practitioners on the Swedish island of Gotland. The doctors attended comprehensive lectures on the causes, classification, and treatment of depressive illnesses; they also learned about more specific areas of clinical concern, such as the diagnosis and treatment of children, adolescents, and the elderly. Follow-up studies showed that the doctors who had participated in the intensive educational program were better able to identify patients with depression and were more accurate in the treatments they prescribed. The overall suicide rate on the island decreased more than did the rate for Sweden as a whole; specifically, the proportion of suicides due to depressive illness decreased. Although the methods used to determine changes in the suicide rate have been debated by some researchers, as has the durability of the change, the results have been impressive to many public health physicians. They have been encouraged by the potential of an educational program to make an impact on a problem that has remained more resistant to change than virtually any other major cause of death.

Doctors who are in frequent and direct contact with very suicidal patients are in a more obvious position to prevent suicides than general practitioners are. Medical staff in emergency rooms, for example, treat patients who have attempted suicide and therefore are at high risk for eventually killing themselves. The American Foundation for Suicide Prevention has developed a poster to be placed in emergency rooms across the United States that highlights, for both nonspecialists and psychiatrists, the major clinical predictors of suicide, as well as minimal steps that should be taken by clinicians to decrease the chance of its occurring. Reaching out to those doctors and patients, it is hoped, will save at least some, if not many, lives.

Widespread screening of patients in more general medical practices, however, has not been shown to be particularly effective; neither the Centers for Disease Control and Prevention in the United States nor the Canadian Task Force set up to study the feasibility of such a screening process recommends it. In the future, though, it may well be that automated interviews conducted with a computer, which do not place a heavy burden on the limited time of general practitioners and which, research indicates, elicit more accurate reports of suicidal ideation and alcohol consumption than those obtained by clinicians, will be used routinely.

Identifying and treating people at high risk for suicide involves not only doctors, of course, but many other individuals, organizations, and intervention strategies as well. National Depression Screening Day, which began as a pilot program at a local hospital in Massachusetts, has, since 1991, reached out to a more self-selected group of individuals from the public. In October of each year, in thousands of clinics, hospitals, libraries, businesses, and shopping malls across America, people fill out a brief depression checklist. If they request a referral for treatment, or if their depression score indicates they should be more thoroughly evaluated by a clinician, they are. (Twenty percent of those screened are severely depressed,

TODAY'S SUICIDE ATTEMPTER COULD BE TOMORROW'S SUICIDE

ATTEMPTERS AT GREATEST RISK FOR SUICIDE . . .

Suicidal History	Still thinking of suicide
	Have made a prior suicide attempt
Mental State	Depressed, manic, hypomanic, severely anxious, or have a mixture of these states
	Substance abuse alone, or in association with a mood disorder
	Irritable, agitated, threatening violence to others, delusional, or hallucinating
Demographics	Male
	Living alone

DO NOT DISCHARGE SUCH A PATIENT WITHOUT A PSYCHIATRIC EVALUATION

LOOK FOR SIGNS OF CLINICAL DEPRESSION

Depressed mood most of the time
Loss of interest or pleasure in usual activities
Weight loss or gain
Can't sleep or sleeps too much
Restless or slowed-down
Fatigue, loss of energy
Feels worthless or guilty
Low self-esteem, disappointed with self
Feels hopeless about future
Can't concentrate, indecisive
Recurring thoughts of death
Irritable, upset by little things

LOOK FOR SIGNS OF MANIA OR HYPOMANIA COMBINED WITH DEPRESSION

Elated, expansive or irritable mood
Inflated self-esteem, grandiosity
Decreased need for sleep
More talkative than usual, pressured speech
Racing thoughts
Abrupt topic changes when talking
Distractible
Excessive participation in multiple activities
Agitated or restless
Hypersexual, spends foolishly, uninhibited remarks

BEFORE DISCHARGING A PATIENT, CHECK THAT . . .

- **Firearms** and lethal **medications** have been secured or removed
- A **supportive person** is available
- A **follow-up appointment** with a mental health professional has been scheduled
- The patient has the **name and number** of a clinician who can be called in an emergency

Emergency-room poster
(Adapted from American Foundation for Suicide Prevention)

but of those only one in ten is in treatment.) More than 400,000 people, many of them at significant risk for suicide, have participated in the screening program since it began. When a similar depression symptom checklist was published recently in nationally syndicated *Parade* magazine, along with a telephone contact number, more than 100,000 telephone calls were received within two weeks. Only a small minority of those who called were in treatment.

In the future, there will almost certainly be biological tests to assess suicidal risk. These tests—whether for specific genetic markers, measures of serotonergic functioning, or neuroimaging studies designed to detect neurochemical and anatomical changes associated with an increased risk of suicide—will at best predict only partially. All are likely to be fraught with clinical and ethical problems. There will inevitably be ambiguities and inaccuracies in interpreting test results and uncertainty about their specificity and predictiveness. There also will be psychological consequences for the individuals who are tested, as well as for their families (and perhaps employment and insurance repercussions, as well), and there are bound to be issues surrounding the cost of and fair access to the tests. If and when these biological tests become available, however, and if they add to our ability to predict suicide or ascertain those at high risk, they will be a tremendous advance on what we now can do.

For the moment, we know that some groups of individuals are much more likely to kill themselves than others: those who have previously made serious attempts; those who suffer from depression, manic-depression, alcoholism, schizophrenia, or personality disorders; patients who have recently been released from psychiatric hospitals; young men in jails or prisons, especially those who are mentally ill, isolated, or living in overcrowded spaces; police officers; gamblers; the unemployed; homosexual and bisexual men (who have a higher risk for suicide attempts but not as clearly as for suicide); Native Americans; Alaskan adolescents; and, increasingly, young

African-American males. Worldwide, young women in China and adolescent boys in Micronesia are among those at particularly high risk for suicide.

Schools, communities, and national governments have tried, in very different ways, to deal with the problem of suicide prevention in these high-risk groups, as well as in more general populations. Results have been mixed. Most school-based suicide awareness programs, though clearly well intentioned, have not been effective and, in some instances, have been inaccurate, misleading, and even damaging. Some investigators report an improvement in children's knowledge and beliefs about suicide and others cite a decrease in suicidal behavior. Studies commissioned by the governments of Australia, Canada, and the United States have, however, questioned the utility of currently used programs designed to increase awareness about suicide and its prevention. The Australian review, for example, concluded that the data "do not support the promotion of curriculum based suicide prevention programs, and certainly do not support the mandating of such programs in our secondary schools." Canadians, likewise, found "insufficient evidence to support curriculum-based suicide prevention programs for adolescents," and a comprehensive American survey of youth suicide prevention programs found "no justification" to mandate such programs.

Why these discouraging findings? Is the problem with existing programs, or is it inherent in most educational efforts for this age group? Identifiable problems with existing programs and examples of success suggest an unrealized potential for school-based intervention.

An extensive and withering analysis of school-based programs, published a few years ago in *The American Psychologist*, focused on several specific criticisms:

Many curriculum-based programs are not clearly founded on current empirical knowledge of the risk factors of adolescent suicide. By deemphasizing or denying the fact that most adolescents who commit suicide are mentally ill, these programs misrepresent the facts. In their attempt to destigmatize suicide in this way they may be, in fact, normalizing the behavior and reducing potentially protective taboos. . . . The incidence of adolescent suicide is sometimes exaggerated in suicide prevention programs because one of the programs' goals is to increase awareness and concern about the problem. . . . The danger of exaggeration is that students may perceive suicide as a more common, and therefore more acceptable act. . . . Magnifying the incidence of the problem is one indication that the developers of curriculum-based programs have not heeded the substantial literature on the imitation or contagion effect in adolescent suicide. Another is the common use of print or visual media to present case histories of adolescents who have attempted or committed suicide. The purpose is to teach students how to identify friends who may be at risk for suicidal behavior. However, the method may have a paradoxical effect in that students may closely identify with the problems portrayed by the case examples and may come to see suicide as the logical solution to their own problems. . . . Finally, at the most practical level, suicide prevention programs may never reach their target population, adolescents most at risk for suicide. Incarcerated and runaway youths, as well as dropouts, have extremely high rates of suicide.

Other researchers and clinicians have criticized school-based programs for the diffuseness of the audience they aim to reach (all students, rather than those at highest risk), as well as the inaccuracy of the information given about suicide. An in-depth study of 115 school-based suicide prevention programs for adolescents discovered that most of them were only two hours or less in duration and that the majority of the programs focused almost exclusively on a "stress model" of suicide; that is, a model that assumes suicide is a response to extreme stress and that in essence, given sufficient stress, suicide could happen to anyone. Only 4 percent of the programs they reviewed presented the perspective that suicide is usually a consequence of mental illness. Disturbingly, the reviewers also discovered that "students who indicated having made a prior suicide attempt (approximately 11% of the sample) reacted in a generally more negative fashion to suicide prevention curricula. A greater proportion found the program less interesting or helpful, and were troubled by the program. . . . [A] greater proportion of prior attempters who attended a program than attempters who didn't attend said they would not want to reveal suicidal preoccupations to others, stated they did not believe that they could be helped by a mental health professional, and that suicide was a reasonable solution to problems."

The results of such programs, although discouraging, point out some of the difficulties that need to be resolved. It is clear that the medical dictum of "First, do no harm" needs to be at the heart of any thinking about school programs designed to prevent suicide. It is important, as well, that school administrations avoid romanticizing suicide and that they place the primary emphasis of their educational and screening efforts on recognition and treatment of mental illness and substance abuse.

David Shaffer and his colleagues at Columbia University in New York have developed a promising program that systematically screens high school students for known predictors of suicide. (There are no lectures given about suicide, and no responsibility is placed on teachers or students to "act like mental health professionals.") If, when a student fills out a brief self-report questionnaire, the responses indicate that he or she may be at risk, he or she then completes a computerized diagnostic interview. The computer generates a diagnostic impression that is given to the clinician, who, in the third and final stage of the process, personally interviews the student. On the basis of this interview, the clinician determines whether the student should be referred for treatment. A case manager gets in touch with the parents if treatment is necessary and helps to facilitate follow-up care.

The Columbia program has been very effective in locating students at risk for suicide and getting them into treatment. (Of the students who were identified through the screening process as suffering from major depression, only a third were in treatment. Of those who had actually attempted suicide, only half were receiving treatment.) The screening system is now being used by more than seventy groups worldwide, including schools in South Africa and Australia, as well as in the United States.

Community-based suicide prevention programs, such as the Samaritans in Britain and the Suicide Prevention Centers in America, have not had a demonstrable effect on suicide rates. An early study suggested a possible lowering of the suicide rate in communities that maintained Suicide Prevention Centers, but virtually every study since has found little or no impact. This lack of effect is counterintuitive in many ways, but not entirely surprising: Suicide Prevention Centers and crisis hotlines, although very helpful to many people, tend not to be used by the most severely depressed or suicidal individuals. Additionally, many suicides are impulsive, which generally precludes contacting anyone. An analysis of the types of patients and callers to Suicide Prevention Centers suggests that the majority are in need of help but are not suicidal.

Suicide prevention is not just a clinical problem. Society must deal with the potentially infectious repercussions of suicide, especially among the young, and must somehow try to keep a single tragedy from progressing to deaths of others. The contagious quality of suicide, or the tendency for suicides to occur in clusters, has been observed for centuries and is at least partially responsible for some of the ancient sanctions against the act of suicide. Epidemics of suicide occurred among soldiers and citizens during Greek and Roman times, for instance, as well as among worshipers of Odin in Viking society. Occasionally, decisive action on the part of a leader prevented further catastrophe.

Six hundred years before Christ, for example, the king of Rome ended a suicide epidemic among soldiers by declaring that the bodies of all suicides were to be nailed to a cross and put on public display. In the fourth century B.C., to stop a widespread epidemic of suicide among young Greek women, a local magistrate decreed that "the body of every young woman who hanged herself should be dragged naked through the streets by the same rope with which she committed the deed." The epidemic soon stopped. Centuries later, a similar law was passed to halt a suicide epidemic among young women in Marseilles. Again, the threat of public exposure and nakedness appeared to stop the wave of self-inflicted deaths.

One grenadier in the army of Napoleon Bonaparte killed himself, and then another did. Napoleon moved swiftly to stop the spread of suicide in his troops by issuing an order:

> The grenadier Groblin has committed suicide, from a disappointment in love. He was, in other respects, a worthy man. This is the second event of the kind that has happened in this corps within a month. The First Consul directs that it shall be notified in the order of the day of the guard, that a soldier ought to know how to overcome the grief and melancholy of his passions; that there is as much true courage in bearing mental affliction manfully as in remaining unmoved under the fire of a battery. To abandon oneself to grief without resisting, and to kill oneself in order to escape from it, is like abandoning the field of battle before being conquered.

The order worked; no suicides were reported for a long time afterward.

The tendency for suicide to incite imitation, especially if

the death is highly publicized or romanticized, is persistent. In September 1774, Goethe published *The Sorrows of Young Werther*, a book that portrayed a young man who shot himself over the love of a woman. It became a best-seller, as well as the impetus for a spate of suicides: young men were found dead by gunshot, dressed in blue frock coats and yellow waistcoats, with a copy of Goethe's novel nearby. In an attempt to stop the epidemic of suicides, the book was banned in Italy, Germany, and Denmark. In 1974, the sociologist David Phillips coined the phrase "Werther effect" to describe the phenomenon of suicide contagion.

Suicide is contagious among family members, as well as among strangers or acquaintances. Olive Anderson describes this in her book *Suicide in Victorian and Edwardian England*:

> There are many examples of a particular method of suicide running in a family. Experienced coroners knew that one suicide was apt to breed another of the same type, and some made it a rule never to return the razor, cup or gun used for suicide to the relatives, even when they asked for them as a memento, since a suicide instrument had a dangerous fascination. They tried, too, to stop local publicity being given to a suicide in the neighbourhood by an exotic method or in an unusual place. Opinions differed over whether or not the act of suicide itself was likely to be the result of "emotional contagion," but all agreed that the precise method or place chosen was often the result of imitation. Nor was the field of contagion necessarily limited to the local neighbourhood. The nation-wide publicity given by the press to outstanding sensational or "human interest" stories wherever they took place was repeatedly shown to be baneful and regretted.

There has been no shortage of suicide clusters in recent years: they have occurred in psychiatric hospitals and clinics; in suburban America—Plano, Texas; Leominster, Massachusetts; Clear Lake, Texas; Mankato, Minnesota; Bucks County, Pennsylvania; Fairfax County, Virginia; South Boston; New Jersey; South Dakota—and on college campuses (there were, for example, six suicides within three months at Michigan State University). There have been suicide outbreaks in Alaskan Eskimo villages, on Canadian Indian reservations, in Japan, in England, and in virtually every country that keeps records of such death patterns. Suicide clustering is primarily, but by no means entirely, a phenomenon of the young. Its mechanisms are diverse and contested. Imitation plays an important role, of course, but presumably a suicide disinhibits or triggers suicidal behavior only in an already vulnerable individual (in a study of two clusters of suicides in Texas, for example, one in which eight adolescents enrolled in the same school district committed suicide within a fifteen-month period and another in which six adolescents killed themselves within a two-to-three-month period, those who committed suicide were more likely than control subjects to have had a history of suicide attempts, threats, and self-destructive behavior). Implausibility also weighs in. Adolescents often imagine that the attention or retaliation denied to them in life may come their way through death or that suicide is made more acceptable by its having been carried out by others more famous or accomplished.

Many researchers believe that highly publicized media accounts of suicide lead to an increase in suicidal behavior, while others are less certain. Most agree that the strongest impact is on teenagers and concur that the content of the story and the style in which it is reported—be it through newspapers, radio, television, or film—have an influence for better or worse. In Austria, after members of the media consulted with suicide experts, the sensationalized coverage of suicide epidemics sharply declined. In Hungary, beginning in the early 1980s, the media have given less coverage to prominent or sensational suicides and more to the link between mental illness and suicide; the German media have also focused more on the relationship between suicide and psychiatric disorders.

In 1994, in an attempt to minimize the possibility of suicide contagion, the Centers for Disease Control and Prevention published recommendations for the media. The guidelines, while acknowledging that "suicide is often newsworthy, and it will probably be reported," also emphasized that "all parties should understand that a scientific basis exists for concern that news coverage of suicide may contribute to the causation of suicide" and that "public officials and the news media should carefully consider what is to be said and reported regarding suicide." Specifically, the public health facility's staff outlined certain aspects of news coverage that can promote suicide contagion:

- **Presenting simplistic explanations for suicide.** Suicide is never the result of a single factor or event, but rather results from a complex interaction of many factors and usually involves a history of psychosocial problems. Public officials and the media should carefully explain that the final precipitating event was not the only cause of a given suicide. Most persons who have committed suicide have had a history of problems that may not have been acknowledged during the acute aftermath of the suicide. Cataloguing the problems that could have played a causative rode in a suicide is not necessary, but acknowledgment of these problems is recommended.
- **Engaging in repetitive, ongoing, or excessive reporting of suicide in the news.** Repetitive and ongoing coverage, or prominent coverage, of a suicide tends to promote and maintain a preoccupation with suicide among at-risk persons, especially among persons fifteen to twenty-four years of age. This preoccupation appears to be associated with suicide con-

tagion. Information presented to the media should include the association between such coverage and the potential for suicide contagion. Public officials and media representatives should discuss alternative approaches for coverage of newsworthy suicide stories.

- **Providing sensational coverage of suicide.** By its nature, news coverage of a suicidal event tends to heighten the general public's preoccupation with suicide. This reaction is also believed to be associated with contagion and the development of suicide clusters. Public officials can help minimize sensationalism by limiting, as much as possible, morbid details in their public discussions of suicide. News media professionals should attempt to decrease the prominence of the news report and avoid the use of dramatic photographs related to the suicide (e.g., photographs of the funeral, the deceased person's bedroom, and the site of the suicide).

- **Reporting "how-to" descriptions of suicide.** Describing technical details about the method of suicide is undesirable. For example, reporting that a person died from carbon monoxide poisoning may not be harmful; however, providing details of the mechanism and procedures used to complete the suicide may facilitate initiation of the suicidal behavior by other at-risk persons.

- **Presenting suicide as a tool for accomplishing certain ends.** Suicide is usually a rare act of a troubled or depressed person. Presentation of suicide as a means of coping with personal problems (e.g., the breakup of a relationship or retaliation against parental discipline) may suggest suicide as a potential coping mechanism to at-risk persons. Although such factors often seem to trigger a suicidal act, other psychopathological problems are almost always involved. If suicide is presented as an effective means of accomplishing a specific end, it may be perceived by a potentially suicidal person as an attractive solution.

- **Glorifying suicide or persons who commit suicide.** News coverage is less likely to contribute to suicide contagion when reports of community expressions of grief (e.g., public eulogies, flying flags at half-mast, and erecting permanent public memorials) are minimized. Such actions may contribute to suicide contagion by suggesting to susceptible persons that society is honoring the suicidal behavior of the deceased person, rather than mourning the person's death.

- **Focusing on the suicide completer's positive characteristics.** Empathy for family and friends often leads to a focus on reporting the positive aspects of a suicide completer's life. For example, friends or teachers may be quoted as saying the deceased person "was a great kid" or "had a bright future" while avoiding mentioning the troubles and problems the deceased person had. As a result, statements venerating the deceased person are often reported in the news. However, if the suicide completer's problems are not acknowledged along with these laudatory statements, suicidal behavior may appear attractive to other at-risk persons, especially those who rarely receive positive reinforcement for desirable behaviors.

Through guidelines of this sort, and through other initiatives, the Centers for Disease Control and Prevention has demonstrated the potential benefits of active leadership from public health authorities.

Society also has other ways of curbing suicide, most notably by limiting access to deadly methods. Many of the safeguards we now try to put into place have been used by other cultures in earlier times. Olive Anderson traces the threads of modern suicide prevention to eighteenth- and nineteenth-century attempts to set up social agencies to provide help for those in danger of killing themselves. By the end of the eighteenth century, for example, English police regularly patrolled London parks and bridges to thwart suicide attempts, and by the mid-nineteenth century laws aimed at limiting the availability of poisons—the Arsenic Act of 1851 and the Sale of Poisons and the Pharmacy Act of 1868—had been passed. The development of new technologies inevitably led to new methods of suicide—carbolic acid for cleaning, potassium cyanide for photography, gas cookers, newly developed pesticides, and railways—and legislation was hard pressed to keep up. Firearms could be regulated, and were, but razors, ropes, and railway lines could not.

The twentieth century has seen many attempts to curtail access to fatal methods: a drastic lowering in the carbon monoxide content of domestic gas; the introduction of catalytic converters; major restrictions on the prescription of barbiturates and other potentially deadly drugs; and the development of less toxic antidepressant medications. These changes have shifted the pattern of methods used for suicide, but debate rages over whether, if deprived of one method, a suicidal person will simply reach out for a different one. The answer is unclear. Certainly, detoxification of gas and limitations on access to deadly drugs have caused suicide rates to fall in some countries. People do not automatically switch to another method, but there are some who do. The extent of the substitution of one suicide method for another is not entirely clear, and any increase or decrease in suicide rate is seldom attributable to just one thing. During perestroika, for example, Soviet premier Mikhail Gorbachev instituted a massive, if short-lived, campaign to decrease alcohol consumption; prices shot up and sales of alcohol plummeted. So did the suicide rate, which fell by 35 percent between the years of 1984 and 1988. Given the impact of alcohol on depression and impulsive behavior, it would be surprising if the ebb in suicide rates were not to some extent due to the restrictions on alcohol use. Yet during this same time there were also extraordinary social changes in the former USSR—changes that, however, *increased* overall mortality rates in other segments of the population. It is hard to disentangle complicated social influences from their disparate effects on the public health.

Gun control (and, to a lesser extent, alcohol restriction) are fiercely partisan issues. Passions run feverishly high in the United States, for example, whenever the topic of gun control is raised. But in 1996, 60 percent of the suicides in this country were carried out with guns; indeed, the number of suicides by firearm exceeded the number of firearm homicides. In study after study, a gun in the home has been shown to be significantly associated with a higher risk of suicide, especially among the young. Impulsivity, when coupled with an accessible and deadly method, adds to the psychological and psychiatric vulnerability in this age group.

Public health officials, trauma surgeons, emergency room doctors, medical examiners, and mental health professionals have voiced professional outrage over the proliferation of handguns and assault weapons. It is they who cannot staunch the bleeding from bullet wounds, who must fill out the death certificates, inform the parents, or dictate the autopsy reports. The American Academy of Pediatricians, the American Pediatric Surgical Association, and the American Trauma Society, among others, have adopted or proposed policies for the control of the skyrocketing increase in suicides and homicides from firearm violence. A survey of one thousand surgeons and internists, published in 1998, found that 84 percent of the surgeons and 72 percent of the internists thought that physicians should be more actively involved in firearm injury prevention, including the prevention of suicide. Most said they had received little or no education on the subject, but virtually all of them expressed a desire to receive training that would help them deal with the issue.

The American public shares many of the same concerns. A national survey of adults conducted in 1998 found that 88 percent favor childproofing guns (installing trigger locks or guaranteeing safe gun storage); 71 percent, the personalization of guns (so-called smart guns, which will fire only after "recognizing" the owner's fingerprints, hand size, or specific radio transmissions from a wristband); 82 percent, the use of magazine safeties (which prevent a gun's firing if the magazine or clip is removed); and 73 percent, the use of devices that indicate whether a gun's chamber is loaded. These seem like intelligent, if minimal, actions for society to take. It is hard to imagine any justification for making it easy for a child or an adolescent to kill himself.

The Swedish National Program to Develop Suicide Prevention has set specific priorities for reducing the availability of other "instruments of suicide." In transportation, they recommend introducing modified ignition locks that open only when the driver's exhaled air contains no alcohol; introducing idling shutoff devices activated by high carbon monoxide concentrations; extending exhaust emissions controls to include carbon monoxide as well; introducing better-designed exhaust systems to prevent carbon monoxide suicides; making air bags standard on all cars; designing locomotive front ends so that, on impact, a person will be pushed aside instead of run over; equipping with various forms of protective device those subway stations that have a high frequency of accidents and suicidal acts; and setting up protection (fences or nets) and SOS telephones at particularly frequent suicide sites (tall buildings, bridges). For weapons, it recommends safety grips on guns; separate storage of weapons and ammunition; taking suicide risk into account in drawing up regulations for weapon possession; and limited access to weapons for suicidal people.

Finally, for prescription drugs, it recommends developing less toxic drugs, as well as suitable forms of administration and packaging; cautious prescription routines; careful follow-up of patients; and efforts to restrict possession of toxic prescription drugs by suicidal people.

Sweden, along with several other countries, including Norway, Finland, New Zealand, and Australia, has developed a comprehensive strategy to reduce the rate of suicide. Most of these national strategies include a strong component of public and media education; a focus on increasing the awareness and treatment of alcoholism, depression, and other mental illnesses; reduction of access to deadly methods; and intensified training of health and other professionals. The World Health Organization has outlined six basic steps for the prevention of suicide, most of which center on reducing the availability of methods: more effective treatment of mental disorders, gun possession control, detoxification of domestic gas, detoxification of car emissions, control of toxic substance availability, and toning down suicide reports in the media.

Several years ago, the United Kingdom set a specific goal for its national health campaign: to reduce, by the year 2000, the rate of suicide by 15 percent. The Royal College of Psychiatrists has run an active Defeat Depression campaign throughout Britain. Its goals have been to reduce the stigma associated with depression, to educate the public about depression and its treatments, and to encourage those suffering from depression to seek treatment earlier rather than later. Preliminary studies indicate that public attitudes toward depression and psychological counseling have improved but that many people still regard antidepressants as less effective than counseling or as potentially addictive. It is too soon to know what effects the efforts of the British government, and those of the Royal College of Psychiatrists, will have on the suicide rate. There is also in Britain, as in most countries, a gap between the availability of mental health services and the public's awareness of that availability. In April 1999, the Mental Health Foundation in London released the results of a survey taken of three thousand people who had been asked to locate the telephone number they would call if they, or someone they knew, needed immediate psychiatric care. Fifty percent of the respondents were unable to locate the contact number of a local or national hot line or their local social services; 30 percent could not find the telephone number of their local National Health Service mental health service.

The United States waited until the last months of the twentieth century to propose a coherent and comprehensive national strategy to prevent suicide. There were, of course, many excellent suicide prevention programs in place throughout the country, but there had been no unifying concept or sustained and funded national leadership. In 1997, Senator Harry Reid of Nevada, whose father killed himself and whose state consistently has had the highest suicide rate in the nation, introduced a resolution in the U.S. Senate. Unanimously passed, it read in part:

Resolved, That the Senate—
1. recognizes suicide as a national problem and declares suicide prevention to be a national priority;
2. acknowledges that no single suicide prevention program or effort will be appropriate for all populations or communities;
3. encourages initiatives dedicated to—
   A. preventing suicide;
   B. responding to people at risk for suicide and people who have attempted suicide;
   C. promoting safe and effective treatment for persons at risk for suicidal behavior;
   D. supporting people who have lost someone to suicide; and
   E. developing an effective national strategy for the prevention of suicide; and
4. encourages the development and the promotion of

accessibility and affordability, of mental health services, to enable all persons at risk for suicide to obtain the services, without fear of any stigma.

The Senate resolution was an eloquent and important beginning and acted as a catalyst for many government health agencies, suicide prevention programs, mental health advocacy groups, and an imaginative, active grassroots organization, the Suicide Prevention Advocacy Network, which is an alliance of community activists, many of whom have lost a family member to suicide. Working with Senator Reid, this network provided much of the impetus for a recent consensus meeting, which developed a national strategy for suicide prevention. These groups were brought together under the leadership of the Surgeon General of the United States, David Satcher, a physician and former director of the Centers for Disease Control and Prevention. Satcher is a natural leader, one whose intelligence and compassion have eased the way for building the kind of coalition necessary to put together a national strategy on suicide prevention. His 1999 *Surgeon General's Report on Suicide* is the first published on the subject in the two hundred years of his office. The report calls for an increase in public awareness of suicide and its risk factors; an improvement in population-based and clinical services; and an investment in the advancement of the science of suicide prevention.

The federal government has made a good start on the problem of suicide, but the effort will not go far without support from the public and without funding from the Congress and the state legislatures. Nor is major success at suicide prevention a realistic goal if treatment for mental illness remains unaffordable and out of the reach of millions of Americans because health insurance is poor or nonexistent; if hospital stays for the severely mentally ill are limited to days, rather than weeks; or if society continues to be unaware of the suffering of so many people in its midst. Streets and jails are no places for the mentally ill.

The challenges to policy remain substantial. But increasing numbers of successful approaches promise important gains for directed public action. Much remains to be learned about how to prevent suicide. But, as the Surgeon General's report convincingly argues, much can now be done.

SHORTLY BEFORE he killed himself, D.C. Council Chairman John Wilson spoke to the Mental Health Association about suicide and mental illness in the black community. "Suicide," he said, "is the number one killer among young black people, but we call it gunfire. . . . We don't even like to talk about it. We've got to change the way America feels about depression." He was right, as usual.

I miss John Wilson very much, and I can still hear him saying in his passionate, inimitable way, *We can't put it all in God's hands. God's busy.*

CHAPTER 10

A Half-Stitched Scar

— THOSE LEFT BEHIND —

> . . . Time does not heal,
> It makes a half-stitched scar
> That can be broken and again you feel
> Grief as total as in its first hour.
>
> —ELIZABETH JENNINGS

SEVERAL MONTHS ago my husband and I were having dinner with an old friend of his, a psychiatrist, who toward the end of the evening asked me what I was working on. I told him I was writing a book about suicide, and this, as is not uncommonly the case, seemed to unbell the cat. A short silence followed. Then he said, with the remarkable certainty of someone whose thin understanding of suicide is belied by thirty years of private practice, "I was suicidal once, when I was eighteen. But I decided I couldn't commit suicide because it would be so terrible for my family and friends. I certainly couldn't now. I'm a doctor. Think what it would be like for my patients. How incredibly selfish!" A slight sense of moral superiority hung in the air.

I kicked my husband's shins under the table to encourage him to ask for the bill, and then I reminded his friend, who knew it well, that I had tried years earlier to kill myself, and nearly died in the attempt, but did not consider it either a selfish or a not-selfish thing to have done. It was simply the end of what I could bear, the last afternoon of having to imagine waking up the next morning only to start all over again with a thick mind and black imaginings. It was the final outcome of a bad disease, a disease it seemed to me I would never get the better of. No amount of love from or for other people—and there was a lot—could help. No advantage of a caring family and fabulous job was enough to overcome the pain and hopelessness I felt; no passionate or romantic love, however strong, could make a difference. Nothing alive and warm could make its way in through my carapace. I knew my life to be a shambles, and I believed—incontestably—that my family, friends, and patients would be better off without me. There wasn't much of me left anymore, anyway, and I thought my death would free up the wasted energies and well-meant efforts that were being wasted in my behalf.

All of what our colleague said was true, however. Suicide is awful beyond expression for those who have to spend their lives with its reality. No one who is a parent or child, a brother or a sister, a friend, a doctor or a patient would say otherwise. Most would agree with him that it is, on the face of it, a selfish act; most have yelled in their hearts, if not out loud, "How could you have done this to me?" All have asked themselves over and over again, and then a thousand times beyond, *Why? What could I have done differently? Why?*

The sting of death is always, as Arnold Toynbee writes, "less sharp for the person who dies than it is for the bereaved survivors." This is, he said, "the capital fact about the relation between living and dying. There are two parties to the suffering that death inflicts; and, in the apportionment of this suffering, the survivor takes the brunt."

Those who are left behind in the wake of suicide are left to deal with the guilt and the anger, to sift the good memories from the bad, and to try to understand an inexplicable act. Most of all, they are left to miss a parent or child whose life was threaded to theirs from its very beginning, mourn a spouse whose bed and love and trust they shared, or grieve the loss of a confidant with whom they spent long days and evenings of friendship.

How can killing oneself, in the context of other lives, ever be seen as anything but a highly personal, cruel, and thoughtless act? Yet suicide is tangential to reason and consideration and is almost always an irrational choice, the seemingly best way to end the pain, the futility, the voices, or the hopelessness. Decisions about suicide are not fleeting thoughts that can be willed away in deference to the best interests of others. Suicide wells up from cumulative anguish or is hastened by impulse; however much it may be set in or set off by the outer world, the suicidal mind tends not to mull on the well-being and future of others. If it does, it conceives for them a brighter future due to the fact that their lives are rid of an ill, depressed, violent, or psychotic presence. A young chemist, before committing suicide, put it succinctly: "The question of suicide and selfishness to close friends and relatives is one that I can't answer or even give an opinion on. It is obvious, however, that I have pondered it and decided I would hurt them less dead than alive."

SUICIDE IS a death like no other, and those who are left behind to struggle with it must confront a pain like no other. They are left with the shock and the unending "what if's." They are left with anger and guilt and, now and again, a terrible sense of relief. They are left to a bank of questions from others, both asked and unasked, about Why; they are left to the silence of others, who are horrified, embarrassed, or unable to cobble together a note of condolence, an embrace, or a comment; and they are left with the assumption by others—and themselves— that more could have been done.

Family members and friends are, most painfully, left to ask of themselves, What will I do without him? How can I live without her? A month after his death, two years ago now, an older woman wrote me a letter that began, "My 21 year old grandson shot and killed himself. We were very close and I loved him more than life itself. He started treatment too late and wouldn't take his medicine. . . . His death leaves a hole in my heart that can never be filled." It is the hole in the heart that is such a terrible thing. Once the shock has abated, the guilt wrestled with, and peace made, it is the hole in the heart, the missing of the person, that stays. This suicide shares with other kinds of death.

Although it might seem otherwise, most aspects of bereavement after suicide are not notably different from the reactions of those who lose members of their family or friends to death in other ways: to chronic illness, an accident, homicide. All are hit with shock, denial, anger, depression, intense loneliness, and a pervasive sense of loss. But a few things intrinsic to suicide set it apart. Because the death is often sudden and unexpected—though by no means always; perhaps half of suicides are at least somewhat expected (one person told an investigator, for example, "When I got the phone call that he had done it, my first thought was: so this is it.")—families haven't the opportunity to become accustomed to the possibility of death, make amends, or say good-bye.

The initial denial that often accompanies death is frequently compounded by a denial of the nature of the death. Parents who ultimately accept the loss of a child may continue to deny that the death was a suicide. This is particularly true for the parents of young children or adolescents who kill themselves. The medical examiner for the state of Maryland told me that even if an adolescent writes a suicide note and dies by hanging or by a gunshot wound to the head, some parents continue to insist that the death was an accident. (The inevitable ambiguities involved in overdose deaths, drownings, and single-passenger automobile accidents make parental acceptance of suicide in these cases even harder.)

Other matters compound the nightmare: suicide is often

violent, which means that family members either discover or must identify severely mutilated or damaged bodies; police need to be involved in the death scene, which adds an additional criminal-like and disquieting element; and insurance investigators, in whose hands financial futures are held, often make matters worse by intrusive and offensive questioning. Friends and neighbors may or may not respond to a suicide death with the same level of consolation and community support that most other deaths command, and in fact, one-third of family members report they felt stigmatized by suicide.

Guilt is a usual and corrosive presence after suicide: parents, siblings, children, husbands, wives, friends, colleagues, and the most casual of acquaintances remember and ruminate on all things done and left undone: the arguments, the slights, the unreturned telephone calls, the doctor not notified, the guns or drugs not removed from the house, the psychiatric hospitalization postponed or resisted. Many suicides occur in an already highly stressed and fragile personal world, a world fraught with anxiety, frayed tempers, overdrawn bank accounts, and ill will. Persistent psychiatric illness is not kind to those who have it, nor is it kind to those who must live with those who have it. Anger, mistrust, and agitation are part and parcel of manic-depression, depression, schizophrenia, and alcohol and drug abuse. However great the love may have been for the person who commits suicide, it is likely that the most sustaining relationships were, at the time of death, frazzled, drained, or severed entirely. The absolute hopelessness of suicidal depression is, by its nature, contagious, and it renders those who would help impotent to do so. By the time suicide occurs, those who kill themselves may resemble only slightly children or spouses once greatly loved and enjoyed for their company. It is a chilling, but not surprising, reality that one in ten family members admits relief that suicide has brought to an end the agony for all concerned. In one study, parents whose children had died in accidents were compared with parents whose children had killed themselves. Both groups of parents were asked, among other things, if the children's deaths had brought any unexpected benefits to the family:

> An equal number of parents from both the suicide and accident groups said that the death did have a positive impact on their families. Those from the accident group felt that the suffering had brought the family closer together. Parents in the suicide group believed that the positive effect was due to the calm that came back into their lives from not having to worry all the time. This was mostly the experience of families who had a son, suffering from mental illness or substance abuse, which had caused great stress and tension within the family. The suicide, as painful as it might be for all the family members, was perceived as a relief from all the difficulties and suffering for themselves and their son.

Death by suicide is not a gentle deathbed gathering: it rips apart lives and beliefs, and it sets its survivors on a prolonged and devastating journey. The core of this journey has been described as an *agonizing questioning*, a tendency to ask repeatedly why the suicide occurred and what its meaning should be for those who are left. One parent explained to a researcher, "I'd wake up at night envisioning it—him sitting there with a gun to his head. And then I'd wake up a lot trying to get an answer or figure out what was going through his head when he was doing this." Another said simply, "The thoughts are always there, you know. You wake up and wonder 'why?' "

Parents of children who commit suicide are left particularly devastated. For months, if not years, they are overwhelmed not only by the loss of a child but by guilt as well: a sense of having failed the child at the most critical time of his life, of being insensitive to the extent of his pain, or of overlooking final cues. Many fathers and mothers repeatedly question their competence as parents and experience a deep sense of shame, as well as anger and guilt. Unbridled terror that another child might also commit suicide is common, as is overprotectiveness of the surviving children. Iris Bolton, director of a counseling center in Atlanta and author of a book about her son's suicide, writes that after her twenty-year-old son died of a self-inflicted gunshot wound she was haunted by "Why? Why wasn't I home? Why my son?" and felt as though her car had a huge sign on it reading "My son committed suicide. I am a failure." She worried, as many parents do, about the impact of the suicide on her remaining sons and observed that her husband dealt with his grief far more privately than she did. With a minister, she started a support group for parents and found in it the beginning of a life without her son, as well as an acceptance of the fact that she and all parents of children who kill themselves are "mortally and irrevocably wounded." (Mothers in particular are vulnerable to depression after a child's suicide. One in five becomes significantly depressed within six months of the death.) She also observed that mothers and fathers tend to respond to suicide differently:

> During the past ten years I have met many mothers and fathers who have experienced suicide. Most have similar feelings. One difference between the sexes is that fathers more often talk about the lost *future* with the child, while mothers feel that they have lost their *present* time. Nancy Hogan, a nurse and grief educator from Illinois, explains this by saying that, since the father spends much of his time working away from the home and providing for the future of his children, his loss comes partly from the fact that he has no future with this child. He had planned for the child's graduation or perhaps walking his daughter down the aisle at her wedding. His work may now have lost its meaning. The mother may be involved with the day-to-day activities of the child,

such as carpools, organizing clothes, school, basketball practice, etc. She has lost her "present time" with the deceased child. The losses are equally painful, but they are different.

In the preface to her book *My Son . . . My Son,* Bolton laid out the dilemma that she and all parents who lose a child to suicide face:

> *I don't know why.*
> *I'll never know why.*
> *I don't have to know why.*
> *I don't like it.*
> *What I have to do is make a choice*
> *about my living.*

Before they get to that point, however, parents go through acute disbelief, suffering, and bewilderment describable only by them. I am still haunted by the words of a colleague and friend whose nineteen-year-old son died of a self-inflicted gunshot wound. An extraordinarily warm, lively, and caring mother and clinician, she said, still in shock after her son's death, "I feel like a mother animal. I keep searching for my baby."

The impact of a suicide on the lives of brothers and sisters has been almost entirely ignored in the clinical research literature, an omission made the more remarkable by the closeness of emotional ties between siblings and the possibility that they may be more likely to kill themselves because of shared genes and environment. The surviving children also now share the suffering and heightened anxieties of devastated parents. Clinically, siblings experience not only the enormous loss that the death of a brother or sister brings but guilt and a sense of responsibility as well. The nature of the death lends itself to unkind speculation and stigmatization by other children and feelings of vulnerability that this might happen to them as well.

A three-year follow-up study of the siblings of twenty adolescents who died by suicide found, however, that in general there appeared to be relatively few long-term adverse psychological consequences to the surviving children. But in the first six months after the death, depression was common; one in four of the siblings, in fact, became clinically depressed. Not surprisingly, siblings who had a family or personal history of a psychiatric disorder were far more likely to become depressed than those who did not. Younger children—perhaps because they were more influenced by the life of an older child or perhaps because they spent more time at home—were more obviously affected than older siblings. Adolescents, when asked about the impact of a sibling's suicide, often say they feel they "grew up quickly" or "matured more rapidly" as the result of the death.

The suicide of an adolescent is often considered to be a newsworthy event, and when handled in an insensitive or sensationalist manner by the media it can be a further source of pain and embarrassment to the siblings and parents. Karen Dunne-Maxim, now the project director for the New Jersey Central Region Youth Suicide Prevention Project, recalls the horror that she and the rest of her family felt when the local newspaper reported simply that her sixteen-year-old brother, Tim, "dove" in front of a commuter train. No information was given about the rest of his life, which made the manner of his death more important than the loss of his life. The family asked *Newsday*, a Long Island newspaper, if it would include a description of Tim as they had known him, and it did:

He never missed a year on the honor roll. He was editor of the Junior High yearbook and produced his own anti-war film that was presented at the Rockville Center Library. He received awards for playing the cello and had recently been mountain climbing with the Boy Scouts in Switzerland. He was brilliant and sensitive and the question will always remain with those who loved him—Why did he die?

Surprisingly little is known not only about the impact of suicide on siblings but also about its impact on friends. There is next to nothing written about how close friends and colleagues make sense of or deal with the suicide of someone they know well or have worked with. Anecdotal and clinical experience suggests that guilt—How could I have not noticed how depressed he was?; If only I had called (or written, or dropped by her house); If only I had let his wife or doctor know—is common, as is denial that suicide was the real cause of death. Most people know little about suicide or the psychiatric illnesses most closely associated with it and therefore flail about, trying to make sense of an often senseless act. They inevitably focus on the events of life—broken or difficult relationships, financial concerns, job-related stress—as the reasons for suicide. In some instances, employers use the occasion to educate the surviving staff about the most common causes of suicide and provide information about depression and how to obtain help if it is necessary, but this, unfortunately, is unusual. More commonly, the cause of death is skirted around or not discussed, and speculation outstrips accurate information and compassion.

Denial of suicide by family members can make a bad situation even worse for friends and fellow workers. A colleague of mine, an eminent scientist who suffered from manic-depressive illness, killed himself a few years ago. His wife, understandably distraught, refused to believe that he had committed suicide. She made it clear that suicide was not to be mentioned at his funeral or memorial service and, unknowingly, made it very hard for his fellow professors, graduate students, and laboratory staff to deal with his death and move on with their lives. Even a year later, his students and colleagues found it difficult to discuss the suicide of this intense, imaginative, and charismatic man. One of his students said, "He was larger than life. He gave all of us life and joy in our work; his enthusiasm filled the lab. I'm finally getting back to my experiments, but it all seems grayer now. I still believe I ought to have been able to save him. He would have done as much for me." The student paused for a long time, trying not to cry, and then said, "But I guess he didn't, did he?"

THE SUICIDE of a husband or wife brings with it all the intensity and complexity of marriage, and the loss is inevitably shaded not just by the closeness of the relationship but by whatever arguments, physical violence, financial strains, and emotional withdrawal may have been imposed on it by psychiatric illness or drug or alcohol abuse. Preexisting marital problems or separations generally worsen the already powerful sense of guilt or responsibility the surviving spouse feels. To the person who has shared a suicide's bed or borne his children, the decision to commit suicide is a particularly personal rejection. And because suicide is usually seen by others as a preventable or avoidable death, spouses often bear the brunt of community gossip and family blame. The inevitable involvements with the police immediately following death, with the not-so-subtle awareness of murder having to be ruled out, do not improve the situation.

If, as is frequently the case, there has been a prolonged history of severe mental illness in the spouse who commits suicide, the toll it has taken on the marriage—in anger, resentment, sexual infidelity, hopelessness, physical and verbal abuse, or estrangement—will cause some spouses to feel, in addition to their despair, an unnerving sense of relief. One husband's immediate reaction after the suicide of his wife, who had suffered from recurrent depression for twelve years, reflects this ambivalence: "I had the strange feeling of being three persons," he said. "One was the person in shock. The second person felt a strange sense of relief: no more psychiatrists, pills, shock therapy and hospitals. A third person witnessed the other two: 'Look at that fool weeping and yelling, and look at the other fool already experiencing relief after twelve years of sympathetic suffering.' "

Although the spouses of those who commit suicide experience sharper guilt and a stronger sense of being blamed for the death than do spouses whose husbands or wives die in accidents (even though they, too, have been widowed under sudden and unexpected circumstances), most research finds that the long-term psychological outcome is similar for both groups. An ultimately good adjustment is made by the majority of surviving spouses, especially by those who are young. Most go through an initial period of depression after the suicide but then go on to remarry and bring up their children with less difficulty than might be imagined. Less difficulty does not mean no difficulty, however, and the healing is exceedingly hard and takes a very long time.

Josephine Pesaresi, a social worker in New Jersey, was left a widow with three children aged ten, fifteen, and sixteen after her husband, a psychiatrist, died of a self-inflicted gunshot wound during a severe, agitated depression. She describes the days and months that followed:

> From the first moment, people wanted to know why. Why? Why? God, how I came to hate that question. I was somehow expected to be able to explain a happening that had just torn the heart out of me. The stigma, the awful stigma that is associated with suicide, compounded the excruciating pain we were experiencing. . . .
>
> As the realization of the loss began to set in, so too did the guilt and blame. I blamed myself for not realizing the depth of my husband's suffering and for not hospitalizing him. Our children felt guilt about their relationship with him. Our son was in the middle of

adolescence and had been arguing with his father. Our older daughter said she had sensed disaster and should have followed her instincts to stay close to her father that day instead of going swimming. Our younger daughter felt she should not have left the room where her father was to listen to a tape in her room.

The guilt and "if onlys" escalated and seemed to be endless, especially for me. My husband's parents, who were very close to us before the suicide, blamed me for my husband's depression and refused to enter our home. . . .

After my husband's death, my children and I had an unspoken contract. If I would crawl out of my hole, put on some clothes, shop for food, and drive them to their activities and school, they, too, would continue with their lives as best they could. However, I had to keep my end of the bargain—no fudging and no substitute mothers. We were all hurting, but if any of us were going to do it, we were going to do it together. They drove a hard bargain with me. It was torture, and they made me furious, but I got in that damned car and they did too. I knew that my husband had left me with the unfinished job of raising three children conceived in love and commitment. Somehow we would get each other through—and we did. Humor even began to creep back into our lives. Our older daughter gave me a plaque to keep by my bed which said, "Shall we call in a consultant or louse it up ourselves?"

Children, although devastated and permanently marked by the suicide of a parent, for the most part survive the death without severe or enduring pathology. Like adults in the wake of suicide, however, many children experience profound grief, guilt, and anxiety that can persist for many months, if not years. In some instances, particularly if the child has a history of psychiatric disturbance, the reaction may be severe and long-lasting. An eleven-year-old boy, for instance, was evaluated at a clinic approximately one year after his father's suicide: "This thin, wan, passive boy appeared withdrawn, apathetic, lifeless," the admitting doctor wrote. "He hung his head, staring at the floor out of unseeing eyes. Greatly preoccupied, he rarely initiated any remark, was painfully slow to respond. His gestures were of utter resignation and defeat, although occasionally he picked at his arm and lip. When he spoke it was of his immense loneliness, his guilt regarding his father's suicide, his inability to be of help to his family following the suicide, and his own worthlessness."

The initial communication, or lack of communication, about the circumstances of a parent's death can be critical to a child's ability to accept and deal with suicide. The range in sensitivity of the surviving parent may be great, as a study conducted in Britain points out: on the one hand, a father told his sons, "Mummy was very depressed, unhappy and tired and so took her own life by taking too many tablets"; at the other extreme, one mother said to her three-year-old, "The silly fool's gone and put his head in the gas oven." Josephine Pesaresi, the social worker whose husband, a psychiatrist, shot himself, told her children, within minutes of his death, "He had a sickness that was like a cancer which could not be cured."

It is important that children be told the truth as completely and quickly as they are able to take it in. Efforts to "protect" or "shield" a child almost invariably come back to haunt him or her by creating a web of distortions and misperceptions and a "conspiracy of silence." The true circumstances of death, if hidden, may in any event be quickly revealed by conversations with other children or overheard remarks between adults. Learning the truth later rather than sooner can be an additional and unnecessary damage, and one that prevents the child from understanding the reality of his own or his parent's experience. Television writer and director Christopher Lukas, whose mother, grandmother, uncle, aunt, and brother (the writer

Anthony Lukas) committed suicide, discusses the conspiracy of silence and dishonesty surrounding his mother's death in his book *Silent Grief*, written with psychologist Henry Seiden:

> On a hot August afternoon in 1941, when I was six years old, and she was thirty-three, my mother walked out of her psychiatrist's house in Connecticut, stepped into the garden, and cut her throat. My father, a successful lawyer—though an unhappy man—was summoned from his New York office to deal with the death. Also at the psychiatrist's house that day was my grandmother. She had been taking my mother to the psychiatrist that summer; the visits were the culmination of years of manic-depressive bouts. There was some disagreement between my mother's mother and my father on what to tell the children—me at home, and my eight-year-old brother, away at camp. My father won the argument: For ten years the nature of my mother's death was kept a secret from us, though all our relatives and most of their friends knew that she had committed suicide.
>
> When I was finally told the truth, at the age of sixteen, my father and I were sitting in a railroad station on another hot August day. I was about to catch a train, and I have always believed that my father chose that moment to tell me because he could not bear to hold a prolonged conversation on the subject. "Why?" I querulously inquired. "She was sick," my father replied, making it clear that was all he had to say on the subject. We didn't talk about it again for many years.

Joshua Logan, director and writer of the films *Mister Roberts, Picnic, South Pacific, Bus Stop*, and *Sayonara*, suffered from manic-depressive illness much of his adult life. Following one of his hospitalizations, he made an appointment to see a new psychiatrist and started to recite his childhood history:

In discussing my childhood I heard myself saying, almost as if by rote, "My father died of pneumonia in a hospital in Chicago when I was three years old."

After a slight pause, Dr. Moore said quietly, "Your father cut his throat with a pocket knife in a sanatorium in Chicago. I think it's about time you knew that, Mr. Logan."

I was so astounded that I asked him to repeat the statement three or four times, and then demanded to know how he could know facts I had never heard of in my life. . . .

I couldn't wait to leave Dr. Moore's office and took a taxi to my apartment, where I rushed to call my Uncle Will in Louisiana.

"Yes, Josh," said Will, "it's true."

"But," I said, "they always told me he died of pneumonia."

"He did die of pneumonia. It was the blood from his throat that went into his lungs."

"But why didn't anyone tell me? Why didn't my mother tell me?"

"She never wanted you to know, Josh. I can't tell you why, except I imagine she thought it would be too painful for you."

"It's not painful, Will, it's a relief, because at last I know the truth. The boil has been lanced and the sore is clean. In fact, I'm feeling better than I have in a very long time. Now I know my father, and for the first time in my life. I feel close to him for the first time. He must have been very much like me."

"He was," said Will. "Very much. And I hope you won't tell your mother you know."

For some, like Joshua Logan, the truth about his father's suicide came as a relief and helped him make sense of both his father and himself. Others remain haunted by the thought of suicide, obsessed by their parent's violent end, and fearful of what it means to their own lives. John Berryman, who like his father and his father's sister killed himself, wrote in his poem "Of Suicide": "Reflexions on suicide, & on my father possess me / . . . Of suicide I continually think." In a poem written after Ernest Hemingway's suicide he said, "Save us from shotguns & father's suicides / . . . Mercy! my father; do not pull the trigger / or all my life I'll suffer from your anger / killing what you began." But his most powerful statement on his father's suicide was in yet another poem from *The Dream Songs:*

> *The marker slants, flowerless, day's almost done,*
> *I stand above my father's grave with rage,*
> *often, often before*
> *I've made this awful pilgrimage to one*
> *who cannot visit me, who tore his page*
> *out: I come back for more,*
>
> *I spit upon this dreadful banker's grave*
> *who shot his heart out in a Florida dawn*

HOW DO PEOPLE survive such impassable grief and rage? How do they keep from being so destroyed by guilt and sorrow that they sacrifice the remainder of their own lives for the one lost earlier to suicide? There are many ways: the support of family and friends, religious faith, the passage of time, psychotherapy, or counseling, but one of the most effective has been through the establishment of self-help groups for those who have survived another's suicide. The American Foundation for Suicide Prevention and the American Association of Suicidology are the major national organizations in the United States that offer, in addition to scientific, advocacy, and education programs, a wide network of local support groups. These groups allow those who have been through the suicide of a friend or family member to get together and exchange support, information, and encouragement about carving out a meaningful future. Listening to others who have survived kindred straits and eventually helping newer members to do the same is invaluable in learning to survive and do well with life. Many of the suicide survivors go on to become actively involved in school and church education programs, hoping to raise awareness about suicide and the psychiatric illnesses that can lead to it. Others work at the state and national level to change legislation or to increase funding for suicide prevention programs and related research. All try to redeem some good from the awfulness they have known; and most succeed.

Still, most are left to ask why it happened. Scottish writer Lewis Grassic Gibbon, who himself attempted suicide when he was a young man, writes of this in *Sunset Song*, the first book in his trilogy *A Scots Quair.* He describes the struggles of his protagonist, Chris Guthrie, in trying to come to terms with her mother's suicide:

> Just as the last time she'd climbed to the loch: and when had that been? She opened her eyes and thought, and tired from that and closed down her eyes again and gave a queer laugh. The June of last year it had been, the day when mother had poisoned herself and the twins.
>
> So long as that and so near as that, you'd thought of the hours and days as a dark, cold pit you'd never escape. But you'd escaped, the black damp went out of the sunshine and the world went on, the white faces and whispering ceased from the pit, you'd never be the same again, but the world went on and you went with it. It was not mother only that died with the twins, something died in your heart and went down with her to lie in Kinraddie kirkyard—the child in your heart died then, the

bairn that believed the hills were made for its play, every road set fair with its warning posts, hands ready to snatch you back from the brink of danger when the play grew over-rough. That died, and the Chris of the books and the dreams died with it, or you folded them up in their paper of tissue and laid them away by the dark, quiet corpse that was your childhood. . . .

Then Mistress Munro washed down the body that was mother's and put it in a nightgown, her best, the one with blue ribbons on it that she hadn't worn for many a year; and fair she made her and sweet to look at, the tears came at last when you saw her so, hot tears wrung from your eyes like drops of blood. But they ended quick, you would die if you wept like that for long, in place of tears a long wail clamoured endless, unanswered inside your head *Oh, mother, mother, why did you do it?*

Epilogue

I was naive to underestimate how disturbing it would be to write this book. I knew, of course, that it would mean interviewing people about the most painful and private moments of their lives, and I also knew that I would inevitably be drawn into my own private dealings with suicide over the years. Neither prospect was an attractive one, but I wanted to do something about the untolled epidemic of suicide and the only thing I knew to do was to write a book about it. I am by temperament an optimist, and I thought from the beginning that there was much to be written about suicide that was strangely heartening.

As a clinician, I believed there were treatments that could save lives; as one surrounded by scientists whose explorations of the brain are elegant and profound, I believed our basic understanding of its biology was radically changing how we think about both mental illness and suicide; and as a teacher of young doctors and graduate students, I felt the future held out great promise for the intelligent and compassionate care of the suicidal mentally ill.

All of these things I still believe. Indeed, I believe them more strongly than I did when I first began doing the background research for this book two years ago. The science is of the first water; it is fast-paced, and it is laying down, pixel by pixel, gene by gene, the dendritic mosaic of the brain. Psychologists are deciphering the motivations for suicide and piecing together the final straws—the circumstances of life—that so dangerously ignite the brain's vulnerabilities. And throughout the world, from Scandinavia to Australia, public health officials are mapping a clearly reasoned strategy to cut the death rate of suicide.

Still, the effort seems unhurried. Every seventeen minutes in America, someone commits suicide: Where is the public concern and outrage? I have become more impatient as a result of writing this book and am more acutely aware of the problems that stand in the way of denting the death count. I cannot rid my mind of the desolation, confusion, and guilt I have seen in the parents, children, friends, and colleagues of those who kill themselves. Nor can I shut out the images of the autopsy photographs of twelve-year-old children or the prom photographs of adolescents who within a year's time will put a pistol in their mouths or jump from the top floor of a university dormitory building. Looking at suicide—the sheer numbers, the pain leading up to it, and the suffering left behind—is harrowing. For every moment of exuberance in the science, or in the success of governments, there is a matching and terrible reality of the deaths themselves: the young deaths, the violent deaths, the unnecessary deaths.

Like many of my colleagues who study suicide, I have seen time and again the limitations of our science, been privileged to see how good some doctors are and appalled by the callousness and incompetence of others. Mostly, I have been impressed by how little value our society puts on saving the lives of those who are in such despair as to want to end them. It is a societal illusion that suicide is rare. It is not. Certainly the mental illnesses most closely tied to suicide are not rare. They are common conditions, and, unlike cancer and heart disease, they disproportionately affect and kill the young.

A FEW WEEKS after I nearly died from a suicide attempt, I went to the Episcopal church across the street from the UCLA campus. I was a parishioner there, however occasional, and in light of being able to walk in through the door instead of being carried in by six, I thought I would see what was left of my relationship with God. To make it easier, I purchased a ticket to a Bach recital that was being performed in the chapel. I went to the church early; my mind was still dull, and everything in it and in my heart was frayed and exhausted. But I knelt anyway, in spite or because of this, and spoke into my hands the only prayer I really know or care very much about. The beginning was rote and easy: "God be in my head, and in my understanding," I said to myself or God, "God be in mine eyes, and in my *looking." Somehow, despite the thickening of my mind, I got through most of the rest of it. But then I blanked out entirely as I got to the end, struggling to get through what had started as an act of reconciliation with God. The words were nowhere to be found.*

I imagined for a while that my forgetting was due to the remnants of the poisonous quantities of lithium I had taken, but suddenly the final lines came up into my consciousness: "God be at mine end, and at my departing." I felt a convulsive sense of shame and sadness, a kind I had not known before, nor have I known it since. Where had God been? I could not answer the question then, nor can I answer it now. I do know, however, that I should have been dead but was not— and that I was fortunate enough to be given another chance at life, which many others were not.

While writing this book, I kept on my desk a photograph and a fragment of a poem. The photograph is of a young, good-looking cadet at the Air Force Academy, standing next to a jet fighter. Writing about this young man's suicide was perhaps the most difficult part of writing this book. I started the essay on a clear winter day in the library at the University of St. Andrews in Scotland, where I teach for a few weeks each year. I was able to read his medical records only for brief periods before I had to get up, walk over to the window, and look out at the North Sea in a futile attempt to pull from it a meaning that would make more tolerable the awfulness of it all. I would then return to the medical notes that charted out the inexorable course of the illness that would kill him. The photograph at first haunted, then consoled me; I found great pleasure in knowing Drew Sopirak.

The fragment of the poem I kept on my desk was one that drew me to life. It is the last line from Douglas Dunn's "Disenchantments":

Look to the living, love them, and hold on.

Appendix
Notes
Acknowledgments
Index

Appendix

RESOURCES FOR INFORMATION ABOUT SUICIDE,
MENTAL ILLNESS, AND ALCOHOL AND
DRUG ABUSE

American Association of Suicidology

4201 Connecticut Avenue, N.W., Suite 408
Washington, DC 20008
(202) 237-2280
Fax: (202) 237-2282
www.suicidology.org

American Foundation for Suicide Prevention

120 Wall Street, 22nd Floor
New York, NY 10005
(888) 333-2377
Fax: (212) 363-6237
www.afsp.org

Anxiety Disorders Association of America

(301) 231-9350
Fax: (301) 231-7392
www.adaa.org

Centers for Disease Control and Prevention

National Center for Injury Control and Prevention
www.cdc.gov/ncipc

Child and Adolescent Bipolar Foundation

www.cabf.org

Depression and Related Affective Disorders Association

The Johns Hopkins Hospital, Meyer 3-181
600 North Wolfe Street
Baltimore, MD 21287

(410) 955-4647
Fax: (410) 614-3241
www.med.jhu.edu/drada

Health Resources and Services Administration
www.hrsa.dhhs.gov

National Alliance for Research on Schizophrenia and Depression

60 Cutter Mill Road, Suite 404
Great Neck, NY 11021
(516) 829-0091
Fax: (516) 487-6930
www.mhsource.com/narsdad.html

National Alliance for the Mentally Ill

200 North Glebe Road, Suite 1015
Arlington, VA 22203
Help line: (800) 950-6264
Front desk: (703) 524-7600
Fax: (703) 524-9094
www.nami.org

National Depressive and Manic-Depressive Association

730 North Franklin Street, Suite 501
Chicago, IL 60610
(800) 826-3632
Fax: (312) 642-7243
www.ndmda.org

National Institute on Alcohol Abuse and Alcoholism

6000 Executive Boulevard, Willco Building
Bethesda, MD 20892
www.niaaa.nih.gov

National Institute of Mental Health

6001 Executive Boulevard
Bethesda, MD 20892
(800) 421-4211
www.nimh.nih.gov

National Institute of Mental Health Suicide Research Consortium

www.nimh.nih.gov/research/suicide.htm

National Institute on Drug Abuse

6001 Executive Boulevard
Bethesda, MD 20892
(800) 644-6432
www.nida.nih.gov

National Mental Health Association

1201 Prince Street
Alexandria, VA 22314
(800) 969-6642
Fax: (703) 684-5968
www.nmha.org

National Mental Illness Screening Project

One Washington Street, Suite 304
Wellesley Hills, MA 02481
(800) 573-4433 (Depression Screening)
Fax: (781) 431-7447
www.nmisp.org

Substance Abuse and Mental Health Services

www.samhsa.gov

Suicide Prevention Advocacy Network

5034 Odin's Way
Marietta, GA 30068
(888) 649-1366
Fax: (770) 642-1419
www.spanusa.org

Surgeon General of the United States

www.surgeongeneral.gov

Notes

1 · DEATH LIES NEAR AT HAND

11 "A tiny blade": Seneca, "To Lucilius: On Providence." Seneca (4 B.C.–A.D. 65), Roman statesman and philosopher, was forced to take his own life after having been accused of conspiracy by Nero, emperor of Rome. Three years later Nero, too, was forced to commit suicide.

12 The Cro-Magnons, we believe: W. F. Allman, *The Stone Age Present: How Evolution Has Shaped Modern Life—From Sex, Violence, and Language to Emotions, Morals, and Communities* (New York: Simon & Schuster, 1994); Ian Tattersall, *Becoming Human: Evolution and Human Uniqueness* (New York: Harcourt Brace, 1998).

12 and the hunting apes: B. B. Beck, *Animal Tool Behavior* (New York: Garland Press, 1980); W. C. McGrew, *Chimpanzee Material Culture* (Cambridge, England: Cambridge University Press, 1992); R. Byrne, *The Thinking Ape: Evolutionary Origins of Intelligence* (Oxford: Oxford University Press, 1995).

12 Several—for example, the Eskimo: S. Bromberg and C. K. Cassel, "Suicide in the Elderly: The Limits of Paternalism," *Journal of the American Geriatrics Society*, 31 (1983): 698–703.

13 Among the Yuit Eskimos: A. H. Leighton and C. C. Hughes, "Notes on Eskimo Patterns of Suicide," *Southwestern Journal of Anthropology*, 11 (1955): 327–338.

13 Most of these deaths: G. Rosen, "History in the Study of Suicide," *Psychological Medicine*, 1 (1971): 267–285; T. J. Marzen, M. K. O'Dowd, D. Crone, and T. J. Balch, "Suicide: A Constitutional Right?" *Duquesne Law Review*, 24 (1985), 1–242; Anton van Hooff, *From Autothanasia to Suicide: Self-Killing in Classical Antiquity* (London: Routledge, 1990); M. Crone, "Historical Attitudes Toward Suicide," *Duquesne Law Review* (Special Issue: A Symposium on Physician-Assisted Suicide), 35 (1996), 7–42.

13 Gladiators thrust wooden sticks: Seneca, "On the Proper Time to Slip the Cable," *Epistulae Morales*, vol. 4, trans. R. M. Gummere (Cambridge, Mass.: Harvard University Press, 1967).

14 The Catholic Church: Charles Moore, *A Full Inquiry Into the Subject of Suicide*, vol. 1 (London: Rivington, 1790), pp. 306–325; George Rosen, "History in the Study of Suicide."

14 St. Augustine: St. Augustine, *The City of God*, trans. Marcus Dods, vol. 1, (New York: Hafner, 1948) Book 1, pp. 31–39. For an excellent recent history of suicide in western culture, see G. Minois, *History of Suicide: Voluntary Death in Western Culture*, trans. L. G. Cochrane (Baltimore: Johns Hopkins, 1999).

14 so as "not to bury the wicked": H. Cohn, "Suicide in Jewish Legal and Religious Tradition," *Mental Health and Society,* 3 (1976): 129–136, p. 136.

14 The Semachot: D. M. Posner, "Suicide and the Jewish Tradition," in E. J. Dunne, J. L. McIntosh, and K. Dunne-Maxim, eds., *Suicide and Its Aftermath* (New York: W. W. Norton, 1987), pp. 159–162. The Semachot is quoted on p. 160.

14 "The general rule": Cohn, "Suicide in Jewish Legal and Religious Tradition."

14 In Islamic law, suicide: Y. Al-Najjar, "Suicide in Islamic Law," in H. Winnick and L. Miller, eds., *Aspects of Suicide in Modern Civilization* (Jerusalem: Academic Press, 1978), pp. 28–33.

15 "keep the corpses down": C. Gittings, *Death, Burial and the Individual in Early Modern England* (London: Routledge, 1988).

15 In early Massachusets,: Howard I. Kushner, *American Suicide: A Psychocultural Exploration* (New Brunswick, N.J.: Rutgers University Press, 1991).

15 they then sank his body: P. V. Glob, *The Bog People: Iron-Age Man Preserved,* trans. Rupert Bruce-Mitford (Ithaca, N.Y.: Cornell University Press, 1988), pp. 148–151.

15 "The deceased was washed": K. A. Achte and J. Lönnqvist, "Death and Suicide in Finnish Mythology and Folklore," in N. Speyer, R. F. W. Diekstra, and K. J. M. van de Loo, eds., *Proceedings of the International Conference for Suicide Prevention* (Amsterdam; Swets & Zeitlinger, 1973), pp. 317–323, p. 321.

16 In France, the body: G. Rosen, "History in the Study of Suicide."

16 In parts of Germany: Henry Romilly Fedden, *Suicide: A Social and Historical Study* (London: Peter Davies, 1938), p. 37.

16 Early Norwegian laws: Nils Retterstol, *Suicide: A European Perspective* (Cambridge, England: Cambridge University Press, 1993), p. 20.

16 "an irreparable deed": Ibid., p. 21.

16 "individual submission to Satan": Kushner, *American Suicide.*

16 "gibbeted and . . . left to rot": Mark Williams, *Cry of Pain: Understanding Suicide and Self-Harm* (London: Penguin, 1997).

16 Rather than suffering: Ibid.

17 "Whensoever any affliction": John Donne, *Biathanatos.* A modern-spelling edition with introduction and comment by Michael Rudick and M. Pabst Battin (New York: Garland, 1982), p. 39.

17 Two recent authors: Williams, *Cry of Pain;* Kushner, *American Suicide.* Roy Porter's *Mind-Forg'd Manacles: A History of Madness in England from the Restoration to the Regency* (Cambridge, Mass.: Harvard University Press, 1987) is also an excellent historical account of suicide.

17 in mid-seventeenth-century England: Williams, *Cry of Pain.*

17 the Boston Coroners' Juries made: Kushner, *American Suicide.*

18 Dorothy Bradford . . . "accidentally fell overboard": Samuel Eliot Morison, Introduction to William Bradford, *Of Plymouth Plantation: 1620–1647* (New York; Alfred A. Knopf, 1996), p. xxiv.

18 Bradford himself does not mention: Bradford, ibid.

18 Most European countries formally decriminalized: J. Neeleman, "Suicide as a Crime in the U.K.: Legal History, International Comparisons and Present Implications," *Acta Psychiatrica Scandinavica,* 94 (1996): 252–257.

18 "I am the resurrection and the life": The Book of Common Prayer (Oxford: Oxford University Press), pp. 394–395.
18 the Order for the Burial of the Dead: Ibid., p. 388.
20 "desperately sensitive and confused": A. Alvarez, "Literature in the Nineteenth and Twentieth Centuries," in S. Perlin, ed., *A Handbook for the Understanding of Suicide* (Northvale, N.J.: Jason Aronson, 1975), p. 59.
21 "Judging whether life": A. Camus, *The Myth of Sisyphus and Other Essays* (New York: Vintage, 1995), p. 3.
21 Study after study has shown: R. M. A. Hirschfeld and G. L. Klerman, "Treatment of Depression in the Elderly," *Geriatrics*, 127 (1979): 51–57; B. D. Lebowitz, J. L. Pearson, L.S. Schneider, et al., "Diagnosis and Treatment of Depression in Late Life: Consensus Statement Update," *Journal of the American Medical Association*, 278 (1997), 1186–1190.
21 suicide rates in the elderly are alarmingly high: Y. Conwell, R. Melanie, and E. D. Caine, "Completed Suicide at Age 50 and Over," *Journal of the American Geriatric Society*, 38 (1990: 640–644; N. J. Osgood, *Suicide in Later Life* (New York: Lexington Books, 1992); D. C. Clark, "Narcissistic Crises of Aging and Suicidal Despair," *Suicide and Life-Threatening Behavior*, 23 (1993): 21–26; M. M. Henriksson, M. J. Marttunen, E. T. Isometsä, et al., "Mental Disorders in Elderly Suicide," *International Psychogeriatrics*, 7 (1995): 275–286; Y. Conwell, P. R. Duberstein, C. Cox, et al., "Relationships of Age and Axis I Diagnoses in Victims of Completed Suicide: A Psychological Autopsy Study," *American Journal of Psychiatry*, 153 (1996): 1001–1008; Gary J. Kennedy, ed., *Suicide and Depression in Late Life* (New York: John Wiley, 1996); H. Hendin, "Suicide, Assisted Suicide, and Medical Illness," *Journal of Clinical Psychiatry* 60 (Suppl. 2) (1999): 46–50.
21 physician-assisted suicide: For thoughtful but opposing discussions of the subject, see H. Hendin, *Seduced by Death: Doctors, Patients and the Dutch Cure* (New York: W. W. Norton, 1997), and C. F. McKhann, *A Time to Die: The Place for Physician Assistance* (New Haven: Yale University Press, 1999).
21 Suicide in the young: R. N. Anderson, K. D. Kochanek, and S. L. Murphy, "Advance Report of Final Mortality Statistics, 1995," *Monthly Vital Statistics Report*, 45 (11) (Suppl. 2) (Hyattsville, Md.: National Center for Health Statistics, 1997), DHHS Publication No. (PHS) 97–1120.
21 The 1995 National College: Division of Adolescent and School Health, National Center for Chronic Disease Prevention and Health Promotion, "Youth Risk Behavior Surveillance: National College Health Risk Behavior Survey—United States, 1995," *Morbidity and Mortality Weekly Report*, 46 (1997): No. SS-6.
22 One in five high school students: "Youth Risk Behavior Surveillance—United States, 1997," *Morbidity and Mortality Weekly Report*, 47 (1997): No. SS-3.
22 the same as those reported for high school students: L. Kann, C. W. Warren, W. A. Harris, J. L. Collins, B. I. Williams, J. G. Ross, and L. J. Kolbe, "Youth Risk Behavior Surveillance—United States, 1995," *Morbidity and Mortality Weekly Report*, 45 (1996): No. SS-4; L. Kann, C. W. Warren, W. A. Harris, J. L. Collins, K. A. Douglas, M. E. Collins, B. I. Williams, J. G. Ross, and L. J. Kolbe, "Youth Risk Behavior Surveillance—United States, 1993," *Morbidity and Mortality Weekly Report*, 44 (1995): No. SS-1.

23 Data for graph: For Vietnam War deaths: United States Department of Defense, Washington Headquarters Services, Directorate for Information Operations and Reports, July 1998. For HIV deaths and suicide: R. N. Anderson, K. D. Kochanek, and S. L. Murphy, "Report of Final Mortality Statistics, 1995," *Monthly Vital Statistics Report*, 45 (11, Suppl. 2) (Hyattsville, Md.: National Center for Health Statistics, 1997); additional statistics compiled by Dr. Alex Crosby, Centers for Disease Control and Prevention, Atlanta, Ga.; Ken Kochanek, M.A., Centers for Disease Control and Prevention (National Center for Health Statistics, Hyattsville, Md.); Dr. Harry Rosenberg, also at the National Center for Health Statistics.

24 Thirty thousand Americans: L. F. McCraig and B. J. Strussman, "National Hospital Ambulatory Care Survey: 1996. Emergency Department Summary Advance Data from Vital and Health Statistics," no. 293 (Hyattsville, Md.: National Center for Health Statistics, 1997).

25 "There is . . . in this humour": Robert Burton, *The Anatomy of Melancholy*, vol. 1 (London: J. M. Dent, 1932), pp. 431–432.

2 · To Measure the Heart's Turbulence

26 "to discover the elusive boundaries": Henry Romilly Fedden, *Suicide: A Social and Historical Study* (London: Peter Davies, 1938), p. 9.

26 The early Greeks: D. Daube, "The Linguistics of Suicide," *Suicide and Life-Threatening Behavior*, 7 (1977): 132–182.

27 Centuries of books: John Donne, *Biathanatos* (New York: Garland, 1982; first published 1647); David Hume, *Of Suicide* (1784, posthumous), in A. Macintyre, ed., *Hume's Ethical Writings* (New York: Macmillan, 1956); Emile Durkheim, *Suicide: A Study in Sociology* (New York: Free Press, 1951; first published 1897); Albert Camus, *The Myth of Sisyphus and Other Essays* (New York: Alfred A. Knopf, 1955); J. D. Douglas, *The Social Meanings of Suicide* (Princeton, N.J.: Princeton University Press, 1967); Jacques Choron, *Suicide* (New York: Scribners, 1972); M. P. Battin and D. J. Mays, eds., *Suicide: The Philosophical Issues* (New York: St. Martin's Press, 1980); R. Maris, *Pathways to Suicide* (Baltimore: Johns Hopkins University Press, 1981); Edwin Shneidman, *Definition of Suicide* (New York: John Wiley, 1985); Gavin J. Fairbairn, *Contemplating Suicide: The Language and Ethics of Self Harm* (London: Routledge, 1995).

27 All suicide classification: A. T. Beck, J. H. Davis, C. J. Frederick, S. Perlin, A. D. Pokorny, R. E. Schulman, R. H. Seiden, and B. J. Wittlin, "Classification and Nomenclature," in H. L. P. Resnick and B. C. Hathorne, eds., *Suicide Prevention in the Seventies* (Washington, D.C.: U.S. Government Printing Office, 1973), pp. 7–12; T. E. Ellis, "Classification of Suicidal Behavior: A Review and Step Toward Integration," *Suicide and Life-Threatening Behavior*, 18 (1988): 358–371.

27 Suicide is defined: M. L. Rosenberg, L. E. Davidson, J. C. Smith, A. L. Berman, H. Buzbee, G. Ganter, G. A. Gay, B. Moore-Lewis, D. H. Mills, D. Murray, P. W. O'Carroll, and D. Jobes, "Operational Criteria for the Determination of Suicide," *Journal of Forensic Sciences*, 32 (1988): 1445–1455; P. W. O'Carroll, A. L. Berman, R. W. Maris, E. K. Moscicki, B. L. Tanney, and M. M. Silverman, "Beyond the Tower of Babel: A

Nomenclature for Suicide," *Suicide and Life-Threatening Behavior,* 26 (1996): 237–252.

27 The World Health Organization: World Health Organization, *Prevention of Suicide,* Public Health Paper No. 35 (Geneva: World Health Organization, 1968).

27 Legal and financial issues: S. W. Abbott, "Death Certification," Albert H. Buck, ed., *Reference Handbook of the Medical Sciences,* (New York: William Wood, (1901); Edwin S. Shneidman, *Deaths of Man* (New York: Quadrangle, 1973); D. Jacobs and M. Klein-Benheim, "The Psychological Autopsy: A Useful Tool for Determining Proximate Causation in Suicide Cases," *Bulletin of the American Academy of Psychiatry and Law,* 23 (1995): 165–182.

28 Earlier estimates suggested: L. Dublin, *Suicide* (New York: Ronald Press, 1963); National Center for Health Statistics, *Suicide in the United States, 1950–1964;* United States Public Health Service Publication No. 1000, Series 20:1, Rockville, Md., 1967; J. M. Toolan, "Suicide in Children and Adolescents," *American Journal of Psychotherapy,* 29 (1975): 339–344; R. E. Litman, "Psychological Aspects of Suicide," in W. J. Curran, A. L. McGarry, and C. S. Petty, eds., *Modern Legal Medicine: Psychiatry and Forensic Science* (Philadelphia: F. A. Davis, 1980); D. A. Jobes and A. L. Berman, "Response Biases and the Impact of Psychological Autopsies on Medical Examiners' Determination of Mode of Death," paper presented to the 17th Meeting of the American Association of Suicidology, Anchorage, Alaska, 1984.

28 more recent studies indicate: A. B. Ford, N. B. Rushforth, N. Rushforth, C. S. Hirsch, and L. Adelson, "Violent Death in a Metropolitan County: II. Changing Patterns in Suicides (1959–1974)," *American Journal of Public Health,* 69 (1979): 459–464; D. A. Brent, J. A. Perper, and C. J. Allman, "Alcohol, Firearms, and Suicide Among the Young," *Journal of the American Medical Association,* 257 (1987): 3369–3372; G. Kleck, "Miscounting Suicides," *Suicide and Life-Threatening Behavior,* 18 (1988): 219–236; E. K. Moscicki, "Epidemiology of Suicidal Behavior," *Suicide and Life-Threatening Behavior,* 25 (1995): 22–35; A. Ohberg and J. Lönnqvist, "Suicides Hidden Among Undetermined Deaths," *Acta Psychiatrica Scandinavica,* 98 (1998): 214–218.

28 The evidence may be explicit: D. A. Jobes, A. L. Berman, and A. R. Josselson, "Improving the Validity and Reliability of Medical-Legal Certifications of Suicide," *Suicide and Life-Threatening Behavior,* 17 (1987): 310–325, p. 323.

29 In Canadian studies: G. K. Jarvis and H. C. Northcott, "Religion and Differences in Mortality and Morbidity," *Social Science and Medicine,* 25 (1987): 813–824; G. K. Jarvis, M. Boldt, and J. Butt, "Medical Examiners and Manner of Death," *Suicide and Life-Threatening Behavior,* 21 (1991): 115–133.

29 In one investigation, Danish coroners: M. W. Atkinson, N. Kessel, and J. B. Dalgaard, "The Comparability of Suicide Rates," *British Journal of Psychiatry,* 127 (1975): 247–256.

29 Coroners and medical examiners: B. Walsh, D. Walsh, and B. Whelan, "Suicide in Dublin: II. The Influence of Some Social and Medical Factors

on Coroners' Verdicts," *British Journal of Psychiatry*, 126 (1975): 309–312; J. Maxwell Atkinson, *Discovering Suicide: Studies in the Social Organization of Sudden Death* (Pittsburgh: University of Pittsburgh Press, 1978); M. C. Bradley, "Changing Patterns of Suicide in Leeds, 1979 to 1985," *Medical Science Law*, 27 (1987): 201–206; M. Speechley and K. M. Stavraky, "The Adequacy of Suicide Statistics for Use in Epidemiology and Public Health," *Canadian Journal of Public Health*, 82 (1991): 38–42.

29 Indeed, most drownings: T. T. Noguchi, *Coroner* (New York: Simon and Schuster, 1983); A. L. Berman, "Forensic Suicidology and the Psychological Autopsy," A. A. Leenaars, ed., in *Suicidology: Essays in Honor of Edwin S. Shneidman* (Northvale, N.J.: Jason Aronson, 1993), pp. 248–266.

30 "For just as it is difficult": J. Maxwell Atkinson, *Discovering Suicide: Studies in the Social Organization of Sudden Death* (Pittsburgh: University of Pittsburgh Press, 1978), pp. 124–125.

30 Deaths in single-car accidents: D. P. Phillips and T. E. Ruth, "Adequacy of Official Suicide Statistics for Scientific Research and Public Policy," *Suicide and Life-Threatening Behavior*, 23 (1993): 307–319; A. Ohberg, A Penttila, and J. Lönnqvist, "Driver Suicides," *British Journal of Psychiatry*, 171 (1997): 468–472.

30 The most important cause: I. M. K. Ovenstone, "A Psychiatric Approach to the Diagnosis of Suicide and Its Effect upon the Edinburgh Statistics," *British Journal of Psychiatry*, 123 (1973): 15–21; M. W. Atkinson, N. Kessel, and J. B. Dalgaard, "The Comparability of Suicide Rates," *British Journal of Psychiatry*, 127 (1975): 247–256; B. M. Barraclough, "Reliability of Violent Death Certification in One Coroner's District," *British Journal of Psychiatry*, 132 (1978): 39–41; R. E. Litman, "500 Psychological Autopsies," *Journal of Forensic Science*, 34 (1989): 638–646; M. Speechley and K. M. Stavraky, "The Adequacy of Suicide Statistics for Use in Epidemiology and Public Health," *Canadian Journal of Public Health*, 82 (1991): 38–42; P. N. Cooper and C. M. Milroy, "The Coroner's System and Under-reporting of Suicide," *Medical Science Law*, 35 (1995), 319–326.

30 Self-poisoning deaths: R. D. T. Farmer, "Assessing the Epidemiology of Suicide and Parasuicide," *British Journal of Psychiatry*, 153 (1988): 16–20.

31 This technique: P. Friedman, "Suicide Among Police: A Study of Ninety-Three Suicides Among New York City Policemen, 1934–1940," in E. S. Shneidman, ed., *Essays in Self-Destruction* (New York: Science House, 1967), pp. 414–449.

31 The study, now a classic: E. R. Robins, G. E. Murphy, R. H. Wilkinson, S. Gassner, and J. Kayes, "Some Clinical Considerations in the Prevention of Suicide Based on a Study of 134 Successful Suicides," *American Journal of Public Health*, 49 (1959): 888–899; Eli Robins, *The Final Months: A Study of the Lives of 134 Persons Who Committed Suicide* (New York: Oxford University Press, 1981).

31 as a method of clinical: E. S. Shneidman and N. L. Farberow, "Sample Investigations of Equivocal Deaths," in N. L. Farberow and E. S. Shneidman, eds., *The Cry for Help* (New York: McGraw-Hill, 1961), pp. 118–128; R. E. Litman, T. J. Curphey, E. S. Shneidman, et al., "Investigations of Equivocal Suicides," *Journal of the American Medical Association*, 184 (1963): 924–929; T. J. Curphey, "The Forensic Pathologist and the Multidiscipli-

nary Approach to Death," in E. S. Shneidman, ed., *Essays in Self-Destruction* (New York: Science House, 1967), pp. 110–117; E. S. Shneidman, "Suicide, Lethality and the Psychological Autopsy," E. S. Shneidman and M. Ortega, eds., *Aspects of Depression* (Boston: Little, Brown, 1969).

32 Members of the Suicide Team: The list of inquiry topics is from E. S. Shneidman, *Deaths of Man* (Baltimore: Penguin, 1974), p. 135.

32 "In practically any coroner's office": N. L. Farberow and E. S. Shneidman, eds., *The Cry for Help* (New York: McGraw-Hill, 1965), p. 121.

34 The psychological autopsy: J. Beskow, B. Runeson, and U. Asgard, "Psychological Autopsies: Methods and Ethics," *Suicide and Life-Threatening Behavior*, 20 (1990): 307–323; D. C. Clark and S. L. Horton-Deutsch, "Assessment *in Absentia*: The Value of the Psychological Autopsy Method for Studying Antecedents of Suicide and Predicting Future Suicides," in R. W. Maris, A. L. Berman, J. T. Maltsberger, and R. I. Yufit, eds., *Assessment and Prevention of Suicide*, (New York: Guilford, 1992, pp. 144–181.

34 It has proven especially useful: T. L. Dorpat and H. S. Ripley, "A Study of Suicide in the Seattle Area," *Comprehensive Psychiatry*, 1 (1960): 349–359; B. M. Barraclough, J. Bunch, B. Nelson, and P. Sainsbury, "A Hundred Cases of Suicide: Clinical Aspects," *British Journal of Psychiatry*, 125 (1974): 355–373; C. L. Rich, D. Young, and R. C. Fowler, "San Diego Suicide Study: 1. Young Versus Old Subjects," *Archives of General Psychiatry*, 43 (1986): 577–582; D. A. Brent, J. A. Perper, C. E. Goldstein, D. J. Kolko, M. J. Allan, C. J. Allman, and J. P. Zelenak, "Risk Factors for Adolescent Suicide: A Comparison of Adolescent Suicide Victims with Suicidal Inpatients," *Archives of General Psychiatry*, 45 (1988): 581–588.

34 These indirect, or "subintentional,": Edwin Shneidman, *Definition of Suicide* (New York: John Wiley, 1985), p. 21.

35 chronic alcohol or drug abuse: Karl Menninger, *Man Against Himself* (New York: Harcourt, Brace and Co., 1938); Norman Farberow, ed., *The Many Faces of Suicide* (New York: McGraw-Hill, 1980).

35 Twenty-five years ago: E. S. Paykel, J. K. Myers, J. J. Lindenthal, and J. Tanner, "Suicidal Feelings in the General Population: A Prevalence Study," *British Journal of Psychiatry*, 124 (1974) 460–469.

35 National Institute of Mental Health: Lee N. Robins and Darrel A. Regier, eds., *Psychiatric Disorders in America: The Epidemiologic Catchment Area Study* (New York: Free Press, 1991).

36 Of the 18,500 individuals: E. K. Moscicki, P. O'Carroll, B. Z. Locke, D. S. Rae, A. G. Roy, and D. A. Regier, "Suicidal Ideation and Attempts: The Epidemiologic Catchment Area," in U.S. DHHS, *Report of the Secretary's Task Force on Youth Suicide*: vol. 4, *Strategies for the Prevention of Youth Suicide* (Washington, D.C.: U.S. Government Printing Office, 1988); E. K. Moscicki, "Epidemiologic Surveys as Tools for Studying Suicidal Behavior: A Review," *Suicide and Life-Threatening Behavior*, 19 (1989): 131–146.

36 Other investigations conducted: J. J. Schwab, J. Warheit, and C. E. Holzer, "Suicidal Ideation and Behaviour in a General Population," *Diseases of the Nervous System*, 33 (1972): 745–749; T. Hällstrom, "Life-Weariness, Suicidal Thoughts and Suicidal Attempts Among Women in Gothenburg, Sweden," *Acta Psychiatrica Scandinavica*, 56 (1977): 15–20; D. S. Vandivort and B. Z. Locke, "Suicide Ideation: Its Relation to Depression, Suicide, and

Suicide Attempt," *Suicide and Life-Threatening Behavior,* 9 (1979): 205–218; E. L. Goldberg, "Depression and Suicide Ideation in the Young Adult," *American Journal of Psychiatry,* 138 (1981): 35–40; R. Ramsay and C. Bagley, "The Prevalence of Suicidal Behaviors, Attitudes and Associated Social Experiences in an Urban Population," *Suicide and Life-Threatening Behavior,* 15 (1985): 151–167.

36 The most comprehensive study: "Youth Risk Behavior Surveillance: National College Health Risk Behavior Survey—United States, 1995," *Morbidity and Mortality Weekly Report,* 46 (1997): No. SS-6.

36 Other research, conducted in Europe: L. E. Craig and R. J. Senter, "Student Thoughts About Suicide," *Psychological Record,* 22 (1972): 355–358; C. V. Leonard and D. E. Flinn, "Suicidal Ideation and Behavior in Youthful Nonpsychiatric Populations," *Journal of Consulting and Clinical Psychology,* 38 (1972): 366–371; D. C. Murray, "Suicidal and Depressive Feelings Among College Students," *Psychological Reports,* 33 (1973): 175–181; B. L. Mishara, A. H. Baker, and T. T. Mishara, "The Frequency of Suicide Attempts: A Retrospective Approach Applied to College Students," *American Journal of Psychiatry,* 133 (1976): 841–844; J. L. Bernard and M. Bernard, "Factors Related to Suicidal Behavior Among College Students and the Impact of Institutional Response," *Journal of College Student Personnel,* 23 (1982): 409-413; B. L. Mishara, "College Students' Experience with Suicide and Reactions to Suicidal Verbalizations: A Model for Prevention." *Journal of Community Psychology,* 10 (1982): 142–150; M. D. Rudd, "The Prevalence of Suicidal Ideation Among College Students," *Suicide and Life-Threatening Behavior,* 19 (1989): 173–183; P. W. Meilman, J. A. Pattis, and D. Kraus-Zeilmann, "Suicide Attempts and Threats on One College Campus: Policy and Practice," *Journal of American College Health,* 42 (1994): 147–154.

36 High school students also: Youth Risk Behavior Surveillance—United States, 1997, Centers for Disease Control and Prevention, CDC Surveillance Summaries, August 14, 1998. *Morbidity and Mortality Weekly Report,* 47 (1998): No. SS-3.

37 more than 50 percent of New York: J. M. Harkavy Friedman, G. M. Asnis, M. Boeck, and J. DiFiore, "Prevalence of Specific Suicidal Behaviors in a High School Sample," *American Journal of Psychiatry,* 144 (1987): 1203-1206.

37 20 percent of Oregon high school: P. M. Lewinsohn, P. Rohde, and J. P. Seeley, "Adolescent Suicidal Ideation and Attempts: Prevalence, Risk Factors, and Clinical Implications," *Clinical Psychology: Science and Practice,* 3 (1996): 25–46.

37 One in twenty French boys: M. Choquet and H. Menke, "Suicidal Thoughts During Early Adolescence: Prevalence, Associated Troubles and Help-Seeking Behavior," *Acta Psychiatrica Scandinavica,* 81 (1989): 170–177.

37 In Canada, one in ten: M. Choquet, V. Kovess, and N. Poutignat, "Suicidal Thoughts Among Adolescents: An Intercultural Approach," *Adolescence,* 28 (1993): 649–659.

37 Another Canadian study: R. T. Joffe, D. R. Offord, and M. H. Boyle, "Ontario Child Health Study," *American Journal of Psychiatry,* 145 (1988): 1420–1423.

37 it is of further concern: T. M. Achenbach and C. S. Edelbrock, *Manual for*

the *Child Behavior Checklist and Revised Child Behavior Profile* (Burlington: University of Vermont Department of Psychiatry, 1983); T. M. Achenbach and C. S. Edelbrock, *Manual for the Youth Self-Report and Profile* (Burlington: University of Vermont Department of Psychiatry, 1987); J. M. Rey and K. D. Bird, "Sex Differences in Suicidal Behavior of Referred Adolescents," *British Journal of Psychiatry*, 158 (1991): 776–781.

38 Parents also seriously underestimate: D. M. Velting, D. Shaffer, M. S. Gould, R. Garfinkel, P. Fisher, and M. Davies, "Parent-Victim Agreement in Adolescent Suicide Research," *Journal of the American Academy of Child and Adolescent Psychiatry*, 37 (1998): 1161–1166.

38 Cynthia Pfeffer: C. R. Pfeffer, "Suicidal Fantasies in Normal Children," *Journal of Nervous and Mental Disease*, 173 (1985): 78–84, p. 80.

39 "One night": Evelyn Waugh, *A Little Learning. The First Volume of an Autobiography* (London: Chapman & Hall, 1964), pp. 229–230.

40 There is, in fact, no consistent: D. J. Pallis and P. Sainsbury, "The Value of Assessing Intent in Attempted Suicide," *Psychological Medicine*, 6 (1976): 487–492; A. S. Henderson, J. Hartigan, J. Davidson, G. N. Lance, P. Duncan-Jones, K. M. Koller, K. Ritchie, H. McAuley, C. L. Williams, and W. Slaghuis, "A Typology of Parasuicide," *British Journal of Psychiatry*, 131 (1977): 631–641; E. S. Paykel and E. Rassaby, "Classification of Suicide Attempters by Cluster Analysis," *British Journal of Psychiatry*, 133 (1978): 45–52; S. Henderson and G. N. Lance, "Types of Attempted Suicide," *Acta Psychiatrica Scandinavica*, 59 (1979): 31–39; K. Hawton, M. Osborn, J. O'Grady, and D. Cole, "Classification of Adolescents Who Take Overdoses," *British Journal of Psychiatry*, 140 (1982): 124–131; D. J. Pallis, J. S. Gibbons, and D. W. Pierce, "Estimating Suicide Risk Among Attempted Suicides: II. Efficiency of Predictive Scales After the Attempt," *British Journal of Psychiatry*, 144 (1984): 139–148; D. A. Brent, "Correlates of the Medical Lethality of Suicide Attempts in Children and Adolescents," *Journal of the American Academy for Child and Adolescent Psychiatry*, 26 (1987): 87–89; A. Kurz, H. J. Möller, G. Baindl, F. Bürk, A Torhorst, C. Wächtler, and H. Lauter, "Classification of Parasuicide by Cluster Analysis: Types of Suicidal Behaviour, Therapeutic and Prognostic Implications," *British Journal of Psychiatry*, 150 (1987): 520–525; H. Hjelmeland, "Verbally Expressed Intentions of Parasuicide: 1. Characteristics of Patients with Various Intentions," *Crisis*, 16 (1995): 176–180; E. Arensman and J. F. M. Kerkhof, "Classification of Attempted Suicide: A Review of Empirical Studies, 1963–1993," *Suicide and Life-Threatening Behavior*, 26 (1996): 46–65.

40 A Suicide Intent Scale: R. W. Beck, J. B. Morris, and A. T. Beck, "Cross-Validation of a Suicide Intent Scale," *Psychological Reports*, 34 (1974): 445–446.

44 In addition to scales: P. R. McHugh and H. Goodell, "Suicidal Behavior: A Distinction in Patients with Sedative Poisoning Seen in a General Hospital," *Archives of General Psychiatry*, 25 (1971): 456–464; A. D. Weisman and J. W. Worden, "Risk-Rescue Rating in Suicide Assessment," *Archives of General Psychiatry*, 26 (1972): 553–560; L. B. Potter, M. Kresnow, K. E. Powell, Patrick W. O'Carroll, R. K. Lee, R. F. Frankowski, A. C. Swann, T. L. Bayer, M. H. Bautista, and M. G. Briscoe, "Identification of Nearly

Fatal Suicide Attempts: Self-Inflicted Injury Severity Form," *Suicide and Life-Threatening Behavior,* 28 (1998): 174–186.

45 between 1 and 4 percent: J. J. Schwab, G. J. Warheit, and C. E. Holzer, "Suicide Ideation and Behavior in a General Population," *Diseases of the Nervous System,* 33 (1972): 745–748; E. S. Paykel, J. K. Myers, J. J. Lindenthal, and J. Tanner, "Suicidal Feelings in the General Population: A Prevalence Study," *British Journal of Psychiatry,* 124 (1974): 460–469; R. Ramsay and C. Bagley, "The Prevalence of Suicidal Behaviors, Attitudes and Associated Social Experiences in an Urban Population," *Suicide and Life-Threatening Behavior,* 15 (1985): 151–167; E. K. Moscicki, P. O'Carroll, D. S. Rae, B. Z. Locke, A. Roy, and D. A. Regier, "Suicide Attempts in the Epidemiologic Catchment Area Study," *Yale Journal of Biology and Medicine,* 61 (1988): 259–268; J. Hintikka, H. Viinamäki, A. Tanskanen, O. Kontula, and K. Koskela, "Suicidal Ideation and Parasuicide in the Finnish General Population," *Acta Psychiatrica Scandinavica,* 98 (1998): 23–27; D. J. Statham, A. C. Heath, P. A. F. Madden, K. K. Bucholz, L. Bierut, S. H. Dinwiddie, W. S. Slutske, M. P. Dunne, and N. G. Martin, "Suicidal Behaviour: An Epidemiological and Genetic Study," *Psychological Medicine,* 28 (1998): 839–855; M. M. Weissman, R. C. Bland, G. J. Canino, S. Greenwald, H.-G. Hwu, P. R. Joyce, E. G. Karam, C.-K. Lee, J. Lellouch, J.-P. Lepine, S. C. Newman, M. Rubio-Stipec, J. E. Wells, P. J. Wickramartne, H.-U. Wittchen, and E.-K. Yeh, "Prevalence of Suicide Ideation and Suicide Attempts in Nine Countries," *Psychological Medicine,* 29 (1999): 9–17.

45 Adolescents, on the other hand: B. L. Mishara, A. H. Baker, and T. T. Mishara, "The Frequency of Suicide Attempts: A Retrospective Approach Applied to College Students," *American Journal of Psychiatry,* 133 (1976): 841–844; J. M. Harkavy Friedman, G. M. Asnis, M. Boeck, and J. Di Fiore, "Prevalence of Specific Suicidal Behaviors in a High School Sample," *American Journal of Psychiatry,* 144 (1987): 1203–1206; R. T. Joffe, D. R. Offord, and M. H. Boyle, "Ontario Child Health Study: Suicidal Behavior in Youth Age 12–16 Years," *American Journal of Psychiatry,* 145 (1988): 1420–1423; M. D. Rudd, "The Prevalence of Suicidal Ideation Among College Students," *Suicide and Life-Threatening Behavior,* 19 (1989): 173–183; C. W. M. Kienhorst, E. J. DeWilde, J. van den Bout, R. F. W. Diekstra, and W. H. G. Wolters, "Characteristics of Suicide Attempters in a Population-Based Sample of Dutch Adolescents," *British Journal of Psychiatry,* 156 (1990): 243–248; P. J. Meehan, J. A. Lamb, L. E. Saltzman, and P. W. O'Carroll, "Attempted Suicide Among Young Adults: Progress Toward a Meaningful Estimate of Prevalence," *American Journal of Psychiatry,* 149 (1992): 41–44; P. M. Lewinsohn, P. Rohde, and J. R. Seeley, "Adolescent Suicidal Ideation and Attempts: Prevalence, Risk Factors, and Clinical Implications," *Clinical Psychology: Science and Practice,* 3 (1996): 25–46; "Youth Risk Behavior Surveillance: National College Health Risk Behavior Survey—United States, 1995," *Morbidity and Mortality Weekly Report,* 46 (1997): No. SS-6; C. Rey Gex, F. Narring, C. Ferron, and P. A. Michaud, "Suicide Attempts Among Adolescents in Switzerland: Prevalence, Associated Factors and Comorbidity," *Acta Psychiatrica Scandinavica,* 98 (1998): 28–33; "Youth Risk Behavior Surveillance—United States, 1997," Centers for Disease Control and Prevention, CDC Surveillance Summa-

ries, August 14, 1998, *Morbidity and Mortality Weekly Report*, 47 (1998): No. SS-3.

45 Myrna Weissman: M. M. Weissman, "The Epidemiology of Suicide Attempts, 1960 to 1971," *Archives of General Psychiatry*, 30 (1974): 737–746.

45 There may also be a tendency: R. D. Goldney, S. Smith. A. H. Winefield, M. Tiggeman, and H. R. Winefield, "Suicidal Ideation: Its Enduring Nature and Associated Morbidity," *Acta Psychiatrica Scandinavica*, 83 (1991): 115–120.

46 There are an estimated: E. S. Shneidman and N. L. Farberow, "Statistical Comparison Between Attempted and Committed Suicides," in N. L. Farberow and E. S. Shneidman, eds., *The Cry for Help* (New York: McGraw-Hill, 1961), pp. 19–47; E. Stengel, *Suicide and Attempted Suicide* (Baltimore: Penguin, 1964); D. Parkin and E. Stengel, "Incidence of Suicidal Attempts in an Urban Community," *British Medical Journal*, 2 (1965): 133–138; I. M. K. Ovenstone, "Spectrum of Suicidal Behaviours in Edinburgh," *British Journal of Preventive and Social Medicine*, 27 (1973): 27–35; M. McIntire, C. R. Angle, R. L. Wikoff, and M. L. Schlicht, "Recurrent Adolescent Suicidal Behavior," *Pediatrics*, 60 (1977): 605–608; K. R. Petronis, J. F. Samuels, and E. K. Moscicki, "An Epidemiologic Investigation of Potential Risk Factors for Suicide Attempts," *Social Psychiatry and Psychiatric Epidemiology*, 35 (1990): 193–199; R. F. W. Diekstra and W. Gulbinat, "The Epidemiology of Suicidal Behavior: A Review of Three Continents," *World Health Statistical Quarterly*, 46 (1993): 52–68; C. M. Pearce and G. Martin, "Predicting Suicide Attempts Among Adolescents," *Acta Psychiatrica Scandinavica*, 90 (1994): 324–328; A. Schmidtke, "Perspective: Suicide in Europe," *Suicide and Life-Threatening Behavior*, 27 (1997): 127–136.

46 And many, if not most: R. Siani, N. Garzotto, C. Zimmerman Tansella, and M. Tansella, "Predictive Scales for Parasuicide Repetition: Further Results," *Acta Psychiatrica Scandinavica*, 59 (1979): 17–23; N. Kreitman and P. Casey, "Repetition of Parasuicide: An Epidemiological and Clinical Study," *British Journal of Psychiatry*, 153 (1988): 792–800; E. D. Myers, "Predicting Repetition of Deliberate Self-Harm: A Review of the Literature in the Light of a Current Study," *Acta Psychiatrica Scandinavica*, 77 (1988): 314–319; A. Öjehagen, G. Regnell, and L. Träskman-Bendz, "Deliberate Self-Poisoning: Repeaters and Nonrepeaters Admitted to an Intensive Care Unit," *Acta Psychiatrica Scandinavica*, 84 (1991): 266–271; H. Hjelmeland, "Repetition of Parasuicide: A Predictive Study," *Suicide and Life-Threatening Behavior*, 26 (1996): 395–404; U. Bille-Brahe, A. Kerkhof, D. De Leo, A. Schmidtke, P. Crepet, J. Lönnqvist, K. Michel, E. Salander-Renberg, T. C. Stiles, D. Wasserman, B. Aagaard, H. Egebo, and B. Jensen, "A Repetition-Prediction Study of European Parasuicide Populations: A Summary of the First Report from Part II of the WHO/EURO Multicentre Study on Parasuicide," *Acta Psychiatrica Scandinavica*, 95 (1977): 81–86.

46 Women in the United States: R. N. Anderson, K. D. Kochanek, and S. L. Murphy, "Advance Report of Final Mortality Statistics, 1995," *Monthly Vital Statistics Report*, 45 (Hyattsville, Md.: National Center for Health Statistics, 1997), DHHS Publication No. (PHS) 97–1120.

46 The reasons for this: D. Lester, "The Distribution of Sex and Age Among Completed Suicides," *International Journal of Social Psychiatry*, 28 (1982):

256–260; A. R. Rich, J. Kirkpatrick-Smith, R. L. Bonner, and F. Jans, "Gender Differences in the Psychosocial Correlates of Suicidal Ideation Among Adolescents," *Suicide and Life-Threatening Behavior,* 22 (1992): 364–373; E. K. Moscicki, "Gender Differences in Completed and Attempted Suicides," *Annals of Epidemiology,* 4 (1994): 152–158; M. A. Young, L. F. Fogg, W. A. Scheftner, and J. A. Fawcett, "Interactions of Risk Factors in Predicting Suicide," *American Journal of Psychiatry,* 151 (1994): 434–435; Silva Sara Canetto and David Lester, eds., *Women and Suicidal Behavior* (New York: Springer, 1995); S. S. Canetto, "Gender and Suicidal Behavior: Theories and Evidence," in R. W. Maris, M. M. Silverman, and S. S. Canetto, eds., *Review of Suicidology* (New York: Guilford, 1997), pp. 138–167; G. E. Murphy, "Why Women Are Less Likely Than Men to Commit Suicide," *Comprehensive Psychiatry,* 39 (1998): 165–175.

46 Women and girls, for example: M. M. Weissman, P. J. Leaf, C. E. Holzer III, J. K. Myers, and G. L. Tischler, "The Epidemiology of Depression: An Update on Sex Differences in Rates," *Journal of Affective Disorders,* 7 (1984): 179–188; J. E. Fleming, D. R. Offord, and M. H. Boyle, "The Ontario Child Health Study: Prevalence of Childhood and Adolescent Depression in the Community," *British Journal of Psychiatry,* 155 (1989): 647–654; C. Z. Garrison, K. L. Jackson, F. Marsteller, R. McKeown, and C. Addy, "A Longitudinal Study of Depressive Symptomatology in Young Adolescents," *Journal of the American Academy of Child and Adolescent Psychiatry,* 29 (1990): 581–585.

46 This higher rate of depression: M. Weissman and M. Olfson, "Depression in Women: Implications for Health Care Research," *Science,* 269 (1995): 799–801; M. Weissman, R. C. Bland, G. J. Canino, C. Faravelli, S. Greenwald, H.-G. Hwu, P. R. Joyce, E. G. Karam. C.-K. Lee, J. Lellouch, J.-P. Lépine, S. C. Newman, M. Rubio-Stipec, J. E. Wells, P. J. Wickramaratne, H.-U. Wittehen, and E.-K. Yeh, "Cross-National Epidemiology of Major Depression and Bipolar Disorder," *Journal of the American Medical Association,* 276 (1996): 293–299.

46 There is also evidence: H. White and J. M. Stillion, "Sex Differences in Attitudes Toward Suicide: Do Males Stigmatize Males?" *Psychology of Women Quarterly,* 12 (1988): 357–366.

47 *American Journal of Insanity:* E. K. Hunt, "Statistics of Suicide in the United States," *American Journal of Insanity,* 1 (1845): 225–234.

47 between those who attempt suicide: E. Robins, G. E. Murphy, R. H. Wilkinson Jr., S. Gassner, and J. Kays, "Some Clinical Considerations in the Prevention of Suicide Based on a Study of 134 Successful Suicides," *American Journal of Public Health,* 49 (1959): 888–899; T. L. Dorpat and H. S. Ripley, "A Study of Suicide in the Seattle Area," *Comprehensive Psychiatry,* 1 (1960): 349–359; B. Barraclough, J. Bunch, B. Nelson, and P. Sainsbury, "A Hundred Cases of Suicide: Clinical Aspects," *British Journal of Psychiatry,* 125 (1974): 355–373; I. M. K. Ovenstone and N. Kreitman, "Two Syndromes of Suicide," *British Journal of Psychiatry,* 124 (1974): 336–345.

47 long-term (ten- to forty-year) follow-up studies: P. B. Schneider, *La Tentative de suicide: Étude statistique, clinique, psychologique et catamnestique* (Neuchâtel and Paris: Delachauz et Niestlé, 1954); O Otto, "Suicidal Acts by Children and Adolescents," *Acta Psychiatrica Scandinavica,* 233 (Suppl.),

1972; K. G. Dahlgren, "Attempted Suicides—35 Years Afterwards," *Suicide and Life-Threatening Behavior,* 7 (1977): 75–79; O. Ekeberg, O. Ellingsen, and D. Jacobsen, "Mortality and Causes of Death in a 10-Year Follow-up of Patients Treated for Self-Poisonings in Oslo," *Suicide and Life-Threatening Behavior,* 24 (1994): 398–405.

47 Predicting who: J. A. Motto, "Suicide Attempts: A Longitudinal View," *Archives of General Psychiatry,* 13 (1965): 516–520; S. Greer and H. A. Lee, "Subsequent Progress of Potentially Lethal Suicide Attempts," *Acta Psychiatrica Scandinavica,* 43 (1967): 361–371; J. Tuckman and W. F. Youngman, "Assessment of Suicide Risk in Attempted Suicides," in H. L. P. Resnik, ed., *Suicidal Behaviors: Diagnosis and Management* (Boston: Little, Brown, 1968), pp. 190–197; J. Lönnqvist, P. Niskanen, K. A. Achte, and L. Ginman, "Self-Poisoning with Follow-up Considerations," *Suicide and Life-Threatening Behavior,* 5 (1975): 39–46; G. Paerregaard, "Suicide Among Attempted Suicides: A 10-Year Follow-up," *Suicide and Life-Threatening Behavior,* 5 (1975): 140–144; A. T. Beck, R. A. Steer, M. Kovacs, and B. Garrison, "Hopelessness and Eventual Suicide: A 10 Year Prospective Study of Patients Hospitalized with Suicidal Ideation," *American Journal of Psychiatry,* 142 (1985): 559–563; J. Cullberg, D. Wasserman, and C. G. Stefansson, "Who Commits Suicide After a Suicide Attempt?" *Acta Psychiatrica Scandinavica,* 77 (1988): 598–603.

47 "Do I deserve credit": Robert Lowell, "Suicide," lines 46–55; *Day by Day* (London: Faber and Faber, 1978), p. 16.

48 Suicide, which kills: *Morbidity and Mortality Weekly Report,* 46 (1997), p. 942.

48 A recent World Health Organization report: World Health Organization, *The World Health Report 1999* (Geneva: World Health Organization, 1999).

48 British researchers: P. Sainsbury, J. Jenkins, and A. Levey, "The Social Correlates of Suicide in Europe," in R. D. T. Farmer and S. R. Hirsch, eds., *The Suicide Syndrome* (London: Croom Helm, 1980), pp. 38–53; U. Åsgård, P. Nordström, and G. Råbäck, "Birth Cohort Analysis of Changing Suicide Risk by Sex and Age in Sweden 1952 to 1981," *Acta Psychiatrica Scandinavica,* 76 (1987): 456–463; S. P. Kachur, L. B. Potter, S. P. James, and K. E. Powell, *Suicide in the United States, 1980–1992* (Atlanta, Ga.: National Center for Injury Prevention and Control, 1995).

48 The strong trend toward higher: E. M. Brooke, *Suicide and Attempted Suicide,* Public Health Paper No. 58 (Geneva: World Health Organization, 1974); C. Jennings and B. Barraclough, "Legal and Administrative Influences on the English Suicide Rate Since 1900," *Psychological Medicine,* 10 (1980): 407–418; G. E. Murphy and R. D. Wetzel, "Suicide Risk by Birth Cohort in the United States, 1949 to 1974," *Archives of General Psychiatry,* 37 (1980): 519–523; O. Hagnell, J. Lanke, B. Rorsman, and L. Ojesjo, "Are We Entering an Age of Melancholy? Depressive Illness in a Prospective Epidemiological Study over 25 Years: The Lundby Study, Sweden," *Psychological Medicine,* 12 (1982): 279–289; G. L. Klerman, P. W. Lavori, J. Rice, T. Reich, J. Endicott, N. C. Andreasen, M. B. Keller, and R. M. A. Hirschfeld, "Birth Cohort Trends in Rates of Major Depressive Disorder Among Relatives of Patients with Affective Disorder," *Archives of General Psychiatry,* 42 (1985): 689–695; R. T. Rubin, "Mood Changes During Adolescence," in J. Bancroft and J. Reinisch, eds., *Adolescence and Puberty*

(Oxford: Oxford University Press, 1990); L. N. Robins and D. A. Regier, eds., *Psychiatric Disorders in America: The Epidemiologic Catchment Area Study* (New York: Free Press, 1991); N. D. Ryan, D. E. Williamson, S. Iyengar, H. Orvaschel, T. Reich, R. E. Dahl, and J. Puig-Antich, "A Secular Increase in Child and Adolescent Onset Affective Disorder," *Journal of American Academy of Child Psychiatry,* 31 (1992): 600–605; J. L. McIntosh, "Generational Analyses of Suicide: Baby Boomers and 13ers," *Suicide and Life-Threatening Behavior,* 24 (1994): 334–342; C. Pritchard, "New Patterns of Suicide by Age and Gender in the United Kingdom and the Western World 1974–1992: An Indicator of Social Change?" *Social Psychiatry Psychiatric Epidemiology,* 31 (1996): 227–234.

49 Data for graphs: World Bank, *World Development Report 1993: Investing in Health* (New York: Oxford University Press for the World Bank, 1993); C. J. L. Murray and A. D. Lopez, *The Global Burden of Disease* (Cambridge, Mass.: Harvard University Press, 1996).

50 American and Finnish studies: P. Räsänen, H. Hakko, M. Isohanni, S. Hodgins, M.-R. Järvelin, and J. Tiihonen, "Maternal Smoking During Pregnancy and Risk of Criminal Behavior Among Adult Male Offspring in the Northern Finland 1966 Birth Cohort," *American Journal of Psychiatry,* 156 (1999): 857–862; M. M. Weissman, V. Warner, P. J. Wickramartne, and D. B. Kandel, "Maternal Smoking During Pregnancy and Psychopathology in Offspring Followed to Adulthood," *Journal of the American Academy of Child and Adolescent Psychiatry,* 38 (1999): 892–899.

Essay · This Life, This Death

55 "Minds of men fashioned": "The U.S. Air Force Song," ll. 10–13, 15–16, 28. Words and music by Robert Crawford. (Copyright © 1939, 1942, 1951 by Carl Fischer, Inc.)

68 "And He will raise you": from "On Eagle's Wings," refrain and l. 1 of verse 3. Text and music, 1979, New Dawn Music. Lyrics by Michael Joncas (adapted from Psalm 91).

69 "As we soar": from "One More Roll," by Commander Jerry Coffee (Hanoi, 1968).

69 "We will run": "We Will Rise Again," refrain. Text and music by David Haas, text based upon Isaiah 40, 41. OCP Publications, 1985.

3 · Take Off the Amber, Put Out the Lamp

73 "It is time": Quoted in Viktoria Schweitzer, *Tsvetaeva* (New York: Farrar, Straus and Giroux, 1992), p. 377. Russian poet Marina Tsvetaeva (1892–1941) wrote these lines six months before she killed herself. Her friend Boris Pasternak said of her that she was "determined, militant, indomitable. In her life and in her work she rushed impetuously, eagerly, and almost rapaciously toward the achievement of finality and definiteness." Her work, he wrote, was "immense, violent" and a "great triumph for Russian poetry." Boris Pasternak, *I Remember: Sketches for an Autobiography* (Cambridge, Mass.: Harvard University Press, 1983), pp. 109–110.

74 "Suicide notes," he writes: E. Shneidman, *Voices of Death* (New York: Bantam Books, 1980), p. 58.

75 Perhaps one in four does: A review of sixteen studies of rates of suicide notes finds that the percentage of those leaving notes ranges between 10 and 42; the three largest studies of suicides (sample sizes 3,127, 1,418, and 1,033) report rates of 30, 23, and 21 percent, respectively. The most frequently cited study of suicide notes (E. S. Shneidman and N. L. Farberow, "Some Comparisons Between Genuine and Simulated Suicide Notes in Terms of Mowrer's Concepts of Discomfort and Relief," *Journal of General Psychology*, 56 [1957]: 251–256) found that 15 percent of the 721 suicides had left notes. See also J. Tuckman, R. J. Kleiner, and M. Lavell, "Emotional Content of Suicide Notes," *American Journal of Psychiatry*, 116 (1959): 59–63; L. B. Bourque, B. Cosand, and J. Kraus, "Comparison of Male and Female Suicide in a Defined Community," *Journal of Community Health*, 9 (1983): 7–17; J. A. Posener, A. LaHaye, and P. N. Cheifetz, "Suicide Notes in Adolescence," *Canadian Journal of Psychiatry*, 1989 (34): 171–176; N. Heim and D. Lester, "Do Suicides Who Write Notes Differ from Those Who Do Not? A Study of Suicides in West Berlin," *Acta Psychiatrica Scandinavica*, 82 (1990): 372–373; R. Chynoweth, "The Significance of Suicide Notes," *Australian and New Zealand Journal of Psychiatry*, 11 (1997): 197–200.

75 Lo, my name is abhorred: C. Thomas, "First Suicide Note?" *British Medical Journal*, July 26, 1980, pp. 284–285.

76 Goodbye, my friend: Sergei Esenin, quoted in Gordon McVay, *Esenin: A Life* (Ann Arbor, Mich.: Ardis, 1976), p. 288.

77 Paul Celan, for example: Quoted in J. Felstiner, *Paul Celan: Poet, Survivor, Jew* (New Haven: Yale University Press, 1995), p. 287.

77 "The cadence of suffering": Quoted in D. Lajolo, *An Absurd Vice: A Biography of Cesare Pavese* (New York: New Directions, 1983), p. 238.

77 notes ranged in length: I. O'Donnell, R. Farmer, and J. Catalan, "Suicide Notes," *British Journal of Psychiatry*, 163 (1993): 45–48, p. 47.

77 only an explicit warning: A. Leenaars, *Suicide Notes: Predictive Clues and Patterns* (New York: Human Sciences Press, 1988), pp. 232, 255.

77 The reasons given: A. Capstick, "Recognition of Emotional Disturbance and the Prevention of Suicide," *British Medical Journal*, 1 (1960): 1179–1181; S. L. Cohen and J. E. Fiedler, "Content Analysis of Multiple Messages in Suicide Notes," *Life-Threatening Behavior*, 4 (1974) 75–95.

77 Young children are less specific: J. A. Posener, A. LaHaye, and P. N. Cheifetz, "Suicide Notes in Adolescence"; B. Grøholt, Ø. Ekeberg, L. Wichstrøm, and T. Haldorsen, "Youth Suicide in Norway, 1990–1992: A Comparison Between Children and Adolescents Completing Suicide and Age- and Gender-Matched Controls," *Suicide and Life-Threatening Behavior*, 27 (1997): 250–263.

78 "No one is to blame": Quoted in E. R. Ellis and G. N. Allen, *Traitor Within: Our Suicide Problem* (New York: Doubleday, 1961), p. 183.

78 The majority of all suicide notes: J. Tuckman, R. J. Kleiner, and M. Lavell, "Emotional Content of Suicide Notes," *American Journal of Psychiatry*, 116 (1959): 59–63.

78 "I used to love you": Cited in H. Wolf, "Suicide Notes," *American Mercury*, 24 (1931): 264–272, p. 265.

78 "I hate you": Tuckman et al., "Emotional Content of Suicide Notes," p. 60.

78 Suicide notes in general: E. S. Shneidman and N. L. Farberow, "Some

Comparisons Between Genuine and Simulated Suicide Notes in Terms of Mowrer's Concepts of Discomfort and Relief," *Journal of General Psychology*, 56 (1957): 251–256; L. A. Gottschalk and G. C. Gleser, "An Analysis of the Verbal Content of Suicide Notes," *British Journal of Medical Psychology*, 33 (1960): 195; D. E. Spiegel and C. Neuringer, "Role of Dread in Suicidal Behavior," *Journal of Abnormal and Social Psychology*, 66 (1963): 507–511; D. M. Ogilvie, P. J. Stone, and E. S. Shneidman, "Some Characteristics of Genuine Versus Simulated Suicide Notes," *Bulletin of Suicidology*, March 1969, 27–32; R. I. Yufit, B. Benzies, M. E. Fonte, and J. A. Fawcett, "Suicide Potential and Time Perspective," *Archives of General Psychiatry*, 23 (1970): 158–163; S. Arbeit and S. J. Blatt, "Differentiation of Simulated and Genuine Suicide Notes," *Psychological Reports*, 33 (1973): 283–297; D. Lester, "Temporal Perspective and Completed Suicide," *Perceptual and Motor Skills*, 36 (1973): 760; A. A. Leenaars and W. D. G. Balance, "A Predictive Approach to Freud's Formulations Regarding Suicide," *Suicide and Life-Threatening Behavior*, 14 (1984): 275–283; D. Lester, "Can Suicidologists Distinguish Between Suicide Notes from Completers and Attempters?" *Perceptual and Motor Skills*, 79 (1994): 1498.

79 "To whom it may concern": Quoted in Ellis and Allen, *Traitor Within*, p. 62.

79 "Dear Dear Betty": Wolf, "Suicide Notes," p. 264.

80 "I am known to Mr. Herschell": Anonymous, *American Journal of Insanity*, 13 (1857): 401–402, p. 401.

81 "On the one hand": Ibid., p. 402.

81 "I wish I could explain it": Suicide note reproduced in A. A. Leenaars, *Suicide Notes: Predictive Clues and Patterns* (New York: Human Sciences Press, 1988), pp. 247–248.

82 "I will be of no use": Wolf, "Suicide Notes," p. 271.

82 "21st.—Slept horribly": *Autobiography of Benjamin Robert Haydon*, with an Introduction and Epilogue by Edmund Blunden (London: Oxford University Press, 1927; autobiography first published 1853), p. 399.

83 "The world I am living in now": Quoted in M. Iga, *The Thorn in the Chrysanthemum: Suicide and Economic Success in Modern Japan* (Berkeley: University of California Press, 1986), pp. 82–83.

83 "Do not grieve for me": Quoted in James Curtis, *James Whale: A New World of Gods and Monsters* (Boston: Faber and Faber, 1998), pp. 384–385.

84 The awareness of the damage done: H. Warnes, "Suicide in Schizophrenics," *Diseases of the Nervous System*, 29 (1968): 35–40; R. E. Drake, C. Gates, P. G. Cotton, and A. Whitaker, "Suicide Among Schizophrenics: Who Is at Risk?" *Journal of Nervous and Mental Disease*, 172 (1984): 613–617; C. Dingman and T. McGlashan, "Discriminating Characteristics of Suicides: Chestnut Lodge Follow-up Sample Including Patients with Affective Disorder, Schizophrenia and Schizoaffective Disorder," *Acta Psychiatrica Scandinavica*, 74 (1986): 91–97; A. Roy, "Suicide in Schizophrenia," in A. Roy, ed., *Suicide* (Baltimore: Williams & Wilkins, 1986), pp. 97–112; A. A. Salama, "Depression and Suicide in Schizophrenic Patients," *Suicide and Life-Threatening Behavior*, 18 (1988): 379–384; J. F. Westermeyer, M. Harrow, and J. T. Marengo, "Risk for Suicide in Schizophrenia and Other Psychotic and Nonpsychotic Disorders," *Journal of Nervous and Mental Disorders*, 179 (1991): 259–266; X. F. Amador, J. Har-

kavy Friedman, C. Kasapis, S. A. Yale, M. Flaum, and J. M. Gorman, "Suicidal Behavior in Schizophrenia and Its Relationship to Awareness of Illness," *American Journal of Psychiatry*, 153 (1996): 1185–1188; K. J. Kaplan and M. Harrow, "Positive and Negative Symptoms as Risk Factors for Later Suicidal Activity in Schizophrenics Versus Depressives," *Suicide and Life-Threatening Behavior*, 26 (1996): 105–121; C. D. Rossau and P. B. Mortensen, "Risk Factors for Suicide in Patients with Schizophrenia: Nested Case-Control Study," *British Journal of Psychiatry*, 171 (1997): 355–359.

84 "It was so queer": Quoted in *Randall Jarrell's Letters: An Autobiographical and Literary Selection* (Boston: Houghton Mifflin, 1985), Mary Jarrell, ed., p. 516.

84 "I feel certain": Virginia Woolf, March 18 (?), 1941, in Virginia Woolf, *The Letters*, vol. 6, eds. N. Nicolson and J. Trautman (London: Hogarth Press, 1975–1980), p. 481.

84 "Dearest, I want to tell you": Virginia Woolf, March 28, 1941, ibid., pp. 486–487.

85 "Everyone who has known me": Quoted in Bruce Kellner, *The Last Dandy: Ralph Barton* (Columbia: University of Missouri Press, 1991), p. 213.

86 "A suicide's excuses": A. Alvarez, *The Savage God: A Study of Suicide* (London: Weidenfeld and Nicolson, 1971), p. 97.

87 In classical antiquity: Anton van Hooff, *From Autothanasia to Suicide: Self-Killing in Classical Antiquity* (London: Routledge, 1990).

87 By the nineteenth century, Bierre de Boismont: Data from Bierre de Boismont cited in Henry Romilly Fedden, *Suicide: A Social and Historical Study* (London: Peter Davies, 1938), p. 344.

87 Tom Wehr and his colleagues: T. A. Wehr, D. A. Sack, and N. E. Rosenthal, "Sleep Reduction as a Final Common Pathway in the Genesis of Mania," *American Journal of Psychiatry*, 144 (1987): 201–204; S. Malkoff-Schwartz, E. Frank, B. Anderson, J. T. Sherrill, L. Siegel, D. Patterson, and D. J. Kupfer, "Stressful Life Events and Social Rhythm Disruption in the Onset of Manic and Depressive Bipolar Episodes," *Archives of General Psychiatry*, 55 (1998): 702–707.

88 People, when manic or depressed: C. Hammen, "Generation of Stress in the Course of Unipolar Depression," *Journal of Abnormal Psychology*, 100 (1991): 555–561; X.-J. Cui and G. E. Vaillant, "Does Depression Generate Negative Life Events?" *Journal of Nervous and Mental Disease*, 185 (1997): 145–150.

88 no consistent strong relationship: R. D. Goldney and P. W. Burvill, "Trends in Suicidal Behaviour and Its Management," *Australian and New Zealand Journal of Psychiatry*, 14 (1980): 1–15; D. M. Shepherd and B. M. Barraclough, "Work and Suicide: An Empirical Investigation," *British Journal of Psychiatry*, 136 (1980): 469–478; S. Platt, "Unemployment and Suicidal Behaviour: A Review of the Literature," *Social Science and Medicine*, 19 (1984): 93–115; H. J. Cormier and G. L. Klerman, "Unemployment and Male-Female Labor Force Participation as Determinants of Changing Suicide Rates of Males and Females in Quebec," *Social Psychiatry*, 20 (1985): 109–114; A. Beautrais, P. R. Joyce, and R. T. Mulder, "Unemployment and Serious Suicide Attempts," *Psychological Medicine*, 28 (1998): 209–218.

88 Most research finds: G. W. Brown and J. L. T. Birley, "Crises and Life Changes and the Onset of Schizophrenia," *Journal of Health and Social Behavior,* 9 (1968): 203–214; A. Ambelas, "Psychologically Stressful Life Events in the Precipitation of Manic Episodes," *British Journal of Psychiatry,* 135 (1979): 15–21; D. L. Dunner, V. Patrick, and R. R. Fieve, "Life Events and Onset of Bipolar Disorder," *American Journal of Psychiatry,* 136 (1979): 508–511; A. Ambelas, "Life Events and Mania: A Special Relationship?" *British Journal of Psychiatry,* 150 (1987): 235–240; R. Day, J. A. Neilsen, A. Korten, et al., "Stressful Life Events Preceding the Acute Onset of Schizophrenia: A Cross-National Study from the World Health Organization," *Culture, Medicine and Psychiatry,* 11 (1987): 123–206; A. Ellicott, C. Hammen, M. Gitlin, G. Brown, and K. Jamison, "Life Events and Course of Bipolar Disorder," *American Journal of Psychiatry,* 147 (1990): 1194–1198; F. K. Goodwin and K. R. Jamison, *Manic-Depressive Illness* (New York: Oxford University Press, 1990); P. Bebbington, S. Wilkins, P. Jones, A. Foerster, R. Murray, B. Toone, and S. Lewis, "Life Events and Psychosis: Initial Results from the Camberwell Collaborative Psychosis Study," *British Journal of Psychiatry,* 162 (1993): 72–79.

88 although the influence: R. M. Post, D. Rubinow, and J. C. Ballenger, "Conditioning and Sensitisation in the Longitudinal Course of Affective Illness," *British Journal of Psychiatry,* 149 (1986): 191–201; R. M. Post, "Transduction of Psychosocial Stress into the Neurobiology of Recurrent Affective Disorder," *American Journal of Psychiatry,* 149 (1992): 999–1010.

88 Patients with mood disorders: A. Breier, "Stress, Dopamine, and Schizophrenia: Evidence for a Stress-Diathesis Model," in C. M. Mazure, ed., *Does Stress Cause Psychiatric Illness?* (Washington, D.C.: American Psychiatric Press, 1995), pp. 67–86; B. P. Dohrenwend, P. E. Shrout, B. G. Link, A. E. Skodol, and A. Stueve, "Life Events and Other Possible Psychosocial Risk Factors for Episodes of Schizophrenia and Major Depression: A Case-Control Study," in Mazure, ed., *Does Stress Cause Psychiatric Illness?,* pp. 43–65.

88 Psychologist Sherry Johnson: S. L. Johnson and I. Miller, "Negative Life Events and Time to Recovery from Episodes of Bipolar Disorder," *Journal of Abnormal Psychology,* 106 (1997): 449–457.

89 Sudden heartbreak: E. S. Paykel and D. Dowlatshahi, "Life Events and Mental Disorder," in S. Fisher and J. Reason, eds., *Handbook of Life Stress, Cognition, and Health* (New York: J. Wiley and Sons, 1988), pp. 241–263; M. Heikkinen, H. Aro, and J. Lönnqvist, "Life Events and Social Support in Suicide," *Suicide and Life-Threatening Behavior,* 23 (1993): 343–358; E. Isometsä, M. Heikkinen, M. Henriksson, H. Aro, and J. Lönnqvist, "Recent Life Events and Completed Suicide in Bipolar Affective Disorder: A Comparison with Major Depressive Suicides," *Journal of Affective Disorders,* 33 (1995): 99–106.

89 Difficulties and conflicts: G. E. Murphy and E. Robins, "Social Factors in Suicide," *Journal of the American Medical Association,* 199 (1967): 303–308; G. E. Murphy, J. W. Armstrong, S. L. Hermele, J. R. Fischer, and W. W. Clendenin, "Suicide and Alcoholism: Interpersonal Loss Confirmed as a Predictor," *Archives of General Psychiatry,* 36 (1979): 65–69; G. E. Murphy, "Suicide in Alcoholism," in A. Roy, ed., *Suicide* (Baltimore: Williams &

Wilkins, 1986), pp. 89–96; C. L. Rich, R. C. Fowler, L. A. Fogarty, and D. Young, "San Diego Suicide Study: III. Relationship Between Diagnoses and Stressors," *Archives of General Psychiatry*, 45 (1988): 589–592.

89 Sometimes the reasons: T. F. Dugan and M. L. Belfer, "Suicide in Children," in D. Jacobs and H. N. Brown, eds., *Suicide: Understanding and Responding: Harvard Medical School Perspectives* (Madison, Conn.: International Universities Press, 1990), pp. 201–220, p. 201.

89 In a large Finnish study: M. Heikkinen, H. Aro, and J. Lönnqvist, "The Partners' Views on Precipitant Stressors in Suicide," *Acta Psychiatrica Scandinavica*, 85 (1992): 380–384.

89 Young or adolescent boys: D. Shaffer, "Suicide in Childhood and Adolescence," *Journal of Child Psychology and Psychiatry*, 15 (1974): 275–291; C. L. Rich, D. Young, and R. C. Fowler, "San Diego Suicide Study: I. Young vs. Old Subjects," *Archives of General Psychiatry*, 43 (1986): 577–582; D. J. Poteet, "Adolescent Suicide: A Review of 87 Cases of Completed Suicide in Shelby County, Tennessee," *American Journal of Forensic Medicine and Pathology*, 8 (1987): 12–17; D. A. Brent, J. A. Perper, C. E. Goldstein, D. J. Kolke, M. J. Allan, C. J. Allmen, and J. P. Zelenak, "Risk Factors for Adolescent Suicide: A Comparison of Adolescent Suicide Victims with Suicidal Inpatients," *Archives of General Psychiatry*, 45 (1988): 581–588; H. H. Hoberman and B. D. Garfinkel, "Completed Suicide in Youth," *Canadian Journal of Psychiatry*, 33 (1988): 494–504; D. A. Brent, J. A. Perper, G. Moritz, M. Baugher, C. Roth, L. Balach, and J. Schweers, "Stressful Life Events, Psychopathology, and Adolescent Suicide: A Case Control Study," *Suicide and Life-Threatening Behavior*, 23 (1993): 179–187; L. Davidson, M. L. Rosenberg, J. A. Mercy, J. Franklin, and J. T. Simmons, "An Epidemiologic Study of Risk Factors in Two Teenage Suicide Clusters," *Journal of the American Medical Association*, 262 (1989): 2687–2692; M. Marttunen, H. M. Aro, and J. K. Lönnqvist, "Precipitant Stressors in Adolescent Suicide," *Journal of the Academy of Child and Adolescent Psychiatry*, 32 (1993): 1178–1183; M. S. Gould, P. Fisher, M. Paridas, M. Flory, and D. Shaffer, "Psychosocial Risk Factors of Child and Adolescent Completed Suicide," *Archives of General Psychiatry*, 53 (1996): 1155–1162.

90 David Shaffer: D. Shaffer, "Suicide in Childhood and Adolescence," *Journal of Child Psychology and Psychiatry*, 15 (1974): 275–291; M. Shafii, S. Carrigan, J. R. Whittinghill, and A. Derrick, "Psychological Autopsy of Completed Suicide in Children and Adolescents," *American Journal of Psychiatry*, 142 (1985): 1061–1064; R. C. Fowler, C. L. Rich, and D. Young, "San Diego Suicide Study: II. Substance Abuse in Young Cases," *Archives of General Psychiatry*, 43 (1986): 962–965; D. Shaffer, A. Garland, M. Gould, P. Fisher, and P. Trautman, "Preventing Teenage Suicide: A Critical Review," *Journal of the American Academy of Child and Adolescent Psychiatry*, 27 (1988): 675–687; D. A. Brent, J. A. Perper, C. E. Goldstein, D. J. Kolke, M. J. Allan, C. J. Allman, and J. P. Zelenak, "Risk Factors for Adolescent Suicide: A Comparison of Adolescent Suicide Victims with Suicidal Inpatients," *Archives of General Psychiatry*, 45 (1988): 581–588; D. Shaffer, "The Epidemiology of Teen Suicide: An Examination of Risk Factors," *Journal of Clinical Psychiatry*, 49 (1988): 36–41; M. Shafii, J. Steltz-Lenarsky, A. M. Derrick, C. Beckner, and R. Whittinghill, "Comorbidity of Mental Disorders in the Post-Mortem

Diagnosis of Completed Suicide in Children and Adolescents," *Journal of Affective Disorders*, 15 (1988): 227–233; B. Runeson, "Mental Disorders in Youth Suicide: DSM-III-R Axes I and I," *Acta Psychiatrica Scandinavica*, 79 (1989): 490–497; F. E. Crumley, "Substance Abuse and Adolescent Suicidal Behavior," *Journal of the American Medical Association*, 263 (1990): 3051–3056; M. Kovacs, D. Goldston, and C. Gatsonis, "Suicidal Behaviors and Childhood-Onset Depressive Disorders: A Longitudinal Investigation," *Journal of the American Academy of Child and Adolescent Psychiatry*, 32 (1993): 8–20; M. J. Marttunen, H. M. Aro, M. M. Henriksson, and J. K. Lönnqvist, "Antisocial Behaviour in Adolescent Suicide," *Acta Psychiatrica Scandinavica*, 89 (1994): 167–173; D. Shaffer, M. S. Gould, P. Fisher, P. Trautman, D. Moreau, M. Kleinman, and M. Flory, "Psychiatric Diagnosis in Child and Adolescent Suicide," *Archives of General Psychiatry*, 53 (1996): 339–348; B. M. Wagner, R. E. Cole, and P. Schwartzman, "Comorbidity of Symptoms Among Junior and Senior High School Suicide Attempters," *Suicide and Life-Threatening Behavior*, 26 (1996) 300–307; B. Grøholt, Ø. Ekeberg, L. Wichstrøm, and T. Haldorsen, "Youth Suicide in Norway, 1990–1992," *Suicide and Life-Threatening Behavior*, 27 (1997): 250–263.

90 The fact that most parents: D. M. Velting, D. Shaffer, M. S. Gould, R. Garfinkel, P. Fisher, and M. Davies, "Parent-Victim Agreement in Adolescent Suicide Research," *Journal of the Academy of Child and Adolescent Psychiatry*, 37 (1998): 1161–1166.

90 Recent research shows: M. M. Weissman, S. Wolk, R. B. Goldstein, D. Moreau, P. Adams, S. Greenwald, C. M. Klier, N. D. Ryan, R. E. Dahl, and P. Wickramaratne, "Depressed Adolescents Grow Up," *Journal of the American Medical Association*, 281 (1999): 1707–1713.

90 "Once . . . he wrote a poem": Quoted in J. J. Norwich, *Christmas Crackers* (London: Penguin, 1982), p. 105.

92 Neuropsychologists and clinicians: These studies are reviewed in "Thought Disorder, Perception, and Cognition," in F. K. Goodwin and K. R. Jamison, *Manic-Depressive Illness* (New York: Oxford University Press, 1990), pp. 247–280.

92 are less able: C. Neuringer, "Rigid Thinking in Suicidal Individuals," *Journal of Consulting and Clinical Psychology*, 76 (1964): 91–100; M. Levenson and C. Neuringer, "Problem Solving Behavior in Suicidal Adolescents," *Journal of Consulting and Clinical Psychology*, 37 (1971): 433–436; A. Patsiokas, G. Clum, and R. Luscomb, "Cognitive Characteristics of Suicide Attempters," *Journal of Consulting and Clinical Psychology*, 3 (1979): 478–484; R. L. Bonner and A. R. Rich, "Toward a Predictive Model of Suicidal Ideation and Behavior," *Suicide and Life-Threatening Behavior*, 17 (1987): 50–63; B. C. McLeavey, R. J. Daly, C. M. Murray, J. O'Riordan, and M. Taylor, "Interpersonal Problem-Solving Deficits in Self-Poisoning Patients," *Suicide and Life-Threatening Behavior*, 17 (1987): 33–49; I. Orbach, E. Rosenheim, and E. Hary, "Some Aspects of Cognitive Functioning in Suicidal Children," *Journal of the American Academy of Child and Adolescent Psychiatry*, 26 (1987): 181–185; D. E. Schotte and G. A. Clum, "Problem-Solving Skills in Suicidal Psychiatric Patients," *Journal of Consulting and Clinical Psychology*, 55 (1987): 49–54; A. Bartfai, I.-M. Winborg, P. Nordström, and M. Åsberg, "Suicidal Behavior and Cognitive Flexibility:

Design and Verbal Fluency After Attempted Suicide," *Suicide and Life-Threatening Behavior,* 20 (1990): 254–266; J. Evans, J. M. G. Williams, S. O'Loughlin, and K. Howells, "Autobiographical Memory and Problem-Solving Strategies of Parasuicide Patients," *Psychological Medicine,* 22 (1992): 399–405; W. Mraz and M. A. Runco, "Suicide Ideation and Creative Problem Solving," *Suicide and Life-Threatening Behavior,* 24 (1994): 38–47.

92 Their thinking is more: V. J. Henken, "Banality Reinvestigated: A Computer-Based Content Analysis of Suicidal and Forced Death Documents," *Suicide and Life-Threatening Behavior,* 6 (1976): 36–43; Antoon A. Leenaars, *Suicide Notes: Predictive Clues and Patterns* (New York: Human Sciences Press, 1988); I. O'Donnell, R. Farmer, and J. Catalan, "Suicide Notes," *British Journal of Psychiatry,* 163 (1993): 45–48.

92 When suicidal patients: J. M. G. Williams and K. Broadbent, "Autobiographical Memory in Attempted Suicide," *Journal of Abnormal Psychology,* 95 (1986): 144–149; J. M. G. Williams and B. Dritschel, "Emotional Disturbance and the Specificity of Autobiographical Memory," *Cognition and Emotion,* 2 (1988): 221–234; J. Evans, J. M. G. Williams, S. O'Loughlin, and K. Howells, "Autobiographical Memory and Problem-Solving Strategies of Parasuicide Patients," *Psychological Medicine,* 22 (1992): 399–405.

93 When asked to think: A. K. MacLeod, G. S. Rose, and J. M. G. Williams, "Components of Hopelessness About the Future in Parasuicide," *Cognitive Therapy and Research,* 17 (1993): 441–455; A. K. MacLeod, B. Pankhania, M. Lee, and D. Mitchell, "Parasuicide, Depression and the Anticipation of Positive and Negative Future Experiences," *Psychological Medicine,* 27 (1997): 973–977.

93 a sense of responsibility: M. Linehan, J. Goodstein, S. Nielsen, and J. Chiles, "Reasons for Staying Alive When You Are Thinking of Killing Yourself: The Reasons for Living Inventory," *Journal of Consulting and Clinical Psychology,* 51 (1983): 276–286.

93 "This is my last experiment": Quoted in Ellis and Allen, *Traitor Within,* pp. 175–176.

93 The drawing is taken from A. L. Berman and D. A. Jobes, *Adolescent Suicide: Assessment and Intervention* (Washington, D.C.: American Psychological Association, 1991), pp. 133–134.

94 Aaron Beck and his colleagues: A. T. Beck, M. Kovacs, and A. Weissman, "Hopelessness and Suicidal Behavior," *Journal of the American Medical Association,* 234 (1975): 1146–1149; A. E. Kazdin, N. H. French, A. S. Unis, K. Esveldt-Dawson, and R. B. Sherick, "Hopelessness, Depression, and Suicidal Intent Among Psychiatrically Disturbed Inpatient Children," *Journal of Consulting and Clinical Psychology,* 51 (1983): 504–510; A. T. Beck, R. A. Steer, M. Kovacs, and B. Garrison, "Hopelessness and Eventual Suicide: A 10-Year Prospective Study of Patients Hospitalized with Suicidal Ideation," *American Journal of Psychiatry,* 142 (1985): 559–563; A. T. Beck, G. Brown, and R. A. Steer, "Prediction of Eventual Suicide in Psychiatric Inpatients by Clinical Ratings of Hopelessness," *Journal of Consulting and Clinical Psychology,* 57 (1989): 309–310; A. T. Beck, G. Brown, B. J. Berchick, B. L. Stewart, and R. A. Steer, "Relationship Between Hopelessness and Ultimate Suicide: A Replication with Psychiatric Outpatients," *American Journal of Psychiatry,* 147 (1990): 190–195.

94 Jan Fawcett: J. Fawcett, W. A. Sheftner, L. Fogg, D. C. Clark, M. A. Young, D. Hedeker, and R. Gibbons, "Time-Related Predictors of Suicide in Major Affective Disorder," *American Journal of Psychiatry*, 147 (1990): 1189–1194.

94 "October 9th": Excerpts from the journals of Dawn Renee Befano, October 1995.

4 · THE BURDEN OF DESPAIR

98 "One forgets emotions": Graham Greene, *A Sort of Life*, p. 127. Graham Greene (1904–1991), like his grandfather, suffered from manic-depression. As a schoolboy, he carved open his leg and attempted to poison himself with deadly nightshade and aspirin; while an undergraduate, he played Russian roulette six times within a period of six months. "I have never understood," he wrote in *The End of the Affair*, "why people who can swallow the enormous improbability of a personal God boggle at a personal Devil." These events are described in Greene's memoir, *A Sort of Life* (London: Penguin Books, 1962; first published 1951), pp. 64–68 and 92–96, and in Norman Sherry's biography, *The Life of Graham Greene, Volume I: 1904–1939* (London: Jonathan Cape, 1989), pp. 85–91 and 154–160. The direct quote is from *The End of the Affair*, p. 59.

98 "Miserableness is like": Graham Greene, letter to Vivien Dayrell-Browning, 1926 (quoted in Norman Sherry, *The Life of Graham Greene, Volume 1, 1904–1939* [New York: Viking Penguin, 1989], p. 276).

98 "I tried out other forms": Graham Greene, *A Sort of Life* (London: Penguin, 1972; first published 1971), p. 64.

99 "I felt nothing": Ibid., p. 91.

99 "I slipped a bullet": Ibid., pp. 93–94.

100 Study after study: E. Robins, G. E. Murphy, R. H. Wilkinson, S. Gassner, and J. Kayes, "Some Clinical Considerations in the Prevention of Suicide Based on a Study of 134 Successful Suicides," *American Journal of Public Health*, 49 (1959): 888–899; T. L. Dorpat and H. S. Ripley, "A Study of Suicide in the Seattle Area," *Comprehensive Psychiatry*, 1 (1960): 349–350; B. M. Barraclough, J. Bunch, B. Nelson, and P. Sainsbury, "A Hundred Cases of Suicide: Clinical Aspects," *British Journal of Psychiatry*, 125 (1974): 355–373; O. Hagnell and B. Rorsman, "Suicide and Endogenous Depression with Somatic Symptoms in the Lundby Study," *Neuropsychobiology*, 4 (1978): 180–187; J. Beskow, "Suicide and Mental Disorder in Swedish Men," *Acta Psychiatrica Scandinavica*, 277 (Suppl.) (1979): 1–138; O. Hagnell and B. Rorsman, "Suicide in the Lundby Study: A Comparative Investigation of Clinical Aspects," *Neuropsychobiology*, 5 (1979): 61–73; R. Chynoweth, J. I. Tonge, and J. Armstrong, "Suicide in Brisbane—A Retrospective Psychosocial Study," *Australian and New Zealand Journal of Psychiatry*, 14 (1980): 37–45; R. C. Fowler, C. L. Rich, and D. Young, "San Diego Suicide Study: II. Substance Abuse in Young Cases," *Archives of General Psychiatry*, 43 (1986): 962–965; D. W. Black, "The Iowa Record-Linkage Experience," *Suicide and Life-Threatening Behavior*, 19 (1989): 78–89; B. L. Tanney, "Mental Disorders, Psychiatric Patients, and Suicide," in R. W. Maris, A. L. Berman, J. T. Maltsberger, and R. I. Yufit, eds., *Assessment and Prediction of Suicide* (New York: Guilford, 1992), pp. 277–320; A. T. A. Cheng, "Mental

Illness and Suicide: A Case-Control Study in East Taiwan," *Archives of General Psychiatry*, 52 (1995): 594–603; T. Foster, K. Gillespie, and R. McClelland, "Mental Disorders and Suicide in Northern Ireland," *British Journal of Psychiatry*, 170 (1997): 447–452; J. Angst, F. Angst, and H. H. Stassen, "Suicide Risk in Patients with Major Depressive Disorder," *Journal of Clinical Psychiatry*, (Suppl. 2) (1999): 57–62.

100 High rates of psychopathology: M. M. Weissman, "The Epidemiology of Suicide Attempts, 1960–1971," *Archives of General Psychiatry*, 30 (1974): 737–746; D. J. Pallis and P. Sainsbury, "The Value of Assessing Intent in Attempted Suicide," *Psychological Medicine*, 6 (1976): 487–492; J. G. B. Newson-Smith and S. R. Hirsch, "Psychiatric Symptoms in Self-Poisoning Patients," *Psychological Medicine*, 9 (1979): 493–500; P. Urwin and J. L. Gibbons, "Psychiatric Diagnosis in Self-Poisoning Cases," *Psychological Medicine*, 9 (1979): 501–507; R. D. Goldney, K. S. Adam, J. C. O'Brien, and P. Termansen, "Depression in Young Women Who Have Attempted Suicide: An International Replication Study," *Journal of Affective Disorders*, 3 (1981): 327–337; K. Hawton and J. Catalán, *Attempted Suicide: A Practical Guide to its Nature and Management* (Oxford: Oxford University Press, 1982); K. Michel, "Suicide Risk Factors: A Comparison of Suicide Attempters with Suicide Completers," *British Journal of Psychiatry*, 150 (1987): 78–82; A. L. Beautrais, P. R. Joyce, R. T. Mulder, D. M. Fergusson, B. J. Deavoll, and S. K. Nightingale, "Prevalence and Comorbidity of Mental Disorders in Persons Making Serious Suicide Attempts: A Case-Control Study," *American Journal of Psychiatry*, 153 (1996): 1009–1014; K. Suominen, M. Henriksson, J. Suokas, E. Isometsä, A. Ostamo, and J. Lönnqvist, "Mental Disorders and Comorbidity in Attempted Suicide," *Acta Psychiatrica Scandinavica*, 94 (1996): 234–240.

100 Work done by Clare Harris: E. C. Harris and B. Barraclough, "Suicide as an Outcome for Mental Disorders: A Meta-Analysis," *British Journal of Psychiatry*, 170 (1997): 205–228.

102 one-third of the patients: A. Stenbeck, K. A. Achté, and R. N. Rimón, "Physical Disease, Hypochondria and Alcohol Addiction in Suicides Committed by Mental Hospital Patients," *British Journal of Psychiatry*, 111 (1965): 933–937.

102 Two things seem to be true: T. L. Dorpat, W. F. Anderson, and H. S. Ripley, "The Relationship of Physical Illness to Suicide," In H. L. P. Resnick, ed., *Suicidal Behaviors: Diagnosis and Management* (Boston: Little, Brown, 1968), pp. 209–219.

103 most of the medical conditions: F. A. Whitlock, "Suicide and Physical Illness," in A. Roy, ed., *Suicide* (Baltimore: Williams & Wilkins, 1986), pp. 151–170; E. C. Harris and B. M. Barraclough, "Suicide as an Outcome for Medical Disorders," *Medicine* 73 (1994): 281–296; P. R. McHugh, "Suicide and Medical Afflictions," *Medicine*, 73 (1994): 297–298.

103 a three- to eightfold decrease: E. C. Harris and B. Barraclough, "Suicide as an Outcome for Medical Disorder," *Medicine*, 73 (1994): 281–296.

104 "airless and without exits": A. Alvarez, *The Savage God* (New York: W. W. Norton, 1990; first published 1971), p. 293.

104 "I have been and am": Sylvia Plath, *The Journals of Sylvia Plath*, T. Hughes and F. McCullough, eds. (New York: Dial Press, 1982), p. 240.

104 "The next thing": Alan Garner, *The Voice That Thunders: Essays and Lectures* (London: Harvill Press, 1997), pp. 208–209.

105 "What I had begun": William Styron, *Darkness Visible: A Memoir of Madness* (New York: Random House, 1990), p. 50.

106 "becomes changed": Hugo Wolf, quoted in F. Walker, *Hugo Wolf: A Biography* (London: J. M. Dent & Sons, 1968), p. 359.

106 "tireless, madly sanguine": Robert Lowell, "Near the Unbalanced Aquarium," in R. Giroux, ed., *Robert Lowell: Collected Prose* (New York: Farrar, Straus and Giroux, 1987), p. 353.

106 the "Columbus": V. Mayakovsky, quoted in V. Markov, *The Longer Poems of Velimir Khlebnikov* (Westport: Conn.: Greenwood Press, 1975), p. 23.

106 "Working with number": Ibid., pp. 362–363.

109 "The condition of my mind": E. Reiss, *Konstitutionelle Verstimmung und Alanisch-Depressive Irresein: Klinische Untersuchungen über den Zusammenhang von Veranlagung und Psychose* (Berlin: J. Springer, 1910).

109 One person in a hundred: F. K. Goodwin and K. R. Jamison, *Manic-Depressive Illness* (New York: Oxford University Press, 1990); L. N. Robins and D. A. Regier, *Psychiatric Disorders in America: The Epidemiologic Catchment Area Study* (New York: Free Press, 1991); R. C. Kessler, D. R. Rubinow, C. Holmes, J. M. Abelson, and S. Zhao, "The Epidemiology of DSM-III-R Bipolar I Disorder in a General Population Survey," *Psychological Medicine*, 27 (1997): 1079–1089.

109 at least twice as common: M. M. Weissman, R. C. Bland, G. J. Canino, C. Faravelli, S. Greenwald, H.-G. Hwu, P. R. Joyce, E. G. Karam, C.-K. Lee, J. Lellouch, J.-P. Lépine, S. C. Newman, M. Rubio-Stipec, E. Wells, P. J. Wickramaratne, H.-U. Wittchen, and E.-K. Yeh, "Cross-National Epidemiology of Major Depression and Bipolar Disorder," *Journal of the American Medical Association*, 276 (1996): 293–299; J. Angst, "The Prevalence of Depression," in M. Briley and S. A. Montgomery, eds., *Antidepressant Therapy: At the Dawn of the Third Millennium* (St. Louis: Mosby, 1998), pp. 191–212.

109 Bipolar illness is generally: F. K. Goodwin and K. R. Jamison, *Manic-Depressive Illness* (New York: Oxford University Press, 1990); D. A. Regier, M. E. Farmer, D. S. Raye, B. Z. Locke, S. J. Keith, L. L. Judd, and F. K. Goodwin, "Co-Morbidity of Mental Disorders with Drug and Alcohol Abuse: Results from the Epidemiologic Catchment Area (ECA) Study," *Journal of the American Medical Association*, 264 (1990): 2511–2518; D. F. MacKinnon, K. R. Jamison, and J. R. DePaulo, "Genetics of Manic-Depressive Illness," *Annual Review of Neuroscience*, 20 (1997): 355–373.

110 Suicide attempts are disproportionately high: G. F. Johnson and G. Hunt, "Suicidal Behavior in Bipolar Manic-Depressive Patients and Their Families," *Comprehensive Psychiatry*, 20 (1979): 159–164; K. R. Jamison, "Suicide and Bipolar Disorders," *Annals of the New York Academy of Sciences*, 487 (1986): 301–315; Y. W. Chen and S. C. Dilsaver, "Lifetime Rates of Suicide Attempts Among Subjects with Bipolar and Unipolar Disorders Relative to Subjects with Other Axis I Disorders," *Biological Psychiatry*, 39 (1996): 896–899; F. K. Goodwin and K. R. Jamison, *Manic-Depressive Illness* (New York: Oxford University Press, 1990); S.-Y. Tsai, C.-C. Chen, and E.-K. Yeh, "Alcohol Problems and Long-Term Psychosocial Outcome in Chinese Patients with Bipolar Disorder," *Journal of Affective Disorders*, 46 (1997):

143–150; R. C. Kessler and E. E. Walters, "Epidemiology of DSM-III-R Major Depression and Minor Depression Among Adolescents and Young Adults in the National Comorbidity Survey," *Depression and Anxiety*, 7 (1998): 3–14. S. G. Simpson and K. R. Jamison, "The Risk of Suicide in Patients with Bipolar Disorders," *Journal of Clinical Psychiatry*, 60 (Suppl. 2) (1999): 53–56.

110 Individuals with mood disorders: E. Vieta, E. Nieto, C. Gastó, and E. Cirera, "Serious Suicide Attempts in Affective Patients," *Journal of Affective Disorders*, 24 (1992): 147–152.

110 For those with mood disorders: A. R. Beisser and J. E. Blanchette, "A Study of Suicides in a Mental Hospital," *Diseases of the Nervous System*, 22 (1961): 365–369; K. A. Achté, A. Stenback, and H. Teravainen, "On Suicides Committed During Treatment in Psychiatric Hospitals," *Acta Psychiatrica Scandinavica*, 42 (1966): 272–284.

110 Mild or moderate depressions: J. R. Morrison, "Suicide in a Psychiatric Practice Population," *Journal of Clinical Psychiatry*, 43 (1982): 348–352; R. L. Martin, C. R. Cloninger, and S. B. Guze, "Mortality in a Follow-up of 500 Psychiatric Outpatients: I. Total Mortality," *Archives of General Psychiatry*, 42 (1985): 47–54; G. W. Blair-West, G. W. Mellsop, and M. L. Eyeson-Annan, "Down-Rating Lifetime Suicide Risk in Major Depression," *Acta Psychiatrica Scandinavica*, 95 (1997): 259–263.

110 Swedish researchers: O. Hagnell, J. Lanke, and B. Rorsman, "Suicide Rates in the Lundby Study: Mental Illness as a Risk Factor for Suicide," *Neuropsychobiology*, 7 (1981): 248–253.

110 The severity of depression: T. L. Dorpat and H. S. Ripley, "A Study of Suicide in the Seattle Area," *Comprehensive Psychiatry*, 1 (1960): 349–359; M. Arato, E. Demeter, Z. Rihmer, and E. Somogyi, "Retrospective Psychiatric Assessment of 200 Suicides in Budapest," *Acta Psychiatrica Scandinavica*, 77 (1988): 454–456; M. M. Henriksson, H. M. Aro, M. J. Marttunen, et al., "Mental Disorders and Comorbidity in Suicide," *American Journal of Psychiatry*, 150 (1993): 935–940; E. T. Isometsä, M. M. Henriksson, H. M. Aro, M. E. Heikkinen, K. I. Kuoppasalmi, and J. K. Lönnqvist, "Suicide in Major Depression," *American Journal of Psychiatry*, 151 (1994): 530–536; S. C. Dilsaver, Y.-W. Chen, A. C. Swann, A. M. Shoaib, and K. J. Krajewski, "Suicidality in Patients with Pure and Depressive Mania," *American Journal of Psychiatry*, 151 (1994): 1312–1315.

111 Suicide appears to be: D. L. Dunner, E. S. Gershon, and F. K. Goodwin, "Heritable Factors in the Severity of Affective Illness," *Biological Psychiatry*, 11 (1976): 31–42; M. T. Tsuang, "Suicide in Schizophrenics, Manics, Depressives, and Surgical Controls," *Archives of General Psychiatry*, 35 (1978): 153–155; T. H. McGlashan, "Chestnut Lodge Follow-up Study: III. Long-Term Outcome of Schizophrenia and Affective Disorders," *Archives of General Psychiatry*, 41 (1984): 586–601; J. Endicott, J. Nee, N. Andreasen, P. Clayton, M. Keller and W. Coryell, "Bipolar II: Combine or Keep Separate?" *Journal of Affective Disorders*, 8 (1985): 17–28; R. L. Martin, C. R. Cloninger, S. B. Guze, and P. Clayton, "Mortality in a Follow-up of 500 Psychiatric Outpatients," *Archives of General Psychiatry*, 42 (1985): 58–66; A. Weeke and M. Vaeth, "Excessive Mortality of Bipolar and Unipolar (Manic-Depressive) Patients," *Journal of Affective Disorders*, 11 (1986): 227–234; Z. Rihmer, J. Barsi, M. Arató, and E. Demeter, "Suicide in Subtypes of Pri-

mary Major Depression," *Journal of Affective Disorders*, 18 (1990): 221–225; S. C. Newman and R. C. Bland, "Suicide Risk Varies by Subtype of Affective Disorder," *Acta Psychiatrica Scandinavica*, 83 (1991): 420–426.

111 more common in major depression: S. B. Guze and E. Robins, "Suicide and Primary Affective Disorders," *British Journal of Psychiatry*, 117 (1970): 437–438; G. Winokur and M. Tsuang, "The Iowa 500: Suicide in Mania, Depression, and Schizophrenia," *American Journal of Psychiatry*, 132 (1975): 650–651; W. Coryell, R. Noyes, and J. Clancy, "Excess Mortality in Panic Disorder: A Comparison with Primary Unipolar Depression," *Archives of General Psychiatry*, 39 (1982): 701–703; M. Berglund and K. Nilsson, "Mortality in Severe Depression," *Acta Psychiatrica Scandinavica*, 76 (1987): 372–380; D. W. Black, G. Winokur, and A. Nasrallah, "Suicide in Subtypes of Major Affective Disorder: A Comparison with General Population Suicide Mortality," *Archives of General Psychiatry*, 44 (1987): 878–880; F. K. Goodwin and K. R. Jamison, *Manic-Depressive Illness* (New York: Oxford University Press, 1990).

111 "The patients, therefore": E. Kraepelin, *Manic-Depressive Insanity and Paranoia*, trans. R. M. Barclay, ed. G. M. Robertson (New York: Arno Press, 1976; first published 1921), p. 25.

112 Paranoia, extreme irascibility: J. Himmelhoch, D. Mulla, J. F. Neil, T. P. Detre, and D. J. Kupfer, "Incidence and Significance of Mixed Affective States in a Bipolar Population," *Archives of General Psychiatry*, 33 (1976): 1062–1066; F. K. Goodwin and K. R. Jamison, *Manic-Depressive Illness* (New York: Oxford University Press, 1990); S. L. McElroy, P. E. Keck, H. G. Pope, J. I. Hudson, G. L. Faedda, and A. C. Swann, "Clinical and Research Implications of the Diagnosis of Dysphoric or Mixed Mania or Hypomania," *American Journal of Psychiatry*, 149 (1992): 1633–1644.

112 "I walk from room to room": Anne Sexton, handwritten notes dated "February 16th or so [probably 1957]," Dr. Orne file, restricted collection; quoted in Diane Wood Middlebrook, *Anne Sexton: A Biography* (Boston: Houghton Mifflin, 1991), p. 36.

112 "I went to bed & wept": Edgar Allan Poe, letter to Annie L. Richmond, November 16, 1848, in John Wand Ostrom, ed., *The Letters of Edgar Allan Poe*, vol. 2 (Cambridge, Mass.: Harvard University Press, 1948), pp. 401–403.

112 Mixed states: G. R. Jameison, "Suicide and Mental Disease: A Clinical Analysis of One Hundred Cases," *Archives of Neurology and Psychiatry*, 36 (1936): 1–12; K. R. Jamison, "Suicide and Bipolar Disorders," *Annals of New York Academy of Sciences*, 487 (1986): 301–315; S. C. Silsaver, Y.-W. Chen, A. C. Swann, A. M. Shoaib, and K. J. Krajewski, "Suicidality in Patients with Pure and Depressive Mania," *American Journal of Psychiatry*, 151 (1994): 1312–1315; S. M. Strakowski, S. L. McElroy, P. E. Keck, and S. A. West, *American Journal of Psychiatry*, 153 (1996): 674–676; J. F. Goldberg, J. L. Garno, A. C. Leon, J. H. Kocsis, and L. Portera, "Association of Recurrent Suicidal Ideation with Nonremission from Acute Mixed Mania," *American Journal of Psychiatry*, 155 (1998): 1753–1755.

113 "The patient cannot": Kraepelin, *Manic-Depressive Insanity and Paranoia*, pp. 64–65, 164.

113 Psychosis, the presence: D. W. Goodwin, P. Alderson, and R. Rosenthal,

"Clinical Significance of Hallucinations in Psychiatric Disorders," *Archives of General Psychiatry*, 24 (1971): 76–80; W. Coryell and M. T. Tsuang, "Primary Unipolar Depression and the Prognostic Importance of Delusions," *Archives of General Psychiatry*, 39 (1982): 1181–1184; D. E. Frangos, G. Athanassenas, S. Tsitourides, P. Psilolignos, and N. Katsanou, "Psychotic Depressive Disorder: A Separate Entity?" *Journal of Affective Disorders*, 5 (1983): 259–265; S. P. Roose, A. H. Glassman, B. T. Walsh, S. Woodring, and J. Vital-Herne, "Depression, Delusions, and Suicide," *American Journal of Psychiatry*, 140 (1983): 1159–1162; M. Wolfersdorf, F. Keller, B. Steiner, and G. Hole, "Delusional Depression and Suicide," *Acta Psychiatrica Scandinavica*, 76 (1987): 359–363; D. W. Black, G. Winokur, and A. Nasrallah, "Effect of Psychosis on Suicide Risk in 1,593 Patients with Unipolar and Bipolar Affective Disorders," *American Journal of Psychiatry*, 145 (1988): 849–852; C. L. Rich, M. S. Motooka, R. C. Fowler, and D. Young, "Suicide by Psychotics," *Biological Psychiatry*, 23 (1988): 595–601; J. F. Westermeyer, M. Harrow, and J. T. Marengo, "Risk for Suicide in Schizophrenia and Other Psychotic and Nonpsychotic Disorders," *Journal of Nervous and Mental Disease*, 179 (1991): 259–266; K. J. Kaplan and M. Harrow, "Positive and Negative Symptoms as Risk Factors for Later Suicidal Activity in Schizophrenics Versus Depressives," *Suicide and Life-Threatening Behavior*, 26 (1996): 105–121; P. E. Quinlan, C. A. King, G. L. Hanna, and N. Ghaziuddin, "Psychotic Versus Nonpsychotic Depression in Hospitalized Adolescents," *Depression and Anxiety*, 6 (1997): 40–42.

113 depressed patients with auditory hallucinations: D. Hellerstein, W. Frosch, and H. W. Koenigsberg, "The Clinical Significance of Command Hallucinations," *American Journal of Psychiatry*, 144 (1987): 219–221.

113 Psychotic patients do, however: E. Isometsä, M. Henriksson, H. Aro, M. Heikkinen, K. Kuoppasalmi, and J. Lönnqvist, "Suicide in Psychotic Major Depression," *Journal of Affective Disorders*, 3 (1994): 187–191.

114 People with depression or manic-depression: G. R. Jameison, "Suicide and Mental Disease: A Clinical Analysis of One Hundred Cases," *Archives of Neurology and Psychiatry*, 36 (1936): 1–12; S. Guze and E. Robins, "Suicide and Primary Affective Disorders," *British Journal of Psychiatry*, 117 (1970): 437–438; J. B. Copas, D. L. Freeman-Browne, and A. A. Robin, "Danger Periods for Suicide in Patients Under Treatment," *Psychological Medicine*, 1 (1971): 400–404; M. T. Tsuang and R. F. Woolson, "Excess Mortality in Schizophrenia and Affective Disorders," *Archives of General Psychiatry*, 35 (1978): 1181–1185; G. F. Johnson and G. Hunt, "Suicidal Behavior in Bipolar Manic-Depressive Patients and Their Families," *Comprehensive Psychiatry*, 20 (1979): 159–164; A. Weeke, "Causes of Death in Manic-Depressives," in M. Schou and E. Strömgren, eds., *Origin, Prevention and Treatment of Affective Disorders* (London: Academic Press, 1979), pp. 289–299; A. Roy, "Risk Factors for Suicide in Psychiatric Patients," *Archives of General Psychiatry*, 39 (1982): 1089–1095; D. W. Black, G. Winokur, and A. Nasrallah, "Mortality in Patients with Primary Unipolar Depression, Secondary Unipolar Depression, and Bipolar Affective Disorder: A Comparison with General Population Mortality," *International Journal of Psychiatry and Medicine*, 17 (1987): 351–360; J. Fawcett, W. Scheftner, D. Clark, D. Hedeker, R. Gibbons, and W. Coryell, "Clinical

Predictors of Suicide in Patients with Major Affective Disorders: A Controlled Prospective Study," *American Journal of Psychiatry*, 144 (1987): 35–40; D. W. Black, "The Iowa Record-Linkage Experience," *Suicide and Life-Threatening Behavior*, 19 (1989): 78–89; A. Roy, "Features Associated with Suicide Attempts in Depression: A Partial Replication," *Journal of Affective Disorders*, 27 (1993): 35–38; B. Ahrens, A. Berghöfer, T. Wolf, and B. Müller-Oerlinghausen, "Suicide Attempts, Age and Duration of Illness in Recurrent Affective Disorders," *Journal of Affective Disorders*, 36 (1995): 43–49; H. Brodaty, C. M. MacCuspie-Moore, L. Tickle, and G. Lusocombe, "Depression, Diagnostic Sub-Type and Death: A 25-Year Follow-up Study," *Journal of Affective Disorders*, 46 (1997): 233–242.

114 one of the highest-risk periods: Sir T. S. Clouston, *Clinical Lectures on Mental Disease*, 5th ed. (London: Churchill, 1898); J. Barfield Adams, "Suicide—From a General Practitioner's Point of View," *The Practitioner*, 44 (1915): 470–478; D. K. Henderson and R. D. Gillespie, *A Textbook of Psychiatry* (London: Oxford University Press, 1927); E. Stengel, "The Risk of Suicide in States of Depression," *Medical Press*, 234 (1955): 182–184; J. B. Copes, D. L. Freeman-Browne, and A. A. Robin, "Danger Periods for Suicide in Patients Under Treatment," *Psychological Medicine*, 1 (1971): 400–404; J. B. Copas and M. J. Fryer, "Density Estimation and Suicide Risk in Psychiatric Treatment," *Statistical Society*, 143 (1980): 167–176; P. Barner-Rasmussen, "Suicide in Psychiatric Patients in Denmark, 1971–1981: II. Hospitalization Utilization and Risk Groups," *Acta Psychiatrica Scandinavica*, 73 (1986): 449–455; E. Schweizer, A. Dever, and C. Clary, "Suicide upon Recovery from Depression: A Clinical Note," *Journal of Nervous and Mental Disease*, 176 (1988): 633–636.

115 "We should be careful": Benjamin Rush, *Medical Inquiries and Observations upon the Diseases of the Mind* (Philadelphia: Kimber & Richardson, 1812), pp. 239–240.

116 "The electricity manifests itself": Michael Hurd, *The Ordeal of Ivor Gurney* (Oxford: Oxford University Press, 1984), p. 158.

116 "There is a dreadful hell": "To God," ll. 8–9, 12, in P. J. Kavanagh, ed., *Collected Poems of Ivor Gurney* (Oxford: Oxford University Press, 1984), p. 156.

116 "There is one who all day": from "An Appeal for Death," ll. 1, 22, in Kavanagh, ed., *Collected Poems of Ivor Gurney*, pp. 181–182.

116 Schizophrenia is the most severe: R. J. Wyatt, R. C. Alexander, M. F. Egan, and D. G. Kirch, "Schizophrenia: Just the Facts. What Do We Know? How Well Do We Know It? *Schizophrenia Research*, 1 (1988): 3–18; L. N. Robins and D. A. Regier, eds. *Psychiatric Disorders in America: The Epidemiologic Catchment Area Study* (New York: Free Press, 1991); American Psychiatric Association, *Diagnostic and Statistical Manual of Mental Disorders*, 4th ed. (Washington, D.C.: American Psychiatric Association, 1994); I. I. Gottesman, "Complications to the Complex Inheritance of Schizophrenia," *Clinical Genetics*, 46 (1994): 116–123; P. Asherson, R. Mant, and P. McGuffin, "Genetics and Schizophrenia," in S. R. Hirsch and D. R. Weinberger, *Schizophrenia* (Oxford: Blackwell Science, 1995), pp. 253–274.

117 It is malevolent: A. Roy, "Suicide in Schizophrenia," in A. Roy, ed., *Suicide* (Baltimore: Williams & Wilkins, 1986), pp. 97–112; C. B. Caldwell and I. I. Gottesman, "Schizophrenia—A High-Risk Factor for Suicide:

Clues to Risk Reduction," *Suicide and Life-Threatening Behavior,* 22 (1992): 479–493.

117 death's heads: Emil Kraepelin, *Dementia Praecox and Paraphrenia,* trans. R. M. Barclay, ed. G. M. Robertson (Huntington, N.Y.: Robert E. Krieger, 1971; first published in English 1919), p. 14.

118 "I lay motionless": Carol S. North, *Welcome, Silence: My Triumph over Schizophrenia* (New York: Simon and Schuster, 1987), p. 116.

119 "The reality for myself": R. Bayley, "First Person Account: Schizophrenia," *Schizophrenia Bulletin,* 22 (1996): 727–729.

120 For many, mood is also affected: S. G. Siris, "Depression and Schizophrenia," in S. R. Hirsch and D. R. Weinberger, *Schizophrenia* (Oxford: Blackwell Science, 1995), pp. 128–145.

120 at least one in four: R. E. Drake and P. G. Cotton, "Depression, Hopelessness and Suicide in Chronic Schizophrenia," *British Journal of Psychiatry,* 148 (1986): 554–559; A. A. Salama, "Depression and Suicide in Schizophrenic Patients," *Suicide and Life-Threatening Behavior,* 18 (1988): 379–384; K. K. Cheng, C. M. Leung, W. H. Lo, and T. H. Lam, "Risk Factors of Suicide Among Schizophrenics," *Acta Psychiatrica Scandinavica,* 81 (1990): 220–224; A. M. Dassori, J. E. Mezzich, and M. Keshavan, "Suicidal Indicators in Schizophrenia," *Acta Psychiatrica Scandinavica,* 81 (1990): 409–413; J. S. Jones, D. J. Stein, B. Stanley, J. R. Guido, R. Winchel, and M. Stanley, "Negative and Depressive Symptoms in Suicidal Schizophrenics," *Acta Psychiatrica Scandinavica,* 89 (1994): 81–87; H. Heilä, E. Isometsä, M. M. Henriksson, M. E. Heikkinen, M. J. Marttunen, and J. K. Lönnqvist, "Suicide and Schizophrenia: A Nationwide Psychological Autopsy Study on Age- and Sex-Specific Clinical Characteristics of 92 Suicide Victims with Schizophrenia," *American Journal of Psychiatry,* 154 (1997): 1235–1242; C. D. Rossau and P. B. Mortensen, "Risk Factors for Suicide in Patients with Schizophrenia: Nested Case-Control Study," *British Journal of Psychiatry,* 171 (1997): 355–359.

120 intensely irritable, and restless: P. E. Yarden, "Observations on Suicide in Chronic Schizophrenia," *Comprehensive Psychiatry,* 15 (1974): 325–333; C. W. Dingman and T. H. McGlashan, "Discriminating Characteristics of Suicide," *Acta Psychiatrica Scandinavica,* 74 (1986): 91–97; D. G. Wilkinson, "The Suicide Rate in Schizophrenia," *British Journal of Psychiatry,* 140 (1982): 138–141; P. Allebeck, A. Varla, E. Kristjansson, and B. Wistedt, "Risk Factors for Suicide Among Patients with Schizophrenia," *Acta Psychiatrica Scandinavica,* 76 (1987): 414–419; A. M. Dassori, J. E. Mezzich, and M. Keshavan, "Suicidal Indicators in Schizophrenia," *Acta Psychiatrica Scandinavica,* 81 (1990): 409–413.

120 30 to 40 percent: A. Roy, "Suicide in Schizophrenia," in A. Roy, ed., *Suicide* (Baltimore: Williams & Wilkins, 1986), pp. 97–112; L. N. Robins and D. A. Regier, eds., *Psychiatric Disorders in America: The Epidemiologic Catchment Area Study* (New York: Free Press, 1991); C. B. Caldwell and I. I. Gottesman, "Schizophrenia—A High-Risk Factor for Suicide: Clues to Risk Reduction," *Suicide and Life-Threatening Behavior,* 22 (1992): 479–493; R. Chatterton, "Parasuicide in People with Schizophrenia," *Australian and New Zealand Journal of Mental Health Nursing,* 4 (1995): 83–86; G. L. Haas, "Suicidal Behavior in Schizophrenia," in R. W. Maris, M. M. Silverman,

and S. S. Canetto, eds., *Review of Suicidology, 1997* (New York: Guilford, 1997), pp. 202–236

120 the single best predictor: J. W. Shaffer, S. Perlin, C. W. Schmidt, and J. H. Stephens, "The Prediction of Suicide in Schizophrenia," *Journal of Nervous and Mental Disease*, 159 (1974): 349–355; G. Wilkinson and N. A. Bacon, "A Clinical and Epidemiological Survey of Parasuicide and Suicide in Edinburgh Schizophrenics," *Psychological Medicine*, 14 (1984): 899–912; P. Allebeck, A. Varla, E. Kristjansson, and B. Wistedt, "Risk Factors for Suicide Among Patients with Schizophrenia," *Acta Psychiatrica Scandinavica*, 76 (1987): 414–419; G. L. Haas, "Suicidal Behavior in Schizophrenia," in R. W. Maris, M. M. Silverman, and S. S. Canetto, eds. *Review of Suicidology* (New York: Guilford, 1997), pp. 202–236. Roy, "Suicide in Schizophrenia."

120 in the early stages: M. T. Tsuang and R. F. Woolson, "Excess Mortality in Schizophrenia and Affective Disorders," *Archives of General Psychiatry*, 35 (1978): 1181–1185; D. W. Black and G. Winokur, "Prospective Studies of Suicide and Mortality in Psychiatric Patients," *Annals of the New York Academy of Sciences*, 487 (1986): 106–113; C. A. Johns, M. Stanley, and B. Stanley, "Suicide in Schizophrenia," *Annals of the New York Academy of Sciences*, 487 (1986): 294–300; D. Wiersma, F. J. Nienhuis, C. J. Slooff, and R. Giel, "Natural Course of Schizophrenic Disorders: A 15-Year Followup of a Dutch Incidence Cohort," *Schizophrenia Bulletin*, 24 (1998): 75–85.

120 recently released: G. S. Stein, "Dangerous Episodes Occurring Around the Time of Discharge of Four Chronic Schizophrenics," *British Journal of Psychiatry*, 141 (1982): 586–589; Roy, "Suicide in Schizophrenia"; D. W. Black and R. Fisher, "Mortality in DSM-III-R Schizophrenia," *Schizophrenia Research*, 7 (1992): 109–116; C. D. Rossau and P. B. Mortensen, "Risk Factors for Suicide in Patients with Schizophrenia: Nested Case-Control Study," *British Journal of Psychiatry*, 171 (1997): 355–359.

121 Although hallucinations and delusions: A. Breier and B. M. Astrachan, "Characterization of Schizophrenic Patients Who Commit Suicide," *American Journal of Psychiatry*, 141 (1984): 206–209; G. Wilkinson and N. A. Bacon, "A Clinical and Epidemiological Survey of Parasuicide and Suicide in Edinburgh Schizophrenics," *Psychological Medicine*, 14 (1984): 899–912; Roy, "Suicide in Schizophrenia"; D. Hellerstein, W. Frosch, and H. W. Koenigsberg, "The Clinical Significance of Command Hallucinations," *American Journal of Psychiatry*, 144 (1987): 219–221; K. J. Kaplan and M. Harrow, "Positive and Negative Symptoms as Risk Factors for Later Suicidal Activity in Schizophrenics Versus Depressives," *Suicide and Life-Threatening Behavior*, 26 (1996): 105–121; W. S. Fenton, T. H. McGlashan, B. J. Victor, and C. R. Blyler, "Symptoms, Subtype, and Suicidality in Patients with Schizophrenia Spectrum Disorders," *American Journal of Psychiatry*, 154 (1997): 199–204.

121 Although the eating disorders: D. B. Herzog, M. B. Keller, and P. W. Lavori, "Outcome in Anorexia Nervosa and Bulimia Nervosa: A Review of the Literature," *Journal of Nervous and Mental Disease*, 176 (1988): 131–143; E. D. Eckert, K. A. Halmi, P. Marchi, et al., "Ten-Year Follow-up of Anorexia Nervosa: Clinical Course and Outcome," *Psychological Medicine*, 25 (1995): 143–156.

121 A review of more than thirty studies: A. Gardner and C. Rich, "Eating Dis-

orders and Suicide," in R. Yufit, ed., *Proceedings of the 21st Annual Meeting of the American Association of Suicidology* (Denver: American Association of Suicidology, 1988), pp. 171–172; P. K. Keel, J. E. Mitchell, K. B. Miller, T. L. Davis, and S. J. Crow, "Long-Term Outcome of Bulimia Nervosa," *Archives of General Psychiatry*, 56 (1999): 63–69.

121 Anxiety disorders, on the other hand: J. Fawcett, W. A. S. Scheftner, L. Fogg, D. C. Clark, M. A. Young, D. Hedeker, and R. Gibbons, "Time-Related Predictors of Suicide in Major Affective Disorder," *American Journal of Psychiatry*, 147 (1990): 1189–1194; E. C. Harris and B. Barraclough, "Suicide as an Outcome for Mental Disorders: A Meta-Analysis," *British Journal of Psychiatry*, 170 (1997): 205–228.

121 The defining symptoms: P. J. Clayton, W. M. Grove, W. Coryell, et al., "Follow-up and Family Study of Anxious Depression," *American Journal of Psychiatry*, 148 (1991): 1512–1517.

121 Panic attacks are also: M. M. Weissman, G. L. Klerman, J. S. Markowitz, and R. Ouellette, "Suicidal Ideation and Suicide Attempts in Panic Disorder and Attacks," *New England Journal of Medicine*, 321 (1989): 1209–1214; M. G. Warshaw, A. O. Massion, L. G. Peterson, L. A. Pratt, and M. B. Keller, "Suicidal Behavior in Patients with Panic Disorder: Retrospective and Prospective Data," *Journal of Affective Disorders*, 34 (1994): 235–247; C. D. Horning and R. J. McNally, "Panic Disorder and Suicide Attempt: A Reanalysis of Data from the Epidemiologic Catchment Area Study," *British Journal of Psychiatry*, 167 (1995): 76–79; M. M. Weissman, "Comorbidity and Suicide Risk," *British Journal of Psychiatry*, 167 (1995): 819–820; E. C. Harris and B. Barraclough, "Suicide as an Outcome for Mental Disorders: A Meta-Analysis," *British Journal of Psychiatry*, 170 (1997): 205–228.

121 Severe anxiety: J. Fawcett, W. A. S. Scheftner, L. Fogg, D. C. Clark, M. A. Young, D. Hedeker, and R. Gibbons, "Time-Related Predictors of Suicide in Major Affective Disorder," *American Journal of Psychiatry*, 147 (1990): 1189–1194.

122 suicide is rare: N. L. Gittleson, "The Relationship Between Obsessions and Suicidal Attempts in Depressive Psychosis," *British Journal of Psychiatry*, 112 (1966): 889–890; C. M. Rosenberg, "Complications of Obsessional Neurosis," *British Journal of Psychiatry*, 114 (1968): 477–478; R. A. Woodruff, P. J. Clayton, and S. B. Guze, "Suicide Attempts and Psychiatric Diagnosis," *Diseases of the Nervous System*, 33 (1972): 617–621; C. E. Hollingsworth, P. E. Tanguay, L. Grossman, and P. Pabst, "Long-Term Outcome of Obsessive-Compulsive Disorder in Childhood," *Journal of the American Academy of Child Psychiatry*, 19 (1980): 134–144; W. Coryell, R. Noyes, and D. House, "Mortality Among Outpatients with Anxiety Disorders," *American Journal of Psychiatry*, 143 (1986): 508–510.

122 unless it is extremely severe: E. Kringlen, "Obsessional Neurotics: A Long-Term Follow-Up," *British Journal of Psychiatry*, 111 (1965): 709–722; P. Hay, P. Sachdev, S. Cumming, et al., "Treatment of Obsessive-Compulsive Disorder by Psychosurgery," *Acta Psychiatrica Scandinavica*, 87 (1993): 197–207.

122 Impulsivity and violence: M. R. Fryer, A. J. Frances, T. Sullivan, S. W. Hurt, and J. Clarkin, "Suicide Attempts in Patients with Borderline Personality Disorder," *American Journal of Psychiatry*, 145 (1988): 737–739; B.-Å. Armelius and G. Kullgren, "Pc-Modelling as an Instrument to Identify

Patterns of Traits and Behaviors Associated with Completed Suicide in Borderline Personality Disorder," in G. Kullgren, ed., *Clinical Studies on the Borderline Concept with Special Reference to Suicidal Behavior* (Umeå, Sweden: Umeå University Medical Dissertations, 1987), p. 204, cited in B. Runeson and J. Beskow, "Borderline Personality Disorder in Young Swedish Suicides," *Journal of Nervous and Mental Disease*, 179 (1991): 153–156; D. A. Brent, B. Johnson, S. Bartle, et al., "Personality Disorder, Tendency to Impulsive Violence, and Suicidal Behavior in Adolescents," *Journal of the American Academy of Child and Adolescent Psychiatry*, 32 (1993): 69–75; B. S. Brodsky, K. M. Malone, S. P. Ellis, R. A. Dulit, and J. J. Mann, "Characteristics of Borderline Personality Disorder Associated with Suicidal Behavior," *American Journal of Psychiatry*, 154 (1997): 1715–1719; A. T. A. Cheng, A. H. Mann, and K. A. Chan, "Personality Disorder and Suicide: A Case-Control Study," *British Journal of Psychiatry*, 170 (1997): 441–446.

123 When the unstable elements: M. R. Fryer, A. J. Frances, T. Sullivan, S. W. Hurt, and J. Clarkin, "Suicide Attempts in Patients with Borderline Personality Disorder," *American Journal of Psychiatry*, 145 (1988): 737–739; E. M. Corbitt, K. M. Malone, G. L. Haas, and J. J. Mann, "Suicidal Behavior with Minor Depression and Comorbid Personality Disorders," *Journal of Affective Disorders*, 39 (1996): 61–72; E. T. Isometsä, M. M. Henriksson, M. E. Heikkinen, H. M. Aro, M. J. Marttunen, K. I. Kuoppasalmi, and J. K. Lönnqvist, "Suicide Among Subjects with Personality Disorders," *American Journal of Psychiatry*, 153 (1996): 667–673; M. H. Stone, "Paradoxes in the Management of Suicidality in Borderline Patients," *American Journal of Psychotherapy*, 47 (1993): 255–272; P. H. Soloff, "Risk Factors for Suicidal Behavior in Borderline Personality Disorder," *American Journal of Psychiatry*, 151 (1994): 1316–1323; J. Davis, P. Janicak, and F. Ayd, "Psychopharmacotherapy of the Personality-Disordered Patient," *Psychiatric Annals*, 25 (1995): 614–620.

123 Nearly three-quarters: T. H. McGlashan. "The Chesnut Lodge Follow-up Study: III. Long-Term Outcome of Borderline Personalities," *Archives of General Psychiatry*, 43 (1986): 2–30; J. Paris, R. Brown, and D. Nowlis, "Long-Term Follow-up of Borderline Patients in a General Hospital," *Comprehensive Psychiatry*, 28 (1987): 530–535; M. H. Stone, D. K. Stone, and S. Hurt, "The Natural History of Borderline Patients Treated by Intensive Hospitalization," *Psychiatric Clinics of North America*, 10 (1987): 185–206.

123 more than 40 percent: B. S. Runeson, J. Beskow, and M. Waern, "The Suicidal Process in Suicides Among Young People," *Acta Psychiatrica Scandinavica*, 93 (1996): 35–42.

123 "During the first hours": H. A. Wishnie, "Inpatient Therapy with Borderline Patients," in J. E. Mack, ed., *Borderline States in Psychiatry* (New York: Grune & Straton, 1975), pp. 47–48.

126 The reasons for this: P. M. Marzuk and J. J. Mann, "Suicide and Substance Abuse," *Psychiatric Annals*, 18 (1988): 639–646.

127 Alcohol and drugs, used: T. W. Estroff and M. S. Gold, "Medical and Psychiatric Complications of Cocaine Abuse with Possible Points of Pharmacological Treatment," *Advances in Alcohol and Substance Abuse*, 5 (1986): 61–76; J. M. Himmelhoch and M. E. Garfinkel, "Sources of Lithium Resistance in Mixed Mania," *Psychopharmacology Bulletin*, 22 (1986): 613–620;

F. K. Goodwin and K. R. Jamison, *Manic-Depressive Illness* (New York: Oxford University Press, 1990).

128 mental illness usually precedes: D. B. Kandel and M. Davies, "Adult Sequelae of Adolescent Depressive Syndromes," *Archives of General Psychiatry,* 43 (1986): 255–262; K. A. Christie, J. D. Burke, D. A. Regier, D. S. Rae, J. H. Boyd, and B. Z. Locke, "Epidemiologic Evidence for Early Onset of Mental Disorders and Higher Risk of Drug Abuse in Young Adults," *American Journal of Psychiatry,* 145 (1988): 971–75; R. C. Kessler, "The National Comorbidity Survey: Preliminary Results and Future Directions," *International Journal of Methods in Psychiatric Research,* 5 (1995): 139–151; R. C. Kessler, C. B. Nelson, K. A. McGonagle, M. J. Edlund, R. G. Frank, and P. J. Leaf, "The Epidemiology of Co-Occurring Addictive and Mental Disorders: Implications for Prevention and Service Utilization," *American Journal of Orthopsychiatry,* 50 (1996): 36–43.

128 "I am constitutionally sensitive": J. W. Robertson, *Edgar A. Poe: A Psychopathic Study* (New York: G. P. Putnam, 1923), p. 82.

128 Two of every three: L. N. Robins and D. A. Regier, eds., *Psychiatric Disorders in America* (New York: Free Press, 1991).

128 those who are both: P. Nicholls, G. Edwards, and E. Kyle, "Alcoholics Admitted to Four Hospitals in England: General and Cause-Specific Mortality," *Quarterly Journal Studies of Alcohol,* 35 (1974): 841–855; M. Berglund, "Suicide in Alcoholism," *Archives of General Psychiatry,* 41 (1984): 888–891; A. C. Whitters, R. J. Cadoret, and R. B. Widmer, "Factors Associated with Suicide Attempts in Alcohol Abusers," *Journal of Affective Disorders,* 9 (1985): 19–23; D. W. Black, W. Yates, F. Potty, R. Noyes, and K. Brown, "Suicidal Behavior in Alcoholic Males," *Comprehensive Psychiatry,* 27 (1986): 227–233; A. Roy and M. Linnoila, "Alcoholism and Suicide," *Suicide and Life-Threatening Behavior,* 16 (1986): 244–273; M. A. Schuckit, "Primary Men Alcoholics with Histories of Suicide Attempts," *Journal of Studies on Alcohol,* 47 (1986): 78–81; G. Winokur and D. W. Black, "Psychiatric and Medical Diagnoses as Risk Factors for Mortality in Psychiatric Patients: A Case-Control Study," *American Journal of Psychiatry,* 144 (1987): 208–211; D. Hasin, B. Grant, and J. Endicott, "Treated and Untreated Suicide Attempts in Substance Abuse Patients," *Journal of Nervous and Mental Disease,* 176 (1988): 289–294; M. Hesselbrock, V. Hesselbrock, K. Syzmanski, and M. Weidenman, "Suicide Attempts and Alcoholism," *Journal of Studies on Alcohol,* 49 (1988): 436–442; M. M. Henriksson, H. M. Aro, M. J. Marttunen, M. E. Heikkinen, E. T. Isometsä, K. I. Kuoppasalmi, and J. K. Lönnqvist, "Mental Disorders and Comorbidity in Suicide," *American Journal of Psychiatry,* 150 (1993): 935–940; M. D. Rudd, P. F. Dahm, and M. H. Rajals, "Diagnostic Comorbidity in Persons with Suicidal Ideation and Behavior," *American Journal of Psychiatry,* 150 (1993): 928–934; E. Johnsson and M. Fridell, "Suicide Attempts in a Cohort of Drug Abusers: A 5-Year Follow-Up Study," *Acta Psychiatrica Scandinavica,* 96 (1997): 362–366; L. Tondo, R. J. Baldessarini, J. Hennen, G. P. Minnai, P. Salis, L. Scamonatti, M. Masia, C. Ghiani, and P. Mannu, "Suicide Attempts in Major Affective Disorder Patients with Comorbid Substance Use Disorders," *Journal of Clinical Psychiatry* (Suppl. 2) (1999): 63–69.

129 "He knew he was standing": John Berryman, cited in Paul Mariani, *Dream*

Song: The Life of John Berryman (New York: William Morrow, 1990), pp. 466–467.

5 • WHAT MATTERS IT, IF ROPE OR GARTER

130 "Since we can die": Thomas Chatterton, "Suicide." Chatterton (1752–1770), an English poet, wrote "Suicide" a few months before he swallowed a fatal dose of arsenic. "Cease my anguish'd soul," he wrote not long before he died, "And this last act of wretchedness forgive." He was seventeen.

130 "In whatever direction": Seneca, "To Norvatus on Anger" (III. xv. 3–xvi.), p. 295.

131 "He plunged a dagger": S. B. Nuland, *How We Die: Reflections on Life's Final Chapter* (New York: Alfred A. Knopf, 1994), p. 158.

131 "Razors pain you": D. Parker, *The Poetry and Short Stories of Dorothy Parker* (New York: Modern Library, 1994), p. 62.

132 "When Dorothy was sufficiently recovered": M. Meade, *Dorothy Parker: What Fresh Hell Is This?* (New York: Penguin USA, 1989), p. 107.

132 "I know a hundred ways to die": Edna St. Vincent Millay, *Collected Poems*, ed. Norma Millay (New York: Harper & Row, 1956), p. 264.

133 called his servant: Forbes Winslow, *The Anatomy of Suicide* (London: H. Renshaw, 1840; reprinted by Longwood Press, Boston, 1978), p. 298.

133 drinking boiling water: J. P. Gray, "Suicide," *American Journal of Insanity*, 35 (1878): 37–73, p. 66.

134 One of Karl Menninger's patients: K. A. Menninger, "Psychoanalytic Aspects of Suicide," *International Journal of Psychoanalysis*, 14 (1933): 376–390.

134 "four spoons, three knives": Henry Romilly Fedden, *Suicide: A Social and Historical Study* (London: Peter Davies, 1938), p. 305.

134 there have been several reports: R. J. Frances, T. Wikstrom, and V. Alcena, "Contracting AIDS as a Means of Committing Suicide," *American Journal of Psychiatry*, 142 (1985): 656; D. K. Flavin, J. E. Franklin, and R. J. Frances, "The Acquired Immune Deficiency Syndrome (AIDS) and Suicidal Behavior in Alcohol-Dependent Homosexual Men," *American Journal of Psychiatry*, 143 (1986): 1440–1442.

134 This baffling endgame: A. Feuer, "Drawing a Bead on a Baffling Endgame: Suicide by Cop," *New York Times*, June 21, 1998.

134 "The cuckolded householder": Thomas Lynch, *The Undertaking: Life Studies from the Dismal Trade* (London: Jonathan Cape, 1997), p. 173.

135 Anton van Hooff: A. van Hooff, *From Autothanasia to Suicide: Self-Killing in Classical Antiquity* (London: Routledge, 1990).

136 "To die were best": Euripides, "Helena," ll. 298–303.

136 By the late nineteenth century: E. Morselli, *Suicide: An Essay on Comparative Moral Statistics* (London: Kegan Paul, 1881): E. Durkheim, *Suicide: A Study in Sociology*, trans. J. A. Spaulding and G. Simpson (New York: Free Press, 1951; first published 1897).

137 "The calm, / Cool face": Langston Hughes, "Suicide's Note," in A. Rampersad and D. Roessel, eds., *The Collected Poems of Langston Hughes* (New York: Alfred A. Knopf, 1994), p. 55.

137 "Thus," wrote sociologist: Durkheim, *Suicide: A Study in Sociology*, p. 290.

137 "Even away from their own country": Morselli, *Suicide: An Essay on Comparative Moral Statistics*, p. 327.

137 English, Scottish, and Irish immigrants: P. Burvill, M. McCall, T. Woodings, and N. Stenhouse, "Comparison of Suicide Rates and Methods in English, Scots and Irish Immigrants in Australia," *Social Science and Medicine*, 17 (1983): 705–708.

137 In Belgium, for example: G. F. G. Moens, M. J. M. Loysch, and H. van de Voorde, "The Geographical Pattern of Methods of Suicide in Belgium: Implications for Prevention," *Acta Psychiatrica Scandinavica*, 77 (1988): 320–327.

137 Poisoning and hanging: R. Desjarlais, L. Eisenberg, B. Good, and A. Kleinman, *World Mental Health: Problems and Priorities in Low-Income Countries* (New York: Oxford University Press, 1995).

137 a study of suicide methods: D. Lester, "Changes in the Methods Used for Suicide in 16 Countries from 1960 to 1980," *Acta Psychiatrica Scandinavica*, 81 (1990): 260–261.

138 "The first thing I considered": Quoted by M. Iga, *The Thorn in the Chrysanthemum: Suicide and Economic Success in Modern Japan* (Berkeley and Los Angeles: University of California Press, 1986), pp. 82–83.

139 Freud conjectured: S. Freud, "The Psychogenesis of a Case of Homosexuality in a Woman," *The Standard Edition of the Complete Psychological Works*, trans. and ed. J. Strachey (London: Hogarth Press, 1955), vol. 18, pp. 147–172.

139 Personality traits: D. Lester, "Factors Affecting Choice of Method for Suicide," *Journal of Clinical Psychology*, 26 (1970): 437; D. Lester, "Personality Correlates Associated with Choice of Method for Suicide," *Personality*, 1 (1970): 261–264; D. Lester, "Choice of Method for Suicide and Personality: A Study of Suicide Notes," *Omega*, 2 (1971): 76–80; N. Lukianowicz, "Suicidal Behavior," *Psychiatrica Clinica*, 7 (1974): 159–171; K. Noreik, "Attempted Suicide and Suicide in Functional Psychoses," *Acta Psychiatrica Scandinavica*, 52 (1975): 81–106; D. Lester and A. T. Beck, "What the Suicide's Choice of Method Signifies," *Omega*, 113 (1980–81): 271–277; D. Lester, "Excitor-Inhibitor Scales of the MMPI and Choice of Method for Suicide," *Perceptual and Motor Skills*, 66 (1988): 218; D. Lester, "Determinants of Choice of Method for Suicide and the Person/Situation Debate in Psychology," *Perceptual and Motor Skills*, 85 (1997): 497–498.

139 The availability of the method: M. Tousignant and B. L. Mishara, "Suicide and Culture: A Review of the Literature (1979–1980)," *Transcultural Psychiatric Research Review*, 18 (1981): 5–32; J. R. Bowles, "Suicide and Attempted Suicide in Contemporary Western Samoa," in F. X. Hezel, D. H. Rubinstein, and G. H. White, eds., *Culture, Youth and Suicide in the Pacific: Papers from an East-West Center Conference* (Honolulu: East-West Center, 1985), pp. 15–35; L. R. Berger, "Suicides and Pesticides in Sri Lanka," *American Journal of Public Health*, 78 (1988): 826–828; W. H. Lo and T. M. Leung, "Suicide in Hong Kong," *Australian and New Zealand Journal of Psychiatry*, 19 (1985): 287–292; K. T. Hau, "Suicide in Hong Kong 1971–1990: Age Trend, Sex Ratio, and Method of Suicide," *Social Psychiatry and Psychiatric Epidemiology*, 28 (1993): 23–27; D. Lester, "Suicide by Jumping in Singapore as a Function of High-Rise Apartment Availability," *Perceptual and Motor*

Skills, 79 (1994): 74; R. Desjarlais, L. Eisenberg, B. Good, and A. Kleinman, *World Mental Health: Problems and Priorities in Low-Income Countries* (New York: Oxford University Press, 1995).

140 potentially lethal medications: D. Jacobsen, K. Frederichsen, K. M. Knutsen, Y. Sorum, T. Talseth, and O. R. Odegaard, "A Prospective Study of 1212 Cases of Acute Poisoning: General Epidemiology," *Human Toxicology*, 3 (1984): 93–106; E. Isometsä, M. Henriksson, and J. Lönnqvist, "Completed Suicide and Recent Lithium Treatment," *Journal of Affective Disorders*, 26 (1992): 101–104; D. Waddington and I. P. McKenzie, "Overdose Rates in Lithium-Treated Versus Antidepressant-Treated Outpatients," *Acta Psychiatrica Scandinavica*, 90 (1994): 50–52.

141 Forensic pathologists, for example: C. E. Rhyne, D. I. Templer, L. G. Brown, and N. B. Peters, "Dimensions of Suicide: Perceptions of Lethality, Time, and Agony," *Suicide and Life-Threatening Behavior*, 25 (1995): 373–380.

141 American adolescents: H. E. Harris and W. C. Myers, "Adolescents' Misconceptions of the Dangerousness of Acetaminophen in Overdose," *Suicide and Life-Threatening Behavior*, 27 (1997): 274–277.

141 One study conducted in the 1970s: A. Marks, "Sex Differences and Their Effect upon Cultural Evaluations of Methods of Self-Destruction," *Omega*, 8 (1977): 65–70.

141 Fear of disfigurement: D. Lester, "Why Do People Choose Particular Methods for Suicide?" *Activitas Nervosa Superior*, 30 (1988): 312–314.

141 Age also plays a role: K. Hawton, M. Osborn, J. O'Grady, et al. "Classification of Adolescents Who Take Overdoses," *British Journal of Psychiatry*, 140 (1982): 124–131; D. A. Brent, "Correlates of Medical Lethality of Suicide Attempts in Children and Adolescents," *Journal of the American Academy of Child Psychiatry*, 26 (1987): 87–89; M. L. Rosenberg, J. C. Smith, L. E. Davidson, and J. M. Conn, "The Emergence of Youth Suicide: An Epidemiologic Analysis and Public Health Perspective," *Annual Review of Public Health*, 8 (1987): 417–440; H. M. Hoberman and B. D. Garfinkel, "Completed Suicide in Youth," *Canadian Journal of Psychiatry*, 33 (1988): 494–504; I. O'Donnell and R. D. T. Farmer, "Suicidal Acts on Metro Systems: An International Perspective," *Acta Psychiatrica Scandinavica*, 86 (1992): 60–63; J. L. McIntosh, "Methods of Suicide," in R. W. Maris, A. L. Berman, J. T. Maltsberger, and R. I. Yufit, eds., *Assessment and Prediction of Suicide* (New York: Guilford Press, 1992), pp. 381–397; Centers for Disease Control, "Suicide Among Children, Adolescents, and Young Adults—United States, 1980–1992," *Journal of the American Medical Association*, 274 (1995): 451–452; D. De Leo, D. Conforti, and G. Carollo, "A Century of Suicide in Italy: A Comparison Between the Old and the Young," *Suicide and Life-Threatening Behavior*, 27 (1997): 239–249.

141 The type and degree: H. Hendin, "The Psychodynamics of Suicide," *Journal of Nervous and Mental Disease*, 136 (1963): 236–244; F. G. Guggenheim and A. D. Weisman, "Suicide in the Subway: Publicly Witnessed Attempts of 50 Cases," *Journal of Nervous and Mental Disease*, 155 (1972): 404–409; K. Lindekilde and A. G. Wang, "Train Suicide in the County of Fyn 1979–1982," *Acta Psychiatrica Scandinavica*, 72 (1985): 150–154; R. L. Symonds, "Psychiatric Aspects of Railway Fatalities," *Psychological Medicine*,

15 (1985): 609–621; R. Jacobson, M. Jackson, and M. Berelowitz, "Self-Incineration: A Controlled Comparison of Inpatient Suicide Attempts. Clinical Features and History of Self-Harm," *Psychological Medicine*, 16 (1986): 107–116; M. J. Shkrum and K. A. Johnston, "Fire and Suicide: A Three Year Study of Self-Immolation Deaths," *Journal of Forensic Sciences*, 37 (1992): 208–221.

142 "sometimes noble and weighty": Morselli, *Suicide: An Essay on Comparative Moral Statistics*, p. 352.

142 "psychological constellation": L. I. Dublin, *Suicide: A Sociological and Statistical Study* (New York: Ronald Press, 1963).

143 read a newspaper report: S. J. Surtees, D. C. Taylor, and R. W. Cooper, "Suicide and Accidental Death at Beachy Head," *Eastbourne Medical Gazette*, 2 (1976): 22–24; S. J. Surtees, "Suicide and Accidental Death at Beachy Head," *British Medical Journal*, 284 (1982): 321–324.

144 Publicity given to particular ways: D. J. Pounder, "Suicide by Leaping from Multistorey Car Parks," *Medical Science and Law*, 25 (1985): 179–188; R. H. Haynes, "Suicide in Fiji: A Preliminary Study," *British Journal of Psychiatry*, 145 (1984): 433–438; M. Pinguet, *Voluntary Death in Japan*, trans. R. Morris (Cambridge, England: Polity Press, 1993); D. J. Somasundaram and S. Rajadurai, "War and Suicide in Northern Sri Lanka," *Acta Psychiatrica Scandinavica*, 91 (1995): 1–4.

144 publication of *Final Exit:* P. M. Marzuk, K. Tardiff, C. S. Hirsch, A. C. Leon, M. Stajic, N. Hartwell, and L. Portera, "Increase in Suicide by Asphyxiation in New York City After the Publication of *Final Exit,*" *New England Journal of Medicine*, 329 (1993): 1508–1510; P. M. Marzuk, K. Tardiff, and A. C. Leon, "Increase in Fatal Suicidal Poisonings and Suffocations in the Year *Final Exit* Was Published: A National Study," *American Journal of Psychiatry*, 151 (1994): 1813–1814.

145 "In a free society": J. R. Ashton and S. Donnan, "Suicide by Burning as an Epidemic Phenomenon: An Analysis of 82 Deaths and Inquests in England and Wales in 1978–9," *Psychological Medicine*, 11 (1981): 735–739.

145 an almost mythic belief: Y. Takahashi, *"Aokigahara-jukai:* Suicide and Amnesia in Mt. Fuji's Black Forest," *Suicide and Life-Threatening Behavior*, 18 (1988): 164–175.

147 "The suicide epidemic": E. R. Ellis and G. N. Allen, *Traitor Within: Our Suicide Problem* (New York: Doubleday, 1961), pp. 98–99.

148 a language and mythology soon grew up: R. H. Seiden and M. C. Spence, "A Tale of Two Bridges: Comparative Suicide Incidence on the Golden Gate and San Francisco–Oakland Bay Bridges," *Crisis*, 2 (1982): 32–40.

149 the trauma rips: M. Lafave, A. J. LaPorta, J. Hutton, and P. L. Mallory, "History of High-Velocity Impact Water Trauma at Letterman Army Medical Center: A 54-Year Experience with the Golden Gate Bridge," *Military Medicine*, 160 (1995): 197–199.

149 "There is a kind of form to it": D. H. Rosen, "Suicide Survivors: A Follow-up of Persons Who Survived Jumping from the Golden Gate and San Francisco–Oakland Bay Bridges," *Western Journal of Medicine*, 122 (1975): 289–294, p. 292.

149 "Why do you make it so easy?": Quoted in G. H. Colt, *The Enigma of Suicide* (New York: Summit, 1991), p. 334.

149 an idea resisted: P. Fimrite, "Anti-Suicide Fence Sample on Display," *San Francisco Chronicle*, 10 June 1998.

149 Five to 10 percent: E. Robins, G. E. Murphy, R. H. Wilkinson, S. Gassner, and J. Kayes, "Some Clinical Considerations in the Prevention of Suicide Based on a Study of 134 Successful Suicides," *American Journal of Public Health*, 49 (1959): 888–899; K. A. Achté, A. Stenbäck, and H. Teräväinen, "On Suicides Committed During Treatment in Psychiatric Hospitals," *Acta Psychiatrica Scandinavica*, 42 (1969): 272–284; R. Hessö, "Suicide in Norwegian, Finnish, and Swedish Psychiatric Hospitals," *Archives of Psychiatry and Neurological Sciences*, 224 (1977): 119–127; J. L. Crammer, "The Special Characteristics of Suicide in Hospital Inpatients," *British Journal of Psychiatry*, 145 (1984): 460–476; U. B. Sunqvist-Stensman, "Suicides in Close Connection with Psychiatric Care: An Analysis of 57 Cases in a Swedish County," *Acta Psychiatrica Scandinavica*, 76 (1987): 15–20; M. Wolfersdorf, F. Keller, P.-O. Schmidt-Michel, C. Weiskittel, R. Vogel, and G. Hole, "Are Hospital Suicides on the Increase?," *Social Psychiatry and Psychiatric Epidemiology*, 23 (1988): 207–216; E. C. Harris and B. Barraclough, "Suicide as an Outcome for Mental Disorders: A Meta-Analysis," *British Journal of Psychiatry*, 170 (1997): 205–228.

151 "Only too often the patients": E. Kraepelin, *Manic-Depressive Insanity and Paranoia*, trans. R. M. Barclay, ed. G. M. Robertson (New York: Arno Press, 1976; first published 1921), p. 88.

151 twisted cords around the neck: G. R. Jameison and J. H. Wall, "Some Psychiatric Aspects of Suicide," *Psychiatric Quarterly*, 7 (1933): 211–229.

152 "A maid in a green uniform": S. Plath, *The Bell Jar* (New York: Harper & Row, 1971), p. 153.

152 Hanging and jumping are by far: K. A. Achté, A. Stenbäck, and H. Teräväinen, "On Suicides Committed During Treatment in Psychiatric Hospitals," *Acta Psychiatrica Scandinavica*, 42 (1969): 272–284; N. L. Farberow, S. Ganzler, F. Cutter, and D. Reynolds, "An Eight-Year Survey of Hospital Suicides," *Life-Threatening Behavior*, 1 (1971): 184–202; A. R. Beisser and J. E. Blanchette, "A Study of Suicides in a Mental Hospital," *Diseases of the Nervous System*, 22 (1961): 365–369; A. K. Shah and T. Ganesvaran, "Inpatient Suicides in an Australian Mental Hospital," *Australian and New Zealand Journal of Psychiatry*, 31 (1997): 291–298; K. A. Busch, D. C. Clark, J. Fawcett, and H. M. Kravitz, "Clinical Features of Inpatient Suicide," *Psychiatric Annals*, 23 (1993): 256–262; F. Proulx, A. D. Lesage, and F. Grunberg, "One Hundred Inpatient Suicides," *British Journal of Psychiatry*, 171 (1997): 247–250; V. Sharma, E. Persad, and K. Kueneman, "A Closer Look at Inpatient Suicide," *Journal of Affective Disorders*, 47 (1998): 123–129.

152 Jan Fawcett and Katie Busch: personal communication with Dr. Jan Fawcett, Rush–Presbyterian–St. Luke's Medical Center, Chicago, May 1998.

152 Research indicates: H. G. Morgan, *Death Wishes? The Assessment and Management of Deliberate Self-Harm* (New York: Wiley, 1979); P. H. Salmons, "Suicide in High Buildings," *British Journal of Psychiatry*, 145 (1984): 469–472; H. G. Morgan and P. Priest, "Suicide and Other Unexpected Deaths Among Psychiatric Inpatients," *British Journal of Psychiatry*, 158 (1991): 368–374; J. A. Dennehey, L. Appleby, C. S. Thomas, et al., "Case

Control Study of Suicides by Discharged Psychiatric Patients," *British Medical Journal*, 312 (1996): 1580; K. A. Busch, D. C. Clark, J. Fawcett, and H. M. Kravitz, "Clinical Features of Inpatient Suicide," *Psychiatric Annals*, 23 (1993): 256–262; H. G. Morgan and R. Stanton, "Suicide Among Psychiatric Inpatients in a Changing Clinical Scene," *British Journal of Psychiatry*, 171 (1997): 561–563; V. Sharma, E. Persad, and K. Kueneman, "A Closer Look at Inpatient Suicide," *Journal of Affective Disorders*, 47 (1998) 123–129.

ESSAY · THE LION ENCLOSURE

154 "The Woman at the Washington Zoo": Randall Jarrell (1914–1965) wrote this poem while living in Washington, D.C., in the 1950s. He and his wife frequently visited the zoo, and he drove past it almost every day on his way through Rock Creek Park to his job at the Library of Congress. Jarrell, when asked about the central character in "The Woman at the Washington Zoo," described her as having a despair "beyond expression . . . inside the mechanical official cage of her life, her body, she lives invisibly; no one feeds this animal, reads out its name, pokes a stick through the bars at it—the cage is empty . . . she has become her own cage" ("The Woman at the Washington Zoo," pp. 319–327, reprinted in Randall Jarrell, *Kipling, Auden & Co.: Essays and Reviews: 1935–1964* [New York: Farrar, Straus and Giroux, 1980], pp. 324–325). Jarrell received the National Book Award for his collection of poems *The Woman at the Washington Zoo*. In 1965, after being hospitalized for manic-depressive illness and an attempted suicide, Jarrell was killed by an oncoming car at night. The circumstances of his death provoked considerable debate about whether it had been an accident or suicide. (J. Meyers, "The Death of Randall Jarrell," *The Virginia Quarterly Review*, Summer 1982, pp. 450–467; *Randall Jarrell's Letters*, ed. Mary Jarrell [Boston: Houghton Mifflin, 1985]; W. H. Pritchard, *Randall Jarrell: A Literary Life* [New York: Farrar, Straus and Giroux, 1990]; K. R. Jamison, *Touched with Fire: Manic-Depressive Illness and the Artistic Temperament* [New York: Free Press, 1993]).

155 instinct would dictate: George B. Schaller, *The Serengeti Lion: A Study of Predator-Prey Relations* (Chicago: University of Chicago Press, 1972).

155 The *Washington Post:* The *Washington Post* published five news stories about the death of Margaret Davis King, March 6–10, 1995, and the *Arkansas Democrat-Gazette* published articles on March 7, 8, and 10, 1995.

155 "Suddenly," wrote journalist: Phil McCombs, "In the Lair of the Urban Lion," *Washington Post*, March 7, 1995.

158 We have released: W. R. Breakey, P. J. Fischer, M. Kramer, et al., "Health and Mental Health Problems of Homeless Men and Women in Baltimore," *Journal of the American Medical Association*, 10 (1989): 1352–1357; E. Susser, R. Moore, and B. Link, "Risk Factors for Homelessness," *American Journal of Epidemiology* 15 (1993): 546–556; T. K. J. Craig and P. W. Timms, "Homelessness and Schizophrenia," in S. R. Hirsch and D. R. Weinberger, eds., *Schizophrenia* (Oxford: Blackwell Science, 1995), pp. 664–684.

158 They die younger: C. H. Alstrom, R. Lindelius, and I. Salum, "Mortality Among Homeless Men," *British Journal of Addiction*, 70 (1975): 245–252;

Centers for Disease Control, "Deaths Among the Homeless," *Mortality and Morbidity Weekly Report*, 36 (1987): 297–299; Centers for Disease Control, "Deaths Among Homeless Persons—San Francisco, 1985–1990," *Mortality and Morbidity Weekly Report*, 40 (1991): 877–880; J. R. Hibbs, L. Benner, L. Klugman, R. Spencer, I. Macchia, A. K. Mellinger, and D. Fife, "Mortality in a Cohort of Homeless Adults in Philadelphia," *New England Journal of Medicine* 331 (1994): 304–309.

158　In a 1986 editorial: R. J. Wyatt and E. G. De Renzo, "Scienceless to Homeless," *Science*, 234 (1986): 1309.

6 · A PLUNGE INTO DEEP WATERS

163　"It was, he said": Edgar Allan Poe, *The Fall of the House of Usher.* Problems with alcohol and a lifetime of virulent moods eventually caught up with Edgar Allan Poe (1809–1849), who attempted suicide the year before he died.

163　"But it is always a question": Virginia Woolf, *The Diary of Virginia Woolf,* vol 3. Virginia Woolf (1882–1941), in whose family there was a great deal of depressive illness, committed suicide after years of struggling with manic-depression.

163　Human conduct: J. Ordronaux, "On Suicide," *American Journal of Insanity,* 20 (1864): 380–401, p. 380."

164　"Observations show that": Ibid., p. 381.

164　"With reference to suicide": F. Winslow, *The Anatomy of Suicide* (Boston: Longwood Press, 1978; first published 1840), p. 152.

165　"Captains C. L. and J. L.": B. Rush, *Medical Inquiries and Observations upon the Diseases of the Mind* (New York: Kimber and Richardson, 1812).

166　"There is nothing more firmly established": C. W. Pilgrim, "Insanity and Suicide," *American Journal of Insanity,* 63 (1907): 349–360, p. 359.

167　"The evil results": J. M. S. Wood and A. R. Urquhart, "A Family Tree Illustrative of Insanity and Suicide," *Journal of Mental Science,* 47 (1901): 764–767, p. 767.

167　"A man named Edgar Jay Briggs": *Medical Record,* 60 (1901): 660–661.

167　More recently, in Iraq: F. Dabbagh, "Family Suicide," *British Journal of Psychiatry,* 130 (1977): 159–161.

168　Many other "suicide families": For example, L. B. Shapiro, "Suicide: Psychology and Familial Tendency—Report of a Family of Suicides with History and Discussion," *Journal of Nervous and Mental Disease,* 81 (1935): 547–553; Khin-Maung-Zaw, "A Suicidal Family," *British Journal of Psychiatry,* 139 (1981): 68–69.

168　a strong genetic basis: I. I. Gottesman and J. Shields, *Schizophrenia and Genetics: A Twin Vantage Point* (New York: Academic Press, 1972); S. S. Kety, D. Rosenthal, P. H. Wender, F. Schulsinger, and B. Jacobsen, "Mental Illness in the Biological and Adoptive Families of Individuals Who Have Become Schizophrenic," *Behaviour Genetics,* 6 (1976): 219–225; I. I. Gottesman and J. Shields, *Schizophrenia: The Epigenetic Puzzle* (Cambridge: Cambridge University Press, 1982); K. S. Kendler and A. M. Gruenberg, "An Independent Antigen of the Danish Adoption Study of Schizophrenia: VI. The Relationship Between Psychiatric Disorders as Defined by DSM-

III in the Relatives and Adoptees," *Archives of General Psychiatry*, 41 (1984): 555–564; P. McGuffin, A. E. Farmer, I. I. Gottesman, R. M. Murray, and A. Reveley, "Twin Concordance for Operationally Defined Schizophrenia: Confirmation of Familiality and Heritability," *Archives of General Psychiatry*, 41 (1984): 541–545; I. I. Gottesman and A. Bertlesen, "Confirming Unexpressed Genotypes for Schizophrenia—Risks in the Offspring of Fischer's Danish Identical and Fraternal Discordant Twins," *Archives of General Psychiatry*, 46 (1989): 867–872; M. T. Tsuang and S. V. Faraone, *The Genetics of Mood Disorders* (Baltimore: Johns Hopkins, 1990); P. Tienari, "Gene-Environment Interaction in Adoptive Families," in H. Hafner and W. Gattaz, eds., *Search for the Causes of Schizophrenia* (Berlin: Springer, 1990), pp. 126–143; W. H. Berrettini, T. N. Ferraro, L. R. Goldin, D. E. Weeks, S. Detera-Wadleigh, J. I. Nurnberger, and E. S. Gershon, "Chromosome 18 DNA Markers and Manic-Depressive Illness: Evidence for a Susceptibility Gene," *Proceedings of the National Academy of Sciences, USA*, 91 (1994): 5918–5921; P. Asherson, R. Mant, and P. McGuffin, "Genetics and Schizophrenia," in S. R. Hirsch and D. R. Weinberger, eds., *Schizophrenia* (Oxford: Blackwell Science, 1995), pp. 253–274; O. C. Stine, J. Xu, R. Koskela, F. J. McMahon, M. Gschwend, C. Friddle, C. D. Clark, M. G. McInnis, S. G. Simpson, T. S. Breschel, E. Vishio, K. Riskin, H. Feilotter, E. Chen, S. Shen, S. Folstein, D. A. Meyers, D. Botstein, T. G. Marr, and J. R. DePaulo, "Evidence for Linkage of Bipolar Disorder to Chromosome 18 with a Parent-of-Origin Effect," *American Journal of Human Genetics*, 57 (1995): 1384–1395; N. B. Freimer, V. I. Reus, M. A. Escamilla, L. A. McInnes, M. Spesny, P. Leon, S, K. Service, L. Smith, S. Silva, E. Rojas, A. Gallegos, L. Meza, E. Fournier, S. Baharloo, K. Blankenship, D. J. Tyler, S. Batki, S. Vinogradov, J. Weissenbach, S. H. Barondes, and L. A. Lodewijk, "Genetic Mapping Using Haplotype, Association and Linkage Methods Suggests a Locus for Severe Bipolar Disorder (BPI) at 18q22-q23," *Nature Genetics*, 12 (1996): 436–441; E. S. Gershon, J. A. Badner, S. D. Detera-Wadleigh, T. N. Ferraro, and W. H. Berrettini, "Maternal Inheritance and Chromosome 18 Allele Sharing in Unilineal Bipolar Illness Pedigrees," *Neuropsychiatric Genetics*, 67 (1996): 202–207; D. F. MacKinnon, K. R. Jamison, and J. R. DePaulo, "Genetics of Manic Depressive Illness," *Annual Review of Neuroscience*, 20 (1997): 355–373; S. H. Barondes, *Mood Genes: Hunting for Origins of Mania and Depression* (New York: W. H. Freeman, 1998).

169 more than thirty family studies: Among them are N. Farberow and M. Simon, "Suicide in Los Angeles and Vienna: An Intercultural Study of Two Cities," *Public Health Report*, 84 (1969): 389–403; F. Stallone, D. L. Dunner, J. Ahearn, and R. R. Fieve, "Statistical Predictions of Suicide in Depressives," *Comprehensive Psychiatry*, 21 (1980): 381–387; C. Tishler, P. McKenry, and K. Morgan, "Adolescent Suicide Attempts: Some Significant Factors," *Suicide and Life-Threatening Behavior*, 11 (1981): 86–92; B. D. Garfinkel, A. Froese, and J. Hood, "Suicide Attempts in Children and Adolescents," *American Journal of Psychiatry*, 139 (1982): 1257–1261; G. E. Murphy and R. D. Wetzel, "Family History of Suicidal Behavior Among Suicide Attempters," *Journal of Nervous and Mental Disease*, 170 (1982): 86–90; K. M. Myers, P. Burke, and E. McCauley, "Suicidal Behavior Among Suicide Attempters," *Journal of Nervous and Mental Disease*, 170 (1982):

86–90; C. R. Pfeffer, G. Solomon, R. Plutchik, M. S. Mizruchi, and A. Weiner, "Suicidal Behavior in Latency-Age Psychiatric Inpatients: A Replication and Cross Validation," *Journal of the American Academy of Child Psychiatry*, 21 (1982): 564–569; A. Roy, "Family History of Suicide," *Archives of General Psychiatry*, 40 (1983): 971–974; M. T. Tsuang, "Risk of Suicide in Relatives of Schizophrenics, Manics, Depressives, and Controls," *Journal of Clinical Psychiatry*, 44 (1983): 396–400; J. A. Egeland and J. N. Sussex, "Suicide and Family Loading for Affective Disorders," *Journal of the American Medical Association*, 254 (1985): 915–918; A. Roy, "Family History of Suicide in Manic-Depressive Patients," *Journal of Affective Disorders*, 8 (1985): 187–189; M. Shafii, S. Carrigan, R. Whittinghill, and A. Derrick, "Psychological Autopsy of Completed Suicides in Children and Adolescents," *American Journal of Psychiatry*, 142 (1985): 1061–1064; M. Kerfoot, "Deliberate Self-Poisoning in Childhood and Early Adolescence," *Journal of Child Psychology and Psychiatry*, 29 (1988): 335–343; D. Shaffer, "The Epidemiology of Teen Suicide: An Examination of Risk Factors," *Journal of Clinical Psychiatry*, 49 (1988): 36–41; B. Mitterauer, "A Contribution to the Discussion of the Role of the Genetic Factor in Suicide, Based on Five Studies in an Epidemiologically Defined Area (Province of Salzburg, Austria)," *Comprehensive Psychiatry*, 31 (1990): 557–565; S. B. Sorenson and C. M. Rutter, "Transgenerational Patterns of Suicide Attempt," *Journal of Consulting and Clinical Psychology*, 59 (1991): 861–866; C. R. Pfeffer, L. Normandin, and T. Kakuma, "Suicidal Children Grow Up: Suicidal Behavior and Psychiatric Disorders Among Relatives," *Journal of American Academy of Child and Adolescent Psychiatry*, 33 (1994): 1087–1097; K. Malone, G. Haas, J. Sweeney, and J. Mann, "Major Depression and the Risk of Attempted Suicide," *Journal of Affective Disorders*, 34 (1995): 173–185; D. A. Brent, J. Bridge, B. A. Johnson, and J. Connolly, "Suicidal Behavior Runs in Families: A Controlled Family Study of Adolescent Suicide Victims," *Archives of General Psychiatry*, 53 (1996): 1145–1152; B. A. Johnson, D. A. Brent, J. Bridge, and J. Connolly, "The Familial Aggregation of Adolescent Suicide Attempts," *Acta Psychiatrica Scandinavica*, 97 (1998): 18–24; D. J. Statham, A. C. Heath, P. A. F. Madden, K. K. Bucholz, L. Bierut, S. H. Dinwiddie, W. S. Slutske, M. P. Dunne, and N. G. Martin, "Suicidal Behaviour: An Epidemiological and Genetic Study," *Psychological Medicine*, 28 (1998): 839–855.

169 suicide in a violent manner: P. Linkowski, V. de Maertelaer, and J. Mendlewicz, "Suicidal Behaviour in Major Depressive Illness," *Acta Psychiatrica Scandinavica*, 72 (1985): 233–238; G. N. Papadimitriou, P. Linkowski, C. Delarbre, and J. Mendlewicz, "Suicide on the Paternal and Maternal Sides of Depressed Patients with a Lifetime History of Attempted Suicide," *Acta Psychiatrica Scandinavica*, 83 (1991): 417–419; A. Roy, "Features Associated with Suicide Attempts in Depression: A Partial Replication," *Journal of Affective Disorders*, 27 (1993): 35–38.

169 the Old Order Amish: J. A. Egeland and J. N. Sussex, "Suicide and Family Loading for Affective Disorders," *Journal of the American Medical Association*, 254 (1985): 915–918.

170 "racing one's horse and carriage": J. A. Egeland, A. M. Hostetter, and S. K. Eshleman, "Amish Study: III. The Impact of Cultural Factors on Diagnosis of Bipolar Illness," *American Journal of Psychiatry*, 140 (1983): 67–71, p. 68.

170 replicated in an Austrian study: B. Mitterauer, M. Leibetseder, W. F. Pritz, and G. Sorgo, "Comparisons of Psychopathological Phenomena of 422 Manic-Depressive Patients with Suicide-Positive and Suicide-Negative Family History," *Acta Psychiatrica Scandinavica*, 77 (1988): 438–442; B. Mitterauer, "A Contribution to the Discussion of the Role of the Genetic Factor in Suicide, Based on Five Studies in an Epidemiologically Defined Area (Province of Salzburg, Austria)," *Comprehensive Psychiatry*, 31 (1990): 557–565; B. A. Johnson, D. A. Brent, J. Bridge, and J. Connolly, "The Familial Aggregation of Adolescent Suicide Attempts," *Acta Psychiatrica Scandinavica*, 97 (1998): 18–24.

171 nearly four hundred pairs: W. Haberlandt, "Aportación a la Genética del Suicidio," *Filio Clínica Internacional*, 17 (1967): 319–322; N. Juel-Nielsen and T. Videbech, "A Twin Study of Suicide," *Acta Geneticae Medicae et Gemellologiae*, 19 (1970): 307–310; A. Roy, G. Rylander, and M. Sarchiapone, "Genetics of Suicide: Family Studies and Molecular Genetics," *Annals of the New York Academy of Sciences*, 836 (1997): 135–157; A. Roy, D. Nielsen, G. Rylander, M. Sarchiapone, and N. Segal, "Genetics of Suicide in Depression," *Journal of Clinical Psychiatry* (Suppl. 2) (1999): 12–17.

171 In a different study: A Roy, N. L. Segal, and M. Sarchiapone, "Attempted Suicide Among Living Co-Twins of Twin Suicide Victims," *American Journal of Psychiatry*, 152 (1995): 1075–1076.

171 concordance rate observed for manic-depression: P. McGuffin and R. Katz, "The Genetics of Depression and Manic-Depressive Disorder," *British Journal of Psychiatry*, 155 (1989): 294–304; M. T. Tsuang and S. V. Faraone, *The Genetics of Mood Disorders* (Baltimore: Johns Hopkins, 1990); L. Rifkin and H. Gurling, "Genetic Aspects of Affective Disorders," in R. Horton and C. Katona, eds., *Biological Aspects of Affective Disorders* (London: Academic Press, 1991), pp. 305–334; D. F. MacKinnon, K. R. Jamison, and J. R. DePaulo, "Genetics of Manic Depressive Illness," *Annual Review of Neuroscience*, 20 (1997): 355–373; A. G. Cardno, E. J. Marshall, B. Coid, A. M. Macdonald, T. R. Ribchester, N. J. Davies, P. Venturi, L. A. Jones, S. W. Lewis, P. C. Sham, I. I. Gottesman, A. E. Farmer, P. McGuffin, A. M. Revely, and R. M. Murray, "Heritability Estimates for Psychotic Disorders," *Archives of General Psychiatry*, 56 (1999): 162–168. (Note: Concordance rates for manic-depressive illness in dizygotic, or fraternal, twins range from 13 to 30 percent.)

171 concordance rate for . . . schizophrenia: E. Kringlen, "Twins—Still Our Best Method," *Schizophrenia Bulletin*, 2 (1976): 429–433; I. I. Gottesman and J. Shields, *Schizophrenia: The Epigenetic Puzzle* (Cambridge, England: Cambridge University Press, 1982); A. E. Farmer, P. McGuffin, and I. I. Gottesman, "Twin Concordance for DSM-III Schizophrenia: Scrutinizing the Validity of the Definition," *Archives of General Psychiatry*, 44 (1987): 634–641; S. Onstad, I. Skre, S. Torgersen, and E. Kringlen, "Twin Concordance for DSM-III-R Schizophrenia," *Acta Psychiatrica Scandinavica*, 83 (1991): 395–402; P. Asherson, R. Mant, and P. McGuffin, "Genetics and Schizophrenia," in S. R. Hirsch and D. R. Weinberger, eds., *Schizophrenia* (Oxford: Blackwell Science, 1995), pp. 253–274. (Note: Concordance rates for schizophrenia in dizygotic, or fraternal, twins are generally in the range of 15 to 20 percent.)

172 The first study: R. Schulsinger, S. Kety, D. Rosenthal, and P. Wender, "A

Family Study of Suicide," in M. Schou and E. Stromgren, eds., *Origins, Prevention and Treatment of Affective Disorders* (New York: Academic Press, 1979), pp. 277–287.

173 more than half of those: M. M. Weissman, J. K. Myers, and W. D. Thompson, "Depression and Treatment in a U.S. Urban Community: 1975–1976," *Archives of General Psychiatry*, 38 (1981): 417–421; S. Shapiro, E. A. Skinner, L. G. Kessler, M. Von Korff, P. S. German, G. L. Tischler, P. J. Leaf, L. Benham, L. Cotler, and D. A. Regier, "Utilization of Health and Mental Health Services: Three Epidemiologic Catchment Area Sites," *Archives of General Psychiatry*, 41 (1984): 971–978; L. N. Robins and D. A. Regier, eds., *Psychiatric Disorders in America: The Epidemiologic Catchment Area Study* (New York: Free Press, 1991).

173 In a second study of Danish adoptees: P. Wender, D. Kety, D. Rosenthal, F. Schulsinger, J. Ortmann, and I. Lunde, "Psychiatric Disorders in the Biological and Adoptive Families of Adopted Individuals with Affective Disorder," *Archives of General Psychiatry*, 43 (1986): 923–929.

174 Ivor Jones and Brian Barraclough: I. H. Jones and B. M. Barraclough, "Auto-Mutilation in Animals and Its Relevance to Self-Injury in Man," *Acta Psychiatrica Scandinavica*, 58 (1978): 40–47, pp. 45–46.

175 Severe self-inflicted injuries: J. D. Christian and H. L. Ratcliffe, "Shock Disease in Captive Wild Animals," *American Journal of Pathology*, 28 (1952): 725–737; H. A. Cross and H. F. Harlow, "Prolonged and Progressive Effects of Partial Isolation on the Behaviour of Macaque Monkeys," *Journal of Experimental Research on Personality*, 1 (1965): 39–49; M. Meyer-Holzapfel, "Abnormal Behaviour in Zoo Animals," in F. W. Fox, ed., *Abnormal Behaviour in Animals* (Philadelphia: Saunders, 1968), pp. 476–503; C. A. Levison, "Development of Head Banging in a Young Rhesus Monkey," *American Journal of Mental Deficiency*, 75 (1970): 323–328; K. A. McColl, "Necropsy Findings in Captive Platypus (*Ornithorhynchus anatinus*) in Victoria, Australia," in M. Fowler, ed., *Wildlife Diseases of the Pacific Basin and Other Countries* (Proceedings of the Fourth International Conference of the Wildlife Disease Association, Sydney, Australia, August 25–29, 1981); M. S. Landi, J. W. Kreider, C. M. Lang, and L. P. Bullock, "Effects of Shipping on the Immune Function in Mice," *American Journal of Veterinary Research*, 43 (1982): 1654–1657.

175 Many ranch mink: G. de Jonge, K. Carlstead, and P. R. Wiepkema, *The Welfare of Ranch Mink*, Publication 010, Centre for Poultry Research and Extension, Beekbergen, Netherlands, 1986.

175 "the severe class": I. H. Jones, "Self-Injury: Toward a Biological Basis," *Perspectives in Biology and Medicine*, 26 (1982): 137–150, p. 138.

175 The agitation and frustration appear: E. M. Boyd, M. Dolman, L. M. Knight, and E. P. Sheppard, "The Chronic Oral Toxicity of Caffeine," *Canadian Journal of Psychology Pharmacology*, 43 (1965): 995–1007; H. A. Cross and H. F. Harlow, "Prolonged and Progressive Effects of Partial Isolation on the Behavior of Macaque Monkeys," *Journal of Experimental Research on Personality*, 1 (1965): 39–49; J. M. Peters, "Caffeine Induced Hemorrhagic Automutilation," *Archives of International Pharmacodynamics*, 169 (1967): 139–146; A. S. Chamove and H. F. Harlow, "Exaggeration of Self-Aggression Following Alcohol Ingestion in Rhesus Monkeys," *Jour-*

nal of Abnormal Psychology, 75 (1970): 207–209; G. Allyn, A. Demye, and I. Begue, "Self-Fighting Syndrome in Macaques: A Representative Case Study," *Primate Medicine*, 17 (1976): 1–22.

176 Prisoners, for example: F. Yaroshevsky, "Self-Mutilation in Soviet Prisons," *Canadian Psychiatric Association Journal*, 20 (1975): 443–446.

176 Rats, when too populous: J. B. Calhoun, *The Ecology and Sociology of the Norway Rat*, Public Health Service Publication no. 1008 (Washington, D.C.: U.S. Government Printing Office, 1963).

176 Cannibalism occasionally erupts: M. P. Simon, "The Influence of Conspecifics on Egg and Larval Mortality in Amphibians," in G. Hausfater and S. B. Hrdy, eds., *Infanticide: Comparative and Evolutionary Perspectives* (New York: Aldine, 1984), pp. 65–86; W. L. Rootes and R. H. Chabreck, "Cannibalism in the American Alligator," *Herpetogica*, 49 (1993): 99–107.

176 Snowshoe hares: R. G. Green, C. L. Larson, and J. F. Bell, "Shock Disease as the Cause of the Periodic Decimation of the Snowshoe Hare," *American Journal of Hygiene*, 30 (1939): 83–102.

176 Prolonged psychopathology: S. J. Suomi, H. F. Harlow, and M. T. McKinney, "Monkey Psychiatrists," *American Journal of Psychiatry*, 128 (1972): 927–932.

176 Lemmings, the poster animals: D. Chitty, *Do Lemmings Commit Suicide? Beautiful Hypotheses and Ugly Facts* (New York: Oxford, 1996).

177 George Schaller observed: G. B. Schaller, *The Serengeti Lion: A Study of Predator-Prey Relations* (Chicago: University of Chicago Press, 1972).

177 "We are strongly predisposed": E. O. Wilson, *On Human Nature* (Cambridge, Mass.: Harvard University Press, 1978), pp. 106, 119.

178 The recently emerging field: D. de Catanzaro, *Suicide and Self-Damaging Behavior: A Sociobiological Perspective* (New York: Academic Press, 1981); R. Gardner, "Mechanisms in Manic-Depressive Disorder: An Evolutionary Model," *Archives of General Psychiatry*, 39 (1982): 1436–1441; D. H. Rubinstein, "A Stress-Diathesis Theory of Suicide," *Suicide and Life-Threatening Behavior*, 16 (1986): 100–115; R. M. Nesse, "Evolutionary Explanations of Emotions," *Human Nature*, 1 (1990): 261–289; P. Gilbert, *Depression: The Evolution of Powerlessness* (New York: Guilford, 1992); M. T. McGuire, I. Marks, R. M. Nesse, and A. Troisi, "Evolutionary Biology: A Basic Science for Psychiatry?" *Acta Psychiatrica Scandinavica*, 86 (1992): 89–96; K. R. Jamison, *Touched with Fire: Manic-Depressive Illness and the Artistic Temperament* (New York: Free Press, 1993); D. R. Wilson, "Evolutionary Epidemiology: Darwinian Theory in the Service of Medicine and Psychiatry," *Acta Biotheoretica*, 41 (1993): 205–218; J. Price, L. Sloman, R. Gardner, P. Gilbert, and P. Rohde, "The Social Competition Hypothesis of Depression," *British Journal of Psychiatry*, 164 (1994): 309–315; D. S. Wilson, "Adaptive Genetic Variation and Human Evolutionary Psychology," *Ethology and Sociobiology*, 15 (1994): 219–235; D. R. Wilson, "The Darwinian Roots of Human Neurosis," *Acta Biotheoretica*, 42 (1994): 49–62; R. M. Brown, E. Dahlen, C. Mills, J. Rick, and A. Biblarz, "Evaluation of an Evolutionary Model of Self-Preservation and Self-Destruction," *Suicide and Life-Threatening Behavior*, 29 (1999): 58–71.

178 the same cognitive and social: M. Hammer and J. Zubin, "Evolution, Culture, and Psychopathology," *Journal of General Psychology*, 78 (1968):

151–164; D. F. Horrobin, A. Ally, R. A. Karmali, M. Karmazyn, M. S. Manka, and R. O. Morgan, "Prostaglandins and Schizophrenia: Further Discussion of the Evidence," *Psychological Bulletin*, 8 (1978): 43–48; L. Sloman, M. Konstantareas, and D. W. Dunham, "The Adaptive Role of Maladaptive Neurosis," *Biological Psychiatry*, 14 (1979): 961–972; J. S. Price and L. Sloman, "The Evolutionary Model of Psychiatric Disorder," *Archives of General Psychiatry*, 41 (1984): 211; S. Vinogradov, I. Gottesman, H. Molses, and S. Nicol, "Negative Association Between Schizophrenia and Rheumatoid Arthritis," *Schizophrenia Bulletin*, 17 (1991): 669–678; D. B. Horrobin, "Schizophrenia: The Illness That Made Us Human," *Medical Hypotheses*, 50 (1998): 269–288; R. J. Wyatt, "Schizophrenia: Closing the Gap Between Genetics, Epidemiology, and Prevention," in E. Susser, A. Brown, and J. Gorman, eds., *Epigenetic Causes of Schizophrenia* (Washington, D.C.: American Psychiatric Association Press, 1999), pp. 241–261.

179 Timothy Crow: T. J. Crow, "Temporal Lobe Asymmetries as the Key to the Etiology of Schizophrenia," *Schizophrenia Bulletin*, 16 (1990): 433–443; T. J. Crow, "Constraints on Concepts of Pathogenesis: Language and the Speciation Process as the Key to the Etiology of Schizophrenia," *Archives of General Psychiatry*, 52 (1995): 1011–1014; T. J. Crow, "A Darwinian Approach to the Origins of Psychosis," *British Journal of Psychiatry*, 167 (1995): 12–25; T. J. Crow, "Is Schizophrenia the Price That *Homo sapiens* Pays for Language?" *Schizophrenia Research*, 28 (1997): 127–141.

179 Depression, characterized as it is: J. Price, L. Sloman, R. J. Gardner, P. Gilbert, and P. Rohde, "The Social Competition Hypothesis of Depression," *British Journal of Psychiatry*, 164 (1994): 309–315; I. H. Jones, D. M. Stoddart, and J. Mallick, "Towards a Sociobiological Model of Depression: A Marsupial Model," *British Journal of Psychiatry*, 166 (1995): 475–479; J. H. G. Williams, "Using Behavioural Ecology to Understand Depression," *British Journal of Psychiatry*, 173 (1998): 453–454.

179 Less dominant animals: P. Gilbert, *Depression: The Evolution of Powerlessness* (New York: Guilford Press, 1992); J. S. Price, L. Sloman, R. Gardner, P. Gilbert, and P. Rohde, "The Social Competition Hypothesis of Depression," *British Journal of Psychiatry*, 164 (1994): 309.

179 "[Icarus] glances up": A. Sexton, "To a Friend Whose Work Has Come to Triumph," in *The Complete Poems of Anne Sexton* (Boston: Houghton Mifflin, 1981), p. 53.

180 uncommonly creative: R. A. Woodruff, L. N. Robins, G. Winokur, and T. Reich, "Manic-Depressive Illness and Social Achievement," *Acta Psychiatrica Scandinavica*, 47 (1971): 237–249; C. Bagley, "Occupational Class and Symptoms of Depression," *Social Sciences and Medicine*, 7 (1973): 327–340; F. K. Goodwin and K. R. Jamison, *Manic-Depressive Illness* (New York: Oxford University Press, 1990), pp. 169–173; W. Coryell, J. Endicott, M. Keller, N. Andreasen, W. Groove, R. M. A. Hirschfeld, and W. Scheftner, "Bipolar Affective Disorder and High Achievement: A Familial Association," *American Journal of Psychiatry*, 146 (1989): 983–988. Anthropologist and physician Melvin Konner has also addressed this issue in *Why the Reckless Survive . . . and Other Secrets of Nature* (New York: Viking, 1990).

180 At least twenty studies: A partial listing of the studies or related discussions include C. Martindale, "Father's Absence, Psychopathology, and Poetic

Eminence," *Psychological Reports*, 31 (1972): 843–847; A. Storr, *The Dynamics of Creation* (London: Secker & Warburg, 1972); W. H. Trethowan, "Music and Mental Disorder," in M. Critchley and R. E. Henson, eds., *Music and the Brain* (London: Heinemann, 1977), pp. 398–442; R. Richards, "Relationships Between Creativity and Psychopathology: An Evaluation and Interpretation of the Evidence," *Genetic Psychology Monographs*, 103 (1981): 261–324; N. C. Andreasen, "Creativity and Mental Illness: Prevalence Rates in Writers and Their First-Degree Relatives," *American Journal of Psychiatry*, 144 (1987): 1288–1292; R. L. Richards, D. K. Kinney, I. Lunde, and M. Benet, "Creativity in Manic-Depressives, Cyclothymes, and Their Normal First-Degree Relatives: A Preliminary Report," *Journal of Abnormal Psychology*, 97 (1988): 281–288; K. R. Jamison, "Mood Disorders and Patterns of Creativity in British Writers and Artists," *Psychiatry*, 52 (1989): 125–134; K. R. Jamison, *Touched with Fire: Manic-Depressive Illness and the Artistic Temperament* (New York: Free Press, 1993); F. Post, "Creativity and Psychopathology: A Study of 291 World-Famous Men," *British Journal of Psychiatry*, 165 (1994): 22–34; J. J. Schildkraut, A. J. Hirshfeld, and J. M. Murphy, "Mind and Mood in Modern Art: II. Depressive Disorders, Spirituality, and Early Deaths in the Abstract Expressionist Artists of the New York School," *American Journal of Psychiatry*, 151 (1994): 482–488; A. M. Ludwig, *The Price of Greatness: Resolving the Creativity and Madness Controversy* (New York: Guilford Press, 1995); F. Post, "Verbal Creativity, Depression, and Alcoholism: An Investigation of One Hundred American and British Writers," *British Journal of Psychiatry*, 168 (1996): 545–555.

181 "But mark how beautiful an order": Percy Bysshe Shelley, *A Defence of Poetry*, in R. Ingpen and W. E. Peck, eds., *The Complete Works of Percy Bysshe Shelley*, vol. 7 (New York: Gordian Press, 1965), p. 126.

181 "Is the shipwrack then a harvest": Gerard Manley Hopkins, "The Wreck of the Deutschland," ll. 248–249 in N. H. MacKenzie, ed., *The Poetical Work of Gerard Manley Hopkins* (Oxford: Clarendon Press, 1990), p. 127.

181 "It isn't possible": Vincent van Gogh to Theo van Gogh, 1888 (undated), in *The Complete Letters of Vincent van Gogh*, vol. 2 (Boston: New York Graphic Society, 1958), p. 542.

181 The source of the data on natural scientists, business leaders, theater people, (international) writers, and international poets is A. Ludwig, *The Price of Greatness* (New York: Guilford Press, 1995); for composers, W. H. Trethowan, "Music and Mental Disorder," in M. Critchley and R. E. Henson, eds., *Music and the Brain* (London: Heinemann, 1977), pp. 398–442; for American poets, unpublished study of Pulitzer Prize winners by K. R. Jamison, 1999; for British poets, K. R. Jamison, *Touched with Fire* (New York: Free Press, 1993); for Japanese writers, Mamoru Iga, *The Thorn in the Chrysanthemum: Suicide and Economic Success in Modern Japan* (Berkeley and Los Angeles: University of California Press, 1986); for American artists (Abstract Expressionists): J. J. Schildkraut, A. J. Hirshfeld, and J. M. Murphy, "Mind and Mood in Modern Art: II. Depressive Disorders, Spirituality, and Early Deaths in the Abstract Expressionist Artists of the New York School," *American Journal of Psychiatry*, 151 (1994): 482–488.

181 Many of these artists, writers, and scientists: A partial list of writers who committed suicide includes Francis Ellingwood Abbott, Ryuunosuke

Akutagawa, Takeo Arishima, James Robert Baker, Thomas Lovell Beddoes, Walter Benjamin, John Berryman, Charles Blount, Barcroft Boake, Tadeusz Borowski, Richard Brautigan, William Clark Brinkley, Charles Buckmaster, Eustace Budgell, Don Carpenter, Paul Celan, Thomas Chatterton, Charles Caleb Colton, Hart Crane, Thomas Creech, John Davidson, Osamu Dazai, Tove Ditlevsen, Michael Dorris, Stephen Duck, Sergey Esenin, Aleksander Fadeyev, John Gould Fletcher, Romain Gary, Adam Lindsay Gordon, Richard Harris, Thomas Heggen, James Leo Herlihy, Ernest Hemingway, Ashihei Hino, Robin Hyde, William Inge, Shungetsu Ikuta, B. S. Johnson, Michioi Katō, Yasunari Kawabata, Bisan Kawakami, Tōkoku Kitamura, Heinrich von Kleist, Arthur Koestler, Jerzy Kosinski, Letitia E. Landon, Primo Levi, Vachel Lindsay, Ross Lockridge Jr., Anthony Lukas, Philipp Mainländer, F. O. Matthiessen, Vladimir Mayakovsky, Charlotte Mew, Hugh Miller, Walter M. Miller Jr., Yukio Mishima, Yves Navarre, Gérard de Nerval, Arthur Nortje, John O'Brien, Cesare Pavese, Sylvia Plath, Qu Yuan, Ferdinand Raimund, Jacques Rigaut, Anne Sexton, Sir John Suckling, Eikō Tanaka, Robert Tannahill, Sara Teasdale, Frank Tilsley, John Kennedy Toole, George Trakl, Marina Tsvetayeva, Frances Vernon, Anna Wickham, Virginia Woolf, Constance Fenimore Woolson, Paolo Yashvili, and Stefan Zweig. There is suggestive evidence of suicide in the deaths of Robert Burton, Eugene Izzi, Randall Jarrell, and Jack London. A partial list of artists who committed suicide includes Ralph Barton, James Carroll Beckwith, Francesco Borromini, Patrick Henry Bruce, Dora Carrington, John Currie, Edward Dayes, Rosso Fiorentino (probably), Richard Gerstl, Mark Gertler, Vincent van Gogh, Arshile Gorky, Benjamin Haydon, William Morris Hunt, Ernst Ludwig Kirchner, Wilhelm Lehmbruck, François Le Moyne, Alfred Maurer, Jules Pascin, Eric Pauelson (Poulsen), Mark Rothko, Jean-Louis Sauce, Jochem Seidel, Nicolas de Staël, Pietro Testa, Henry Tilson, William Walton, Brett Whitely, Johannes Wiedewelt, Ezra Winter, Emanuel de Witte, and Jacob de Wolf. (The suicides of several early painters are discussed by Rudolf and Margot Wittkower in their book *Born Under Saturn* [New York: W. W. Norton, 1963].) Many others, who did not die from suicide, attempted it: among them are writers Anna Akhmatova, A. Alvarez, James Baldwin, Konstantin Batyushkov, Charles Baudelaire, Hayden Carruth, Joseph Conrad, William Cowper, Isak Dinesen, Afansy Fet, F. Scott Fitzgerald, Gustav Fröding, Lewis Grassic Gibbon, Maxim Gorky, Graham Greene, Nikolai Gumilyov, Ivor Gurney, Herman Hesse, J. M. R. Lenz, Osip Mandelstam, Eugene O'Neill, Dorothy Parker, Edgar Allan Poe, Laura Riding, Percy Bysshe Shelley, Francis Thompson, Evelyn Waugh, and Mary Wollstonecraft, and artists Paul Gauguin, George Innes, Frida Kahlo, and Dante Gabriel Rossetti. A number of eminent scientists, mathematicians, and inventors have also committed suicide, including Ludwig Boltzmann, founder of statistical mechanics; Paul Ehrenfest, theoretical physicist; Alan Turing, mathematician and pioneer in computer theory; Emil Fischer, Nobel laureate in chemistry who did fundamental research on sugars and purines, and synthesized caffeine and barbiturates; Paul Kammerer, experimental biologist and author of *The Transformation of Species;* Robert Fitzroy, captain of HMS *Beagle,* hydrographer, and meteorologist; Wallace Carothers, inventor of nylon and coinventor of synthetic rubber; Meriwether Lewis, explorer; and Yataka Taniyama, mathematician. Mathematicians G. H. Hardy and Srinivasa Aaiyanger Remanujan attempted suicide.

181 "The hand that whirls the water": D. Thomas, "The Force That Through the Green Fuse Drives the Flower," ll. 11–13, in *The Collected Poems of Dylan Thomas* (New York: New Directions, 1957).

7 · DEATH-BLOOD

182 "I have a violence in me": Sylvia Plath, journal entry, June 11, 1958. American poet Sylvia Plath (1932–1963) wrote extensively about her black, violent moods in her letters, journals, poems, and autobiographical novel *The Bell Jar*. When she was twenty years old, Plath made a nearly lethal suicide attempt; ten years later she killed herself with carbon monoxide. The poems she wrote just before her death were, said Robert Lowell, "the autobiography of a fever."

184 Reserpine: J. M. Davis, "Central Biogenic Amines and Theories of Depression and Mania," in W. F. Fann, I. Karacan, A. D. Pokorny, and R. L. Williams, eds., *Phenomenology and Treatment of Depression* (New York: Spectrum, 1977).

185 iproniazid: N. S. Kline, "Clinical Experience with Iproniazid (Marsilid)," *Journal of Clinical Experimental Psychopathology* 19 (Suppl. 1) (1962).

186 Rats with low serotonin levels: L. Valzelli, S. Bernasconi, and M. Dalessandro, "Effect of Tryptophan Administration on Spontaneous and P-CPA-Induced Muricidal Aggression in Laboratory Rats," *Pharmacological Research Communications*, 13 (1981): 891–897.

186 "knockout" mice: D. Brunner and R. Hen, "Insights into the Neurobiology of Impulsive Behavior from Serotonin Receptor Knockout Mice," *Annals of the New York Academy of Sciences*, 836 (1997): 81–105.

186 Rats and other animals: N. K. Popova, A. V. Kulikov, E.M. Nikulina, E. Y. Kozlachkova, and G. B. Maslova, "Serotonin Metabolism and Serotonergic Receptors in Norway Rats Selected for Low Aggressiveness Towards Man," *Aggressive Behavior*, 17 (1991): 207–213.

186 Monkeys with low levels: P. T. Mehlman, J. D. Higley, I. Faucher, A. A. Lilly, D. M. Taub, J. Vickers, S. J. Suomi, and M. Linnoila, "Low CSF 5-HIAA Concentrations and Severe Aggression and Impaired Impulse Control in Nonhuman Primates," *American Journal of Psychiatry*, 151 (1994): 1485–1491.

186 If serotonin levels: B. Chamberlain, F. R. Ervin, R. O. Pihl, and S. N. Young, "The Effect of Raising or Lowering Tryptophan Levels on Aggression in Vervet Monkeys," *Pharmacology, Biochemistry and Behavior*, 28 (1987): 503–510; K. A. Miczek and P. Donat, "Brain 5-HT System and Inhibition of Aggressive Behavior," in T. Archer, P. Bevan, and A. Cools, eds., *Behavioral Pharmacology of 5-HT* (Hillsdale, N.J.: Lawrence Erlbaum Associates, 1990), pp. 117–144; P. T. Mehlman, J. D. Higley, I. Faucher, A. A. Lilly, D. M. Taub, S. Suomi, and M. Linnoila, "Low CSF 5-HIAA Concentrations and Severe Aggression and Impaired Impulse Control in Nonhuman Primates," *American Journal of Psychiatry*, 151 (1994): 1485–1491.

186 forty-nine free-ranging rhesus monkeys: J. D. Higley, P. T. Mehlman, S. B.

367

Higley, B. Fernald, J. Vickers, S. G. Lindell, D. M. Taub, S. J. Suomi, and M. Linnoila, "Excessive Mortality in Young Free-Ranging Male Nonhuman Primates with Low Cerebrospinal Fluid 5-Hydroxyindoleacetic Acid Concentrations," *Archives of General Psychiatry*, 53 (1996): 537–543.

187 who share with other: B. Eichelman, "Aggressive Behavior: From Laboratory to Clinic," *Archives of General Psychiatry*, 49 (1992): 488–492; M. Åsberg, "Monoamine Neurotransmitters in Human Aggressiveness and Violence: A Selective Review," *Criminal Behavior and Mental Health*, 4 (1994): 303–327.

187 nonhuman primates and humans: For an excellent review, see J. D. Higley and M. Linnoila, "Low Central Nervous System Serotonergic Activity Is Traitlike and Correlates with Impulsive Behavior: A Nonhuman Primate Model Investigating Genetic and Environmental Influences on Neurotransmission," *Annals of the New York Academy of Sciences*, 836 (1997): 39–56.

187 low CSF 5-HIAA concentrations: Ibid.

187 Primates with low CSF 5-HIAA: P. T. Mehlman, J. D. Higley, I. Faucher, A. A. Lilly, D. M. Taub, J. Vickers, S. J. Suomi, and M. Linnoila, "Correlation of CSF 5-HIAA Concentration with Sociality and the Timing of Emigration in Free-Ranging Primates," *American Journal of Psychiatry*, 152 (1995): 907–913; J. D. Higley, S. T. King, M. F. Hasert, M. Champoux, S. J. Suomi, and M. Linnoila, "Stability of Interindividual Differences in Serotonin Function and Its Relationship to Aggressive Wounding and Competent Social Behavior in Rhesus Macaque Females," *Neuropsychopharmacology*, 14 (1996): 67–76; P. T. Mehlman, J. D. Highley, B. J. Fernald, F. R. Sallee, S. J. Suomi, and M. Linnoila, "CSF 5-HIAA, Testosterone, and Sociosexual Behaviors in Free-Ranging Male Rhesus Macaques in the Mating Season," *Psychiatry Research*, 72 (1997): 89–102.

188 Genes certainly are important: D. Nielsen, D. Goldman, M. Virkkunen, R. Tukola, R. Rawlings, and M. Linnoila, "Suicidality and 5-Hydroxindoleacetic Acid Concentration Associated with a Tryptophan Hydroxylase Polymorphism," *Archives of General Psychiatry*, 51 (1994): 34–38; E. F. Coccaro, C. S. Bergeman, R. J. Kavoussi, and A. D. Seroczynski, "Heritability of Aggression and Irritability: A Twin Study of the Buss-Durkee Aggression Scales in Adult Male Subjects," *Biological Psychiatry*, 41 (1997): 273–284; J. J. Mann, K. M. Malone, D. A. Nielsen, D. Goldman, J. Erdos, and J. Gelernter, "Possible Association of a Polymorphism of the Tryptophan Hydroxylase Gene with Suicidal Behavior in Depressed Patients," *American Journal of Psychiatry*, 154 (1997): 1451–1453; F. Bellivier, M. Leboyer, P. Courtet, C. Buresi, B. Beaufils, D. Samolyk, J.-F. Allilaire, J. Feingold, J. Mallet, and A. Malafosse, "Association Between the Tryptophan Hydroxylase Gene and Manic-Depressive Illness," *Archives of General Psychiatry*, 55 (1998): 33–37; P. Courtet, C. Buresi, M. Abbar, J. P. Boulenger, D. Castelnau, and A. Malafosse, "Association Between the Tryptophan Hydroxylase Gene and Suicidal Behavior," poster presented at the American College of Neuropsychopharmacology Annual Meeting, San Juan, Puerto Rico, December 1998; D. A. Nielsen, M. Virkkunen, J. Lappalainen, M. Eggert, G. L. Brown, J. C. Long, D. Goldman, and M. Linnoila, "A Tryptophan Hydroxylase Gene Marker for Suicidality and Alcoholism," *Archives of General Psychiatry*, 55 (1998): 593–602.

188 Adult male vervet monkeys: M. J. Raleigh, M. T. McGuire, G. L. Brammer, and A. Yuwiler, "Social and Environmental Influences on Blood Serotonin Concentrations in Monkeys," *Archives of General Psychiatry*, 41 (1984): 405–410.

188 Studies of rhesus monkeys: These studies are summarized and referenced in J. D. Higley and M. Linnoila, "Low Central Nervous System Serotonergic Activity Is Traitlike and Correlates with Impulsive Behavior: A Nonhuman Primate Model Investigating Genetic and Environmental Influences on Neurotransmission," *Annals of the New York Academy of Sciences*, 836 (1997): 39–56.

189 While it is unlikely: The argument against oversimplification is well outlined in G. W. Kraemer, D. E. Schmidt, and M. H. Ebert, "The Behavioral Neurobiology of Self-Injurious Behavior in Rhesus Monkeys: Current Concepts and Relations to Impulsive Behavior in Humans," *Annals of the New York Academy of Sciences*, 836 (1997): 12–38.

189 More than half of suicide attempts: A review of eight studies shows that one-third to four-fifths of suicidal acts occurred with little premeditation. The modal figure was two-thirds. See C. L. Williams, J. A. Davidson, and I. Montgomery, "Impulsive Suicidal Behavior," *Journal of Clinical Psychology*, 36 (1980): 90–94.

189 many researchers and clinicians: A. Apter, R. Plutchik, and H. M. van Praag, "Anxiety, Impulsivity and Depressed Mood in Relation to Suicidal and Violent Behavior," *Acta Psychiatrica Scandinavica*, 87 (1993): 1–5; P. Nordström, P. Gustavsson, G. Edman, and M. Åsberg, "Temperamental Vulnerability and Suicide Risk After Attempted Suicide," *Suicide and Life-Threatening Behavior*, 26 (1996): 380–394.

189 Professional handwriting analysts: C. J. Frederick, "An Investigation of Handwriting of Suicide Persons Through Suicide Notes," *Journal of Abnormal Psychology*, 73 (1968): 263–267.

189 Suicidal patients, in addition: M. Weissman, K. Fox, and G. L. Klerman, "Hostility and Depression Associated with Suicide Attempts," *American Journal of Psychiatry*, 130 (1973): 450–455; J. A. Yesavage, "Direct and Indirect Hostility and Self-Destructive Behavior by Hospitalized Depressives," *Acta Psychiatrica Scandinavica*, 68 (1983): 345–350; J. Angst and P. Clayton, "Premorbid Personality of Depressive, Bipolar, and Schizophrenic Patients with Special Reference to Suicidal Issues," *Comprehensive Psychiatry*, 27 (1986): 511–532; A. J. Botsis, C. R. Soldatos, A. Liossi, A. Kokkevi, and C. N. Stephanis, "Suicide and Violence Risk: I. Relationship to Coping Styles," *Acta Psychiatrica Scandinavica*, 89 (1994): 92–96; M. Åsberg, "Neurotransmitters and Suicidal Behavior: The Evidence from Cerebrospinal Fluid Studies," *Annals of the New York Academy of Sciences*, 836 (1998): 158–181; J. J. Mann, C. Waternaux, G. L. Haas, and K. M. Malone, "Toward a Clinical Model of Suicidal Behavior in Psychiatric Patients," *American Journal of Psychiatry*, 156 (1999): 181–189.

190 those who actually killed themselves: B. M. Barraclough, J. Bunch, B. Nelson, and P. Sainsbury, "A Hundred Cases of Suicide: Clinical Aspects," *British Journal of Psychiatry*, 125 (1974): 355–372.

190 homicide is frequently followed: D. J. West, *Murder Followed by Suicide* (London: Heinemann, 1966); J. Hansen and O. Bjarneson, "Homicide in

Iceland," *Forensic Sciences*, 4 (1974): 107–117; S. Dalmer and J. A. Humphrey, "Offender-Victim Relationships in Criminal Homicide Followed by Offenders' Suicide: North Carolina 1972–1977," *Suicide and Life-Threatening Behavior*, 10 (1980): 106–118; H. Petursson and G. H. Gudjonsson, "Psychiatric Aspects of Homicide," *Acta Psychiatrica Scandinavica*, 64 (1981): 363–372; N. H. Allen, "Homicide Followed by Suicide: Los Angeles, 1970–1979," *Suicide and Life-Threatening Behavior*, 13 (1983): 155–165; J. Coid, "The Epidemiology of Abnormal Homicide and Murder Followed by Suicide," *Psychological Medicine*, 13 (1983): 855–860; D. C. Blanchard and R. J. Blanchard, "Affect and Aggression: An Animal Model Applied to Human Behavior," in R. J. Blanchard and D. C. Blanchard, eds., *Advances in the Study of Aggression*, vol. 1 (New York: Academic Press, 1984).

190 Nearly 50 percent of all manic episodes: Based on a review of studies in F. K. Goodwin and K. R. Jamison, *Manic-Depressive Illness* (New York: Oxford University Press, 1990), pp. 35–37; see also G. Winokur, P. J. Clayton, and T. Reich, *Manic Depressive Illness* (St. Louis: C. V. Mosby, 1969).

190 a link between serotonin functioning: In addition to the animal studies cited earlier, see also M. Åsberg, D. Schalling, L. Träskman-Bendz, and A. Wagner, "Psychobiology of Suicide, Impulsivity, and Related Phenomena," in H. Y. Meltzer, ed., *Psychopharmacology: The Third Generation of Progress* (New York: Raven Press, 1987), pp. 655–668; E. F. Coccaro, "Central Serotonin and Impulsive Aggression," *British Journal of Psychiatry*, 155 (1989): 52–62; M. Virkkunen, J. De Jong, J. Bartko, and M. Linnoila, "Psychobiological Concomitants of History of Suicide Attempts Among Violent Offenders and Impulsive Fire Setters," *Archives of General Psychiatry*, 46 (1989): 604–606; G. L. Brown and M. I. Linnoila, "CSF Serotonin Metabolite (5-HIAA) Studies in Depression, Impulsivity, and Violence," *Journal of Clinical Psychiatry*, 51 (1990): 31–41.

191 one of the most replicated findings: G. L. Brown, F. K. Goodwin, J. C. Ballenger, P. F. Goyer, and L. F. Major, "Aggression in Humans Correlates with Cerebrospinal Fluid Amine Metabolites," *Psychiatry Research*, 1 (1979): 131–139; G. L. Brown, F. K. Goodwin, and W. E. Bunney, "Human Aggression and Suicide: Their Relationship to Neuropsychiatric Diagnoses and Serotonin Metabolism," *Advances in Biochemistry and Psychopharmacology*, 34 (1982): 287–307; H. van Praag, "Depression, Suicide, and Metabolism of Serotonin in the Brain," *Journal of Affective Disorders*, 4 (1982): 275–290; C. M. Banki and M. Arató, "Relationship Between Cerebrospinal Fluid Amine Metabolites, Neuroendocrine Findings and Personality Dimensions (Marke-Nyman Scale Factors) in Psychiatric Patients," *Acta Psychiatrica Scandinavica*, 67 (1983): 272–280; P. T. Ninan, D. P. van Kammen, M. Scheinin, M. Linnoila, W. E. Bunney, Jr., and F. K. Goodwin, "CSF 5-Hydroxyindoleacetic Acid Levels in Suicidal Schizophrenic Patients," *American Journal of Psychiatry*, 141 (1984): 566–569; R. Limson, D. Goldman, A. Roy, et al., "Personality and Cerebrospinal Fluid Monoamine Metabolites in Alcoholics and Controls," *Archives of General Psychiatry*, 48 (1991): 437–441.

191 Although some scientists have questioned: W. Annitto and B. Shopsin, "Neuropharmacology of Mania," in B. Shopsin, ed., *Manic Illness* (New

York: Academic Press, 1979), pp. 105–164; D. Healy, "The Fluoxetine and Suicide Controversy: A Review of the Evidence," *CNS Drugs*, 1 (1994): 223–231.

191 more than twenty studies: M. Åsberg, "Neurotransmitters and Suicidal Behavior: The Evidence from Cerebrospinal Fluid Studies," *Annals of the New York Academy of Sciences*, 836 (1997): 158–181.

191 if CSF 5-HIAA is measured: L. Träskman, M. Åsberg, L. Bertilsson, and L. Sjöstrand, "Monoamine Metabolities in CSF and Suicidal Behavior," *Archives of General Psychiatry*, 38 (1981): 631–636; A. Roy, H. Ågren, D. Pickar, M. Linnoila, A. R. Doran, N. R. Cutler, and S. M. Paul, "Reduced CSF Concentrations of Homovanillic Acid and Homovanillic Acid to 5-Hydroxyindoleacetic Acid Ratios in Depressed Patients: Relationship to Suicidal Behavior and Dexamethasone Non-Suppression," *American Journal of Psychiatry*, 143 (1986): 1539–1545; P. Nordström, M. Samuelsson, M. Åberg-Wistedt, C. Nordin, and L. Bertilsson, "CSF 5-HIAA Predicts Suicide Risk After Attempted Suicide," *Suicide and Life-Threatening Behavior*, 24 (1994): 1–9.

191 psychiatric and behavioral syndromes: D. J. Cohen, B. A. Shaywitz, B. Caparulo, J. G. Young, and M. B. Bowers, "Chronic, Multiple Tics of Gilles de la Tourette's Disease: CSF Acid Monoamine Metabolites After Probenecid Administration," *Archives of General Psychiatry*, 35 (1978): 245–250; M. Åsberg, P. Thorén, and L. Bertilsson, "Clomipramine Treatment of Obsessive-Compulsive Disorder—Biochemical and Clinical Aspects," *Psychopharmacology Bulletin*, 18 (1982): 13–21; G. L. Brown, M. H. Ebert, P. F. Goyer, D. C. Jimerson, W. J. Klein, W. E. Bunney, and F. K. Goodwin, "Aggression, Suicide, and Serotonin: Relationships to CSF Amine Metabolites," *American Journal of Psychiatry*, 139 (1982): 741–746; M. Linnoila, M. Virkkunen, M. Scheinin, A. Nuutila, R. Rimon, and F. K. Goodwin, "Low Cerebrospinal Fluid 5-Hydroxyindoleacetic Acid Concentration Differentiates Impulsive from Nonimpulsive Violent Behavior," *Life Sciences*, 33 (1983): 2609–2614; W. H. Kaye, M. H. Ebert, H. E. Gwirtsman, and S. R. Weiss, "Differences in Brain Serotonergic Metabolism Between Nonbulimic and Bulimic Patients with Anorexia Nervosa," *American Journal of Psychiatry*, 141 (1984): 1598–1601; T. R. Insel, E. A. Mueller, I. Alterman, M. Linnoila, and D. L. Murphy, "Obsessive-Compulsive Disorder and Serotonin: Is There a Connection?" *Biological Psychiatry*, 20 (1985): 1174–1188; H. M. Van Praag, "Affective Disorders and Aggression Disorders: Evidence for a Common Biological Mechanism," *Suicide and Life-Threatening Behavior*, 16 (1986): 103–132; M. J. Kruesi, "Cruelty to Animals and CSF 5-HIAA," *Psychiatry Research*, 28 (1989): 115–116; D. C. Jimerson, M. D. Lessem, W. H. Kaye, A. P. Hegg, and T. D. Brewerton, "Eating Disorders and Depression: Is There a Serotonin Connection?" *Biological Psychiatry*, 28 (1990): 443–454; M. J. P. Kruesi, J. L. Rapoport, E. Hibbs, W. Z. Potter, M. Lenane, and G. L. Brown, "Cerebrospinal Monoamine Metabolites, Aggression, and Impulsivity in Disruptive Disorders of Children and Adolescents," *Archives of General Psychiatry*, 47 (1990): 419–426; W. H. Kaye, H. E. Gwirtsman, D. T. George, and M. H. Ebert, "Altered Serotonin Activity in Anorexia Nervosa After Long-Term Weight Restoration: Does Elevated Cerebrospinal Fluid 5-Hydroxyindoleacetic

Acid Level Correlate with Rigid and Obsessive Behavior?" *Archives of General Psychiatry,* 48 (1991): 556–562; R. Limson, D. Goldman, A. Roy, D. Lamparski, B. Ravitz, B. Adinoff, and M. Linnoila, "Personality and Cerebrospinal Fluid Monoamine Metabolites in Alcoholics and Controls," *Archives of General Psychiatry,* 48 (1991): 437–441; D. C. Jimerson, M. D. Lesem, W. H. Kaye, and T. D. Brewerton, "Low Serotonin and Dopamine Metabolite Concentrations in Cerebrospinal Fluid from Bulimic Patients with Frequent Binge Episodes," *Archives of General Psychiatry,* 49 (1992): 132–138; S. E. Swedo, H. L. Leonard, M. J. Kruesi, D. C. Rettew, S. J. Listwak, W. Berettini, M. Stipetic, S. Hamburger, P. W. Gold, W. Z. Potter, and J. L. Rapoport, "Cerebrospinal Fluid Neurochemistry in Children and Adolescents with Obsessive-Compulsive Disorder," *Archives of General Psychiatry,* 49 (1992): 29–36; M. Virkkunen, E. Kallio, R. Rawlings, R. Tokola, R. E. Poland, A. Guidotti, C. Nemeroff, G. Bissette, K. Kalogeras, S. L. Karonen, and M. Linnoila, "Personality Profiles and State Aggressiveness in Finnish Alcoholics, Violent Offenders, Fire Setters, and Healthy Volunteers," *Archives of General Psychiatry,* 51 (1994): 28–33.

192 Smoking cigarettes: R. S. Paffenbarger Jr. and D. P. Asnes, "Chronic Disease in Former College Students: III. Precursors of Suicide in Early and Middle Life," *American Journal of Public Health,* 56 (1966): 1026–1036; P. S. Paffenbarger Jr., S. H. King, and A. L. Wing, "Chronic Disease in Former College Students: IX. Characteristics in Youth That Predispose to Suicide and Accidental Death in Later Life," *American Journal of Public Health,* 59 (1969): 900–908; C. B. Thomas, "Suicide Among Us: II. Habits of Nervous Tension as Potential Predictors," *Hopkins Medical Journal,* 129 (1971): 190–201; C. B. Thomas, "Precursors of Premature Disease and Death: The Predictive Potential of Habits and Family Attitudes," *Annals of Internal Medicine,* 85 (1976): 653–658; K. M. Malone, C. Waternaux, G. L. Haas, and J. J. Mann, "Alcohol Abuse, Cigarette Smoking, Suicidal Behavior and Serotonin Function," *Biological Psychiatry,* 41 (Suppl.) (1997): 9; J. Angst and P. J. Clayton, "Personality, Smoking and Suicide," *Journal of Affective Disorders,* 51 (1998): 55–62; P. Clayton, "Smoking and Suicide," *Journal of Affective Disorders,* 50 (1998): 1–2; J. J. Mann, C. Waternaux, G. L. Haas, and K. M. Malone, "Toward a Clinical Model of Suicidal Behavior in Psychiatric Patients," *American Journal of Psychiatry,* 156 (1999): 181–189.

192 postmortem studies: M. Stanley and B. Stanley, "Biochemical Studies in Suicide Victims: Current Findings and Future Implications," *Suicide and Life-Threatening Behavior,* 19 (1989): 30–42; J. E. Kleinman, T. M. Hyde, and M. M. Herman, "Methodological Issues in the Neuropathology of Mental Illness," in F. E. Bloom and D. J. Kupfer, eds., *Psychopharmacology: The Fourth Generation of Progress* (New York: Raven Press, 1995), pp. 859–864; V. Arango, M. D. Underwood, and J. J. Mann, "Fewer Pigmented Locus Ceruleus Neurons in Suicide Victims: Preliminary Results," *Biological Psychiatry,* 39 (1996): 112–120; V. Arango, M. D. Underwood, and J. J. Mann, "Postmortem Findings in Suicide Victims: Implications for *In Vivo* Imaging Studies," *Annals of the New York Academy of Sciences,* 836 (1997): 269–287; S. E. Bachus, T. M. Hyde, M. Akil, C. Shannon Weickert, M. P. Vawter, and J. E. Kleinman, "Neuropathology of Suicide: A Review and an Approach," *Annals of the New York Academy of Sciences,* 836 (1997):

201–219; J. F. López, D. M. Vázquez, D. T. Chalmers, and S. J. Watson, "Regulation of 5-HT Receptors and the Hypothalamic-Pituitary-Adrenal Axis," *Annals of the New York Academy of Sciences*, 836 (1997): 106–134; G. A. Ordway, "Pathophysiology of the Locus Coeruleus in Suicide," *Annals of the New York Academy of Sciences*, 836 (1997): 233–252; J. J. Mann and V. Arango, "The Neurobiology of Suicidal Behavior," in D. G. Jacobs, *The Harvard Medical School Guide to Suicide Assessment and Intervention* (San Francisco: Jossey-Bass, 1999): 98–114.

193 Rats, if subjected: P. Rosenfeld, Y. R. Gutierrez, A. M. Martin, H. A. Mallet, E. Alleva, and S. Levine, "Maternal Regulation of the Adrenocortical Response in Preweanling Rats," *Physiology and Behavior*, 50 (1991): 661–671; D. M. Vázquez and H. Akil, "Pituitary-Adrenal Response to Ether Vapor in the Weanling Animal: Characterization of the Inhibitory Effect of Glucocorticoids on Adrenocorticotropin Secretion," *Pediatric Research*, 34 (1993): 646–653; S. Levine, "The Ontogeny of the Hypothalamic-Pituitary-Adrenal Axis: The Influence of Maternal Factors," *Annals of the New York Academy of Sciences*, 746 (1994): 275–288; C. O. Ladd, M. J. Owens, and C. B. Nemeroff, "Persistent Changes in Corticotropin-Releasing Factor Neuronal Systems Induced by Maternal Deprivation," *Endocrinology*, 137 (1996): 1212–1218.

193 Autopsy studies: K. Dorovini-Zis and A. P. Zis, "Increased Adrenal Weight in Victims of Violent Suicide," *Endocrinology*, 144 (1987): 1214–1215; C. B. Nemeroff, M. J. Owens, G. Bissette, A. C. Andorn, and M. Stanley, "Reduced Corticotropin Releasing Factor Binding Sites in the Frontal Cortex of Suicide Victims," *Archives of General Psychiatry*, 45 (1988): 577–579; M. Arato, C. M. Banki, G. Bissette, and C. B. Nemeroff, "Elevated CSF CRF in Suicide Victims," *Biological Psychiatry*, 25 (1989): 355–359; J. F. López, M. Palkovits, M. Arato, A. Mansour, H. Akil, and S. J. Watson, "Localization and Quantification of Pro-Opiomelanocortin mRNA and Glucocorticoid Receptor mRNA in Pituitaries of Suicide Victims," *Neuroendocrinology*, 56 (1992): 491–501; E. Szigethy, Y. Conwell, N. T. Forbes, C. Cox, and E. D. Caine, "Adrenal Weight and Morphology in Victims of Completed Suicide," *Biological Psychiatry*, 36 (1994): 374–380.

193 enlargement of the amygdala: L. L. Altshuler, G. Bartzokis, T. Grieder, J. Curran, and J. Mintz, "Amygdala Enlargement in Bipolar Disorder and Hippocampal Reduction in Schizophrenia: An MRI Study Demonstrating Neuroanatomic Specificity," *Archives of General Psychiatry*, 55 (1998): 663–664; S. M. Strakowski, M. P. Del Bello, K. W. Sax, M. E. Zimmerman, P. K. Shear, J. M. Hawkins, and E. R. Larson, "Brain Magnetic Resonance Imaging of Structural Abnormalities in Bipolar Disorder," *Archives of General Psychiatry*, 56 (1999): 254–260.

193 increase in white-matter lesions: R. M. Dupont, T. L. Jernigan, and N. Butters, "Subcortical Abnormalities Detected in Bipolar Affective Disorder Using Magnetic Resonance Imaging," *Archives of General Psychiatry*, 47 (1990): 55–59; V. W. Swayze, N. C. Andreasen, R. J. Alliger, J. C. Ehrhardt, and W. T. Yuh, "Structural Brain Abnormalities in Bipolar Affective Disorder: Ventricular Enlargement and Focal Signal Hyperintensities," *Archives of General Psychiatry*, 47 (1990): 1054–1059; G. S. Figiel, K. R. R. Krishnan, V. P. Rao, M. Doraiswamy, E. H. Ellinwood, C. B. Nemeroff,

D. Evans, and O. Boyko, "Subcortical Hyperintensities on Brain Magnetic Resonance Imaging: A Comparison of Normal and Bipolar Subjects," *Journal of Neuropsychiatry and Clinical Neuroscience,* 3 (1991): 18–22; S. M. Strakowski, B. T. Woods, M. Tohen, D. R. Wilson, A. W. Douglass, and A. L. Stoll, "MRI Subcortical Hyperintensities in Mania at First Hospitalization," *Biological Psychiatry,* 33 (1993): 204–206; E. P. Ahearn, D. C. Steffens, F. Cassidy, S. A. Van Meter, J. M. Provenzale, M. F. Seldin, R. H. Weisler, and K. R. R. Krishnan, "Family Leukoencephalopathy in Bipolar Disorder," *American Journal of Psychiatry,* 155 (1998): 1605–1607.

193 severe depletions: D. Öngür, W. C. Drevets, and J. L. Price, "Glial Reduction in the Subgenual Prefrontal Cortex in Mood Disorders," *Proceedings of the National Academy of Sciences USA,* 95 (1998): 13290–13295.

194 brains of patients with chronic schizophrenia: A. B. Levy, N. Kurtz, and A. S. Kling, "Association Between Cerebral Ventricular Enlargement and Suicide Attempts in Chronic Schizophrenia," *American Journal of Psychiatry,* 141 (1984): 438–439.

194 white-matter lesions: O. L. Lopez, J. T. Becker, C. F. Reynolds, C. A. Jungreis, S. Weinman, and S. T. De Kosky, "Psychiatric Correlates of MR Deep White Matter Lesions in Probable Alzheimer's Disease," *Journal of Neuropsychiatry and Clinical Neurosciences,* 9 (1997): 246–250.

194 hyperintensities in the periventricular region: Personal communication from Dr. Eileen Ahearn, March 8, 1999.

194 Concerned by reports: D. Jacobs, H. Blackburn, M. Higgins, D. Reed, H. Iso, G. McMillan, J. Neaton, J. Nelson, J. Potter, B. Rifkind, J. Rossouw, R. Shekelle, and S. Yusuf, "Report of the Conference on Low Blood Cholesterol: Mortality Associations," *Circulation,* 86 (1992): 1046–1060; M. F. Muldoon and S. B. Manuck, "Health Through Cholesterol Reduction: Are There Unforeseen Risks?" *Annals of Behavioral Medicine,* 14 (1992): 101–108; J. D. Neaton, H. Blackburn, D. Jacobs, L. Kuller, D. J. Lee, R. Sherwin, J. Shih, J. Stamler, and D. Wentworth, "Serum Cholesterol Level and Mortality Findings for Men Screened in the Multiple Risk Factor Intervention Trial," *Archives of Internal Medicine,* 152 (1992): 1490–1500; M. F. Muldoon, J. Rossouw, S. B. Manuck, C. J. Glueck, J. R. Kaplan and P. Kaufmann, "Low or Lowered Cholesterol and Risk of Death from Suicide and Trauma," *Metabolism,* 42 (Suppl. 1) (1993): 45–56.

194 Not every study: For reviews of the cholesterol-suicide link, see P. F. Boston, S. M. Durson, and M. A. Reveley, "Cholesterol and Mental Disorder," *British Journal of Psychiatry,* 169 (1996): 682–689; and M. Hillbrand and R. T. Spitz, eds., *Lipids, Health, and Behavior* (Washington, D.C.: American Psychological Association, 1997).

194 simply an artifact: K. Hawton, P. Cowen, D. Owens, et al., "Low Serum Cholesterol and Suicide," *British Journal of Psychiatry,* 162 (1993): 818–825.

194 a few studies: N. Takei, H. Kunugi, S. Nanko, H. Aoki, R. Iyo, and H. Kazamatsuri, "Low Serum Cholesterol and Suicide Attempts," *British Journal of Psychiatry,* 164 (1994): 702–703; J. Fawcett, K. A. Busch, D. Jacobs, H. M. Kravitz, and L. Fogg, "Suicide: A Four-Pathway Clinical-Biochemical Model," *Annals of the New York Academy of Sciences,* 836 (1997): 288–301.

194 Other scientists: J. R. Kaplan, S. B. Manuck, M. Fontenot, M. F. Muldoon,

C. A. Shively, and J. J. Mann, "The Cholesterol-Serotonin Hypothesis: Interrelationships Among Dietary Lipids, Central Serotonergic Activity, and Social Behavior in Monkeys," in M. Hillbrand and R. T. Spitz, eds., *Lipids, Health, and Behavior* (Washington, D.C.: American Psychological Association, 1997), pp. 139–165; J. R. Kaplan, M. F. Muldoon, S. B. Manuck, and J. J. Mann, "Assessing the Observed Relationship Between Low Cholesterol and Violence-Related Mortality," *Annals of the New York Academy of Sciences,* 836 (1997): 57–80.

195 important lipid players: M. E. Virkkunen, D. F. Horrobin, D. K. Jenkins, and M. S. Manku, "Plasma Phospholipids, Essential Fatty Acids and Prostaglandins in Alcoholic, Habitually Violent and Impulsive Offenders," *Biological Psychiatry,* 22 (1987): 1087–1096; T. Hirayama, *Life-Style and Mortality* (Basel: Karger, 1990); J. R. Hibbeln and N. Salem, "Dietary Polyunsaturated Fatty Acids and Depression: When Cholesterol Does Not Satisfy," *American Journal of Clinical Nutrition,* 62 (1995): 1–9; J. R. Hibbeln, M. Linnoila, J. C. Umhau, R. Rawlings, D. T. George, and N. Salem, "Essential Fatty Acids Predict Metabolites of Serotonin and Dopamine in Cerebrospinal Fluid Among Healthy Control Subjects and Early- and Late-Onset Alcoholics," *Biological Psychiatry,* 44 (1998): 235–242; J. R. Hibbeln, J. C. Umhau, M. Linnoila, D. T. George, P. R. Ragan, S. E. Shoaf, M. R. Vaughan, R. Rawlings, and N. Salem, "A Replication Study of Violent and Nonviolent Subjects: Cerebrospinal Fluid Metabolites of Serotonin and Dopamine Are Predicted by Plasma Essential Fatty Acids," *Biological Psychiatry,* 44 (1998): 243–249; D. Horrobin and C. N. Bennett, "New Gene Targets Related to Schizophrenia and Other Psychiatric Disorders: Enzymes, Binding Proteins and Transport Proteins Involved in Phospholipid and Fatty Acid Metabolism," *Prostaglandins, Leukotrienes and Essential Fatty Acids,* 60 (1999): 141–167.

195 Societies that consume: J. R. Hibbeln, "Fish Consumption and Major Depression," *Lancet,* 351 (1998): 1213.

196 Paleolithic and modern: B. S. Eaton and M. Konner, "Paleolithic Nutrition: A Consideration of Its Nature and Current Implications," *New England Journal of Medicine,* 312 (1985): 283–289.

196 fatty acid metabolism and schizophrenia: D. F. Horrobin, "The Membrane Phospholipid Hypothesis as a Biochemical Basis for the Neurodevelopmental Concept of Schizophrenia," *Schizophrenia Research,* 30 (1998): 193–208.

198 Australian aborigines: S. J. Pyne, *World Fire: The Culture of Fire on Earth* (Seattle: University of Washington Press, 1995), p. 31.

198 "Suicide, I suspect": J. Conrad, *Chance: A Tale in Two Parts* (Garden City, N.Y.: Doubleday, Page & Company, 1926), p. 183.

199 John Mann: J. J. Mann, C. Waternaux, G. L. Haas, and K. M. Malone, "Toward a Clinical Model of Suicidal Behavior in Psychiatric Patients," *American Journal of Psychiatry,* 156 (1999): 181–189.

201 "the attacks of manic-depressive insanity": E. Kraepelin, *Manic-Depressive Insanity and Paranoia,* trans. R. M. Barclay, ed. G. M. Robertson (New York: Arno Press, 1976; first published, 1921), p. 181.

202 Suicide, we know, is rare: D. Shaffer, "Suicide in Childhood and Early Adolescence," *Journal of Child Psychology and Psychiatry,* 15 (1974): 275–291;

D. Shaffer and P. Fisher, "The Epidemiology of Suicide in Children and Young Adolescents," *Journal of the American Academy of Child Psychiatry*, 20 (1981): 545–565; C. R. Pfeffer, R. Plutchik, M. S. Mizruchi, and R. Lipkins, "Suicidal Behavior in Child Psychiatric Inpatients and Outpatients and in Nonpatients," *American Journal of Psychiatry*, 143 (1986): 733–738; H. M. Hoberman and B. D. Garfinkel, "Completed Suicide in Youth," *Canadian Journal of Psychiatry*, 33 (1988): 494–504; R. Harrington, H. Rudge, M. Rutter, A. Pickles, and J. Hill, "Adult Outcomes of Childhood and Adolescent Depression," *Archives of General Psychiatry*, 47 (1990): 465–473; M. Kovacs, D. Goldston, and C. Gatsonis, "Suicidal Behaviors and Childhood-Onset Depressive Disorders: A Longitudinal Investigation," *Journal of the American Academy of Child and Adolescent Psychiatry*, 32 (1993): 8–20; U. Rao, M. M. Weissman, J. A. Martin, and R. W. Hammond, "Childhood Depression and Risk of Suicide: A Preliminary Report of a Longitudinal Study," *Journal of the American Academy of Child and Adolescent Psychiatry*, 32 (1993): 21–27; C. R. Pfeffer, S. W. Hurt, T. Kakuma, J. R. Peskin, C. A. Siefker, and S. Nagabhairava, "Suicidal Children Grow Up: Suicidal Episodes and Effects of Treatment During Follow-up," *Journal of the American Academy of Child and Adolescent Psychiatry*, 33 (1994): 225–230; D. N. Klein, P. M. Lewinsohn, and J. R. Seeley, "Hypomanic Personality Traits in a Community Sample of Adolescents," *Journal of Affective Disorders*, 38 (1996): 135–143. There were, however, disturbingly high rates of suicide in young children during the fifteenth through eighteenth centuries in England; see M. MacDonald and T. R. Murphy, *Sleepless Souls: Suicide in Early Modern England* (Oxford: Clarendon Press, 1990), pp. 248–252.

202 believe that death is reversible: M. S. McIntyre and C. A. Angle, "The Child's Concept of Death," paper presented at the Workshop in Methodology, Ambulatory Pediatric Society, Atlantic City, N.J., April 1970; M. W. Speece and S. B. Brent, "Children's Understanding of Death: A Review of Three Components of a Death Concept," *Child Development*, 55 (1984): 1671–1686; C. R. Pfeffer, *The Suicidal Child* (New York: Guilford, 1986); D. Gothelf, A. Apter, A. Brand-Gothelf, N. Offer, H. Ofek, S. Tyano, and C. R. Pfeffer, "Death Concepts in Suicidal Adolescents," *Journal of the American Academy of Child and Adolescent Psychiatry*, 37 (1998): 1279–1286.

202 average age of onset: F. K. Goodwin and K. R. Jamison, *Manic-Depressive Illness* (New York: Oxford University Press, 1990); L. N. Robins and D. A. Regier, *Psychiatric Disorders in America: The Epidemiologic Catchment Area Study* (New York: Free Press, 1991).

202 Gender, as well as age: The nature and extent of gender differences in suicide rates were discussed in Chapter 2 and differences in choice of methods in Chapter 5; see also C. L. Rich, J. E. Ricketts, R. C. Fowler, and D. Young, "Some Differences Between Men and Women Who Commit Suicide," *American Journal of Psychiatry*, 145 (1988): 718–722; S. S. Canetto and D. Lester, eds., *Women and Suicidal Behavior* (New York: Springer, 1995); S. S. Canetto, "Gender and Suicidal Behavior: Theories and Evidence," in R. W. Maris, M. M. Silverman, and S. S. Canetto, *Review of Suicidology, 1997* (New York: Guilford Press, 1997), pp. 138–167.

203 blood levels of serotonin: S. O'Reilly and M. Loncin, "Ceruloplasmin and 5-Hydroxindole Metabolism in Pregnancy," *American Journal of Obstetrics*

and Gynecology, 98 (1967): 8–14; M. Uluitu, L. Dusleag, D. Constantinescu, G. Petcu, G. Catrinescu, and S. Pana, "Serotonin Through Pregnancy: Comparative Researches in Different Species and in Mankind," *Physiologie*, 12 (1975): 275–280.

203 lower rate of suicide: G. J. Kleiner and W. M. Greston, eds., *Suicide in Pregnancy* (London: John Wright, 1984); A. L. Dannenberg, D. M. Carter, H. W. Lawson, D. M. Ashton, S. F. Dorfman, and E. H. Graham, "Homicide and Other Injuries as Causes of Maternal Death in New York City, 1987 through 1991," *American Journal of Obstetrics and Gynecology*, 172 (1995): 1557–1564; P. M. Marzuk, K. Tardiff, A. C. Leon, C. S. Hirsch, L. Portera, N. Hartwell, and M. Irfan Iqbal, "Lower Risk of Suicide During Pregnancy," *American Journal of Psychiatry*, 154 (1997): 122–123.

203 in the year following childbirth: L. Appleby, "Suicide During Pregnancy and in the First Postnatal Year," *British Medical Journal*, 302 (1991): 137–140; L. Appleby, P. B. Mortensen, and E. B. Faragher, "Suicide and Other Causes of Mortality After Post-Partum Psychiatric Admission," *British Journal of Psychiatry*, 173 (1998): 209–211; L. Appleby and G. Turnbull, "Parasuicide in the First Postnatal Year," *Psychological Medicine*, 173 (1998): 209–211.

203 different phases of the mentrual cycle: A. J. Mandell and M. P. Mandell, "Suicide and the Menstrual Cycle," *Journal of the American Medical Association*, 200 (1967): 792–793; R. D. Wetzel, T. Reich, and J. N. McClure, "Phase of the Menstrual Cycle and Self-Referrals to a Suicide Prevention Service," *British Journal of Psychiatry*, 119 (1971): 523–524; E. Baca-García, A. Sánchez González, P. González Diaz-Corralero, I. González Garcia, and J. de Leon, "Menstrual Cycle and Profiles of Suicidal Behaviour," *Acta Psychiatrica Scandinavica*, 97 (1998): 32–35.

203 A London autopsy study: P. C. B. MacKinnon and I. L. MacKinnon, "Hazards of the Menstrual Cycle," *British Medical Journal*, (1956): 555.

203 Autopsies of Hindu women: A. L. Ribeiro, "Menstruation and Crime," *British Medical Journal*, 1 (1962): 640.

203 low levels of estrogen: V. Fourestié, B. de Lignières, F. Roudot-Thoraval, I. Fulli-Lemaire, D. Cremniter, K. Nahoul, S. Fournier, and I.-L. Lejone, "Suicide Attempts in Hypo-Estrogenic Phases of the Menstrual Cycle," *Lancet*, 2 (1986): 1357–1360.

203 more than 180,000: C. Pritchard, "A Comparison of Youth Suicide in Hong Kong, the Developed World, and the People's Republic of China," *Hong Kong Journal of Mental Health*, 22 (1993): 6–16; World Bank, *World Development Report 1993: Investing in Health* (New York: Oxford University Press for the World Bank, 1993); C. J. L. Murray and A. D. Lopez, *The Global Burden of Disease* (Cambridge, Mass.: Harvard University Press, 1996); C. Pritchard, "Suicide in the People's Republic of China Categorized by Age and Gender: Evidence of the Influence of Culture on Suicide," *Acta Psychiatrica Scandinavica*, 93 (1996): 362–367; P. Brown, "No Way Out," *New Scientist*, March 22, 1997, pp. 34–37; E. Rosenthal, "Women's Suicides Reveal Rural China's Bitter Roots," *New York Times*, January 24, 1999.

205 Most suicides occur: E. Morselli, *Suicide: An Essay on Comparative Moral Statistics* (London: Kegan Paul, 1881); C. P. Seager and R. A. Flood, "Suicide in Bristol," *British Journal of Psychiatry*, 111 (1965): 919–932; D. R. Nalin,

"Epidemic of Suicide by Malathion Poisoning in Guyana: Report of 264 Cases," *Tropical Geographical Medicine*, 25 (1973): 8–14; J. R. Aston and S. Donnan, "Suicide by Burning as an Epidemic Phenomenon: An Analysis of 82 Deaths and Inquests in England and Wales in 1978–9," *Psychological Medicine*, 11 (1981): 735–739; D. De Maio, F. Carpenter, and C. Riva, "Evaluation of Circadian, Circsepten and Cirannual Periodicity of Attempted Suicides," *Chronobiologia*, 9 (1982): 185–193; D. W. Johnston and J. P. Waddell, "Death and Injury Patterns: Toronto Subway System," *Journal of Trauma*, 24 (1984): 619–622; P. Williams and M. Tansella, "The Time for Suicide," *Acta Psychiatrica Scandinavica*, 75 (1987): 532–535; R. Hanzlick, K. Masterson, and B. Walker, "Suicide by Jumping from High-Rise Hotels: Fulton County, Georgia, 1967–1986," *American Journal of Forensic Medicine and Pathology*, 11 (1990): 294–297; Y. Motohashi, "Circadian Variation in Suicide Attempts in Tokyo from 1978 to 1985," *Suicide and Life-Threatening Behavior*, 20 (1990): 352–361; G. Maldonado and J. F. Kraus, "Variation in Suicide Occurrence by Time of Day, Day of the Week, Month, and Lunar Phase," *Suicide and Life-Threatening Behavior*, 21 (1991): 174–187; I. O'Donnell and R. D. T. Farmer, "Suicidal Acts on Metro Systems: An International Perspective," *Acta Psychiatrica Scandinavica*, 86 (1992): 60–63; M. Gallerani, F. M. Avato, D. Dal Monte, S. Caracciolo, C. Fersini, and R. Manfredi, "The Time for Suicide," *Psychological Medicine*, 26 (1996): 867–870; L. B. Lerer and R. G. Matzopoulos, "Fatal Railway Injuries in Cape Town, South Africa," *American Journal of Forensic Medicine and Pathology*, 18 (1997): 144–147; C. Altamura, A. VanGastel, R. Pioli, P. Mannu, and M. Maes, "Seasonal and Circadian Rhythms in Suicide in Cagliari, Italy," *Journal of Affective Disorders*, 53 (1999): 77–85.

205 "Shocks and reverses": S. A. K. Strahan, *Suicide and Insanity: A Physiological and Sociological Study* (London: Swan Sonnenschein & Co., 1893), p. 158.

205 Hospital suicides: G. R. Jameison and J. H. Wall, "Some Psychiatric Aspects of Suicide," *Psychiatric Quarterly*, 7 (1933): 211–229; L. S. Lipschutz, "Some Administrative Aspects of Suicide in the Mental Hospital," *American Journal of Psychiatry*, 99 (1942): 181–187; A. D. Pokorny, "Characteristics of Forty-Four Patients Who Subsequently Committed Suicide," *Archives of General Psychiatry*, 2 (1960): 314–323; A. R. Beisser and J. E. Blanchette, "A Study of Suicides in a Mental Hospital," *Diseases of the Nervous System*, 22 (1961): 365–369; P. H. Salmons, "Suicide in High Buildings," *British Journal of Psychiatry*, 145 (1984): 469–472.

206 the well-established diurnal variation: G. Winokur, P. J. Clayton, and T. Reich, *Manic Depressive Illness* (St. Louis: C. V. Mosby, 1969); T. A. Wehr and F. K. Goodwin, eds., *Circadian Rhythms in Psychiatry* (Pacific Grove, Calif.: Boxwood Press, 1983); F. K. Goodwin and K. R. Jamison, *Manic-Depressive Illness* (New York: Oxford University Press, 1990); A. P. R. Moffott, R. E. O'Carroll, J. Bennie, S. Carroll, H. Dick, K. P. Ebmeier, and G. M. Goodwin, "Diurnal Variation of Mood and Neuropsychological Function in Major Depression with Melancholia," *Journal of Affective Disorders*, 32 (1994): 257–269.

206 Cognitive impairment: R. C. Casper, E. Redmond, M. M. Katz, C. B. Shaffer, J. M. Davis, and S. H. Koslow, "Somatic Symptoms in Primary Affective Disorder: Presence and Relationship to the Classification of Depression," *Archives of General Psychiatry*, 42 (1985): 1098–1104.

206 suicide and the lunar cycle: P. K. Jones and S. L. Jones, "Lunar Association with Suicide," *Suicide and Life-Threatening Behavior,* 7 (1977): 31–39; D. Lester, "Temporal Variation in Suicide and Homicide," *American Journal of Epidemiology,* 109 (1979): 517–520; K. MacMahon, "Short-Term Temporal Cycles in the Frequency of Suicide, United States, 1972–1978," *American Journal of Epidemiology,* 117 (1983): 744–750; G. Maldonado and J. F. Kraus, "Variation in Suicide Occurrence by Time of Day, Day of the Week, Month, and Lunar Phase," *Suicide and Life-Threatening Behavior,* 21 (1991): 174–187.

206 before modern lighting: C. L. Raison, H. M. Klein, and M. Steckler, "The Moon and Madness Reconsidered," *Journal of Affective Disorders,* 53 (1999): 99–106.

206 national holidays: D. Lester and A. T. Beck, "Suicide and National Holidays," *Psychological Reports,* 36 (1975): 52; D. P. Phillips and J. Liu, "The Frequency of Suicides Around Major Public Holidays: Some Surprising Findings," *Suicide and Life-Threatening Behavior,* 10 (1980): 41–50; D. P. Phillips and J. S. Wills, "A Drop in Suicides Around Major National Holidays," *Suicide and Life-Threatening Behavior,* 17 (1987): 1–12; S. M. Davenport and J. Birtle, "Association Between Parasuicide and Saint Valentine's Day," *British Medical Journal,* 300 (1990): 783–784; L. A. Panser, D. E. McAlpine, S. L. Wallrichs, D. W. Swanson, W. M. O'Fallon, and L. J. Melton, "Timing of Completed Suicides Among Residents of Olmsted County, Minnesota, 1951–1985," *Acta Psychiatrica Scandinavica,* 92 (1995): 214–219.

206 suicides on Mondays: W. W. K. Zung and R. L. Green, "Seasonal Variation of Suicide and Depression," *Archives of General Psychiatry,* 30 (1974): 89–91; D. Lester, "Temporal Variation in Suicide and Homicide," *American Journal of Epidemiology,* 109 (1979): 517–520; K. Bollen, "Temporal Variations in Mortality," *Demography,* 20 (1983): 45–49; K. MacMahon, "Short-Term Temporal Cycles in the Frequency of Suicide: United States, 1972–1978," *American Journal of Epidemiology,* 117 (1983): 744–750; J. M. Rothberg and F. D. Jones, "Suicide in the U.S. Army," *Suicide and Life-Threatening Behavior,* 17 (1987): 119–132; G. Maldonado and J. F. Kraus, "Variation in Suicide Occurrence by Time of Day, Day of Week, Month, and Lunar Phase," *Suicide and Life-Threatening Behavior,* 21 (1991): 174–187.

206 a "broken-promise" effect: H. Gabennesch, "When Promises Fail: A Theory of Temporal Fluctuations in Suicide," *Social Forces,* 67 (1988): 129–145.

206 In the late 1800s: E. Morselli, *Suicide: An Essay on Comparative Moral Statistics* (London: Kegan Paul, 1881), pp. 56–57.

206 Several years ago: F. K. Goodwin and K. R. Jamison, *Manic-Depressive Illness* (New York: Oxford University Press, 1990); J. Zhang, "Suicides in Beijing, China, 1992–1993," *Suicide and Life-Threatening Behavior,* 26 (1996): 175–180; A. J. Flisher, C. D. H. Parry, D. Bradshaw, and J. M. Juritz, "Seasonal Variation of Suicide in South Africa," *Psychiatry Research,* 66 (1997): 13–22.

207 in the Southern Hemisphere: M. B. Trucco, "Suicídios en el Gran Sanriago: II. Variación Estacional," *Revista Clínica Española,* 105 (1977): 47–49; G. Parker and S. Walter, "Seasonal Variation in Depressive Disorders and Suicidal Deaths in New South Wales," *British Journal of Psychiatry,* 140 (1982):

626–632; K. S. Y. Chew and R. McCleary, "The Spring Peak in Suicides: A Cross-National Analysis," *Social Science and Medicine*, 40 (1995): 223–230; A. J. Flisher, C. D. H. Parry, D. Bradshaw, and J. M. Juritz, "Seasonal Variation of Suicide in South Africa," *Psychiatry Research*, 66 (1979): 13–22.

207 men have one peak: S. M. Kevan, "Perspectives on Season of Suicide: A Review," *Social Science and Medicine*, 14 (1980): 369–378; R. Meares, F. O. Mendelsohn, and J. Milgrom-Friedman, "A Sex Difference in the Seasonal Variation of Suicide Rate: A Single Cycle for Men, Two Cycles for Women," *British Journal of Psychiatry*, 138 (1981): 321–325; S. Näyhä, "The Biseasonal Incidence of Some Suicides," *Acta Psychiatrica Scandinavica*, 67 (1983): 32–42; R. Micciolo, C. Zimmerman-Tansella, P. Williams, and M. Tansella, "Seasonal Variation in Suicide: Is There a Sex Difference?" *Psychological Medicine*, 19 (1989): 199–203; H. Hakko, P. Räsänen, and J. Tiihonen, "Seasonal Variation in Suicide Occurrence in Finland," *Acta Psychiatrica Scandinavica*, 98 (1998): 92–97.

207 Sources of data for graph: Morselli, *Suicide*; Strahan, *Suicide and Insanity*; E. Takahaski, "Seasonal Variation of Conception and Suicide," *Tohoku Journal of Experimental Medicine*, 84 (1964): 215–227; M. MacDonald and T. R. Murphy, *Sleepless Souls: Suicide in Early Modern England* (Oxford: Clarendon Press, 1990); the data for U. S. suicides 1980–1995 were provided by Dr. Alex Crosby of the Centers for Disease Control and Prevention in Atlanta and Ken Kochanek, M.A., Vital Statistics Mortality Branch, National Center for Health Statistics, Hyattsville, Md.

208 This lessening in amplitude: K. Dreyer, "Comparative Suicide Statistics: II. Death Rates from Suicide in Denmark Since 1921, and Seasonal Variations Since 1835," *Danish Medical Bulletin*, 6 (1959): 75–81; W. R. Lyster, "Seasonal Variation in Suicide Rates," *Lancet*, 1 (1973): 725; S. M. Kevan, "Perspectives on Season of Suicide: A Review," *Social Science and Medicine*, 14 (1980): 369–378; R. Meares, F. A. D. Mendelsohn, and J. Milgrom-Friedman, "A Sex Difference in the Seasonal Variation of Suicide Rate: A Single Cycle for Men, Two Cycles for Women," *British Journal of Psychiatry*, 138 (1981): 321–325; H. Hakko, P. Rasanen, and J. Tiihonen, "Secular Trends in the Rates and Seasonality of Violent and Nonviolent Suicide Occurences in Finland During 1980–1995," *Journal of Affective Disorders*, 50 (1998): 49–54; Z. Rihmer, W. Rutz, H. Pihlgren, and P. Pestality, "Decreasing Tendency of Seasonality in Suicide May Indicate Lowering Rate of Depressive Suicides in the Population," *Psychiatry Research*, 81 (1998): 233–240, P. S. F. Yip, A. Chao, and T. P. Ho, "A Re-Examination of Seasonal Variation in Suicide in Australia and New Zealand," *Journal of Affective Disorders*, 47 (1998): 141–150; Z. Rihmer, "Education of Primary Care Providers in the Reduction of Suicide Risk: Does the Gotland Model Work in Hungary Too?" paper presented at Treatment Research with Suicidal Patients Meeting, jointly sponsored by the National Institute of Mental Health and the American Foundation for Suicide Prevention, Washington, D.C., March 1999.

208 The explanations for this "deseasonalization": J. Aschoff, "Annual Rhythms in Man," in J. Aschoff, ed., *Handbook of Behavioral Neurobiology*, vol. 4: *Biological Rhythms* (New York: Plenum, 1981), pp. 475–487.

208 Emile Durkheim observed: Emile Durkheim, *Suicide: A Study in Sociology*

(New York: Free Press, 1951: first published 1897); L. I. Dublin and B. Bunzel, *To Be or Not to Be: A Study of Suicide* (New York: Smith and Hass, 1933); A. J. Flisher, C. D. H. Parry, D. Bradshaw, and J. M. Juritz, "Seasonal Variation of Suicide in South Africa," *Psychiatry Research*, 66 (1997): 13–22.

209 far more pronounced: M. R. Eastwood, J. L. Whitton, P. M. Kramer, and A. M. Peter, "Infradian Rhythm: A Comparison of Affective Disorders and Normal Persons," *Archives of General Psychiatry*, 42 (1985): 295–299; F. K. Goodwin and K. R. Jamison, *Manic-Depressive Illness* (New York: Oxford, 1990).

209 plasma L-tryptophan: L. Wetterberg, D. Eriksson, Y. Friberg, and B. Vango, "Melatonin in Humans: Physiological and Clinical Studies," *Clinica Chimica Acta*, 86 (1978): 169–177; T. H. Oddie, A. H. Klein, T. P. Foley, and D. A. Fisher, "Variation in Values for Iodothyronine Hormones, Thyrotropin, and Thyroxine-Binding Globulin in Normal Umbilical Cord Serum with Season and Duration of Storage," *Clinical Chemistry*, 25 (1979): 1251–1253; P. R. Perez, J. G. Lopez, I. P. Makeos, A. D. Escribano, and M. L. S. Sanchez, "Seasonal Variations in Thyroid Hormones in Plasma," *Revista Clínica Española*, 156 (1980): 245–247; K. M. Behall, D. J. Scholfield, J. G. Hallfrisch, J. L. Kelsay, and S. Reiser, "Seasonal Variation in Plasma Glucose and Hormone Levels in Adult Men and Women," *American Journal of Clinical Nutrition*, 40 (1984): 1352–1356; D. J. Gordon, D. C. Trost, J. Hyde, F. S. Whaley, P. J. Hannan, D. R. Jacobs, and L.-G. Ekelund, "Seasonal Cholesterol Cycles: The Lipid Research Clinics Coronary Primary Prevention Trial Placebo Group," *Circulation*, 76 (1987): 1224–1231; M. Maes, S. Scharpé, R. Verkerk, P. D'Hondt, D. Peeters, P. Cosyns, P. Thompson, F. De Meyer, A. Wauters, and H. Neels, "Seasonal Variation in Plasma L-Tryptophan Availability in Healthy Volunteers: Relationship to Violent Suicide Occurrence," *Archives of General Psychiatry*, 52 (1995): 937–946.

209 The effect of seasonal changes: A. Carlsson, L. Svennerholm, and B. Winblad, "Seasonal and Circadian Monoamine Variations in Human Brains Examined Post Mortem," *Acta Psychiatrica Scandinavica*, 280 (1979): 75–83; J. Aschoff, "Annual Rhythms in Man," in J. Aschoff, ed., *Handbook of Behavioral Neurobiology;* vol. 4: *Biological Rhythms* (New York: Plenum, 1981), pp. 475–487; M. F. Losonczy, R. C. Mohs, and K. L. Davis, "Seasonal Variations of Human Lumbar CSF Neurotransmitter Metabolite Concentrations," *Psychiatry Research*, 12 (1984): 79–87; E. Souêtre, E. Salvati, J. L. Belugou, P. Douillet, T. Braccini, and G. Darcourt, "Seasonal Variation of Serotonin Function in Humans: Research and Clinical Implications," *Annals of Clinical Psychiatry*, 1 (1989): 153–164; V. Lacoste and A. Wirz-Justice, "Seasonal Variation in Normal Subjects: An Update of Variables Current in Depression Research," in N. Rosenthal and M. Blehar, eds., *Seasonal Affective Disorders and Phototherapy* (New York: Guilford Press, 1989), pp. 167–229; M. J. Sarrias, F. Artigas, E. Martínez, and E. Gelpí, "Seasonal Changes of Plasma Serotonin and Related Parameters: Correlation with Environmental Measures," *Biological Psychiatry*, 26 (1989): 695–706; I. Modai, R. Malmgren, L. Wetterberg, P. Eneroth, A. Valevski, and M. Åsberg, "Blood Levels of Melatonin, Serotonin, Cortisol, and Prolactin in Relation to the Circadian Rhythm of Platelet Serotonin Uptake," *Psychiatry*

Research, 43 (1992): 161–166; D. S. Pine, P. D. Trautman, D. Shaffer, L. Cohen, M. Davies, M. Stanley, and B. Parsons, "Seasonal Rhythm of Platelet [³H] Imipramine Binding in Adolescents Who Attempted Suicide," *American Journal of Psychiatry,* 152 (1995): 923–925; R. J. Verkes, G. A. Kerkhof, E. Beld, M. W. Hengeveld, and G. M. J. van Kempen, "Suicidality, Circadian Activity Rhythms and Platelet Serotonergic Measures in Patients with Recurrent Suicidal Behaviour," *Acta Psychiatrica Scandinavica,* 93 (1996): 27–34; K. B. Zajicek, C. S. Price, S. E. Shoaf, P. T. Mehlman, S. J. Suomi, M. Linnoila, and J. Dee Higley, "Seasonal Variation in CSF 5-HIAA Concentrations in Male Rhesus Macaques," *Neuropsychopharmacology,* in press.

209 Hospital admissions for mania: P. Pinel, *A Treatise on Insanity,* trans. D. D. Davis (New York: Hafner, 1806; first published, 1801); E. Esquirol, *A Treatise on Insanity,* trans. E. K. Hunt (Philadelphia: Lea and Blanchard, 1845; first published 1838); D. H. Myers and P. Davies, "The Seasonal Incidence of Mania and Its Relationship to Climate Variables," *Psychological Medicine,* 8 (1978): 433–440; A. C. Pande, "Light-Induced Hypomania," *American Journal of Psychiatry,* 142 (1985): 1146; T. A. Wehr, D. A. Sack, and N. E. Rosenthal, "Sleep Reduction as a Final Common Pathway in the Genesis of Mania," *American Journal of Psychiatry,* 144 (1987): 201–204; P. A. Carney, C. T. Fitzgerald, and C. Monaghan, "Seasonal Variations in Mania," in C. Thompson and T. Silverstone, eds., *Seasonal Affective Disorder* (London: CNS, 1989), pp. 19–27; F. K. Goodwin and K. R. Jamison, *Manic-Depressive Illness* (New York: Oxford University Press, 1990); R. T. Mulder, J. P. Cosgriff, A. M. Smith, and P. R. Joyce, "Seasonality of Mania in New Zealand," *Australian and New Zealand Journal of Psychiatry,* 24 (1990): 187–190; H. K. Sayer, S. Marshall, and G. W. Mellsop, "Mania and Seasonality in the Southern Hemisphere," *Journal of Affective Disorders,* 23 (1991): 151–156; N. Takei, E. O'Callaghan, P. Sham, G. Glover, A. Tamura, and R. Murray, "Seasonality of Admissions in the Psychoses: Effect of Diagnosis, Sex, and Age at Onset," *British Journal of Psychiatry,* 161 (1992): 506–511; K. Kamo, S. Tomitaka, S. Nakadaira, T. Kno, and K. Sakamoto, "Season and Mania," *Japanese Journal of Psychiatry and Neurology,* 47 (1993): 473–474; J. L. Pio-Abreu, "Seasonal Variation in Bipolar Disorder," *British Journal of Psychiatry,* 170 (1997): 483–484.

209 Schizophrenia, likewise: E. Meier, "Die periodischen Jahresschwankungen der internierung Geistes kranker in der Heilanstatt Bürghölzli-Zürich 1900 bis 1920," *Zeitschrift für die Gesamte Neurologie und Psychiatrie,* 76 (1922): 479–507; K. Abe, "Seasonal Fluctuation of Psychiatric Admissions, Based on the Data for Seven Prefectures of Japan for a Seven-Year Period 1955–61, with a Review of the Literature," *Folia Psychiatrica et Neurologica Japonica,* 17 (1963): 101–112; E. H. Hare and S. D. Walter, "Seasonal Variation in Admissions of Psychiatric Patients and Its Relation to Seasonal Variation in Their Birth," *Journal of Epidemiology and Community Health,* 32 (1978): 47–52; M. R. Eastwood and A. M. Peter, "Epidemiology and Seasonal Affective Disorder," *Psychological Medicine,* 18 (1988): 799–806; N. Takei, E. O'Callaghan, P. Sham, G. Glover, A. Tamura, and R. Murray, "Seasonality of Admissions in the Psychoses: Effect of Diagnosis, Sex, and Age at Onset," *British Journal of Psychiatry,* 161 (1992): 506–511; M. Clarke,

P. Moran, F. Keogh, M. Morris, A. Kinsella, D. Walsh, C. Larkin, and E. O'Callaghan, "Seasonal Influences on Admissions in Schizophrenia and Affective Disorder in Ireland," *Schizophrenia Research*, 34 (1998): 143–149.

210 Depressive episodes: E. H. Hare and S. D. Walter, "Seasonal Variation in Admissions of Psychiatric Patients and Its Relation to Seasonal Variation in Their Births," *Journal of Epidemiology and Community Health*, 32 (1978): 47–52; E. Frangos, G. Athanassenas, S. Tsitourides, P. Psilolignos, A. Robos, N. Katsanou, and C. Bulgaris, "Seasonality of the Episodes of Recurrent Affective Psychoses: Possible Prophylactic Interventions," *Journal of Affective Disorders*, 2 (1980): 239–247; Z. Rihmer, "Season of Birth and Season of Hospital Admission in Bipolar Depressed Female Patients," *Psychiatry Research*, 3 (1980): 247–251; G. Parker and S. Walter, "Seasonal Variation in Depressive Disorders and Suicidal Deaths in New South Wales," *British Journal of Psychiatry*, 140 (1982): 626–632; T. D. Brewerton and D. Mclaughlin, "Circannual Cyclicity of Affective Illnesses in Hawaii," paper presented at the Conference on Recent Advances in Affective Disorders, 1986; M. R. Eastwood and A. M. Peter, "Epidemiology and Seasonal Affective Disorder," *Psychological Medicine*, 18 (1988): 799–806; F. K. Goodwin and K. R. Jamison, *Manic-Depressive Illness* (New York: Oxford University Press, 1990); M. Maes, P. Cosyns, H. Y. Meltzer, F. DeMeyer, and D. Peeters, "Seasonality in Violent Suicide but Not Nonviolent Suicide or Homicide," *American Journal of Psychiatry*, 150 (1993): 1380–1385; T. Silverstone, S. Romans, N. Hunt, and H. McPherson, "Is There a Seasonal Pattern of Relapse in Bipolar Affective Disorders? A Dual Northern and Southern Hemisphere Cohort Study," *British Journal of Psychiatry*, 167 (1995): 58–60; C. P. Szabo and M. J. Terre-Blanche, "Seasonal Variation in Mood Disorder Presentation: Further Evidence of This Phenomenon in South African Sample," *Journal of Affective Disorders*, 33 (1995): 209–214; K. Suhail and R. Cochrane, "Seasonal Variations in Hospital Admissions for Affective Disorders by Gender and Ethnicity," *Psychiatry and Psychiatric Epidemiology*, 33 (1998): 211–217.

210 Violent suicides: R. P. Michael and D. Zumpe, "Sexual Violence in the United States and the Role of the Season," *American Journal of Psychiatry*, 140 (1983): 883–886; R. A. Goodman, J. L. Herndon, G. R. Istre, F. B. Jordan, and J. Kelaghan, "Fatal Injuries in Oklahoma: Descriptive Epidemiology Using Medical Examiner Data," *Southern Medical Journal*, 82 (1989): 1128–1134; G. Roitman, E. Orev, and G. Schreiber, "Annual Rhythms of Violence in Hospitalized Affective Patients: Correlation with Changes in the Duration of the Daily Photoperiod," *Acta Psychiatrica Scandinavica*, 82 (1990): 73–76; P. Linkowski, F. Martin, and V. De Maertelaer, "Effect of Some Climatic Factors on Violent and Non-Violent Suicides in Belgium," *Journal of Affective Disorders*, 25 (1992): 161–166; M. Maes, P. Cosyns, H. Y. Meltzer, F. De Meyer, and D. Peeters, "Seasonality in Violent Suicide but Not in Nonviolent Suicide or Homicide," *American Journal of Psychiatry*, 150 (1993): 1380–1385; J. Tiihonen, P. Räsänen, and H. Hakko, "Seasonal Varation in the Occurrence of Homicide in Finland," *American Journal of Psychiatry*, 154 (1997): 1711–1714; H. Hakko, P. Räsänen, and J. Tiihone, "Seasonal Variation in Suicide Occurrence in Finland," *Acta Psychiatrica Scandinavica*, 98 (1998): 92–97; A. Preti and P. Miotto, "Seasonality

in Suicides: The Influence of Suicide Method, Gender and Age on Suicide Distribution in Italy," *Psychiatry Research,* 81 (1988): 219–231.

211 "But these things also are Spring's": Edward Thomas, "But These Things Also," in R. George Thomas, ed., *The Collected Poems of Edward Thomas* (Oxford: Oxford University Press, 1978), p. 127.

ESSAY · THE COLOURING TO EVENTS

214 "private concerns of the household.": Letter from Thomas Jefferson to Meriwether Lewis, February 23, 1801, in D. Jackson, ed., *Letters of the Lewis and Clark Expedition, with Related Documents: 1783–1854,* 2d ed. (Urbana: University of Illinois Press, 1978), vol. 1, p. 2.

215 "The object of your mission": Thomas Jefferson's instructions to Meriwether Lewis, June 20, 1803, in ibid., pp. 61–66.

215 "They embrace years of study": D. Jackson, *Thomas Jefferson and the Stony Mountains: Exploring the West from Monticello* (Urbana: University of Illinois Pess, 1981), p. 139, quoted in Stephen Ambrose, *Undaunted Courage: Meriwether Lewis, Thomas Jefferson, and the Opening of the American West* (New York: Simon & Schuster, 1996), p. 96.

216 "Capt. Lewis is brave": Letter from Thomas Jefferson to Benjamin Rush, February 28, 1803, in Jackson, *Letters of the Lewis and Clark Expedition,* vol. 1, pp. 18–19.

216 After Lewis died: Thomas Jefferson, "Life of Captain Lewis," August 18, 1813, in M. Lewis, *The Lewis and Clark Expedition, the 1814 Edition* (Philadelphia: J. B. Lippincott, 1961), vol. 1, pp. xvi, xviii–xix.

218 "Thursday, May 2nd": From the journals of Meriwether Lewis and William Clark, entries by Meriwether Lewis for May 2 and 3, 1805, in G. E. Moulton and T. W. Dunlay, eds., *The Journals of the Lewis and Clark Expedition,* vol. 4 (Lincoln: University of Nebraska Press, 1987), pp. 100–104.

219 "Few explorers have undertaken": R. D. Burroughs, "The Lewis and Clark Expedition's Botanical Discoveries," *Natural History,* 75 (1966): 57–62, p. 58. See also J. H. Beard, "The Medical Observations and Practice of Lewis and Clark," *The Scientific Monthly,* 20 (1925): 506–526; H. W. Setzer, "Zoological Contributions of the Lewis and Clark Expedition," *Journal of the Washington Academy of Sciences,* 44 (1954): 356–357; D. W. Will, "The Medical and Surgical Practice of the Lewis and Clark Expedition," *Journal of the History of Medicine,* 14 (1959): 273–297; P. R. Cutright, *Lewis and Clark: Pioneering Naturalists* (Urbana: University of Illinois Press, 1969); P. R. Cutright, "Contributions of Philadelphia to Lewis and Clark History," *We Proceeded On,* 6 (1982): 1–43.

219 "Never," declared Thomas: Jefferson, "Life of Captain Lewis," August 18, 1813, in Lewis, *The Lewis and Clark Expedition,* vol. 1, p. xxvi.

220 "I am very often applied": Letter from Thomas Jefferson to Meriwether Lewis, August 16, 1809, in Jackson, *Letters of the Lewis and Clark Expedition,* vol. 2, p. 459.

221 "This day I completed": Meriwether Lewis, journal, August 18, 1805, in Moulton and Dunlay, *The Journals of the Lewis and Clark Expedition,* vol. 5, p. 118.

221 "Several of his Bills": Letter from William Clark to Jonathan Clark, Sep-

tember 1809, published in J. J. Holmberg, " 'I Wish You to See & Know All': The Recently Discovered Letters of William Clark to Jonathan Clark," *We Proceeded On*, 18 (1992): 10.

222 unloaded Lewis's boat: Letter from James Howe to Frederick Bates, September 28, 1809, *Missouri Historical Society Collections*, 4 (1923): 474.

222 "In this condition": Letter from Captain Gilbert C. Russell to Thomas Jefferson, November 26, 1811, in Jackson, *Letters of the Lewis and Clark Expedition*, vol. 2, pp. 573–574.

222 "It is with extreme pain": Letter from James Neelly to Thomas Jefferson, October 18, 1809, in Jackson, *Letters of the Lewis and Clark Expedition*, vol. 2, pp. 467–468.

223 "Governor Lewis, she said": Letter from Alexander Wilson to Alexander Lawson, May 28, 1811, in E. Coues, ed., *History of the Expedition Under the Command of Lewis and Clark* (New York: Dover Reprint, 1965; first published 1893), vol. 1, pp. xliv–xlvi.

225 "I fear O!": Letter from William Clark to Jonathan Clark, October 28, 1809, in Jackson, *Letters of the Lewis and Clark Expedition*, vol. 2, p. 727.

225 "Governor Lewis had": Thomas Jefferson, "Life of Captain Lewis," August 18, 1813, in Lewis, *The Lewis and Clark Expedition*, vol. 1, pp. xxvii–xxviii.

226 But others have felt differently: In addition to O. D. Wheeler, F. W. Seymour, R. Dillon, C. Skinner, and A. Furtwangler, there have been many others weighing in for either murder or suicide. Among these are D. A. Phelps, "The Tragic Death of Meriweather Lewis," *William and Mary Quarterly*, 13 (1956): 305–318; V. Fisher, *Suicide or Murder: The Strange Death of Governor Meriwether Lewis* (Chicago: Sage Books, 1962); P. R. Cutright, "Rest, Rest, Perturbed Spirit," *We Proceeded On*, 12 (1986): 7–16; E. G. Chuinard, "How Did Meriwether Lewis Die? It Was Murder" (pt. 1), *We Proceeded On*, 17 (1991): 4–11; E. G. Chuinard, "How Did Meriwether Lewis Die? It Was Murder" (pt. 2), *We Proceeded On*, 18 (1991): 4–10.

226 "It seems impossible": O. D. Wheeler, *The Trial of Lewis and Clark, 1804–1904* (New York: G. P. Putnam's Sons, 1904), p. 193.

226 "Many believed that Governor Lewis": F. W. Seymour, *Meriwether Lewis* (New York: D. Appleton–Century, 1937), pp. 237–238.

226 "Is it likely": R. Dillon, *Meriwether Lewis: A Biography* (New York: Coward-McCann, 1965), pp. 344, 350.

227 "beclouded": "But, at least, the theory of suicide no longer beclouds his name," wrote C. Skinner in *Adventures in Oregon* (New Haven, 1920), p. 70.

227 "tainted by dishonor": A. Furtwangler, *Acts of Discovery: Visions of America in the Lewis and Clark Journals* (Urbana: University of Illinois Press, 1993).

227 "It seems to me": E. G. Chuinard, "How Did Meriwether Lewis Die? It Was Murder" (pt. 3), *We Proceeded On*, 18 (1992): 4–10, p. 4.

227 "Thomas Jefferson's complicity": D. L. Chandler, *The Jefferson Conspiracies: A President's Role in the Assassination of Meriwether Lewis* (New York: Morrow, 1994), pp. 325–326.

228 there may have been instability: S. M. Drumm, *Luttig's Journal of the Fur Trading Expedition on the Upper Missouri, 1812–1813* (St. Louis: Missouri Historical Society, 1920), pp. 150–151. Meriwether Lewis's mother, Lucy Meriwether Lewis, remarried after the death of Lewis's father. It is unclear

whether the mental instability reported in Dr. John Marks came from the Meriwether or Marks side of the family or both. If it came from the Meriwether side and there was instability on the Lewis side as well, it would not be at all surprising that Meriwether Lewis suffered from a severe form of mental illness.

228 "He had, however, four times": S. E. Ambrose, *Undaunted Courage: Meriwether Lewis, Thomas Jefferson, and the Opening of the American West* (New York: Simon & Schuster, 1996), pp. 358, 481–482.

229 He may well have suffered: A. T. W. Forrester, "Malaria and Insanity," *Lancet,* 1 (1920): 16–17; W. K. Anderson, *Malarial Psychoses and Neuroses* (London: Oxford University Press, 1927); C. C. Turner, "The Neurologic and Psychiatric Manifestations of Malaria," *Southern Medical Journal,* 29 (1936): 578–586; D. H. Funkenstein, "Tertian Malaria and Anxiety," *Psychosomatic Medicine,* 11 (1949): 158–159; R. B. Daroff, J. J. Deller, A. J. Kastl, and W. W. Blocker, "Cerebral Malaria," *Journal of the American Medical Association,* 202 (1967): 119–122; D. W. Mulder and A. J. Dale, "Brain Syndromes Associated with Infection," in A. M. Freedman and H. I. Kaplan, eds., *Comprehensive Textbook of Psychiatry* (Baltimore: Williams & Wilkins, 1967), pp. 775–786; W. W. Blocker, A. J. Kastl, and R. B. Daroff, "The Psychiatric Manifestations of Cerebral Malaria," *American Journal of Psychiatry,* 125 (1968): 192–196; A. J. Kastl, R. B. Daroff, and W. W. Blocker, "Psychological Testing of Cerebral Malaria Patients," *Journal of Nervous and Mental Disease,* 147 (1968): 553–561; R. M. Wintrob, "Malaria and the Acute Psychotic Episode," *Journal of Nervous and Mental Disease,* 156 (1973): 306–317; P. D. Marsden and L. J. Bruce-Chwatt, "Cerebral Malaria," in R. W. Hornabrook, ed., *Topics on Tropical Neurology* (Philadelphia: F. A. Davis, 1975); D. A. Warrell, "Cerebral Malaria," in R. A. Shakir, P. K. Newman, and C. M. Poser, eds., *Tropical Neurology* (London: W. B. Saunders, 1996), pp. 213–245.

229 Douglass Adair and Dawson Phelps: Quoted in V. Fisher, *Suicide or Murder: The Strange Death of Governor Meriwether Lewis* (Chicago: Sage Books, 1962), p. 231.

230 One reader of the *Washington Post:* E. Foxwell, letter to the editor, *Washington Post,* June 29, 1996; K. R. Jamison, letter to the editor, *Washington Post,* July 6, 1996.

230 "He was a man of high energy": Ambrose, *Undaunted Courage,* p. 482.

231 "The breaking of so great a thing": William Shakespeare, *Antony and Cleopatra,* Act V, sc. i, ll. 13–16 (London: J. M. Dent, *The Temple Shakespeare,* 1896), p. 146.

8 · MODEST MAGICAL QUALITIES

235 "For melancholy": Robert Burton, *The Anatomy of Melancholy,* vol. 2. Robert Burton's (1577–1640) *Anatomy of Melancholy* was first published in 1621 and remains to this day one of the most important books on the subject. In it, the author acknowledged that he himself suffered from melancholy; it is reported by others that his mother's brother "died of melancholy." When Burton died in 1640, several of the students at Oxford whispered among themselves that he had "sent up his soul to heaven thro' a slip about his

neck." Another Oxford contemporary concurred, stating that Burton had "ended his dayes in that chamber by hinging him selfe." Whatever the truth of the rumors—and those arguing against suicide point out that Burton would not have been allowed the Christian burial he received had there been definitive evidence that he had killed himself—the epitaph he wrote for his tombstone is provocative: "To whom Melancholy gave life and death." Michael O'Connell, *Robert Burton* (Boston: Twayne Publishers, 1986), pp. 31–33; see also Lawrence Babb, *Sanity in Bedlam: A Study of Robert Burton's Anatomy of Melancholy* (East Lansing: Michigan State University Press, 1959); Bergen Evans, in consultation with George J. Mohr, *The Psychiatry of Robert Burton* (New York: Octagon Books, 1972); Ruth A. Fox, *The Tangled Chain: The Structure of Disorder in* The Anatomy of Melancholy (Berkeley: University of California Press, 1976).

235 "much approved against melancholy": Robert Burton, *The Anatomy of Melancholy*, vol. 2, Pt. 2, Sec. 5 (London: J. M. Dent, 1961; first published 1621), pp. 248–251.

236 communicate their intentions: E. S. Shneidman and N. L. Farberow, "The Logic of Suicide," in E. S. Shneidman and N. L. Farberow, eds., *Clues to Suicide* (New York: McGraw-Hill, 1957); E. Robins, S. Gassner, J. Kayes, R. H. Wilkinson, and G. E. Murphy, "The Communication of Suicidal Intent: A Study of 134 Consecutive Cases of Successful (Completed) Suicide," *American Journal of Psychiatry*, 115 (1959): 724–733; T. L. Dorpat and H. S. Ripley, "A Study of Suicide in the Seattle Area," *Comprehensive Psychiatry*, 1 (1960): 349–359; P. G. Yessler, J. J. Gibbs, and H. A. Becker, "On the Communication of Suicidal Ideas: I. Some Sociological and Behavioral Considerations," *Archives of General Psychiatry*, 3 (1960): 612–631; K. E. Rudestam, "Stockholm and Los Angeles: A Cross-Cultural Study of the Communication of Suicidal Intent," *Journal of Consulting and Clinical Psychology*, 36 (1971): 82–90; B. M. Barraclough, J. Bunch, B. Nelson, and P. Sainsbury, "A Hundred Cases of Suicide: Clinical Aspects," *British Journal of Psychiatry*, 125 (1974): 355–373; J. Beskow, "Suicide and Mental Disorder in Swedish Men," *Acta Psychiatrica Scandinavica*, 277 (Suppl.) (1979): 1–138; C. L. Rich, R. C. Fowler, L. A. Fogarty, and D. Young, "San Diego Suicide Study: III. Relationships Between Diagnoses and Stressors," *Archives of General Psychiatry*, 45 (1988): 589–594; E. T. Isometsä, M. M. Henriksson, H. M. Aro, M. E. Heikkinen, K. I. Kuoppasalmi, and J. K. Lönnqvist, "Suicide in Major Depression," *American Journal of Psychiatry*, 151 (1994): 530–536; E. T. Isometsä, M. M. Henriksson, H. M. Aro, and J. K. Lönnqvist, "Suicide in Bipolar Disorder in Finland," *American Journal of Psychiatry*, 151 (1994): 1020–1024.

237 "If we had found that suicide": E. Robins, G. E. Murphy, R. H. Wilkinson, S. Gassner, and J. Kayes, "Some Clinical Considerations in the Prevention of Suicide Based on a Study of 134 Successful Suicides," *American Journal of Public Health*, 49 (1959): 888–899, p. 897.

237 severe anxiety, agitation, or perturbance: E. S. Shneidman and N. L. Farberow, eds., *Clues to Suicide* (New York: McGraw-Hill, 1957); J. Fawcett, K. A. Busch, D. Jacobs, H. M. Kravitz, and L. Fogg, "Suicide: A Four-Pathway Clinical-Biochemical Model," *Annals of the New York Academy of Sciences*, 836 (1997): 288–301.

238 "Many psychiatrists": W. Styron, *Darkness Visible: A Memoir of Madness* (New York: Random House, 1990), pp. 68–69.
240 its putative capacity: M. H. Sheard, J. L. Marini, and C. I. Bridges, "The Effect of Lithium on Impulsive Aggressive Behavior in Man," *American Journal of Psychiatry*, 133 (1976): 1409–1416; E. A. Wickam and F. V. Reed, "Lithium for the Control of Aggressive and Self-Mutilating Behavior," *International Clinical Psychopharmacology*, 2 (1977): 181–190; A. J. Mandell and S. Knapp, "Asymmetry and Mood, Emergent Properties of Serotonin Regulation," *Archives of General Psychiatry*, 36 (1979): 909–916; S. L. Treiser, C. S. Cascio, T. L. O'Donohue, et al., "Lithium Increases Serotonin Release and Decreases Serotonin Receptors in the Hippocampus," *Science*, 213 (1981): 1529–1531; F. N. Johnson, ed., *The Psychopharmacology of Lithium* (London: Macmillan, 1984); M. H. Sheard, "Clinical Pharmacology of Aggressive Behavior," *Clinical Neuropharmacology*, 11 (1988): 483–492; L. H. D. S. Price, P. L. Charney, P. L. Delgado, and G. R. Heninger, "Lithium and Serotonin Function: Implications for the Serotonin Hypothesis of Depression," *Psychopharmacology*, 100 (1990): 3–12; H. K. Lee, T. B. Reddy, S. Travin, and H. Bluestone, "A Trial of Lithium Citrate for the Management of Acute Agitation of Psychiatric Inpatients: A Pilot Study," *Journal of Clinical Psychopharmacology*, 12 (1992): 361–362; J. F. Dixon and L. E. Hokin, "Lithium Acutely Inhibits and Chronically Up-Regulates and Stabilizes Glutamate Uptake by Presynaptic Nerve Endings in Mouse Cerebral Cortex," *Proceedings of the National Academy of Sciences USA*, 95 (1998): 8363–8368; P. E. Harrison-Read, "Lithium Withdrawal Mania Supports Lithium's Antimanic Action and Suggests an Animal Model Involving Serotonin," *British Journal of Psychiatry*, 172 (1998): 96–97.
240 decrease aggression, agitation: R. W. Cowdry and D. L. Gardner, "Pharmacotherapy of Borderline Personality Disorder," *Archives of General Psychiatry*, 45 (1988): 111–119; T. Kastner, R. Finesmith, and K. Walsh, "Long-Term Administration of Valproic Acid in the Treatment of Affective Symptoms in People with Mental Retardation," *Journal of Clinical Psychopharmacology*, 13 (1993): 448–451; C. L. Bowden, A. M. Brugger, A. C. Swann, J. R. Calabrese, P. G. Janicak, F. Petty, S. D. Dilsaver, J. M. Davis, A. J. Rush, J. G. Small, E. S. Garza-Trevino, S. C. Risch, P. J. Goodnick, and D. D. Morris, "Efficacy of Divalproex vs. Lithium and Placebo in the Treatment of Mania," *Journal of the American Medical Association*, 271 (1994): 918–924; M. Horne and S. E. Lindley, "Divalproex Sodium in the Treatment of Aggressive Behavior and Dysphoria in Patients with Organic Brain Syndromes," *Journal of Clinical Psychiatry*, 56 (1995): 430–431; E. M. Zayas and G. T. Grossberg, "Treating the Agitated Alzheimer Patient," *Journal of Clinical Psychiatry*, 57 (Suppl. 7) (1996): 46–51; D. L. Fogelson and H. Sternbach, "Lamotrigine Treatment of Refractory Bipolar Disorder," *Journal of Clinical Psychiatry*, 58 (1997): 271–273; S. L. McElroy, C. A. Soutullo, P. E. Keck, and G. F. Kmetz, "A Pilot Trial of Adjunctive Gabapentin in the Treatment of Bipolar Disorder," *Annals of Clinical Psychiatry*, 9 (1997): 99–103; R. S. Ryback, L. Brodsky, and F. Munasifi, "Gabapentin in Bipolar Disorder," *Journal of Neuropsychiatry and Clinical Neuroscience*, 9 (1997): 301; C. B. Schaffer and L. C. Schaffer, "Gabapentin

in the Treatment of Bipolar Disorder," *American Journal of Psychiatry*, 154 (1997): 291–292; J. Sporn and G. Sachs, "The Anticonvulsant Lamotrigine in Treatment-Resistant Manic-Depressive Illness," *Journal of Clinical Psychopharmacology*, 17 (1997): 185–189.

240 Patients who had not been treated with lithium: L. Tondo, K. R. Jamison, and R. J. Baldessarini, "Effect of Lithium Maintenance on Suicidal Behavior in Major Mood Disorders," *Annals of the New York Academy of Sciences*, 836 (1997): 339–351.

240 Tondo and his colleagues: L. Tondo, R. J. Baldessarini, G. Floris, F. Silvetti, and N. Rudas, "Lithium Maintenance Treatment Reduces Risk of Suicidal Behavior in Bipolar Disorder Patients," in V. S. Gallicchio and N. J. Birch, eds., *Lithium Biochemical and Clinical Advances* (Cheshire, Conn.: Weidner Publishing Group, 1996), pp. 161–171. See also R. J. Baldessarini, L. Tondo, G. Floris, and N. Rudas, "Reduced Morbidity After Gradually Discontinuing Lithium in Bipolar I and II Disorders: A Replication Study," *American Journal of Psychiatry*, 154 (1997): 548–550; R. J. Baldessarini, L. Tondo, and J. Hennen, "Effects of Lithium Treatment and Its Discontinuation on Suicidal Behavior in Bipolar Manic-Depressive Disorders," *Journal of Clinical Psychiatry*, 60 (Suppl. 2) (1999): 77–84.

240 A 1999 study from Sweden: A. Nilsson, "Lithium Therapy and Suicide Risk," *Journal of Clinical Psychiatry*, 60 (Suppl. 2) (1999): 85–88; B. Ahrens, B. Müller-Oerlinghausen, and P. Grof, "Length of Lithium Treatment Needed to Eliminate the High Mortality of Affective Disorders," *British Journal of Psychiatry*, 163 (Suppl. 21) (1993): 27–29.

241 "Psychiatrists and other practitioners": N. J. Birch and D. P. Srinivasan, "Prevention of Suicide," *Lancet*, 340 (1992): 1233; R. Colgate, "Ranking of Therapeutic and Toxic Side-Effects of Lithium Carbonate," *Psychiatric Bulletin*, 16 (1992): 473–475.

242 to prevent suicide is unproven: F. K. Goodwin, "Anticonvulsant Therapy and Suicide Risk in Affective Disorders," *Journal of Clinical Psychiatry*, 60 (Suppl. 2) (1999): 89–93.

243 "antisuicidal effects": K. Thies-Flechtner, B. Müller-Oerlinghausen, W. Seibert, A. Walther, and W. Greil, "Effect of Prophylactic Treatment on Suicide Risk in Patients with Major Affective Disorders: Data from a Randomized Prospective Trial," *Pharmacopsychiatry* 29 (1996): 103–107, p. 106; B. Müller-Oerlinghausen, B. Ahrens, and A. Berghoefer, "Arguments for a Specific Antisuicidal Effect of Lithium," paper presented at the International Society for Lithium Research, Lexington, Ky., May 1999.

243 "Discontinuing lithium": B. Müller-Oerlinghausen, cited in M. J. Friedrich, "Lithium: Proving Its Mettle for 50 Years," *Journal of the American Medical Association*, 281 (1999): 2271–2273.

244 Sources for graph: D. H. Myers and C. D. Neal, "Suicide in Psychiatric Patients," *British Journal of Psychiatry*, 133 (1978): 38–44; S. W. Gale, A. Mesnikoff, J. Fine, and J. A. Talbot, "A Study of Suicide in State Mental Hospitals in New York City," *Psychiatric Quarterly*, 52 (1980): 201–213; J. Modestin, "Antidepressive Therapy in Depressed Clinical Studies," *Acta Psychiatrica Scandinavica*, 71 (1985): 111–116; Z. Rihmer, J. Barsi, M. Arató, and E. Demeter, "Suicide in Subtypes of Primary Major Depression," *Journal of Affective Disorders*, 18 (1990): 221–225; G. Isacsson, U. Bergman,

and C. L. Rich, "Antidepressants, Depression and Suicide: An Analysis of the San Diego Study," *Journal of Affective Disorders*, 32 (1994): 277–286; E. T. Isometsä, M. M. Henriksson, H. M. Aro, M. E. Heikkinen, K. I. Kuoppasalmi, and J. K. Lönnqvist, "Suicide in Major Depression," *American Journal of Psychiatry*, 151 (1994): 530–536; C. L. Rich and G. Isacsson, "Suicide and Antidepressants in South Alabama: Evidence for Improved Treatment of Depression," *Journal of Affective Disorders*, 45 (1997): 135–142.

245 are almost always excluded: C. M. Beasley, B. E. Dornsief, J. C. Bottomsworth, M. E. Sayler, A. H. Rampey, J. H. Heiligenstein, V. L. Thompson, D. J. Murphy, and D. N. Masica, "Fluoxetine and Suicide: A Meta-Analysis of Controlled Trials of Treatment for Depression," *British Medical Journal*, 303 (1991): 685–692.

245 decrease angry, aggressive, and impulsive behaviors, C. Salzman, A. N. Wolfson, A. Schatzberg, J. Looper, R. Henke, M. Albanese, J. Swartz, and E. Miyawaki, "Effect of Fluoxetine on Anger in Symptomatic Volunteers with Borderline Personality Disorder," *Journal of Clinical Psychopharmacology*, 15 (1995): 23–29; E. F. Coccaro and R. J. Kavoussi, "Fluoxetine and Impulsive Aggressive Behavior in Personality-Disordered Subjects," *Archives of General Psychiatry*, 54 (1997): 1081–1088.

245 a decrease in the number: S. A. Montgomery, D. L. Dunner, and G. C. Dunbar, "Reduction of Suicidal Thoughts with Paroxetine and Comparison with Reference Antidepressants and Placebo," *European Neuropsychopharmacology*, 5 (1995): 5–13; G. Isacsson, U. Bergman, and C. L. Rich, "Epidemiological Data Suggest Antidepressants Reduce Suicide Risk Among Depressives," *Journal of Affective Disorders*, 41 (1996): 1–8; A. Ohberg, E. Vuori, T. Klaukka, and J. Lonnqvist, "Antidepressants and Suicide Mortality," *Journal of Affective Disorders*, 50 (1998): 225–233; R. J. Verkes, R. C. Van der Mast, M. W. Hengeveld, J. P. Tuyl, A. H. Zwinderman, and G. M. J. Van Kempen, "Reduction by Paroxetine of Suicidal Behavior in Patients with Repeated Suicide Attempts but Not Major Depression," *American Journal of Psychiatry*, 155 (1998): 543–547; B. Müller-Oerlinghausen and A. Berghöfer, "Antidepressants and Suicidal Risk," *Journal of Clinical Psychiatry*, 60 (Suppl. 2) (1999): 94–99.

245 woefully underprescribe: B. M. Barraclough, J. Bunch, B. Nelson, and P. Sainsbury, "A Hundred Cases of Suicide: Clinical Aspects," *British Journal of Psychiatry*, 125 (1974): 355–373; P. Tyrer, "Drug Treatment of Psychiatric Patients in General Practice," *British Medical Journal*, 2 (1978): 1008–1010; M. G. Keller, G. L. Klerman, P. W. Lavori, J. Fawcett, W. Coryell, and J. Endicott, "Treatment Received by Depressed Patients," *Journal of the American Medical Association*, 248 (1982): 1848–1855; P. K. Bridges, "And a Small Dose of an Antidepressant Might Help," *British Journal of Psychiatry*, 142 (1983): 626–628; L. F. Prescott and M. S. Highley, "Drugs Prescribed for Self Poisoners" *British Medical Journal*, 290 (1985): 1633–1636; G. Isacsson, G. Boëthius, and U. Bergman, "Low Level of Antidepressant Prescription for People Who Later Commit Suicide: 15 Years of Experience from a Population-Based Drug Database in Sweden," *Acta Psychiatrica Scandinavica*, 85 (1992): 444–448; E. Isometsä, M. Henriksson, and J. Lönnqvist, "Completed Suicide and Recent Lithium Treatment," *Journal of Affective Disorders*, 26 (1992): 101–104; J. Modestin and F. Schwarzen-

bach, "Effect of Psychopharmacotherapy on Suicide Risk in Discharged Psychiatric Inpatients," *Acta Psychiatrica Scandinavica*, 85 (1992): 173–175; E. T. Isometsä, M. M. Henriksson, H. M. Aro, and J. K. Lönnqvist, "Suicide in Bipolar Disorder in Finland," *American Journal of Psychiatry*, 15 (1994): 1020–1024; P. M. Marzuk, K. Tardiff, A. C. Leon, C. S. Hirsch, M. Stajic, N. Hartwell, and L. Portera, "Use of Prescription Psychotropic Drugs Among Suicide Victims in New York City," *American Journal of Psychiatry*, 152 (1995): 1520–1522; S. Henriksson, G. Boëthius, and G. Isacsson, "The Prescription of Drugs to Suicide Cases in a Swedish County, Jämtland, from 1985 Through 1995," data presented to the Annual Meeting of the American Association of Suicidology, Bethesda, Md., April 1998; K. Rost, M. Zhang, J. Fortney, J. Smith, J. Coyne, and G. R. Smith, "Persistently Poor Outcomes of Undetected Major Depression in Primary Care," *General Hospital Psychiatry*, 20 (1998): 12–20; K. H. Suominen, E. T. Isometsä, M. M. Henriksson, A. I. Ostamo, and J. K. Lönnqvist, "Inadequate Treatment for Major Depression Both Before and After Attempted Suicide," *American Journal of Psychiatry*, 155 (1998): 1778–1780; G. Isacsson, P. Holmgren, H. Druid, and U. Bergman, "Psychotropics and Suicide Prevention: Implications from Toxicological Screening of 5281 Suicides in Sweden 1992–1994," *British Journal of Psychiatry*, 174 (1999): 259–265; M. A. Oquendo, K. M. Malone, S. P. Ellis, H. A. Sackeim, and J. J. Mann, "Inadequacy of Antidepressant Treatment for Patients with Major Depression Who Are at Risk for Suicidal Behavior," *American Journal of Psychiatry*, 156 (1999): 190–194.

246 a high rate of suicide: This is reviewed in F. K. Goodwin and K. R. Jamison, *Manic-Depressive Illness* (New York: Oxford University Press, 1990); see also Z. Rihmer, J. Barsi, M. Arató, and E. Demeter, "Suicide in Subtypes of Primary Major Depression," *Journal of Affective Disorders*, 18 (1990); 221–225.

246 perhaps one-third of patients: S. N. Ghaemi, E. E. Boiman, and F. K. Goodwin, "Bipolar Disorder and Antidepressants: A Diagnostic and Treatment Study," paper presented at the American Psychiatric Association Meeting, Toronto, May 1998.

246 survey of pediatricians: This was a survey investigation headed by Jerry Rushton, a pediatrician at the University of North Carolina at Chapel Hill. The results were presented at the Pediatrics Academic Societies Annual Conference in San Francisco in May 1999 and summarized in the *Journal of the American Medical Association*, 281 (1999): 1882.

247 overlapping symptoms: J. Biederman, S. V. Faraone, E. Mick, J. Wozniack, L. Chen, C. Ouellette, A. Marrs, P. Moore, J. Garcia, D. Mennin, and E. Lelon, "Attention Deficit Hyperactivity Disorder and Juvenile Mania: An Overlooked Comorbidity?" *Journal of the American Academy of Child and Adolescent Psychiatry*, 35 (1996): 997–1008; J. Biederman, R. Russell, J. Soriano, J. Wozniak, and S. V. Faraone, "Clinical Features of Children with Both ADHD and Mania: Does Ascertainment Source Make a Difference?" *Journal of Affective Disorders*, 51 (1998): 101–112; G. A. Carlson, "Mania and ADHD: Comorbidity or Confusion," *Journal of Affective Disorders*, 51 (1998): 177–187; B. Geller, M. Williams, B. Zimerman, J. Frazier, L. Beringer, and K. L. Warner, "Prepubertal and Early Adolescent Bipolarity Differentiate from ADHD by Manic Symptoms, Grandiose

Delusions, Ultra-Rapid or Ultradian Cycling," *Journal of Affective Disorders*, 51 (1998): 81–91.

247 Their pre-illness: D. Quackenbush, S. Kutcher, H. Robertson, C. Boulos, and P. Chaban, "Premorbid and Postmorbid School Functioning in Bipolar Adolescents: Description and Suggested Academic Interventions," *Canadian Journal of Psychiatry*, 41 (1996): 16–22; S. Kutcher, H. A. Robertson, and D. Bird, "Premorbid Functioning in Adolescent Onset Bipolar I Disorder: A Preliminary Report from an Ongoing Study," *Journal of Affective Disorders*, 51 (1998): 137–144.

247 controversial and unresolved: F. Rouillon, R. Phillips, E. Serrurier, E. Ansart, and M. J. Gerard, "Prophylactic Efficacy of Maprotiline on Relapses of Unipolar Depression." *L 'Encéphale*, 15 (1989): 527–534; M. H. Teicher, C. Glod, and J. O. Cole, "Emergence of Intense Suicidal Preoccupation During Fluoxetine Treatment," *American Journal of Psychiatry*, 147 (1990): 207–210; A. C. Power and P. J. Cowen, "Fluoxetine and Suicidal Behaviour: Some Clinical and Theoretical Aspects of a Controversy," *British Journal of Psychiatry*, 161 (1992): 735–741; M. H. Teicher, C. A. Glod, and J. O. Cole, "Antidepressant Drugs and the Emergence of Suicidal Tendencies," *Drug Safety*, 8 (1993): 186–212; D. Healy, "The Fluoxetine and Suicide Controversy: A Review of the Evidence," *CNS Drugs*, 1 (1994): 223–231.

247 antidepressants do not increase: S. A. Montgomery and R. M. Pinder, "Do Some Antidepressants Promote Suicide?" *Psychopharmacology*, 92 (1987): 265–266; C. M. Beasley, B. E. Dornseif, J. C. Bosomworth, M. E. Sayler, A. H. Rampey, J. H. Heiligenstein, V. L. Thompson, D. J. Murphy, and D. N. Masica, "Fluoxetine and Suicide: A Meta-Analysis of Controlled Trials of Treatment for Depression," *British Medical Journal*, 303 (1991): 685–692; P. N. Jenner, "Paroxetine: An Overview of Dosage, Tolerability, and Safety," *International Clinical Psychopharmacology*, 6 (Suppl. 4) (1992): 69–80; G. D. Tollefson, J. Fawcett, G. Winokur, C. M. Beasley, J. H. Potvin, D. E. Faries, A. H. Rampey, and M. E. Sayler, "Evaluation of Suicidality During Pharmacologic Treatment of Mood and Nonmood Disorders," *Annals of Clinical Psychiatry*, 5 (1993): 209–224; S. Kasper, S. Schindler, and A. Neumeister, "Risk of Suicide in Depression and Its Implication for Psychopharmacological Treatment," *International Clinical Psychopharmacology*, 11 (1996): 71–79; J. F. Wernicke, M. E. Sayler, S. C. Koke, D. K. Pearson, and G. D. Tollefson, "Fluoxetine and Concomitant Centrally Acting Medication Use During Clinical Trials of Depression: The Absence of an Effect Related to Agitation and Suicidal Behavior," *Depression and Anxiety*, 6 (1997): 31–39; A. C. Leon, M. B. Keller, M. G. Warshaw, T. I. Mueller, D. A. Solomon, W. Coryell, and J. Endicott, "Prospective Study of Fluoxetine Treatment and Suicidal Behavior in Affectively Ill Subjects," *American Journal of Psychiatry*, 156 (1999): 195–201.

248 "possibility of a suicide attempt": *Physicians' Desk Reference* (Montvale, N.J.: Medical Economics Company, 1996), p. 921.

248 The newer SSRIs: H.-J. Möller and E. M. Steinmeyer, "Are Serotonergic Reuptake Inhibitors More Potent in Reducing Suicidality?: An Empircal Study on Paroxetine," *European Neuropsychopharmacology*, 4 (1994): 55–59; D. C. Steffens, K. R. R. Krishnan, and M. J. Helms, "Are SSRIs Better

than TCAs? Comparison of SSRIs and TCAs: A Meta-Analysis," *Depression and Anxiety*, 6 (1997): 10–18; O. Benkert, M. Burkart, and H. Wetzel, "Existing Therapies with Newer Antidepressants—Their Strengths and Weaknesses," in M. Briley and S. A. Montgomery, eds., *Antidepressant Therapy at the Dawn of the Third Millennium* (St. Louis: Mosby, 1998), pp. 213–230; B. Müller-Oerlinghausen and A. Berghöfer, "Antidepressants and Suicidal Risk," *Journal of Clinical Psychiatry*, 60 (Suppl. 2) (1999): 94–99; *Treatment of Depression—Newer Pharmacotherapies*, HCPR Publication No. 99-E014 (Rockville, Md.: Agency for Health Care Policy and Research, 1999).

248 used to good effect: J. R. Cornelius, I. M. Salloum, M. D. Cornelius, J. M. Perel, M. E. Thase, J. G. Ehler, and J. J. Mann, "Fluoxetine Trial in Suicidal Depressed Alcoholics," *Psychopharmacology Bulletin*, 29 (1993): 195–199; J. R. Cornelius, I. M. Salloum, J. G. Ehler, P. J. Jarrett, M. D. Cornelius, J. M. Perel, M. E. Thase, and A. Black, "Fluoxetine in Depressed Alcoholics: A Double-Blind, Placebo-Controlled Trial," *Archives of General Psychiatry*, 54 (1997): 700–705; I. M. Salloum, J. R. Cornelius, M. E. Thase, D. C. Daley, L. Kirisci, and C. Spotts, "Naltrexone Utility in Depressed Alcoholics," *Psychopharmacology Bulletin*, 34 (1998): 111–115.

248 in British women: D. Gunnell, H. Wehner, and S. Frankel, "Sex Differences in Suicide Trends in England and Wales," *Lancet*, 353 (1999): 556–557.

249 "Substance P": M. S. Kramer, N. Cutler, J. Feighner, R. Shrivastava, J. Carman, J. J. Sramek, S. A. Reines, G. Liu, D. Snavely, E. Wyatt-Knowles, J. J. Hale, S. G. Mills, M. MacCoss, C. J. Swain, T. Harrison, R. G. Hill, F. Hefti, E. M. Scolnick, M. A. Cascieri, G. G. Chicchi, S. Sadowski, A. R. Williams, L. Hewson, D. Smith, E. J. Carlson, R. J. Hargreaves, and N. M. J. Rupniak, "Distinct Mechanism for Antidepressant Activity by Blockade of Central Substance P Receptors," *Science*, 281 (1998): 1640–1644.

249 Omega-3 fatty acids: A. L. Stoll, E. Severus, M. P. Freeman, S. Rueter, H. A. Zboyan, E. Diamond, K. K. Cress, and L. B. Marangell, "Omega-3 Fatty Acids in Bipolar Disorder: A Double-Blind Placebo-Conrolled Trial," *Archives of General Psychiatry*, 56 (1999): 407–412.

249 A seventeen-year epidemiological study: T. Hirayama, *Life-Style and Mortality: A Large Census-Based Cohort Study in Japan* (Basel: Karger, 1990).

250 there have been reports: N. Praschak-Rieder, A. Neumeister, B. Hesselmann, M. Willeit, C. Barnas, and S. Kasper, "Suicidal Tendencies as a Complication of Light Therapy for Seasonal Affective Disorder: A Report of Three Cases," *Journal of Clinical Psychiatry*, 58 (1997): 389–392; Y. Meesters and C. A. J. van Houwelinger, "Rapid Mood Swings After Unmonitored Light Exposure," *American Journal of Psychiatry*, 155 (1998): 306; A. M. O'Breasail and S. Argouarch, "Hypomania and St. John's Wort," *Canadian Journal of Psychiatry*, 43 (1998): 746–747. For an excellent overview of St. John's wort, see N. Rosenthal, *St. John's Wort* (New York: HarperCollins, 1998).

250 they can cause akathisia: R. DeAlarcon and M. W. P. Carney, "Severe Depressive Mood Changes Following Slow-Release Intramuscular Fluphenazine Injection," *British Medical Journal*, 3 (1969): 564–567; D. E. Raskin, "Akathisia: A Side-Effect to Be Remembered," *American Journal of*

Psychiatry, 129 (1972): 121–123; K. Shear, A. Frances, and P. Weiden, "Suicide Associated with Akathisia and Depot Fluphenazine Treatment," *Journal of Clinical Psychopharmacology,* 3 (1983): 235–236; R. E. Drake and J. Ehrlich, "Suicide Attempts Associated with Akathisia," *American Journal of Psychiatry,* 142 (1985): 499–501; R. E. Drake, S. J. Bartels, and W. C. Torrey, "Suicide in Schizophrenia: Clinical Approaches," in R. Williams and J. T. Dalby, eds., *Depression in Schizophrenics* (New York: Plenum Press, 1989), pp. 171–183; P. Sachdev, *Akathisia and Restless Legs* (Cambridge, England: Cambridge University Press, 1995).

250 But used carefully: H. Warnes, "Suicide in Schizophrenics," *Diseases of the Nervous System,* 29 (Suppl. 5) (1968): 35–40; D. A. W. Johnson, G. Pasterski, J. M. Ludlow, K. Street, and R. D. W. Taylor, "The Discontinuance of Maintenance Neuroleptic Therapy in Chronic Schizophrenic Patients: Drug and Social Consequences," *Acta Psychiatrica Scandinavica,* 67 (1983): 339–352; T. J. Taiminen, "Effect of Psychopharmacotherapy on Suicide Risk in Psychiatric Inpatients," *Acta Psychiatrica Scandinavica,* 87 (1993): 45–47; H. Y. Meltzer and G. Okayli, "Reduction of Suicidality During Clozapine Treatment of Neuroleptic-Resistant Schizophrenia: Impact on Risk-Benefit Assessment," *American Journal of Psychiatry,* 152 (1995): 183–190; T. P. Hogan and A. G. Awad, "Pharmacotherapy and Suicide Risk in Schizophrenia," *Canadian Journal of Psychiatry,* 28 (1983): 277–281; A. M. Walker, L. L. Lanza, F. Arellano, and K. J. Rothman, "Mortality in Current and Former Users of Clozapine," *Epidemiology,* 8 (1997): 671–677; D. D. Palmer, I. D. Henter, and R. J. Wyatt, "Do Antipsychotic Medications Decrease the Risk of Suicide in Patients with Schizophrenia?" *Journal of Clinical Psychiatry,* 60 (suppl. 2) (1999): 100–103.

251 Electroconvulsive therapy: M. T. Tsuang, G. M. Dempsey, and J. A. Fleming, "Can ECT Prevent Premature Death and Suicide in 'Schizoaffective' Patients?" *Journal of Affective Disorders,* 1 (1979): 167–171; B. L. Tanney, "Electroconvulsive Therapy and Suicide," *Suicide and Life-Threatening Behavior,* 16 (1986): 199–222; D. W. Black, G. Winokur, E. Mohandoss, R. F. Woolson, and A. Nasrallah, "Does Treatment Influence Mortality in Depressives? A Follow-up of 1076 Patients with Major Affective Disorders," *Annals of Clinical Psychiatry,* 1 (1989): 165–173; American Psychiatric Association Task Force on ECT, *The Practice of ECT: Recommendations for Treatment, Training and Privileging* (Washington, D.C.: American Psychiatric Press, 1990); E. T. Isometsä, M. M. Henriksson, M. E. Heikkinen, et al., "Completed Suicide and Recent Electroconvulsive Therapy in Finland," *Convulsive Therapy,* 12 (1996): 152–155; J. Prudic and H. A. Sackeim, "Electroconvulsive Therapy and Suicide Risk," *Journal of Clinical Psychiatry,* 60 (Suppl. 2) (1999): 104–110.

251 "The narcissistic ponderings": J. M. Himmelhoch, "Lest Treatment Abet Suicide," *Journal of Clinical Psychiatry,* 48 (1987): 44–54.

251 A new, noninvasive: M. S. George, E. M. Wassermann, W. A. Williams, A. Callahan, T. A. Ketter, P. Basser, M. Hallett, and R. M. Post, "Daily Repetitive Transcranial Magnetic Stimulation (rTMS) Improves Mood in Depression," *Neuroreport,* 6 (1995): 1853–1856; A. Pascual-Leone, B. Rubio, F. Pallardo, and M. D. Catala, "Beneficial Effect of Rapid-Rate Transcranial Magnetic Stimulation of the Left Dorsolateral Prefrontal

Cortex in Drug-Resistant Depression," *Lancet,* 348 (1996): 233–237; R. H. Belmaker, N. Grisaru, D. Ben-Sharar, and E. Klein, "The Effects of TMS on Animal Modes of Depression, Beta-Adrenergic Receptors and Brain Monoamines," *CNS Spectrums: International Journal of Neuropsychiatric Medicine,* 2 (1997): 26–30; M. S. George, E. M. Wassermann, T. A. Kimbrell, J. J. Little, W. E. Williams, A. L. Danielson, B. D. Greenberg, M. Hallett, and R. M. Post, "Mood Improvement Following Daily Left Prefrontal Repetitive Transcranial Magnetic Stimulation in Patients with Depression: A Placebo-Controlled Crossover Trial," *American Journal of Psychiatry,* 154 (1997): 1752–1756; M. S. George, S. H. Lisanby, and H. A. Sackiem, "Transcranial Magnetic Stimulation: Applications in Neuropsychiatry," *Archives of General Psychiatry,* 56 (1999); 300–311.

252 series of studies: G. L. Klerman, A. De Mascio, M. M. Weissman, B. A. Prusoff, and E. S. Paykel, "Treatment of Depression by Drugs and Psychotherapy," *American Journal of Psychiatry,* 131 (1974): 186–191; A. S. Friedman, "Interaction of Drug Therapy with Marital Therapy in Depressed Patients," *Archives of General Psychiatry,* 32 (1975): 619–637; M. M. Weissman, "The Psychological Treatment of Depression: Evidence for the Efficacy of Psychotherapy Alone, in Comparison with, and in Combination with Pharmacotherapy," *Archives of General Psychiatry,* 36 (1979): 1261–1269; M. M. Weissman, B. A. Prusoff, A. De Mascio, C. Neu, M. Goklaney, and G. L. Klerman, "The Efficacy of Drugs and Psychotherapy in the Treatment of Acute Depressive Episodes," *American Journal of Psychiatry,* 136 (1979): 555–558; D. S. Janowsky and R. J. Neborsky, "Hypothesized Common Mechanism in the Psychotherapy and Psychopharmacology of Depression," *Psychiatric Annals,* 10 (1980): 356–361; I. M. Blackburn, S. Bishop, A. I. M. Glen, L. J. Whalley, and J. E. Christie, "The Efficacy of Cognitive Therapy and Pharmacotherapy, Each Alone and in Combination," *British Journal of Psychiatry,* 139 (1981): 181–189; G. E. Murphy, A. D. Simons, R. D. Wetzel, and P. J. Lustman, "Cognitive Therapy and Pharmacotherapy: Singly and Together in the Treatment of Depression," *Archives of General Psychiatry,* 41 (1984): 33–41; E. Frank and D. J. Kupfer, "Maintenance Treatment of Recurrent Unipolar Depression: Pharmacology and Psychotherapy," in D. Demali and G. Racagni, eds., *Chronic Treatments in Neuropsychiatry* (New York: Raven Press, 1985), pp. 139–151.

252 convincing recent work: S. Cochran, "Preventing Medical Noncompliance in the Outpatient Treatment of Bipolar Affective Disorders," *Journal of Consulting and Clinical Psychology,* 52 (1984): 873–878; K. Jamison, "Manic-Depressive Illness: The Overlooked Need for Psychotherapy," in B. Beitman and G. Klerman, eds., *Integrating Pharmacotherapy and Psychotherapy* (Washington, D.C.: American Psychiatric Association, 1991), pp. 409–420; E. Frank, D. Kupfer, C. Ehlers, T. Monk, C. Cornes, S. Carter, and D. Frankel, "Interpersonal and Social Rhythm Therapy for Bipolar Disorder: Integrating Interpersonal and Behavioral Approaches," *Behavior Therapist,* 17 (1994): 143–149; A. F. Lehman, "Vocational Rehabilitation for Schizophrenia," *Schizophrenia Bulletin,* 21 (1995): 645–656; J. Scott, "Psychotherapy for Bipolar Disorder," *British Journal of Psychiatry,* 167 (1995): 581–588; M. Basco and A. J. Rush, *Cognitive-Behavioral Therapy for Bipolar*

Disorder (New York: Guilford, 1996); I. R. H. Falloon, J. H. Coverdale, and C. Brooker, "Psychosocial Interventions in Schizophrenia: A Review," *International Journal of Mental Health*, 25 (1996): 3–23; D. Miklowitz, "Psychotherapy in Combination with Drug Treatment for Bipolar Disorder," *Journal of Clinical Psychopharmacology*, 16 (Suppl.) (1996): 56–66; D. Miklowitz, E. Frank, and E. George, "New Psychosocial Treatments for the Outpatient Management of Bipolar Disorder," *Psychopharmacology Bulletin*, 32 (1996): 613–621; D. L. Penn and K. T. Mueser, "Research Update on the Psychosocial Treatment of Schizophrenia," *American Journal of Psychiatry*, 153 (1996): 607–617; E. Frank, S. Hlastala, P. Houck, X. M. Tu, T. Monk, A. Mallinger, and D. Kupfer, "Inducing Lifestyle Regularity in Recovering Bipolar Disorder Patients: Results from the Maintenance Therapies in Bipolar Disorder Protocol," *Biological Psychiatry*, 41 (1997): 1165–1173; J. M. Harkavy-Friedman and E. A. Nelson, "Assessment and Intervention for the Suicidal Patient with Schizophrenia," *Psychiatric Quarterly*, 68 (1997): 361–375; I. R. H. Falloon, R. Roncone, U. Malm, and J. H. Coverdale, "Effective and Efficient Treatment Strategies to Enhance Recovery from Schizophrenia: How Much Longer Will People Have to Wait Before We Provide Them?" *Psychiatric Rehabilitation Skills*, 2 (1998): 107–127.

253 "Why do we now give psychiatrists": T. S. Szasz, "A Moral View on Suicide," in D. Jacobs and H. N. Brown, eds., *Suicide: Understanding and Responding* (Madison, Conn.: International Universities Press, 1989), pp. 437–447, pp. 442, 446.

254 The legal complaint: State of New York, County of Onondaga, *Hilde Klein v. Thomas Szasz, M.D.*, August 2, 1994; justice presiding: Hon. Parker J. Stone, J.S.C., Index No. 92-660, RJI No. 33-92-640.

255 "capacity to hear out carefully": N. H. Cassem, "Treating the Person Confronting Death," in A. M. Nicholi, ed., *Harvard Guide to Modern Psychiatry* (Cambridge, Mass.: Belknap Press of Harvard University Press, 1978), pp. 579–606, p. 595.

255 "Because the doctors cared": M. Coate, *Beyond All Reason* (London: Constable, 1964), p. 214.

256 twenty controlled clinical trials: P. M. Salkovskis, C. Atha, and D. Storer, "Cognitive-Behavioral Problem Solving in the Treatment of Patients Who Repeatedly Attempt Suicide: A Controlled Trial," *British Journal of Psychiatry*, 157 (1990): 871–876; M. M. Linehan, H. E. Armstrong, A. Suarez, D. Allmon, and H. L. Heard, "Cognitive Behavioral Treatment of Chronically Parasuicidal Borderline Patients," *Archives of General Psychiatry*, 48 (1991): 1060–1064; M. M. Linehan, H. L. Heard, and H. E. Armstrong, "Naturalistic Follow-up of a Behavioral Treatment for Chronically Parasuicidal Borderline Patients," *Archives of General Psychiatry*, 50 (1993): 971–974; C. Van Heeringen, S. Jannes, W. Buylaert, H. Henderick, D. De Bacquer, and J. van Remoortel, "The Management of Non-Compliance with Referral to Outpatient After-Care Among Attempted Suicide Patients: A Controlled Intervention Study," *Psychological Medicine*, 25 (1995): 963–970; M. M. Linehan, "Behavioral Treatments of Suicidal Behaviors: Definitional Obfuscation and Treatment Outcomes," *Annals of the New York Academy of Sciences*, 836 (1997): 302–328; R. van der Sande, E. Buskens, E. Allart, Y. van

der Graaf, and H. van Engeland, "Psychosocial Intervention Following Suicide Attempt: A Systematic Review of Treatment Interventions," *Acta Psychiatrica Scandinavica*, 96 (1997): 43–50; K. Hawton, E. Arensman, E. Townsend, S. Bremner, E. Feldman, R. Goldney, D. Gunnell, P. Hazell, K. van Heeringen, A. House, D. Owens, I. Sakinofsky, and L. Träskman-Bendz, "Deliberate Self-Harm: Systematic Review of Efficacy of Psychosocial and Pharmacological Treatments in Preventing Repetition," *British Medical Journal*, 317 (1998): 441–447. Preliminary data from the University of Pittsburgh suggest that structured psychotherapy in conjunction with sleep and other forms of biological regulation may reduce active suicidal ideation in bipolar patients (Ellen Frank, Ph.D., personal communication, April 15, 1999).

256 situations of interpersonal conflict: J. Birtchnell, "Some Familial and Clinical Characteristics of Female Suicidal Psychiatric Patients," *British Journal of Psychiatry*, 138 (1981): 381–390; K. Hawton, D. Cole, J. O'Grady, and M. Osborn, "Motivational Aspects of Deliberate Self-Poisoning in Adolescents," *British Journal of Psychiatry*, 141 (1982): 286–291; K. Hawton and J. Catalan, *Attempted Suicide: A Practical Guide to Its Nature and Management* (Oxford: Oxford University Press, 1982); D. James and K. Hawton, "Explanations and Attitudes in Self-Poisoners and Significant Others," *British Journal of Psychiatry*, 146 (1985): 481–485; B. C. McLeavey, R. J. Daly, J. W. Ludgate, and C. M. Murray, "Interpersonal Problem-Solving Skills Training in the Treatment of Self-Poisoning Patients," *Suicide and Life-Threatening Behavior*, 24 (1994): 382–394.

257 Perhaps 20 percent: J. A. Urquhart, "A Call for a New Discipline," *Pharmacology Technology*, 11 (1987): 16–17.

257 in medical conditions such as epilepsy: D. L. Sacket, "The Magnitude of Compliance and Noncompliance," in D. L. Sacket and R. B. Haynes, eds., *Compliance with Therapeutic Regimens* (Baltimore: Johns Hopkins University Press, 1976), pp. 9–25; J. A. Cramer and R. Rosenbeck, "Compliance with Medication Regimens for Mental and Physical Disorders," *Psychiatric Services*, 49 (1988): 196–201.

257 For patients taking antidepressants: J. L. Young, H. V. Zonana, and L. Shepler, "Medication Noncompliance in Schizophrenia: Codification and Update," *Bulletin of the American Academy of Psychiatry and the Law*, 14 (1986): 105–122; F. K. Goodwin and K. R. Jamison, *Manic-Depressive Illness* (New York: Oxford University Press, 1990); W. S. Fenton and T. H. McGlashan, "Schizophrenia: Individual Psychotherapy," in H. I. Kaplan and B. J. Sadock, eds., *Comprehensive Textbook of Psychiatry*, 6th ed., vol. 1, (Baltimore: William & Wilkins, 1995), pp. 1007–1018; S. A. Montgomery and S. Kasper, "Comparison of Compliance Between Serotonin Reuptake Inhibitors and Tricyclic Antidepressants: A Meta-Analysis," *International Clinical Psychopharmaology*, 9 (Suppl. 4) (1995): 33–40; W. S. Fenton, C. R. Blyler, and R. K. Heinssen, "Determinants of Medication Compliance in Schizophrenia: Empirical and Clinical Findings," *Schizophrenia Bulletin*, 23 (1997): 637–651; J. Garavan, S. Browne, M. Gervin, A. Lane, C. Larkin, and E. O'Callaghan, "Compliance with Neuroleptic Medication in Outpatients with Schizophrenia," *Comprehensive Psychiatry*, 39 (1998): 215–219; E. Frank, R. F. Prien, D. J. Kupfer, and L. Alberts, "Implications of

Noncompliance on Research in Affective Disorders," *Psychopharmacology Bulletin*, 21 (1985): 37–42.

257 The one study that directly compared: P. E. Keck, S. L. McElroy, S. M. Strakowski, M. L. Bourne, and S. A. West, "Compliance with Maintenance Treatment in Bipolar Disorder," *Psychopharmacology Bulletin*, 33 (1997): 87–91. An earlier short-term study found essentially no differences in compliance between lithium and valproate; see C. L. Bowden, A. M. Brugger, A. C. Swann, J. R. Calabrese, P. G. Janicak, F. Petty, S. C. Dilsaver, J. M. Davis, A. J. Rush, J. G. Small, E. S. Garza-Treviño, S. C. Risch, P. J. Goodnick, and D. D. Morris, "Efficacy of Divalproex vs. Lithium and Placebo in the Treatment of Mania," *Journal of the American Medical Association*, 271 (1994): 918–924.

257 Compliance rates are even lower: H. M. Bogard, "Follow-up Study of Suicidal Patients Seen in Emergency Room Consultation," *American Journal of Psychiatry*, 126 (1970): 141–144; N. Kreitman, "Reflections on the Management of Parasuicide," *British Journal of Psychiatry*, 125 (1979): 275; H. G. Morgan, C. J. Burns-Cox, H. Pocock, and S. Pottle, "Deliberate Self-Harm: Clinical and Socio-Economic Characteristics of 368 Patients," *British Journal of Psychiatry*, 134 (1979): 335–342; I. F. Litt, W. R. Cuskey, and S. Rudd, "Emergency Room Evaluation of the Adolescent Who Attempts Suicide: Compliance with Follow-up," *Journal of Adolescent Health Care*, 4 (1983): 106–108; E. Taylor and A. Stansfeld, "Children Who Poison Themselves: I. A Clinical Comparison with Psychiatric Controls. II. Prediction of Attendance for Treatment," *British Journal of Psychiatry*, 122 (1984): 1248–1257; G. O'Brien, A. R. Holton, K. Hurren, L. Watt, and F. Hassanyeh, "Deliberate Self-Harm and Predictors of Outpatient Attendance," *British Journal of Psychiatry*, 150 (1987): 246–247; R. B. Vukmir, R. Kremen, D. A. Dehart, and J. Menegazzi, "Compliance with Emergency Department Patient Referral," *American Journal of Emergency Medicine*, 10 (1992): 413–417; P. D. Trautman, N. Stewart, and A. Morishima, "Are Adolescent Suicide Attempters Noncompliant with Outpatient Care?" *Journal of the American Academy of Child and Adolescent Psychiatry*, 32 (1993): 89–94.

257 Psychotherapy increases medication compliance: S. D. Cochran, "Preventing Medical Noncompliance in the Outpatient Treatment of Bipolar Affective Disorders," *Journal of Consulting and Clinical Psychology*, 52 (1984): 873–878; F. K. Goodwin and K. R. Jamison, *Manic-Depressive Illness* (New York: Oxford University Press, 1990); D. J. Miklowitz and M. J. Goldstein, "Behavioral Family Treatment for Patients with Bipolar Affective Disorder," *Behavior Modification*, 14 (1990): 457–489; D. J. Miklowitz and M. J. Goldstein, *Bipolar Disorder: A Family-Focused Treatment Approach* (New York: Guilford, 1997).

257 some, but not all, of the programs: R. Allard, M. Marshall, and M. C. Plante, "Intensive Follow-up Does Not Decrease the Risk of Repeat Suicide Attempts," *Suicide and Life-Threatening Behavior*, 22 (1992): 303–314; C. Van Heeringen, S. Jannes, W. Buylaert, H. Henderick, D. De Bacquer, and J. Van Remoortel, "The Management of Non-Compliance with Referral to Outpatient Aftercare Among Attempted Suicide Patients: A Controlled Intervention Study," *Psychological Medicine*, 25 (1995): 963–970; M. J. Rotheram-Borus, J. Piacentini, R. Roosem Can, F. Grace, C. Cant-

well, D. Castro-Blanco, S. Miller, and J. Feldman, "Enhancing Treatment Adherence with a Specialized Emergency Room Program for Adolescent Suicide Attempters," *Journal of the American Academy of Child and Adolescent Psychiatry*, 35 (1996): 654–663; A. Spirito, "Improving Treatment Compliance Among Adolescent Suicide Attempters," *Crisis*, 17 (1996): 152–154; R. van der Sande, L. Van Rooijen, E. Buskens, E. Allart, K. Hawton, Y. van der Graaf, and H. van Engeland, "Intensive Inpatient and Community Intervention Versus Routine Care After Attempted Suicide: A Randomised Controlled Intervention Study," *British Journal of Psychiatry*, 171 (1997): 35–41; D. C. Daley, I. M. Salloum, A. Zuckoff, L. Kirisci, and M. E. Thase, "Increasing Treatment Adherence Among Outpatients with Depression and Cocaine Dependence: Results of a Pilot Study," *American Journal of Psychiatry*, 155 (1998): 1611–1613; R. Kemp, G. Kirov, B. Everitt, P. Hayward, and A. David, "Randomised Controlled Trial of Compliance Therapy: 18-Month Follow-up," *British Journal of Psychiatry*, 172 (1998): 413–419; D. Spooren, C. Van Heeringen, and C. Jannes, "Strategies to Increase Compliance with Outpatient Aftercare Among Patients Referred to a Psychiatric Emergency Department: A Multi-Centre Controlled Intervention Study," *Psychological Medicine*, 28 (1998): 949–956.

258 Being well informed: These issues are further discussed in K. R. Jamison, "Psychotherapeutic Issues and Suicide Prevention in the Treatment of Bipolar Disorders," in R. E. Hales and A. J. Frances, eds., *American Psychiatric Association Annual Review*, vol. 6 (Washington, D.C.: American Psychiatric Press, 1987), pp. 108–124; K. R. Jamison, "Suicide Prevention in Depressed Women," *Journal of Clinical Psychiatry*, 49 (1988): 42–45; F. K. Goodwin and K. R. Jamison, *Manic-Depressive Illness* (New York: Oxford University Press, 1990).

258 Several recent clinical studies: D. Miklowitz and M. Goldstein, "Behavioral Family Therapy Treatment for Patients with Bipolar Affective Disorder," *Behavioral Modification*, 14 (1990): 457–489; E. Van Gent and F. Zwart, "Psychoeducation of Partners of Bipolar Manic Patients," *Journal of Affective Disorders*, 21 (1991): 15–18; H. J. Moller, "Attempted Suicide: Efficacy of Different Aftercare Strategies," *International Clinical Psychopharmacology*, 6 (Suppl. 6) (1992): 58–59; C. A. King, J. D. Hovey, E. Brand, R. Wilson, and N. Ghaziuddin, "Suicidal Adolescents After Hospitalization: Parent and Family Impacts on Treatment Follow-through," *Journal of the American Academy of Child and Adolescent Psychiatry*, 36 (1997): 85–93; A. Perry, N. Tarrier, R. Morriss, E. McCarthy, and K. Limb, "Randomised Controlled Trial of Efficacy of Teaching Patients with Bipolar Disorder to Identify Early Symptoms of Relapse and Obtain Treatment," *British Medical Journal*, 318 (1999): 149–153.

259 "And, when our lives crack": Sylvia Plath, March 6, 1956, in T. Hughes and F. McCullough, eds., *The Journals of Sylvia Plath* (New York: Ballantine Books, 1983), p. 125.

260 Take your friend or family member seriously: National Depressive and Manic-Depressive Association, *Suicide and Depressive Illness* (Chicago: NDMDA, 1996). Detailed information about mental illness, medication, and suicide for doctors, patients, and family members can be found in R. J. Wyatt, *Practical Psychiatric Practice*, 2d ed. (Washington, D.C.: American Psychiatric Association Press, 1998).

263 "I have a mental disorder": A. Kent, "Perspectives," *Diversity & Distinction*, 2 (1996): 23.

263 "Take a look around": A. Kent, "Balancing Act: A Battle with Manic Depression Inspires One Student to Lead a Crusade for Mental Health Awareness," *Harvard Independent*, March 25, 1999.

9 · AS A SOCIETY

264 "As a society": D. Satcher, "Bringing the Public Health Approach to the Problem of Suicide," *Suicide and Life-Threatening Behavior*, 28 (1998): 325–327, p. 326. David Satcher was appointed by President Clinton in 1998 to the position of Assistant Secretary for Health and Surgeon General of the United States. A physician and scientist, Dr. Satcher previously served as Director of the Centers for Disease Control and Prevention in Atlanta.

265 "What was constant": P. Perl, "A Bridge He Could Not Cross," *Washington Post Magazine*, November 14, 1993.

267 twice as likely to kill themselves: K. D. Rose and I. Rosow, "Physicians Who Kill Themselves," *Archives of General Psychiatry*, 29 (1973): 800–805; C. L. Rich and F. N. Pitts, "Suicide by Male Physicians During a Five-Year Period," *American Journal of Psychiatry*, 136 (1979): 1089–1090; A. H. Rimpelä, M. M. Nurminen, P. O. Pulkkinen, M. K. Rimpelä, and T. Valkonen, "Mortality of Doctors: Do Doctors Benefit from their Medical Knowledge?" *Lancet*, 1 (1987): 84–86; S. Lindeman, E. Läärä, H. Hakko, and J. Lönnqvist, "A Systematic Review on Gender-Specific Suicide Mortality in Medical Doctors," *British Journal of Psychiatry*, 168 (1996): 274–279; K. Juel, J. Mosbech, and E. S. Hansen, "Mortality and Cause of Death Among Danish Physicians, 1973–1992." *Ugeskrift for Læger*, 159 (1997): 6512–6518.

267 Psychiatrists and anesthesiologists: D. L. Bruce, "Causes of Death Among Anesthesiologists: A 20-Year Survey," *Anesthesiology*, 29 (1968): 565–569; A. G. Craig and F. N. Pitts, "Suicide by Physicians," *Diseases of the Nervous System*, 29 (1968): 763–772; D. E. DeSole, P. Singer, and S. Aronson, "Suicide and Role Strain Among Physicians," *International Journal of Social Psychiatry*, 15 (1969): 294–301; C. L. Rich and F. N. Pitts, "Suicide by Psychiatrists: A Study of Medical Specialists Among 18,730 Consecutive Physician Deaths During a Five-Year Period, 1967–1972," *Journal of Clinical Psychiatry*, 41 (1980): 261–263; B. B. Arnetz, L. G. Hörte, A. Hedberg, T. Theorell, E. Allander, and H. Malker, "Suicide Patterns Among Physicians Related to Other Academics as Well as to the General Population," *Acta Psychiatrica Scandinavica*, 75 (1987): 139–143; L. M. Carpenter and A. J. Swerdlow, "Mortality of Doctors in Different Specialties: Findings from a Cohort of 20,000 NHS Hospital Consultants," *Occupational and Environmental Medicine*, 54 (1997): 388–395; S. Lindeman, E. Läärä, J. Hirvonen, and J. Lönnqvist, "Suicide Mortality Among Medical Doctors in Finland: Are Females More Prone to Suicide Than Their Male Colleagues?" *Psychological Medicine*, 27 (1997): 1219–1222.

267 women doctors are three to five: R. C. Steppacher and J. S. Mausner, "Suicide in Male and Female Physicians," *Journal of the American Medical Association*, 228 (1974): 323–328; F. N. Pitts, A. B. Schuller, C. L. Rich, and

A. F. Pitts, "Suicide Among U.S. Women Physicians, 1967–1972," *American Journal of Psychiatry*, 136 (1979): 694–696; F. Pepitone-Arreola-Rockwell, D. Rockwell, and N. Core, "Fifty-Two Medical Student Suicides," *American Journal of Psychiatry*, 138 (1981): 198–201; W. Simon, "Suicide Among Physicians: Prevention and Postvention," *Crisis*, 7 (1986): 1–13; S. M. Schlicht, I. R. Gordon, J. R. B. Ball, and D. G. S. Christie, "Suicide and Related Deaths in Victorian Doctors," *Medical Journal of Australia*, 153 (1990): 518–521; C.-G. Stefansson and S. Wicks, "Health Care Occupations and Suicide in Sweden 1961–1985," *Social Psychiatry and Psychiatric Epidemiology*, 26 (1991): 259–264; S. Lindeman, E. Läärä, H. Hakko, and J. Lönnqvist, "A Systematic Review on Gender-Specific Suicide Mortality in Medical Doctors," *British Journal of Psychiatry*, 168 (1996): 274–279; L. M. Carpenter and A. J. Swerdlow, "Mortality of Doctors in Different Specialties: Findings from a Cohort of 20,000 NHS Hospital Consultants," *Occupational and Environmental Medicine*, 54 (1997): 388–395; S. Lindeman, E. Läärä, J. Hirvonen, and J. Lönnqvist, "Suicide Mortality Among Medical Doctors in Finland: Are Females More Prone to Suicide Than Their Male Colleagues?" *Psychological Medicine*, 27 (1997): 1219–1222.

267 Women psychologists and chemists: P. H. Blachly, H. T. Osterud, and R. Josslin, "Suicide in Professional Groups," *New England Journal of Medicine*, 268 (1963): 1278–1282; F. P. Li, "Suicide Among Chemists," *Archives of Environmental Health*, 19 (1969): 518–520; H. King, "Health in the Medical and Other Learned Professions," *Journal of Chronic Disease*, 23 (1970): 257–281; J. S. Mausner and R. C. Steppacher, "Suicide in Professionals: A Study of Male and Female Psychologists," *American Journal of Epidemiology*, 98 (1973): 436–445; J. Walrath, F. P. Li, S. K. Hoar, M. W. Mead, and J. F. Fraumeni, "Causes of Death Among Female Chemists," *American Journal of Public Health*, 75 (1985): 883–885.

267 Women also probably experience: J. Firth-Cozens, "Sources of Stress in Women Junior House Officers," *British Medical Journal*, 301 (1990): 89–91.

268 stress and depression are common: K. Hsu and V. Marshall, "Prevalence of Depression and Distress in a Large Sample of Canadian Residents, Interns, and Fellows," *American Journal of Psychiatry*, 144 (1987): 1561–1566.

268 and sleep deprivation: T. A. Wehr, D. A. Sack, and N. E. Rosenthal, "Sleep Reduction as a Final Common Pathway in the Genesis of Mania," *American Journal of Psychiatry*, 144 (1987): 201–204; D. E. Duncan, *Residents: The Perils and Promise of Educating Young Doctors* (New York: Scribner, 1996).

268 "things seem inexplicable": S. B. Nuland, *How We Die: Reflections on Life's Final Chapter* (New York: Alfred A. Knopf, 1994), p. 151.

269 Yet nearly a third: B. Barraclough, J. Bunch, B. Nelson, and P. Sainsbury, "A Hundred Cases of Suicide: Clinical Aspects," *British Journal of Psychiatry*, 125 (1974): 355–373; K. Hawton and E. Blackstock, "General Practice Aspects of Self-Poisoning and Self-Injury," *Psychological Medicine*, 6 (1976): 571–575; J. Bancroft, A. Skrimshire, J. Casson, O. Harvard-Watts, and F. Reynolds, "People Who Deliberately Poison or Injure Themselves: Their Problems and Their Contacts With Helping Agencies," *Psychological Medicine*, 7 (1977): 289–303; D. H. Myers and C. D. Neal, "Suicide in Psychiatric Patients," *British Journal of Psychiatry*, 133 (1978): 38–44; J. Beskow, "Suicide and Mental Disorder in Swedish Men," *Acta Psychiatrica*

Scandinavica, 277 (Suppl.) (1979); S. E. Borg and M. Stahl, "Prediction of Suicide: A Prospective Study of Suicides and Control Among Psychiatric Patients," *Acta Psychiatrica Scandinavica*, 65 (1982): 221–232; R. M. Turner, "Parasuicide in an Urban General Practice, 1970–1979," *Journal of the Royal College of General Practice*, 32 (1982): 273–281; K. Petrie, "Recent General Practice Contacts of Hospitalized Suicide Attempters," *New Zealand Medical Journal*, 102 (1989): 130–131; E. T. Isometsä, M. E. Heikkinen, M. J. Marttunen, M. M. Henriksson, H. M. Aro, and J. K. Lönnqvist, "The Last Appointment Before Suicide: Is Suicide Intent Communicated?" *American Journal of Psychiatry*, 152 (1995): 919–922; L. Appleby, T. Amos, U. Doyle, B. Tomenson, and M. Woodman, "General Practitioners and Young Suicides: A Preventive Role for Primary Care," *British Journal of Psychiatry*, 168 (1996): 330–333; A. L. Beautrais, P. R. Joyce, and R. T. Mulder, "Psychiatric Contacts Among Youths Aged 13 Through 24 Years Who Have Made Serious Suicide Attempts," *Journal of the American Academy of Child and Adolescent Psychiatry*, 37 (1998): 504–511; J. Pirkis and P. Burgess, "Suicide and Recency of Health Care Contacts: A Systematic Review," *British Journal of Psychiatry*, 173 (1998): 462–474.

269 Some doctors remain skeptical: R. F. W. Diekstra and M. van Egmond, "Suicide and Attempted Suicide in General Practice, 1979–1986," *Acta Psychiatrica Scandinavica*, 79 (1989): 268–275; A. Macdonald, "The Myth of Suicide Prevention by General Practitioners," *British Journal of Psychiatry*, 163 (1993): 260; H. G. Morgan and M. O. Evans, "How Negative Are We to the Idea of Suicide Prevention?" *Journal of the Royal Society of Medicine*, 87 (1994): 622–625; K. Power, C. Davies, V. Swanson, D. Gordon, and H. Carter, "Case-Control Study of GP Attendance Rates by Suicide Cases with or Without a Psychiatric History," *British Journal of General Practice*, 47 (1997): 211–215.

269 the Swedish Committee for the Prevention and Treatment: W. Rutz, L. von Knorring, and J. Wålinder, "Frequency of Suicide on Gotland After Systematic Postgraduate Education of General Practitioners," *Acta Psychiatrica Scandinavica*, 80 (1989): 151–154; W. Rutz, J. Wålinder, G. Eberhard, G. Holmberg, A.-L. von Knorring, L. von Knorring, B. Wistedt, and A. Åberg-Wistedt, "An Educational Program on Depressive Disorders for General Practitioners on Gotland: Background and Evaluation," *Acta Psychiatrica Scandinavica*, 79 (1989): 19–26; A. Macdonald, "The Myth of Suicide Prevention by General Practitioners," *British Journal of Psychiatry*, 163 (1993): 260; H. G. Morgan and K. Hawton, "Suicide Prevention," *British Journal of Psychiatry*, 164 (1994): 126–127; J. M. G. Williams and R. D. Goldney, "Suicide Prevention in Gotland," *British Journal of Psychiatry*, 165 (1994): 692–698; Z. Rihmer, W. Rutz, and H. Pihlgren, "Depression and Suicide on Gotland: An Intensive Study of All Suicides Before and After a Depression-Training Program for General Practitioners," *Journal of Affective Disorders*, 35 (1995): 147–152.

270 Widespread screening: Canadian Task Force on the Periodic Health Examination, *Canadian Guide to Clinical Preventive Health Care* (Ottawa: Canada Communication Group, 1994), pp. 450–455; United States Preventive Services Task Force, "Screening for Depression," *Guide to Clinical Preventive Services*, 1996; C. P. Schade, E. R. Jones, and B. J. Wittlin, "A Ten-Year

Review of the Validity and Clinical Utility of Depression Screening," *Psychiatric Services*, 49 (1998): 55–61.

270 automated interviews: J. H. Greist, D. H. Gustafson, and F. A. Strauss, "A Computer Interview for Suicide-Risk Prediction," *American Journal of Psychiatry*, 130 (1973): 1327–1332; H. P. Erdman, J. H. Greist, D. H. Gustafson, J. E. Taves, and M. H. Klein, "Suicide Risk Prediction by Computer Interview: A Prospective Study," *Journal of Clinical Psychiatry*, 48 (1987): 464–467; S. Levine, R. J. Ancill, and A. P. Roberts, "Assessment of Suicide Risk by Computer-Delivered Self-Rating Questionnaire: Preliminary Findings," *Acta Psychiatrica Scandinavica*, 80 (1989): 216–220; K. A. Kobak, L. v. H. Taylor, S. L. Dottl, J. H. Greist, J. W. Jefferson, D. Burroughs, J. M. Mantle, D. J. Katzelnick, R. Norton, H. J. Henk, and R. C. Serlin, "A Computer-Administered Telephone Interview to Identify Mental Disorders," *Journal of the American Medical Association*, 278 (1997): 905–910.

270 National Depression Screening Day: D. G. Jacobs, "Depression Screening as an Intervention Against Suicide," *Journal of Clinical Psychiatry*, 60 (Suppl. 2) (1999): 42–45.

272 biological tests: V. Arango, M. D. Underwood, and J. J. Mann, "Postmortem Findings in Suicide Victims: Implications for *in Vivo* Imaging Studies," *Annals of the New York Academy of Sciences*, 836 (1997): 269–287; J. J. Mann, M. Oquendo, M. D. Underwood, and V. Arango, "The Neurobiology of Suicide Risk," *Journal of Clinical Psychiatry*, 60 (Suppl. 2) (1999): 7–11; A. Roy, D. Nielsen, G. Rylander, M. Sarchiapone, and N. Segal, "Genetics of Suicide in Depression," *Journal of Clinical Psychiatry*, 60 (Suppl. 2) (1999): 12–17.

272 young men in jails or prisons: Suicide rates in jails and prisons are three to five times the expected rate: J. E. Smialek and W. U. Spitz, "Death Behind Bars," *Journal of the American Medical Association*, 240 (1978): 2563–2564; D. O. Topp, "Suicide in Prison," *British Journal of Psychiatry*, 134 (1979): 24–27, R. L. Bonner, "Isolation, Seclusion, and Psychosocial Vulnerability as Risk Factors for Suicide Behind Bars," in R. W. Maris, A. L. Berman, J. T. Maltsberger, and R. I Yufit, eds., *Assessment and Prediction of Suicide* (New York: Guilford, 1992), pp. 398–419; A. R. Felthous, "Preventing Jailhouse Suicides," *Bulletin of the American Academy of Psychiatry and Law*, 22 (1994): 477–488; E. Blaauw, A. Kerkhof, and R. Vermunt, "Suicides and Other Deaths in Police Custody," *Suicide and Life-Threatening Behavior*, 27 (1997): 153–163; J. F. Cox and P. C. Morschauser, "A Solution to the Problem of Jail Suicide," *Crisis*, 18 (1977): 178–184; L. M. Hayes and E. Blaauw, "Prison Suicide: A Special Issue," *Crisis*, 18 (1997): 145–192; M. Joukamaa, "Prison Suicide in Finland, 1969–1992," *Forensic Science International*, 89 (1997): 167–174; N. H. Polvi, "Assessing Risk of Suicide in Correctional Settings," in C. D. Webster and M. A. Jackson, eds., *Impulsivity: Theory, Assessment, and Treatment* (New York: Guilford, 1997), pp. 278–301; F. Butterfield, "Prisons Replace Hospitals for the Nation's Mentally Ill," *New York Times*, March 5, 1998.

272 police officers: P. Friedman, "Suicide Among Police: A Study of Ninety-Three Suicides Among New York Policemen, 1934–1940," in E. Shneidman, ed., *Essays in Self-Destruction* (New York: Science House, 1968), pp. 414–449; C. H. Cantor, R. Tyman, and P. J. Slater, "A Historical Survey

of Police Suicide in Queensland, Australia, 1843–1992," *Suicide and Life-Threatening Behavior,* 25 (1995): 499–507; J. M. Violanti, *Police Suicide: Epidemic in Blue* (Springfield, Ill.: Charles C. Thomas, 1996).

272 gamblers: D. P. Phillips, W. R. Welty, and M. M. Smith, "Elevated Suicide Levels Associated with Legalized Gambling," *Suicide and Life-Threatening Behavior,* 27 (1997): 373–377.

272 homosexual and bisexual men: C. L. Rich, R. C. Fowler, D. Young, and M. Blenkush, "The San Diego Suicide Study: Comparison of Gay to Straight Males," *Suicide and Life-Threatening Behavior,* 16 (1986): 448–457; D. Shaffer, P. Fisher, R. Hicks, M. Parides, and M. Gould, "Sexual Orientation in Adolescents Who Commit Suicide," *Suicide and Life-Threatening Behavior,* 25 (Suppl.) (1995): 64–70; C. Bagley and P. Tremblay, "Suicidal Behaviors in Homosexual and Bisexual Males," *Crisis,* 18 (1997): 24–34; G. Remafedi, S. French, M. Story, M. D. Resnick, and R. Blum, "The Relationship Between Suicide Risk and Sexual Orientation: Results of a Population-Based Study," *Americal Journal of Public Health,* 88 (1998): 57–60.

272 Native Americans: J. Fox, D. Manitowabi, and J. A. Ward, "An Indian Community with a High Suicide Rate—5 Years After," *Canadian Journal of Psychiatry,* 29 (1984): 425–427; L. J. D. Wallace, A. D. Calhoun, K. E. Powell, J. O'Neil, and S. P. James, *Homicide and Suicide Among Native Americans, 1979–1992* (Atlanta, Ga.: Centers for Disease Control and Prevention), 1996; M. EchoHawk, "Suicide: The Scourge of Native American People," *Suicide and Life-Threatening Behavior,* 27 (1997): 60–67.

272 Alaskan adolescents: B. D. Gessner, "Temporal Trends and Geographic Patterns of Teen Suicide in Alaska, 1979–1993," *Suicide and Life-Threatening Behavior,* 27 (1997): 264–273.

272 young African-American males: J. T. Gibbs, ed., *Young, Black, and Male in America: An Endangered Species* (Westport, Conn.: Greenwood Press, 1988); D. Shaffer, M. Gould, and R. C. Hicks, "Worsening Suicide Rate in Black Teenagers," *American Journal of Psychiatry,* 151 (1994): 1810–1812; R. L. Taylor, ed., *African-American Youth: Their Social and Economic Status in the United States* (Westport, Conn.: Praeger, 1995); "Suicide Among Black Youths—United States, 1980–1995," *Morbidity and Mortality Weekly Report,* 47 (1998): 193–196.

273 adolescent boys in Micronesia: D. H. Rubinstein, "Epidemic Suicide Among Micronesian Adolescents," *Social Science and Medicine,* 17 (1983): 657–665; D. H. Rubinstein, "Suicide in Micronesia and Samoa: A Critique of Explanations," *Pacific Studies,* 15 (1992): 51–75; D. H. Rubinstein, "Suicidal Behaviour in Micronesia," in K. L. Peng and W.-S. Tseng, eds., *Suicidal Behaviour in the Asia-Pacific Region* (Kent Ridge, Singapore: University of Singapore Press, 1992), pp. 199–230.

273 inaccurate, misleading, and even damaging: J. C. Overholser, A. H. Hemstreet, A. Spirito, and S. Vyse, "Suicide Awareness Programs in the Schools: Effects of Gender and Personal Experience," *Journal of the American Academy of Child and Adolescent Psychiatry,* 28 (1989): 925–930; V. Vieland, B. Whittle, A. Garland, R. Hicks, and D. Shaffer, "The Impact of Curriculum-Based Suicide Prevention Programs for Teenagers: An 18-Month Follow-up," *Journal of the American Academy of Child and Adolescent*

Psychiatry, 30 (1991): 811–815; A. F. Garland and E. Zigler, "Adolescent Suicide Prevention: Current Research and Social Policy Implications," *American Psychologist,* 48 (1993): 169–182; J. J. Mazza, "School-Based Suicide Prevention Programs: Are They Effective?" *School Psychology Review,* 26 (1997): 382–396.

273 Some investigators: J. Ciffone, "Suicide Prevention: A Classroom Presentation to Adolescents," *Social Work,* 38 (1993): 197–203; J. Kalafat and M. Elias, "An Evaluation of School-Based Suicide Awareness Intervention," *Suicide and Life-Threatening Behavior,* 24 (1994): 224–233; L. L. Eggert, E. A. Thompson, J. R. Herting, and L. J. Nicholas, "Reducing Suicide Potential Among High-Risk Youth: Tests of a School-Based Prevention Program," *Suicide and Life-Threatening Behavior,* 25 (1995): 276–296; F. J. Zenere and P. J. Lazarus, "The Decline of Youth Suicidal Behavior in an Urban, Multicultural Public School System Following the Introduction of a Suicide Prevention and Intervention Program," *Suicide and Life-Threatening Behavior,* 27 (1997): 387–403.

273 The Australian review: P. Hazell and R. King, "Arguments for and Against Teaching Suicide Prevention in Schools," *Australian and New Zealand Journal of Psychiatry,* 30 (1996): 633–642, p. 640.

273 Canadians, likewise: J. Ploeg, D. Ciliska, M. Dobbins, S. Hayward, H. Thomas, and J. Underwood, "A Systematic Overview of Adolescent Suicide Prevention Programs," *Canadian Journal of Public Health,* 87 (1996): 319–324.

273 a comprehensive American survey: A. Metha, B. Weber, and L. Dean Webb, "Youth Suicide Prevention: A Survey and Analysis of Policies and Efforts in the 50 States," *Suicide and Life-Threatening Behavior,* 28 (1998): 150–164.

273 "Many curriculum-based programs": A. F. Garland and E. Zigler, "Adolescent Suicide Prevention: Current Research and Social Policy Implications," *American Psychologist,* 48 (1993): 169–182, pp. 174–175.

275 "students who indicated": A. Garland, D. Shaffer, and B. Whittle, "A National Survey of School-Based, Adolescent Suicide Prevention Programs," *Journal of the American Academy of Child and Adolescent Psychiatry,* 28 (1989): 931–934, p. 933.

275 David Shaffer and his colleagues: R. Beamish, "Computers Now Helping to Screen for Troubled Teen-Agers," *New York Times,* December 17, 1998; D. Shaffer and L. Craft, "Methods of Adolescent Suicide Prevention," *Journal of Clinical Psychiatry,* 60 (Suppl. 2) (1999): 70–74.

276 An early study: C. R. Bagley, "The Evaluation of a Suicide Prevention Scheme by an Ecological Method," *Social Science and Medicine,* 2 (1968): 1–14.

276 virtually every study since: I. Weiner, "The Effectiveness of a Suicide Prevention Program," *Mental Hygiene,* 53 (1969): 357–363; D. Lester, "The Myth of Suicide Prevention," *Comprehensive Psychiatry,* 13 (1972): 555–560; B. Bleach and W. L. Clairborn, "Initial Evaluation of Hot-Line Telephone Crisis Centers," *Community Mental Health Journal,* 10 (1974): 387–394; D. Lester, "Effect of Suicide Prevention Centers on Suicide Rates in the United States (Health Services Report, No. 89), 1974, pp. 37–39; R. Apster and M. Hodas, "Evaluating Hotlines with Simulated Calls," *Crisis Intervention,* 6 (1976): 14–21; T. P. Bridge, S. G. Potkin, W. W. K. Zung, and B. J.

Soldo, "Suicide Prevention Centres—Ecological Study of Effectiveness," *Journal of Nervous and Mental Diseases*, 164 (1977): 18–24; C. Jennings, B. M. Barraclough, and J. R. Moss, "Have the Samaritans Lowered the Suicide Rate?—A Controlled Study," *Psychological Medicine*, 8 (1978): 413–422; H. Hendin, *Suicide in America* (new and expanded edition) (New York: W. W. Norton, 1995).

277 "the body of every young woman": F. B. Winslow, *The Anatomy of Suicide* (Boston: Longwood Press, 1978; first published 1840), p. 179.

277 "The grenadier Groblin": Napoleon Bonaparte, quoted in F. B. Winslow, *The Anatomy of Suicide*, p.178.

278 "There are many examples": O. Anderson, *Suicide in Victorian and Edwardian England* (Oxford: Clarendon Press, 1987), pp. 372–373.

278 There has been no shortage: A. L. Kobler and E. Stotland, *The End of Hope: A Social-Clinical Study of Suicide* (New York: Free Press of Glencoe, 1964); J. A. Ward and J. Fox, "A Suicide Epidemic on an Indian Reserve," *Canadian Psychiatric Association Journal*, 22 (1977): 423–426; D. H. Rubinstein, "Epidemic Suicide Among Micronesian Adolescents," *Social Science and Medicine*, 17 (1983): 657–665; S. Fried, "Over the Edge," *Philadelphia Magazine*, October 1984; L. Coleman, *Suicide Clusters* (Boston: Faber and Faber, 1986); J. W. Farrell, M. E. Petrone, and W. E. Parkin, "Cluster of Suicides and Suicide Attempts—New Jersey," *Journal of the American Medical Association*, 259 (1988): 2666–2668; M. S. Gould, S. Wallenstein, and L. Davidson, "Suicide Clusters: A Critical Review," *Suicide and Life-Threatening Behavior*, 19 (1989): 17–29; T. Taiminen, T. Salmenperä, and K. Lehtinen, "A Suicide Epidemic in a Psychiatric Hospital," *Suicide and Life-Threatening Behavior*, 22 (1992): 350–363; N. Jans, "What Makes a Kid Happy One Day, Kill Himself the Next?" *USA Today*, July 16, 1997; S. Rimer, "For Old South Boston, Despair Replaces Hope," *New York Times*, August 17, 1997; J. Ritter, "Six Suicides Rattle Campus in Michigan," *USA Today*, July 10, 1997; P. Belluck, "In Little City Safe from Violence, Rash of Suicides Leaves Scars," *New York Times*, April 5, 1998; M. Jordan, "Overcome with Grief: Japanese Teens Distraught at Rock Star's Death," *Washington Post*, May 8, 1998.

279 in a study of: L. E. Davidson, M. L. Rosenberg, J. A. Mercy, J. Franklin, and J. T. Simmons, "An Epidemiologic Study of Risk Factors in Two Teenage Suicide Clusters," *Journal of the American Medical Association*, 262 (1989): 2687–2692.

279 Many researchers believe: J. A. Motto, "Suicide and Suggestibility—The Role of the Press," *American Journal of Psychiatry*, 124 (1967): 252–256; D. P. Phillips, "The Influence of Suggestion on Suicide: Substantive and Theoretical Implications of the Werther Effect," *American Sociological Review*, 39 (1974): 340–354; D. L. Altheide, "Airplane Accidents, Murder, and the Mass Media: Comments on Phillips," *Social Forces*, 60 (1981): 593–596; K. A. Bollen and D. P. Phillips, "Imitative Suicides: A National Study of the Effects of Television News Stories," *American Sociological Review*, 47 (1982): 802–809; I. M. Wasserman, "Imitation and Suicide: A Reexamination of the Werther Effect," *American Sociological Review*, 49 (1984): 427–436; J. N. Baron & P. C. Reiss, "Same Time, Next Year: Aggregate Analyses of the Mass Media and Violent Behavior," *American Sociological Review*, 50 (1985): 347–363; L. Eisenberg, "Does Bad News About Suicide Beget Bad News?"

New England Journal of Medicine, 315 (1986): 705–707; S. J. Ellis and S. Walsh, "Soap May Seriously Damage Your Health," *Lancet*, 1 (1986): 686; B. P. Fowler, "Emotional Crisis Imitating Television," *Lancet*, 1 (1986): 1036–1037; M. S. Gould and D. Shaffer, "The Impact of Suicide in Television Movies," *New England Journal of Medicine*, 315 (1986): 690–694; D. P. Phillips and L. Cartensen, "Clustering of Teenage Suicides After Television News Stories About Suicide," *New England Journal of Medicine*, 315 (1986): 685–689; D. A. Sandler, P. A. Connell, and K. Welsh, "Emotional Crises Imitating Television," *Lancet*, 1 (1986): 856; A. L. Berman, "Fictional Depiction of Suicide in Television Films and Imitation Effects," *American Journal of Psychiatry*, 145 (1988): 982–986; A. Schmidtke and H. Häfner, "The Werther Effect After Television Films: New Evidence for an Old Hypothesis," *Psychological Medicine*, 18 (1988): 665–676; L. Davidson and M. S. Gould, "Contagion as a Risk Factor for Youth Suicide," in *Report of the Secretary's Task Force on Youth Suicide*, Vol. 2: *Risk Factors for Youth Suicide* (DHHS Publication Number ADM-89-1622), Washington, D.C.: U.S. Government Printing Office, 1989; R. C. Kessler, G. Downey, H. Stipp, and J. R. Milavsky, "Network Television News Stories About Suicide and Short-Term Changes in Total U.S. Suicides," *Journal of Nervous and Mental Diseases*, 177 (1989): 551–555; M. S. Gould, "Suicide Clusters and Media Exposure," in S. J. Blumenthal and D. J. Kupfer, eds., *Suicide over the Life Cycle* (Washington, D.C.: American Psychiatric Press, 1990), pp. 517–532; S. Stack, "Media Impacts on Suicide," in D. Lester, ed., *Current Concepts of Suicide* (Philadelphia: Charles Press, 1990), pp. 107–120; K. Jonas, "Modelling and Suicide: A Test of the Werther Effect," *British Journal of Social Psychology*, 31 (1992): 295–306; S. Simkin, K. Hawton, L. Whitehead, J. Fagg, and M. Eagle, "Media Influence on Parasuicide: A Study of the Effects of a Television Drama Portrayal of Paracetamol Self-Poisoning," *British Journal of Psychiatry*, 167 (1995): 754–759; D. M. Velting and M. S. Gould, "Suicide Contagion," in R. W. Maris, M. M. Silverman, and S. S. Canetto, eds., *Review of Suicidology, 1997* (New York: Guilford, 1997), pp. 96–137.

279 In Hungary: S. Fekete and A. Schmidtke, "The Impact of Mass Media Reports on Suicide and Attitudes Toward Self-Destruction: Previous Studies and Some New Data from Hungary and Germany," in B. L. Mishara, ed., *The Impact of Suicide* (New York: Springer, 1995), pp. 142–155.

280 Centers for Disease Control: P. W. O'Carroll and L. B. Potter, Centers for Disease Control and Prevention, "Suicide Contagion and the Reporting of Suicide: Recommendations from a National Workshop," *Morbidity and Mortality Weekly Record*, 43 (1994): No. SS-6, 9–18, pp. 14–16.

283 Olive Anderson traces: O. Anderson, *Suicide in Victorian and Edwardian England* (Oxford: Clarendon Press, 1987).

283 if deprived of one method: E. Stengel, *Suicide and Attempted Suicide* (Harmondsworth, England: Penguin, 1964); C. Hassall and W. H. Trethowan, "Suicide in Birmingham," *British Medical Journal*, 1 (1972): 717–718; R. G. Oliver, "Rise and Fall of Suicide Rates in Australia: Relation to Sedative Availability," *Medical Journal of Australia*, 2 (1972): 1208–1209; A. Malleson, "Suicide Prevention: A Myth or a Mandate?" *British Journal of Psychiatry*, 122 (1973): 238–239; F. A. Whitlock, "Suicide in Brisbane, 1956 to 1973: The Drug-Death Epidemic," *Medical Journal of Australia*, 1 (1975):

737–743; N. Kreitman, "The Coal Gas Story: United Kingdom Suicide Rates, 1960–71," *British Journal of Preventive and Social Medicine*, 30 (1976): 86–93; M. Boor, "Methods of Suicide and Implications for Suicide Prevention," *Journal of Clinical Psychology*, 37 (1981): 70–75; J. A. Vale and T. J. Meredith, *Poisoning: Diagnosis and Treatment* (London: Update Publications, 1981); N. Kreitman and S. Platt, "Suicide, Unemployment, and Domestic Gas Detoxification in Britain," *Journal of Epidemiology and Community Health*, 38 (1984): 1–6; P. Sainsbury, "The Epidemiology of Suicide," in A. Roy, ed., *Suicide* (Baltimore: Williams & Wilkins, 1986), pp. 17–40; R. V. Clarke and D. Lester, "Toxicity of Car Exhausts and Opportunity for Suicide: Comparison Between Britain and the United States," *Journal of Epidemiology and Community Health*, 41 (1987): 114–120; S. A. Montgomery and R. M. Pinder, "Do Some Antidepressants Promote Suicide?" *Psychopharmacology*, 92 (1987): 265–266; S. A. Montgomery, M. T. Lambert, and S. P. J. Lynch, "The Risk of Suicide and Antidepressants," *International Clinical Psychopharmacology*, 3 (1988): 15–24; P. W. Burvill, "The Changing Pattern of Suicide by Gassing in Australia, 1910–1987: The Role of Natural Gas and Motor Vehicles," *Acta Psychiatrica Scandinavica*, 81 (1989): 178–184; C. H. Cantor and M. A. Hill, "Suicide from River Bridges," *Australian and New Zealand Journal of Psychiatry*, 24 (1990): 377–380; S. Donovan and H. Freeman, "Deaths Related to Antidepressants: A Reconsideration," *Journal of Drug Development*, 3 (1990): 113–120; D. Lester, "The Effect of the Detoxification of Domestic Gas in Switzerland on the Suicide Rate," *Acta Psychiatrica Scandinavica*, 82 (1990): 383–384; M. J. Kelleher, M. Daly, and M. J. A. Kelleher, "The Influence of Antidepressants in Overdose on the Increased Suicide Rate in Ireland Between 1971 and 1988," *British Journal of Psychiatry*, 161 (1992): 625–628; G. Kleck, *Point Blank: Guns and Violence in America* (New York: Aldine de Gruyter, 1992); P. M. Marzuk, A. C. Leon, K. Tardiff, E. B. Morgan, M. Stajic, and J. J. Mann, "The Effect of Access to Lethal Methods of Injury on Suicide Rates," *Archives of General Psychiatry*, 49 (1992): 451–458; G. Isacsson, P. Holmgren, D. Wasserman, and U. Bergman, "Use of Antidepressants Among People Committing Suicide in Sweden," *British Medical Journal*, 308 (1994): 506–509; P. W. O'Carroll and M. M. Silverman, "Community Suicide Prevention: The Effectiveness of Bridge Barriers," *Suicide and Life-Threatening Behavior*, 24 (1994): 89–99; J. G. Edwards, "Suicide and Antidepressants," *British Medical Journal*, 310 (1995): 205–206; S. S. Jick, A. D. Dean, and H. Jick, "Antidepressants and Suicide," *British Medical Journal*, 310 (1995): 215–218; A. Ohberg, J. Lönnqvist, S. Sarna, E. Vuori, and A. Penttila, "Trends and Availability of Suicide Methods in Finland: Proposals for Restrictive Measures," *British Journal of Psychiatry*, 166 (1995): 35–43; M. W. Battersby, J. J. O'Mahoney, A. R. Beckwith, and J. L. Hunt, "Antidepressant Deaths by Overdose," *Australian and New Zealand Journal of Psychiatry*, 30 (1996): 223–228; A. Carlsten, P. Allebeck, and L. Brandt, "Are Suicide Rates in Sweden Associated with Changes in the Prescribing of Medicines?" *Acta Psychiatrica Scandinavica*, 94 (1996): 94–100; A. Ohberg, E. Vuori, I. Ojanperä, and J. Lönnqvist, "Alcohol and Drugs in Suicide," *British Journal of Psychiatry*, 169 (1996): 75–80; M. Öström, J. Thorson, and A. Eriksson, "Carbon Monoxide Suicide from Car Exhausts," *Social Science and Medicine*,

42 (1996): 447–451; J. Neeleman and S. Wessely, "Drugs Taken in Fatal and Non-Fatal Self-Poisoning: A Study in South London," *Acta Psychiatrica Scandinavica*, 95 (1997): 283–287; K. Hawton, "Why Has Suicide Increased in Young Males?" *Crisis*, 19 (1998): 119–124; E. T. Isometsä and J. K. Lönnqvist, "Suicide Attempts Preceding Completed Suicide," *British Journal of Psychiatry*, 173 (1998): 531–535; D. Gunnell, H. Wehner, and S. Frankel, "Sex Differences in Suicide Trends in England and Wales," *Lancet*, 353 (1999): 556–557.

283 During perestroika: I. M. Wasserman, "The Effect of War and Alcohol Consumption Patterns on Suicide: United States, 1910–1933," *Social Forces*, 68 (1989): 513–530; D. Wasserman, A. Värnik, and G. Eklund, "Male Suicides and Alcohol Consumption in the Former USSR," *Acta Psychiatrica Scandinavica*, 89 (1994): 306–313; A. Värnick, D. Wasserman, M. Dankowicz, and G. Eklund, "Marked Decrease in Suicide Among Men and Women in the Former USSR During *Perestroika*," *Acta Psychiatrica Scandinavica*, 98 (Suppl. 394) (1998): 13–19.

284 in 1996, 60 percent: U.S. National Center for Health Statistics, *Vital Statistics of the United States*, Monthly Report, 45 (Washington, D.C.: U.S. Government Printing Office, 1997).

284 a gun in the home: D. A. Brent, J. A. Perper, C. E. Goldstein, D. J. Kolko, M. J. Allan, C. J. Allman, and J. P. Zelenak, "Risk Factors for Adolescent Suicide: A Comparison of Adolescent Suicide Victims with Suicidal Inpatients," *Archives of General Psychiatry*, 45 (1988): 581–588; M. Boor and J. H. Bair, "Suicide Rates, Handgun Control Laws, and Sociodemographic Variables," *Psychological Reports*, 66 (1990): 923–930; D. Lester, "The Availability of Firearms and the Use of Firearms for Suicide: A Study of 20 Countries," *Acta Psychiatrica Scandinavica*, 81 (1990): 146–147; J. H. Sloan, F. P. Rivara, D. T. Reay, J. A. J. Ferris, and A. L. Kellerman, "Firearm Regulations and Rates of Suicide: A Comparison of Two Metropolitan Areas," *New England Journal of Medicine*, 322 (1990): 369–373; D. A. Brent, J. A. Perper, C. J. Allman, G. M. Moritz, and M. E. Wartella, "The Presence and Accessibility of Firearms in the Homes of Adolescent Suicides: A Case-Control Study," *Journal of the American Medical Association*, 266 (1991): 2989–2995; C. Loftin, D. McDowall, B. Wiersema, and T. J. Cottey, "Effects of Restrictive Licensing of Handguns on Homicide and Suicide in the District of Columbia," *New England Journal of Medicine*, 325 (1991): 1615–1620; A. L. Kellerman, F. P. Rivara, G. Somes, D. T. Reay, J. Francisco, J. G. Banton, J. Prodzinski, C. Fligner, and B. B. Hackman, "Suicide in the Home in Relation to Gun Ownership," *New England Journal of Medicine*, 327 (1992): 467–472; D. A. Brent, J. A. Perper, G. Moritz, M. Baugher, J. Schweers, and C. Roth, "Firearms and Adolescent Suicide: A Community Case-Control Study," *American Journal of Diseases of Children*, 147 (1993): 1066–1071; M. Killias, "International Correlations Between Gun Ownership and Rates of Homicide and Suicide," *Canadian Medical Association Journal*, 148 (1993): 1721–1725; D. Hemenway, S. J. Solnick, and D. R. Azrael, "Firearm Training and Storage," *Journal of the American Medical Association*, 273 (1995): 46–50; R. J. Blendon, J. T. Young, and D. Hemenway, "The American Public and the Gun Control Debate," *Journal of the American Medical Association*, 275 (1996): 1719–1722; P. Cummings, T. D. Koepsell, D. C.

Grossman, J. Savarino, and R. S. Thompson, "The Association Between the Purchase of a Handgun and Homicide or Suicide," *American Journal of Public Health*, 87 (1997): 974–978; J. Hintikka, J. Lehtonen, and V. Viinamäki, "Hunting Guns in Homes and Suicides in 15–24 Year–Old Males in Eastern Finland," *Australian and New Zealand Journal of Psychiatry*, 31 (1977): 858–861; M. S. Kaplan and O. Geling, "Firearm Suicides and Homicides in the United States: Regional Variations and Patterns of Gun Ownership," *Social Science and Medicine*, 46 (1998): 1227–1233; M. Miller and D. Hemenway, "The Relationship Between Firearms and Suicide: A Review of the Literature," *Aggression and Violent Behavior*, 4 (1999): 59–75.

284 The American Academy of Pediatricians: L. Adelson, "The Gun and the Sanctity of Human Life: Or the Bullet as Pathogen," *Archives of Surgery*, 127 (1992): 171–176; T. L. Cheng and R. A. Lowe, "Taking Aim at Firearm Injuries," *American Journal of Emergency Medicine*, 11 (1993): 183–186; J. J. Tepas, "Gun Control Legislation: A Major Public Health Issue for Children," *Journal of Pediatric Surgery*, 29 (1994): 369; C. W. Schwab and D. R. Kauder, "Trauma Surgeons on Violence Prevention," *Trauma*, 40 (1996): 671–672.

284 A survey of one thousand surgeons: C. K. Cassel, E. A. Nelson, T. W. Smith, C. W. Schwab, B. Barlow, and N. E. Gary, "Internists' and Surgeons' Attitudes Toward Guns and Firearm Injury Prevention," *Annals of Internal Medicine*, 128 (1998): 224–230.

285 The American public: American Academy of Pediatrics Committee on Adolescence, "Firearms and Adolescents," *Pediatrics*, 89 (1992): 784–787; P. Cummings, D. C. Grossman, F. P. Rivara, and T. D. Koepsell, "State Gun Safe Storage Laws and Child Mortality Due to Firearms," *Journal of the American Medical Association*, 278 (1997): 1084–1086; S. P. Teret, D. W. Webster, J. S. Vernick, T. W. Smith, D. Leff, G. J. Wintemute, P. J. Cook, D. F. Hawkins, A. L. Kellerman, S. B. Sorenson, and S. De Francesco, "Support for New Policies to Regulate Firearms," *New England Journal of Medicine*, 339 (1998): 813–818.

285 The Swedish National Program: The recommendations for reducing the availability of instruments of suicide are taken directly from Swedish National Council for Suicide Prevention, "Support in Suicidal Crises: The Swedish National Program to Develop Suicide Prevention," *Crisis*, 18 (1997): 65–72, p. 71.

286 including Norway, Finland: J. Lönnqvist, "National Suicide Prevention Project in Finland: A Research Phase of the Project," *Psychiatrica Fennica*, 19 (1988): 125–132; J. Lönnqvist, H. Aro, M. Heikkinen, H. Heilä, M. Henriksson, E. Isometsä, K. Kuurne, M. Marttunen, A. Ostamo, M. Pelkonen, S. Pirkola, J. Suokas, and K. Suominen, "Project Plan for Studies on Suicide, Attempted Suicide, and Suicide Prevention," *Crisis*, 16 (1995): 162–175; J. Hakanen and M. Upanne, "Evaluation Strategy for Finland's Suicide Prevention Project," *Crisis*, 17 (1996): 167–174; S. J. Taylor, D. Kingdom, and R. Jenkins, "How Are Nations Trying to Prevent Suicide?: An Analysis of National Suicide Prevention Strategies," *Acta Psychiatrica Scandinavica*, 95 (1997): 457–463.

286 The World Health Organization: World Health Organization, "Consulta-

tion on Strategies for Reducing Suicidal Behaviours in the European Region: Summary Report" (Geneva: World Health Organization, 1990).

286 the United Kingdom: Secretary of State for Health, *The Health of the Nation: A Strategy for Health in England* (London: HMSO, 1992).

286 The Royal College of Psychiatrists: E. S. Paykel, D. Hart, and R. G. Priest, "Changes in Public Attitudes to Depression During the Defeat Depression Campaign," *British Journal of Psychiatry*, 173 (1998): 519–522.

286 There is also in Britain: J. McKerrow, "Community Care for Mentally Ill," *The Times* (London), April 24, 1999.

287 "Resolved, That the Senate": U.S. Senate, "Suicide in America," *Congressional Record*, 143(57) (1998): 1–2.

288 These groups were brought together: D. Satcher, "Bringing the Public Health Approach to the Problem of Suicide," *Suicide and Life-Threatening Behavior*, 28 (1998): 325–327.

288 His 1999 *Surgeon General's Report*: United States Public Health Service, *The Surgeon General's Call to Action to Prevent Suicide* (Washington, D.C., 1999).

288 Nor is major success: H. G. Morgan, "Suicide Prevention: Hazards in the Fast Lane of Community Care," *British Journal of Psychiatry*, 160 (1992): 149–153; M. Goldacre, V. Seagrott, and K. Hawton, "Suicide After Discharge from Psychiatric Inpatient Care," *Lancet*, 342 (1993): 283–286; P. B. Mortensen and K. Juel, "Mortality and Causes of Death in First Admitted Schizophrenic Patients," *British Journal of Psychiatry*, 163 (1993): 183–189; A. Bass, "DMH Sees Increase in Deaths," *Boston Globe*, June 11, 1995; R. McKeon, "The Impact of Managed Care on Suicidal Patients," paper presented to the American Association of Suicidology Annual Meeting, Bethesda, Md., April 1998; J. Rabinowitz, E. J. Bromet, J. Lavelle, K. J. Severance, S. L. Zariello, and B. Rosen, "Relationship Between Type of Insurance and Care During the Early Course of Psychosis," *American Journal of Psychiatry*, 155 (1998): 1392–1397; J. M. Zito, D. J. Safer, S. dos Reis, and M. A. Riddle, "Racial Disparity in Psychotropic Medications Prescribed for Youths with Medicaid Insurance in Maryland," *Journal of the American Academy of Child and Adolescent Psychiatry*, 37 (1998): 179–184.

10 · A HALF-STITCHED SCAR

291 "less sharp": A. Toynbee, A. K. Mant, N. Smart, J. Hinton, S. Yudkin, E. Rhode, R. Heywood, and H. H. Price, *Man's Concern with Death* (St. Louis: McGraw-Hill, 1968), p. 271.

292 "The question of suicide": E. R. Ellis and G. N. Allen, *Traitor Within: Our Suicide Problem* (New York: Doubleday, 1961), p. 176.

293 Although it might seem otherwise: D. Shepherd and B. M. Barraclough, "The Aftermath of Suicide," *British Medical Journal*, 2 (1974): 600–603; A. S. Demi, "Social Adjustment of Widows After a Sudden Death: Suicide and Non-Suicide Survivors Compared," *Death Education*, 8 (1984): 91–111; L. G. Calhoun, C. B. Abernathy, and J. W. Selby, "The Rules of Bereavement: Are Suicidal Deaths Different?" *Journal of Community Psychology*, 14 (1986): 213–218; M. P. H. D. Cleiren, *Adaptation After Bereavement: A Com-*

parative Study of the Aftermath of Death from Suicide, Traffic Accident and Illness for Next of Kin (Leiden: DSWO Press, 1991); B. B. Cohen, "Holocaust Survivors and the Crisis of Aging," *Families in Society*, 72 (1991): 226–231; M. P. H. D. Cleiren, "After the Loss: Bereavement After Suicide and Other Types of Death," in B. L. Mishara, *The Impact of Suicide* (New York: Springer, 1995), pp. 7–39.

294 Friends and neighbors may or may not: L. G. Calhoun, J. W. Selby, and M. E. Faulstich, "Reactions to the Parents of the Child Suicide: A Study of Social Impressions," *Journal of Consulting and Clinical Psychology*, 48 (1980): 535–536; L. G. Calhoun, J. W. Selby, and L. E. Selby, "The Psychological Aftermath of Suicide: An Analysis of Current Evidence," *Clinical Psychology Review*, 2 (1982): 409–420.

294 one-third of family members report: M. I. Solomon, "The Bereaved and the Stigma of Suicide," *Omega*, 13 (1982–83): 377–387.

294 one in ten family members: S. Wallace, *After Suicide* (New York: Wiley, 1973); K. E. Rudestam, "Physical and Psychological Responses to Suicide in the Family," *Journal of Consulting and Clinical Psychology*, 45 (1977): 162–170.

295 "An equal number of parents": M. Séguin, A. Lesage, and M. C. Kiely, "Parental Bereavement After Suicide and Accident: A Comparative Study," *Suicide and Life-Threatening Behavior*, 25 (1995): 489–498, p. 493.

295 "I'd wake up at night": C. J. Van Dongen, "Agonizing Questioning: Experiences of Survivors of Suicide Victims," *Nursing Research*, 39 (1990): 224–229, pp. 226, 227.

295 Many fathers and mothers: A. Herzog and H. L. Resnick, "A Clinical Study of Parental Response to Adolescent Death by Suicide with Recommendations for Approaching Survivors," *British Journal of Social Psychiatry*, 3 (1969): 144–152; K. E. Rudestam, "Physical and Psychological Responses to Suicide in the Family," *Journal of Consulting and Clinical Psychology*, 45 (1977): 162–170; S. M. Vallente and C. L. Halton, "Bereavement Group for Parents Who Suffered a Suicidal Loss of an Adolescent or Youth," *Dépression et Suicide*, (1981): 509–510; T. A. Rando, "Bereaved Parents: Particular Difficulties, Unique Factors and Treatment Issues," *Social Work* (1985): 19–23.

296 Mothers in particular: D. A. Brent, G. Moritz, J. Bridge, J. Perper, and R. Canobbio, "The Impact of Adolescent Suicide on Siblings and Parents: A Longitudinal Follow-up," *Suicidal and Life-Threatening Behavior*, 26 (1996): 253–259.

296 "During the past ten years": I. M. Bolton, "Our Son Mitch," in E. J. Dunne, J. L. McIntosh, and K. Dunne-Maxim, eds., *Suicide and Its Aftermath* (New York: W. W. Norton, 1987), pp. 85–94, p. 92.

297 "I don't know why": I. M. Bolton, *My Son . . . My Son . . . : A Guide to Healing After Death, Loss, or Suicide* (Atlanta: Bolton Press, 1983).

298 relatively few long-term adverse: D. A. Brent, G. Moritz, J. Bridge, J. Perper, and R. Canobbio, "The Impact of Adolescent Suicide on Siblings and Parents."

298 depression was common: D. A. Brent, J. A. Perper, G. Moritz, L. Liotus, J. Schweers, C. Roth, L. Balach, and C. Allman, "Psychiatric Impact of the Loss of an Adolescent Sibling to Suicide," *Journal of Affective Disorders*, 28 (1993): 249–256.

298 Adolescents, when asked: D. Balk, "Adolescents' Grief Reactions and Self-

Concept Perceptions Following Sibling Death," *Journal of Youth and Adolescence*, 12 (1983): 137–161.

298 "He never missed a year": K. Dunne-Maxim, "Survivors and the Media: Pitfalls and Potential," in E. J. Dunne, J. L. McIntosh, and K. Dunne-Maxim, eds., *Suicide and Its Aftermath* (New York: W. W. Norton, 1987), pp. 45–56, p. 47.

300 "I had the strange feeling": T. Organ, "Grief and the Art of Consolation: A Personal Testimony," *The Christian Century*, 96 (1979): 759–762; quoted in J. L. McIntosh, "Survivor Family Relationships: Literature Review," in E. J. Dunne, J. L. McIntosh, and K. Dunne-Maxim, eds., *Suicide and Its Aftermath* (New York: W. W. Norton, 1987), pp. 83–84.

301 long-term psychological outcome: A. C. Cain and I. Fast, "The Legacy of Suicide: Observations on the Pathogenic Impact of Suicide upon Marital Partners," *Psychiatry*, 29 (1966): 406–411; D. Shepherd and B. M. Barraclough, "The Aftermath of Suicide," *British Medical Journal*, 15 June 1974: 600–603; A. S. Demi, "Social Adjustment of Widows After a Sudden Death: Suicide and Non-Suicide Survivors Compared," *Death Education*, 8 (Suppl.) (1984): 91–111; D. E. McNiel, C. Hatcher, and R. Reubin, "Family Survivors of Suicide and Accidental Death: Consequences for Widows," *Suicide and Life-Threatening Behavior*, 18 (1988): 137–148; T. W. Barrett and T. B. Scott, "Suicide Bereavement and Recovery Patterns Compared with Non-suicide Bereavement Patterns," *Suicide and Life-Threatening Behavior*, 20 (1990): 1–15; M. P. H. D. Cleiren, O. Grad, A. Zavasnik, and R. F. W. Diekstra, "Psychosocial Impact of Bereavement After Suicide and Fatal Traffic Accident: A Comparative Two Country Study," *Acta Psychiatrica Scandinavica*, 94 (1996): 37–44.

301 "From the first moment": J. Pesaresi, "When One of Us Is Gone," in E. J. Dunne, J. L. McIntosh, and K. Dunne-Maxim, eds., *Suicide and Its Aftermath* (New York: W. W. Norton, 1987), pp. 104–108, pp. 105, 106.

303 "This thin, wan, passive boy": A. C. Cain and I. Fast, "Children's Disturbed Reactions to Parent Suicide: Distortions of Guilt, Communication, and Identification," in A. C. Cain, ed., *Survivors of Suicide* (Springfield, Ill.: Charles C. Thomas, 1972), pp. 93–111, p. 97.

303 "Mummy was very depressed": D. M. Shepherd and B. M. Barraclough, "The Aftermath of Parental Suicide for Children," *British Journal of Psychiatry*, 129 (1976): 267–276, p. 269.

303 "He had a sickness": Pesaresi, "When One of Us Is Gone," p. 104.

304 "On a hot August afternoon": C. Lukas and H. M. Seiden, *Silent Grief: Living in the Wake of Suicide* (Northvale, N.J.: Jason Aronson, 1997), pp. 3–4.

305 "In discussing my childhood": J. Logan, *Josh: My Up and Down, In and Out Life* (New York: Delacorte, 1976), pp. 386–387.

306 "Reflexions on suicide": J. Berryman, "Of Suicide," in C. Thornbury, ed., *John Berryman: Collected Poems 1937–1971*, (New York, Noonday Press, 1989, 1999), p. 206, ll. 1, 27.

306 "Save us from shotguns": J. Berryman, "235," in *The Dream Songs* (New York: Farrar, Straus and Giroux, 1969), p. 254, ll. 7, 16–18.

306 "The marker slants, flowerless": J. Berryman, "384," in *The Dream Songs* p. 406, ll. 1–8.

307 "Just as the last time": Lewis Grassic Gibbon, *Sunset Song* (Edinburgh: Canongate, 1988; first published 1932), pp. 63, 64.

EPILOGUE

311 "Look to the living": Douglas Dunn, "Disenchantments," in D. Dunn, *Dante's Drum-kit* (London: Faber and Faber, 1993), p. 46.

Acknowledgments

I AM INDEBTED to many people for their help during the writing of this book. Drew Sopirak's parents, Andrew and Allyn, allowed me access to his medical records; talked with me and wrote to me at length about his life and death; shared his writings, drawings, photographs, and books; and encouraged me to talk with his high school friends and teachers, as well as his instructors and fellow cadets from the U.S. Air Force Academy. To the following people I owe my appreciation for their time, interviews, letters, and memories: Lt. Colonel Philip Bossert, Jr., Tom Buckley, Tam Bui, Ellen Fitzgerald, Dr. Joseph Galema, Judy Landis, Janna Mattey, Major Stephen Pluntze, Lt. David Shoemaker, Paul and Kay Spangler, Kerri Whittaker, and Stephen Wood.

The staff of the National Institutes of Health Library were particularly helpful in tracking down the scientific and clinical literature on suicide. I also used extensively the William H. Welch Medical Library of the Johns Hopkins School of Medicine, Georgetown University Library, the University of St. Andrews Library, the London Library (which files its books about suicide on the "Science and Miscellaneous" shelves between "Sugar" and "Sundials"), and the National Gallery of Art Library in Washington, D.C. Mildred L. Amer, who is with the Congressional Research Service of the Library of Congress, assisted in locating information about U.S. Congressmen who died of other than natural causes. Mrs. J. M. Buckberry, Librarian and Archivist of the Royal Air Force College in England, sent me material about the history and literature of aviation.

Dr. Alex Crosby, with the Centers for Disease Control and Prevention in Atlanta; Dr. Eve Mościcki, from the epidemiology branch of the National Institute of Mental Health; and Ken Kochanek, M.A., with the Mortality Branch of the National Center for Health Statistics, were very helpful in providing me with up-to-date suicide statistics. Dr. Robert Gallo and Dr. Farley Cleghorn, with the Institute of Virology at the University of Maryland, and Dr. Harry Rosenberg, Chief of the Mortality Statistics Branch of the Centers for Disease Control and Prevention, provided AIDS mortality statistics. Tom Campbell and Roger Jorstad in the Department of Defense sent me Vietnam War mortality data. Broadcast journalist Paul Berry provided me with background information and videotape footage about his friend John Wilson, the former chairman of the D.C. Council.

Many of my colleagues, along with other individuals, were kind enough to send me manuscripts or works-in-progress; others shared new data, illustrations, or opinions about ongoing research protocols. I am indebted to Dr. Eileen Ahearn, Duke University Medical Center; Dr. Marie Åsberg, the Karolinska Institute in Stockholm; Dr. Susan Bachus, the Clinical Brain Disorders Branch of

Acknowledgments

the National Institute of Mental Health; Dr. Aaron Beck, University of Pennsylvania; Dr. Lanny Berman, American Association of Suicidology; Virginia Betts, R.N., J.D., in the U.S. Surgeon General's office; Dr. Emil Coccaro, University of Chicago; Dr. Francis Collins and his staff at the National Human Genome Research Institute; Dr. Jerry Cott, National Institute of Mental Health; Dr. Joseph Coyle, Harvard Medical School; Dr. Lucy Davidson, Emory University School of Medicine; Lamia Doumato, National Gallery of Art; Karen Dunne-Maxim, R.N.; Colonel Molly Hall, U.S. Air Force; Dr. Dan Herman, New York Psychiatric Institute; Dr. Herb Hendin, New York Medical College and the American Foundation for Suicide Prevention; Dr. Joseph Hibbeln, Laboratory of Membrane Biochemistry and Biophysics, National Institute on Alcohol Abuse and Alcoholism; Dr. J. Dee Higley, Primate Unit, National Institute on Alcohol Abuse and Alcoholism; Liz Hylton, the *Washington Post;* Dr. Steven Hyman, National Institute of Mental Health; Dr. Joanne Leslie, UCLA School of Public Health; Dr. John Mann, Columbia University; the Viscount Norwich; Dr. Barbara Parry, University of Calilfornia, San Diego; Dr. Alec Roy, Veteran Affairs Medical Center, New Jersey; Dr. David Rubinow, National Institute of Mental Health; Dr. Donald Rubenstein, Stanford University and the University of Guam; Dr. Matthew Rudorfer, National Institute of Mental Health; Dr. David Shaffer, Columbia University; Dr. John Smialek, Chief Medical Examiner for the State of Maryland; Dr. Michael Sopher, UCLA Department of Anesthesiology; David Sturtevant, Museum of Fine Arts, Boston; Dr. Ezra Susser, New York Psychiatric Institute; Ian Tattersall, American Museum of Natural History; Dr. E. Fuller Torrey, the Stanley Foundation; Dr. Tom Wehr, National Institute of Mental Health; Dr. Myrna Weissman, Columbia University; and Dr. Peter Whybrow, UCLA School of Medicine.

I am deeply appreciative to my colleagues who carefully reviewed my manuscript and offered numerous and very helpful suggestions: Dr. Samuel Barondes, University of California, San Francisco School of Medicine; Dr. Lucy Davidson, Emory University School of Medicine; Dr. Ellen Frank, University of Pittsburgh School of Medicine; Dr. Dean Jamison, UCLA School of Public Health; Dr. David Kupfer, University of Pittsburgh School of Medicine; Dr. John Mann, Columbia University, College of Physicians and Surgeons; Dr. Charles Nemeroff, Emory University School of Medicine; Dr. Norman Rosenthal, National Institute of Mental Health; and Dr. Anthony Storr of Oxford, England.

I am particularly grateful to the following people for their friendship and support: Dr. Daniel Auerbach, David Mahoney, Dr. Anthony Storr, Dr. and Mrs. James Ballenger, Robert Boorstin, Lucie Bryant, Dr. Raymond De Paulo and my other colleagues at Johns Hopkins, Professor Douglas Dunn, Dr. Robert Faguet and Dr. Kay Faguet, Antonello and Christina Fanna, Mrs. Katharine Graham, Charles and Gwenda Hyman, Earl and Helen Kindle, Dr. Athanasio Koukopoulos, Senator George McGovern, Dr. Paul McHugh, Alain Moreau, Clarke and Wendy Oler, Victor and Harriet Potik, Senator Robert Packwood, Dr. Norman Rosenthal, Dr. Per Vestergaard, Dr. Jeremy Waletzky, Dr. and Mrs. James Watson, and Professor Robert Winter. During a difficult time, Senator Orrin Hatch extended kindness and his friendship, which has meant a great deal to me. So too has the friendship of songwriter Mickey Newbury, whose words and music have been a sad and lovely thread throughout my life for thirty years.

Acknowledgments

Carol Janeway, my editor at Alfred A. Knopf, has been remarkable, and I cannot imagine that I could have had the privilege of working with anyone better. Stephanie Katz, also at Knopf, has been enormously helpful. I am indebted, as well, to Paul Bogaards and William Loverd at Knopf, and to my agent, Maxine Groffsky. William Collins, who has typed all of my manuscripts, has been simply wonderful. Silas Jones has helped me on a nearly daily basis, and I am deeply grateful to him for everything he has done to make my life easier.

As always, I owe my family everything: my mother, Dell Jamison; my father, Marshall Jamison; Danica and Kelda Jamison; Joanne Leslie; Julian, Eliot, and Leslie Jamison; Kin Bing Wu; and my brother, Dean Jamison.

My husband, Richard Wyatt, encouraged me to write this book, read every chapter as I wrote it, and made excellent scientific and clinical suggestions. He understood that the book was not an easy one to write, and he could not have been more loving or supportive. I am very fortunate.

Index

Index

cerebrospinal fluid (CSF), 186–9
  in biology of suicide, 191–2, 195,
    201, 203
Chandler, David Leon, 227
Chatterton, Thomas, 130, 352*n*
Cheng, Andrew, 205
children, 310
  and aftermath of suicides, 291–8,
    300–8
  aggression in, 191
  biology of suicide in, 183, 199, 202
  personality disorders in, 122–3
  predisposition to suicide in, 169–70
  psychology of suicide in, 73, 89
  psychopathology of suicide in, 122–3
  in public health approach to suicide,
    267–9, 273, 284–5
  suicidal thoughts in, 36–8
  suicide attempts in, 99
  suicide rates in, 48–50
  treatment and prevention of suicide
    in, 246–7, 261
  see also adolescents
chimpanzees, 12
China, 47, 140, 203–5, 207, 273
cholesterol, 194–6, 201, 209
Chuinard, E. G., 227
citalopram (Celexa), 241
Clark, Meriwether Lewis, 227
Clark, William, 226–7
  explorations of, 215–17, 219, 229
  on Lewis's death, 220, 225, 228
  on Lewis's finances, 221
Clinton, President William, 156, 400*n*
Coate, Morag, 255–6
cognitive abilities, 92, 179
  in biology of suicide, 193, 202, 206
cohort effect, 45
college students
  contagion of suicide in, 279
  manic-depressive illness in, 55
  psychology of suicide in, 92–3
  suicidal thoughts in, 36
  suicide rates in, 21
  treatment and prevention of suicide
    in, 261–3
conduct disorders, 122
Congress, U.S., 214, 287–8
Conrad, Joseph, 198
cop, suicide by, 134–5
coroners, *see* medical examiners
Cowper, William, 9–10

crime and criminals, *see* laws and legal
    crises
Crow, Timothy, 179
Cry of Pain (Williams), 17
cultures, *see* societies
Curphey, Theodore, 32

Daniel, Book of, 155–6, 158
Dante Alighieri, 14
death and deaths, 42–3, 92, 102, 140,
    158, 237
  in AIDS vs. suicide, 22–4, 48
  leading causes of, 48–50
  in psychology of suicide, 76, 79, 81–
    2, 86–9, 92, 94–6
  suicide notes on, 76, 79, 81–2
decapitation, 133
Demosthenes, 13
Denmark, 29, 172–3, 190, 208, 278
depression, 127
  and aftermath of suicides, 292–4,
    296, 298–9, 301–3
  asking for help during, 4
  in biology of suicide, 184–6, 190–
    202, 205–6, 209–11
  of Burton, 17, 25, 235, 386*n*–7*n*
  comparisons between schizophrenia
    and, 120
  creativity and academic success in,
    180–1
  in defining suicide, 29, 31, 33
  deinstitutionalizing patients with,
    159
  diagnosis of, 246
  in evolutionary reason for suicide,
    174, 178–81
  heredity in, 163, 165–6, 168, 170,
    172–3, 178
  of Lewis, 221, 225, 228–9
  in men vs. women, 46–7
  in psychology of suicide, 75, 81, 84,
    86–92, 94–7
  in psychopathology of suicide, 98–
    115, 117, 120–9, 340*n*
  in public health approach to suicide,
    267–72, 276–7, 281, 284, 286
  recovery from, 114–15, 259
  in rise of suicide rates, 50–1
  in selecting suicide methods and lo-
    cations, 131–2, 149
  severity of, 110–11, 114, 121, 211
  stigma associated with, 286

Index

Index

Socrates, 13
Sopirak, Drew, 54–69
  funeral of, 66–8
  hospitalization of, 54–9, 62–4
  memorial service for, 65–6, 68–9
  notes and journal entries of, 64–5
  suicide of, 54–5, 62, 64–9, 311
Sorrows of Young Werther, The (Goethe), 278
Sort of Life, A (Greene), 98–9, 340n
soul, 25, 78, 109
  in history of suicide, 11, 14–15
  see also carbon monoxide poisonings
South Africa, 207–8, 276
Southern Hemisphere, 207
Soviet roulette, 34
Soviet Union, 283–4
Spence, Mary, 148
spouses, 33, 267
  in aftermath of suicides, 291–2, 294, 296, 299–304
  in predisposition to suicide, 166–7
  in psychology of suicide, 78–80, 84–6
  in psychopathology of suicide, 108, 124–5, 129
  in selecting suicide methods and locations, 134–5
  see also marriages
Sri Lanka, 140, 144
SSRIs, *see* selective serotonin reuptake inhibitors
stabbings, 10, 38, 80
  selection of, 133, 138
starvation, 111, 176
  in history of suicide, 11, 13
  selection of, 133, 135
stress, 56, 81–3, 127, 310
  and aftermath of suicides, 292, 294–5, 299, 302
  in biology of suicide, 183, 192–4, 197–8, 200–1, 204–5, 211
  in defining suicide, 28, 32
  in evolutionary reason for suicide, 173–6, 179
  in predisposition to suicide, 172–3
  in psychology of suicide, 83, 85–9, 91, 93–6
  in psychopathology of suicide, 104–6, 110, 115–21
  in public health approach to suicide, 267–8, 272, 275
  in selecting suicide methods and locations, 131–2, 138, 141–2, 153

  in treatment and prevention of suicide, 236–7, 239, 249, 251–2, 255–6, 258, 261, 263
Stress-Diathesis model, 199
Styron, William, 105–6, 238–9
substance abuse, *see* alcohol and alcoholism; drug abuse
Substance P, 249
suffocations
  in defining suicide, 27, 29
  in psychopathology of suicide, 111–12
  selection of, 131, 133–4, 138, 142, 144
  see also carbon monoxide poisonings
suicidal thoughts, 35–9, 72, 90, 192, 270, 306
  frequency and duration of, 35–6
  line between suicidal actions and, 39–40, 45, 47–8
  psychopathology of, 99, 108–9, 111–12, 114, 116
  in selecting suicide methods and locations, 132, 150–2
  in treatment and prevention of suicide, 237, 252, 256
"Suicide" (Lowell), 47–8
suicide and suicides
  accuracy in reporting of, 28, 50
  aftermath of, 24, 79–80, 142, 290–308
  as altruistic, 13
  ambivalence in, 39
  bizarreness of, 155
  calmness before, 114–15
  commonness of, 100
  complexity of, 18–20, 85
  contagious aspect of, 12, 146–8, 276–82
  deceptiveness in, 115
  definitions of, 26–34, 40, 174
  destructiveness of, 5
  as existential issue, 21
  in history, 11–25, 163–6, 206, 208, 276–7, 283
  impulsiveness in, 189–90, 197–9, 201, 203–4, 237, 292
  individuality of, 100
  intention in, 28–35, 40–4, 110, 113, 115–16, 134–5, 138, 141, 150–1, 189, 198, 202, 237, 254, 292
  media on, 143–6, 149, 155, 157, 278–82, 286, 298–9
  motivations in, 86–94, 199, 204, 309
  in physical presence of another, 123

Index

PERMISSIONS ACKNOWLEDGMENTS

Grateful acknowledgment is made to the following for permission to reprint previously published material:

American Psychological Association: Figure 6, page 133, and Figure 7, page 134, from *Adolescent Suicide* by A. L. Berman and D. A. Jobes, copyright © 1991 by the American Psychological Association. Reprinted by permission of the American Psychological Association.

Ardis Publishers: Excerpt from poem by Sergei Esenin in *Esenin: A Life* by Gordon McVay. Reprinted by permission of Ardis Publishers.

Elizabeth Barnett, Literary Executor, Edna St. Vincent Millay Society: Excerpt from "Not So Far as the Forest (I)" and "From a Very Little Sphinx (IV)" in *Collected Poems* by Edna St. Vincent Millay (New York: HarperCollins Publishers), copyright © 1929, 1939, 1956, 1967 by Edna St. Vincent Millay and Norma Millay Ellis. All rights reserved. Reprinted by permission of Elizabeth Barnett, Literary Executor, Edna St. Vincent Millay Society.

Bolton Press Atlanta: Poem by Iris M. Bolton from *My Son . . . My Son* by Iris M. Bolton (Bolton Press Atlanta, 1983, 1991). Reprinted by permission of Bolton Press Atlanta.

Canongate Books: Excerpt from *Sunset Song* by Lewis Grassic Gibbon (Canongate Classics, imprint of Canongate Books, 1995). Reprinted by permission of Canongate Books, Edinburgh EH1 1TE, United Kingdom.

Chatto & Windus: Excerpt from "An Academic" from *Collected Poems* by Norman MacCaig. Reprinted by permission of Chatto & Windus, an imprint of The Random House Group Ltd., on behalf of the Estate of Norman MacCaig.

Delacorte Press: Excerpt from *Josh: My Up and Down, In and Out Life* by Joshua L. Logan, copyright © 1976 by Joshua L. Logan. Reprinted by permission of Delacorte Press, a division of Random House, Inc.

Farrar, Straus and Giroux, LLC: 4 lines from "#235" and 8 lines from "#384" from *The Dream Songs* by John Berryman, copyright © 1969 by John Berryman, copyright renewed 1997 by Kate Donahue Berryman; excerpt from "Suicide" from *Day by Day* by Robert Lowell, copyright © 1977 by Robert Lowell. Reprinted by permission of Farrar, Straus and Giroux, LLC.

Carl Fischer Music: Excerpt from the lyric "The U.S. Air Force" by Robert Crawford, copyright © 1939, 1942, 1951 by Carl Fischer LLC. All rights reserved. Reprinted by permission of Carl Fischer Music.

Harcourt, Inc.: Excerpts from *The Letters of Virginia Woolf, Volume VI: 1936–1941* by Nigel Nicolson and Joanne Trautmann, copyright © 1980 by Quentin Bell and Angelica Garnett. Reprinted by permission of Harcourt, Inc.

Houghton Mifflin Company and Sterling Lord Literistic, Inc.: Excerpt from "To a Friend Whose Work Has Come to Triumph" from *All My Pretty Ones* by Anne

A NOTE ABOUT THE AUTHOR

KAY REDFIELD JAMISON is Professor of Psychiatry at the Johns Hopkins University School of Medicine, as well as Honorary Professor of English at the University of St. Andrews in Scotland. She is the author of the national best-seller *An Unquiet Mind: A Memoir of Moods and Madness* and coauthor of the standard medical text on manic-depressive illness. She is also the author of *Touched with Fire: Manic-Depressive Illness and the Artistic Temperament*, as well as more than a hundred scientific papers about mood disorders, psychotherapy, psychopharmacology, and suicide. Dr. Jamison, formerly the director of the UCLA Affective Disorders Clinic, is the recipient of numerous national and international scientific awards, including the American Foundation for Suicide Prevention's Research Award. She lives in Washington, D.C., with her husband, Richard Wyatt, a physician and scientist at the National Institutes of Health.

A NOTE ON THE TYPE

This book was set in Janson, a typeface long thought to have been made by the Dutchman Anton Janson, who was a practicing typefounder in Leipzig during the years 1668–1687. However, it has been conclusively demonstrated that these types are actually the work of Nicholas Kis (1650–1702), a Hungarian, who most probably learned his trade from the master Dutch typefounder Dirk Voskens. The type is an excellent example of the influential and sturdy Dutch types that prevailed in England up to the time William Caslon (1692–1766) developed his own incomparable designs from them.

Composed by Creative Graphics,
Allentown, Pennsylvania
Printed and bound by R. R. Donnelley & Sons,
Harrisonburg, Virginia
Designed by Virginia Tan
Graphs by Mark Stein